MW00652126

WHERE THE CONFLICT REALLY LIES

WHERE THE CONFLICT REALLY LIES

Science, Religion, and Naturalism

Alvin Plantinga

OXFORD
UNIVERSITY PRESS

OXFORD
UNIVERSITY PRESS

Oxford University Press, Inc., publishes works that further
Oxford University's objective of excellence
in research, scholarship, and education.

Oxford   New York
Auckland   Cape Town   Dar es Salaam   Hong Kong   Karachi
Kuala Lumpur   Madrid   Melbourne   Mexico City   Nairobi
New Delhi   Shanghai   Taipei   Toronto

With offices in
Argentina   Austria   Brazil   Chile   Czech Republic   France   Greece
Guatemala   Hungary   Italy   Japan   Poland   Portugal   Singapore
South Korea   Switzerland   Thailand   Turkey   Ukraine   Vietnam

Copyright © 2011 Oxford University Press

Published by Oxford University Press, Inc.
198 Madison Avenue, New York, New York 10016

www.oup.com

Oxford is a registered trademark of Oxford University Press

All rights reserved. No part of this publication may be reproduced,
stored in a retrieval system, or transmitted, in any form or by any means,
electronic, mechanical, photocopying, recording, or otherwise,
without the prior permission of Oxford University Press.

Library of Congress Cataloging-in-Publication Data
Plantinga, Alvin.
Where the conflict really lies : science, religion, and naturalism / Alvin Plantinga.
p.   cm.
ISBN 978-0-19-981209-7 (hardcover : alk. paper)
1. Religion and science.   2. Evolution (Biology)—Religious aspects—Christianity.
3. Naturalism—Religious aspects—Christianity.   I. Title.
BL240.3.P53 2011
231.7'65—dc22
2011002532

16 18 17

Printed in the United States of America
on acid-free paper

CONTENTS

Preface   ix

PART I
ALLEGED CONFLICT

1 Evolution and Christian Belief (1)   3
  I Preliminaries   3
  II Dawkins   13

2 Evolution and Christian Belief (2)   31
  I   Dennett's Argument   33
  II Draper's Argument   49
  III Why Do People Doubt Evolution?   52
  IV Kitcher's "Enlightenment Case"   55

3 Divine Action in the World: The Old Picture   65
  I The Problem   69
  II The Old Picture   76

CONTENTS

4 The New Picture   91

    I Quantum Mechanics   92

   II What is the Problem with "Intervention"?   97

  III What *is* Intervention?   108

  IV Intervention and Divine Action at the
Quantum Level   113

   V A Couple of Other Alleged Conflicts   121

PART II

SUPERFICIAL CONFLICT

5 Evolutionary Psychology and Scripture Scholarship   129

    I Evolutionary Psychology   130

   II Evolutionary Psychology and Religion   137

  III Historical Biblical Criticism   152

6 Defeaters?   163

    I Defeaters and Their Nature   164

   II Evidence Base   167

  III Methodological Naturalism   168

  IV Is Simonian Science a Defeater for
Christian Belief?   174

   V Faith and Reason   178

  VI Can Religious Beliefs be Defeated?   183

  VII The Reduction Test   186

PART III
CONCORD

7 Fine-Tuning   193
    I Fine-Tuning   194
    II Objections   199

8 Design Discourse   225
    I Michael Behe and Biological Arguments   225
    II *Perceiving* Design?   236
    III Design *Argument* vs. Design *Discourse*   240
    IV The Difference it Makes   248

9 Deep Concord: Christian Theism and the Deep
    Roots of Science   265
    I Science and the Divine Image   266
    II Reliability and Regularity   271
    III Law   274
    IV Mathematics   284
    V Induction and Learning from Experience   292
    VI Simplicity and Other Theoretical Virtues   296
    VII Contingency and Science as Empirical   299

PART IV
DEEP CONFLICT

10 The Evolutionary Argument Against Naturalism   307
    I Superficial Concord   307
    II Deep Conflict   309

CONTENTS

III The Argument   311
IV The First Premise: Darwin's Doubt   316
V The Argument for Premise (1)   325
VI The Remaining Premises   339
VII Two Concluding Comments   346

Index   351

PREFACE

My overall claim in this book: *there is superficial conflict but deep concord between science and theistic religion, but superficial concord and deep conflict between science and naturalism.*

Now central to the great monotheistic religions—Christianity, Judaism, Islam—is the thought that there is such a person as God: a personal agent who has created the world and is all-powerful, all-knowing, and perfectly good. I take naturalism to be the thought that there is no such person as God, or anything like God. Naturalism is stronger than atheism: you can be an atheist without rising to the full heights (sinking to the lowest depths?) of naturalism; but you can't be a naturalist without being an atheist.

Naturalism is what we could call a worldview, a sort of total way of looking at ourselves and our world. It isn't clearly a religion: the term "religion" is vague, and naturalism falls into the vague area of its application. Still, naturalism plays many of the same roles as a religion. In particular, it gives answers to the great human questions: Is there such a person as God? How should we live? Can we look forward to life after death? What is our place in the universe? How are

PREFACE

we related to other creatures? Naturalism gives answers here: there is no God, and it makes no sense to hope for life after death. As to our place in the grand scheme of things, we human beings are just another animal with a peculiar way of making a living. Naturalism isn't clearly a religion; but since it plays some of the same roles as a religion, we could properly call it a *quasi*-religion.

If my thesis is right, therefore—if there is deep concord between science and Christian or theistic belief, but deep conflict between science and naturalism—then there is a science/religion (or science/quasi-religion) conflict, all right, but it isn't between science and theistic religion: it's between science and *naturalism*.

Many would dispute my claim that there is no serious conflict between religion and science—indeed, many seem to think naturalism or atheism is part of the "scientific worldview." Among them are the "new atheists": Richard Dawkins, Daniel Dennett, Christopher Hitchens, and Sam Harris. These are the Four Horsemen—not of the Apocalypse, nor of Notre Dame, but of atheism; and their aim is to run roughshod over religion. Their objections and complaints are manifold. First, they attribute most of the ills of the world to religion: they point to the Crusades, to witch hunts, to religious wars, to intolerance, to current terrorism, and much else besides. Of course the world's religions do indeed have much to repent; still (as has often been pointed out) the suffering, death, and havoc attributable to religious belief and practice pales into utter insignificance beside that due to the atheistic and secular idiologies of the twentieth century alone.

The Four Horsemen also claim that religious belief is unreasonable and irrational, as silly as believing in the Spaghetti Monster or Superman, or maybe even the Green Lantern. Their claims are loud and strident. They propose to deal with their opponents not by way of reasoned argument and discussion, but by way of ridicule and "naked contempt" (see footnote 24 in chapter 2). Why they choose

x

this route is not wholly clear. One possibility, of course, is that their atheism is adolescent rebellion carried on by other means. Another (consistent with the first) is that they know of no good reasons or arguments for their views, and hence resort to schoolyard tactics. In terms of intellectual competence, the new atheists are certainly inferior to the "old atheists"—Bertrand Russell and John Mackie come to mind. They are also inferior to many other contemporary but less strident atheists—Thomas Nagel, Michael Tooley, and William Rowe, for example. We may perhaps hope that the new atheists are but a temporary blemish on the face of serious conversation in this crucial area.

Be all that as it may, these new atheists unite with the old atheists in declaring that there is deep and irreconcilable conflict between theistic religion—Christian belief, for example—and science. (And here they are joined by some from the opposite end of the spectrum: those Christians who believe that reason and modern science are the enemies of Christian belief.) Now if this were true, it would be both important and unhappy. Modern science is certainly the most striking and impressive intellectual phenomenon of the last half millennium. Think of the development of physics from the time of Isaac Newton to the present: the sheer intellectual brilliance and power of that tradition is astonishing. It involves a large number of extremely talented people, but also an army of less incandescent luminaries—all addressing an evolving set of overlapping questions in such a way that the later answers often build on and carry further the earlier answers. What is particularly striking about modern science (at least to a philosopher) is that it is in this way a *cooperative* venture. (Of course it is also, often, an extremely competitive venture.) Scientists not only collaborate with each other; they regularly build on each other's results.

It's no surprise that this intellectual splendor has also had some unfortunate and unintended side effects. Some treat science as if it were a sort of infallible oracle, like a divine revelation—or if not infallible (since it seems so regularly to change its mind), at any rate such that when it comes to fixing belief, science is the court of last appeal. But this can't be right. First, science doesn't address some of the topics where we most need enlightenment: religion, politics, and morals, for example. Many look to scientists for guidance on matters outside of science, matters on which scientists have no special expertise. They apparently think of scientists as the new priestly class; unsurprisingly, scientists don't ordinarily discourage this tendency. But of course a scientist pontificating on matters outside her field is no better than anyone else pontificating on matters outside her field. Second, science contradicts itself, both over time and at the same time. Two of the most important and overarching contemporary scientific theories are general relativity and quantum mechanics. Both are highly confirmed and enormously impressive; unfortunately, they can't both be correct.

Still, modern science is impressive and amazing. If there were serious conflicts between religion and current science, that would be very significant; initially, at least, it would cast doubt on those religious beliefs inconsistent with current science. But in fact, I will argue, there is no such conflict between Christian belief and science, while there *is* conflict between naturalism and science. My argument goes as follows. In Part I, Alleged Conflict, I note some areas of supposed conflict between science and Christian (and theistic) belief. First, there is evolution. Second, there is the claim that theistic religions endorse miracles or other kind of special divine action, thereby going against science. I argue that these apparent conflicts are *merely* apparent. There is no real conflict between theistic religion and the scientific theory of evolution. What there is, instead, is conflict between theistic religion and a philosophical gloss or add-on to the scientific doctrine of evolution: the claim that evolution is *undirected*, unguided, unorchestrated by God (or anyone else).

I argue next that there is no conflict between science and the thought that there are and have been miracles—for example, miraculous healings, and the chief miracle of Christianity, Jesus' rising from the dead. In particular, I argue that special divine action, including miracles, is not incompatible with the various conservation laws (the conservation of energy, for example), in that these laws apply to systems that are *causally closed*—closed to causal influence from the outside. Any system in which a divine miracle occurs, however, would *not* be causally closed; hence such a system is not addressed by those laws.

In Part II, Superficial Conflict, I point out that there are indeed some areas of *actual* conflict between science and Christian belief. For example, certain theories from evolutionary psychology, and certain theories in scientific scripture scholarship (or "historical Biblical criticism," as I will call it) are inconsistent with Christian belief. Unlike the alleged conflicts in Part I, these are real conflicts. Though real, however, these conflicts are *superficial*; that is because they don't tend to provide defeaters for Christian or theistic belief. The reason, as I argue, is that the scientific evidence base, constrained as it is by methodological naturalism, is only a part of the Christian evidence base. Perhaps certain Christian beliefs are improbable from that partial evidence base; it doesn't follow that they are improbable from a Christian's complete evidence base. If so, however, these theories don't (automatically, at any rate) constitute or provide a defeater for the Christian beliefs with which they conflict. This conflict is therefore properly thought of as superficial.

So far, then, what we see is that there is superficial conflict between Christian belief and science. But there is also concord, as I argue in Part III. In chapters 7 and 8 I consider the "fine-tuning" arguments for theism, pointing out that they offer non-negligible evidence for theistic belief. And in chapter 9, Deep Concord, I point out several ways in which Christian and theistic ways of thinking are deeply hospitable to science.

These all revolve around one central theme: according to Christian belief, God has created us in his image, which includes our being able, like God himself, to have knowledge of ourselves and our world. He has therefore created us and our world in such a way that there is a *match* between our cognitive powers and the world. To use the medieval phrase, there is an *adaequatio intellectus ad rem* (an adequation of the intellect to reality).

In Part IV, Deep Conflict, I argue that the same most emphatically does not go for science and naturalism. Here there is superficial concord, if only because so many distinguished thinkers wrap themselves in naturalism like a politician in the flag, claiming that science is a supporting pillar in the temple of naturalism. But such concord is at best superficial; more exactly, perhaps, it isn't as much superficial as merely alleged.

On the other hand, there is deep and serious conflict between naturalism and science. Taking naturalism to include materialism with respect to human beings, I argue that it is improbable, given naturalism and evolution, that our cognitive faculties are reliable. It is improbable that they provide us with a suitable preponderance of true belief over false. But then a naturalist who accepts current evolutionary theory has a defeater for the proposition that our faculties are reliable. Furthermore, if she has a defeater for the proposition that her cognitive faculties are reliable, she has a defeater for any belief she takes to be produced by her faculties. But of course *all* of her beliefs have been produced by her faculties—including, naturally enough, her belief in naturalism and evolution. That belief, therefore—the conjunction of naturalism and evolution—is one that she can't rationally accept. Hence naturalism and evolution are in serious conflict: one can't rationally accept them both. And hence, as I said above, there is a science/religion conflict (maybe a science/quasi-religion conflict) to be sure, but it is between science and *naturalism*, not science and theistic belief.

I have employed two sizes of print: the main argument goes on in the large print, with more specialized points and other additions in the small. This book is not intended merely for specialists in philosophy. I hope that students with a course or two in philosophy or for that matter anyone with an interest in the subject will find it intelligible and interesting.

Earlier versions of chapters 3 and 4 appeared as "What is 'Intervention'?" in *Theology and Science,* volume 6, number 4 (November, 2008); parts of chapters 5 and 6 appeared earlier in "Games Scientists Play" in *The Believing Primate*, eds. Jeffrey Schloss and Michael Murray (Oxford: Oxford University Press, 2009).

This book originated as Gifford Lectures, entitled "Science and Religion: Conflict or Concord?" in the University of St. Andrews in 2005. I am deeply indebted to the electors for the invitation, and for the consequent opportunity to work out these ideas. I am also indebted to St. Mary's College for wonderful hospitality; here I must mention in particular Alan Torrance and his late wife Jane Torrance, whose gracious kindness to me and my wife was genuinely remarkable.

There are many others to whom I am indebted for wise advice and valuable comment: for example, Mike Bergmann, Robin Collins, Oliver Crisp, Anders Kraal, Trenton Merricks, Brad Monton, Ric Otte, Del Ratzsch, Mike Rea, Elliott Sober, Roger White, Rene van Woudenberg, and Xiangdong Xu. Thanks are also due to a rotating cadre of grad students who read, discussed, and criticized various parts of the manuscript: among them are Andrew Bailey, Brian Boeninger, Kenny Boyce, Isaac Choi, Marcin Iwanicki, Matthew Lee, Dolores Morris, Timothy Pawl, Anne Peterson, Brian Pitts, Chris Porter, Ksenija Puskaric, Bradley Rettler, Josh Rasmussen, Aaron Segal, Amy Seymour, and Luke van Horn. (My apologies to any whom I have inadvertently omitted.) Special thanks are due to Nathan Ballantyne, Kelly Clark, Tom Crisp, and Dan Howard-Snyder, all of whom graciously read and commented on the entire manuscript; Dan Howard-Snyder's comments almost amounted to another book on the subject. I am entirely sensitive to the fact that with so much distinguished help I should have done better.

In 1939, the eminent British philosopher Charlie Dunbar Broad remarked that discussions of the relations between religion and science "had acquired something of the repulsiveness of half cold mutton in half-congealed gravy."[1] Some contemporary forays into the subject, for example by the above Four Horseman, are perhaps less half-cold and half-congealed than overheated and overdone. I'm hoping my contribution to the topic is both more judicious and more appetizing.

---

1. *Philosophy* (1939), p. 131. Quoted in *The Cambridge Companion to Religion and Science*, ed. Peter Harrison (Cambridge: Cambridge University Press, 2010), p. 1.

PART I

ALLEGED CONFLICT

Chapter 1

Evolution and Christian Belief (1)

I PRELIMINARIES

In the first part of this book, I propose to look into alleged conflict between religion and modern science. I'll be concerned in particular with Christian belief and science; most of the alleged conflicts, however, have to do with *theism*, belief that there is such a person as God, rather than with doctrines that separate specifically Christian belief from other theistic religions such as Islam and Judaism. Most of what I say, therefore, will apply to other theistic religions as well as to Christianity. Chapters 1 and 2 will deal with tensions between Christian or theistic belief and evolution. Chapters 3 and 4 will examine the claim that God's acting *specially* in the world (miracles, but other kinds of direct action as well) is incompatible with science. They will also briefly address two further claims: the claim that the so-called scientific worldview (what Peter Unger calls the "Scientiphical worldview") is incompatible with religious belief, and the claim that religion and science are incompatible because the epistemic attitudes characteristic of them are incompatible.[1]

It would be a serious matter if any of these alleged conflicts were genuine. First, science is widely and justly celebrated as a splendid intellectual achievement—perhaps mankind's most splendid effort along these lines; but then any human enterprise in serious conflict

1. See, e.g., Unger's *All the Power in the World* (New York: Oxford University Press, 2005) and chapters 1 and 5 of *Beyond Inanity*, forthcoming.

with it has some explaining to do. Second, science does or should enjoy particularly high regard among Christians. A central feature of Jewish, Christian, and at least some strands of Islamic thought is the doctrine of the *imago dei*; we human beings have been created in the image of God. A central feature of *that* idea is that we resemble God not just in being persons, beings who can think and feel, who have aims and intentions, who form beliefs and act on those beliefs, and the like; we resemble God more particularly in being able to *know* and *understand* something of ourselves, our world, and God himself. Thus Thomas Aquinas:

> Since human beings are said to be in the image of God in virtue of their having a nature that includes an intellect, such a nature is most in the image of God in virtue of being most able to imitate God;
>
> and
>
> Only in rational creatures is there found a likeness of God which counts as an image....As far as a likeness of the divine nature is concerned, rational creatures seem somehow to attain a representation of [that] type in virtue of imitating God not only in this, that he is and lives, but especially in this, that he understands.[2]

Of course the idea of the *imago dei* has been understood in many ways. Some Lutheran and Reformed Creeds (e.g., the Belgic Confession, the Westminister Confession, the Heidelberg Catechism) seem to deny that we human beings still display the image of God; they speak of that image as constituted by "righteousness, knowledge and holiness" (Heidelberg Catechism) and declare that this image was lost (or mostly lost) in the fall. But here there may be less disagreement than meets the eye; the apparent disagreement may be mainly terminological.

2. Aquinas, *Summa Theologiae* Ia q. 93 a. 4; *Summa Theologiae* Ia q.93 a.6.

Some Reformed thinkers distinguish a broad image of God (as with Aquinas, including personhood, rational faculties, knowledge of right and wrong) from a narrow image (righteousness, knowledge of God, and holiness); those who claim that the image of God was lost in the fall are thinking of the narrow image, and presumably would not make the same claim about the broad image. Furthermore, all the creeds presuppose that human beings display that broad image.

Although we are divine image-bearers, our knowledge and understanding is of course partial and fragmentary and often shot through with error; nevertheless, it is real. Taken naively but (so I say) accurately, modern science is an enormously impressive attempt to come to know something about ourselves and our world. (Think, for example, of the development of physics from Newton's day to ours: surely an unexcelled display of cooperative intellectual power and depth.) Modern science is therefore a most impressive way in which humankind communally reflects the divine nature, a striking development of the image of God in humanity. Accordingly it is to be prized by Christians and other theists; but then conflict between religion and science, from that perspective, is initially anomalous, disturbing, perplexing.

Like it or not, however, there is and has been at any rate apparent conflict.[3] Many Christians have at least the vague impression that modern science is somehow unfriendly to religious belief; for other believers it is less a vague impression than a settled conviction. Similarly, many scientists and science enthusiasts argue that there is opposition between serious religious belief and science; indeed, some claim that religious belief constitutes a clear and present danger to science. Still others see religious belief as

---

3. How, exactly (or even approximately) shall we understand *conflict*? Conflict comes in more than one form. There is straightforward inconsistency, there is inconsistency in the presence of obvious truths, there is probabilistic incompatibility, and more. I address these questions in chapters 5 and 6.

steadily dwindling in the face of scientific advance. Tension between religion and science goes back at least to the seventeenth century, where the alleged conflict centered on astronomy.[4] There is the famous Galileo affair, often portrayed as a contest pitting the Catholic hierarchy (representing the forces of repression and tradition, the voice of the Old World, the dead hand of the past, etc.) against the forces of progress and the dulcet voice of sweet reason and science. This way of looking at the matter dates back to Andrew Dixon White and his rancorous *History of the Warfare of Science and Theology*. White, in his characteristically restrained and judicious way, describes Galileo's ecclesiastical opponents as "a seething, squabbling, screaming mass of priests, bishops, archbishops, and cardinals."[5] Of course this way of looking at the matter is enormously simplistic; much more was involved.[6] The dominant Aristotelian thought of the day was heavily a prioristic; hence part of the dispute was about the relative importance, in astronomy, of observation as opposed to a priori thought. Also involved were questions about what the Christian (and Jewish) Bible teaches in

---

4. It is commonly claimed that the Copernican revolution signified a demotion for humanity by virtue of earth's being removed from the center of the universe; that is just one way among others, so goes the claim, in which earth's privileged place in the universe was compromised by the advance of science. This seems to be a mistake; in the earlier Aristotelian scheme of things, being at the center of the universe was definitely not an honor. It was the heavier, grosser elements that sank to the center; in Dante's *Divine Comedy*, the lowest circle of hell is at the very center of the universe; and according to Pico della Mirandola, Earth-dwellers inhabit "the excrementary and filthy parts of the lower world." See Dennis R. Danielson, "The Great Copernican Cliché," *American Journal of Physics* 69 (10) October 2001, pp. 1029ff.

5. White, *History of the Warfare of Science with Theology in Christendom* (New York: D. Appleton and Co., 1898). Quoted in Michael Murray's "Science and Religion in Constructive Engagement" in *Analytic Theology*, ed. Oliver Crisp and Michael Rea (New York: Oxford University Press, 2009), p. 234.

6. John Brooke, *Science and Religion: Some Historical Perspectives* (Cambridge: Cambridge University Press, 1991), pp. 8–9. See also the account of the Galileo affair in Jerome Langford, *Galileo, Science and the Church* (South Bend: St. Augustine's Press, 1998).

this area: does a passage like *Joshua* 10:12–15 (in which Joshua commands the sun to stand still) favor the Ptolemaic (or Tychonic) system over the Copernican? Naturally enough, the usual struggle for power and authority was also present.[7] Nevertheless there certainly did seem to be at least some degree of conflict between the developing modern science and Christian belief, or at any rate ideas closely associated, at the time, with Christian belief.

In the seventeenth century, the main source of debate and conflict was astronomical; since the middle of the nineteenth it has been biological, centering on the theory of evolution. Many Christian fundamentalists and evangelicals find incompatibility between the contemporary Darwinian evolutionary account of our origins and their version of the Christian faith. Many Darwinian fundamentalists (as the late Stephen Jay Gould called them) second that motion: they too claim that Darwinian evolution is flatly inconsistent with classical Christian or even theistic belief. Contemporaries who champion this conflict view include, for example, Richard Dawkins (*The Blind Watchmaker, A Devil's Chaplin*), Daniel Dennett (*Darwin's Dangerous Idea*), and, far to the opposite side, Phillip Johnson (*Darwin on Trial*). In Darwin's own day, this opposition and strife could assume massive proportions. Now Darwin himself was a shy, retiring sort who hated public controversy and confrontation; but given what he had to say, he was often embroiled in violent controversy. Fortunately for him, there was his friend Thomas H. Huxley, who defended Darwin with such fierce tenacity that he came to be called "Darwin's bulldog." Huxley himself continued the canine allusion by referring to some of Darwin's opponents as "curs who will bark and yelp."[8] The canine

---

7. "If any simple explanation existed, it would rather be in terms of the customary ruthlessness of societal authority in suppressing minority opinion, and in Galileo's case with Aristotelianism rather than Christianity in authority" (Stillman Drake, *Galileo* (Oxford: Oxford University Press, 1980), v.

8. Thomas H. Huxley, letter to Darwin, November 23, 1859.

connection has proved resilient, or at least durable, extending all the way to the present, where we have *Discover Magazine* (September 2005) calling Richard Dawkins "Darwin's Rottweiler," and Gould referring (no doubt unkindly) to Daniel Dennett as "Dawkins's lapdog."

Many have claimed, therefore, that there is deep incompatibility between evolution and Christian belief and hence between religion and science; but are they right? To investigate the question we must know how to think of Christian belief. Suppose we take it to be defined or circumscribed by the rough intersection of the great Christian creeds: the Apostle's Creed, the Nicene Creed, and the Athanasian Creed, but also more particular creeds such as the Catholic Baltimore Catechism, the Reformed Heidelberg Catechism, the Belgic Confession and Westminster Confession, Luther's Small Catechism, and the Anglican Thirty-Nine Articles; the result would be something like the "Mere Christianity" of which C. S. Lewis spoke.

In the same way, we must specify how we are to think of evolution. The term covers a multitude—not necessarily a multitude of sins, but a multitude nevertheless. (1) There is the claim that the earth is very old, perhaps some 4.5 billion years old: the *ancient earth thesis*, as we may call it. (2) There is the claim that life has progressed from relatively simple to relatively complex forms (though in terms of sheer bulk or weight the simple forms still vastly overshadow the complex; bacteria outweigh all other living creatures combined). In the beginning there was relatively simple unicellular life, perhaps of the sort represented by bacteria and blue-green algae, or perhaps still simpler unknown forms of life. (Although bacteria are simple compared to some other living beings, they are in fact enormously complex creatures.) Then more complex unicellular life, then relatively simple multi-cellular life such as seagoing worms, coral, and jellyfish, then fish, then amphibia, then reptiles, birds, mammals, and finally, as the current culmination of the whole process, human beings: the *progress thesis*, as we humans may like to call it (jellyfish might have a very different view as to where the whole process culminates). (3) There is the thesis of *descent with modification*: the enormous diversity of the contemporary living world has come about by way of off-spring differing, ordinarily in small and subtle ways, from their parents.

Connected with the thesis of descent with modification is (4) the *common ancestry thesis*: that life originated at only one place on earth, all subsequent life being related by descent to those original living creatures—the claim that, as Gould puts it, there is a "tree of evolutionary descent linking all organisms by ties of genealogy." According to the common ancestry thesis, we are all cousins of each other—and indeed of all living things. Horses, bats, bacteria, oak trees, and even poison ivy—we are all cousins of them all; you and the summer squash in your backyard are cousins under the skin (rind).[9] (5) There is the claim that there is a naturalistic *mechanism* driving this process of descent with modification: the most popular candidate is natural selection operating on random genetic mutation, although some other processes are also sometimes proposed. Since a similar proposal was characteristic of Darwin ("Natural selection," he said, "has been the main but not exclusive means of modification"), call this thesis *Darwinism*.

Finally (although this thesis is not part of evolution strictly so-called), it is often assumed that (6) life itself developed from non-living matter without any special creative activity of God but just by virtue of processes described by the ordinary laws of physics and chemistry: call this the *naturalistic origins thesis*. These six theses are

9. Why not suppose that life has originated in more than one place, so that we needn't all be cousins? This suggestion is occasionally made, but the usual idea is that life originated just once—if only because of the astounding difficulty in seeing how it could have originated (by exclusively natural processes) at all.

of course importantly different from each other. They are also logically independent in pairs, except for the third and fifth theses: the fifth entails the third, in that you can't sensibly propose a mechanism for a process without supposing that the process has indeed occurred. Suppose we use the term "evolution" to denote the first four of these; the fifth thesis, Darwinism, is stronger than evolution (so defined) and points to the mechanism allegedly *underlying* evolution; and the sixth isn't really part of the theory of evolution.

So where does real or apparent conflict arise? Many Christian evangelicals or fundamentalists accept a literal interpretation of the creation account in the first two chapters of Genesis (as well as the genealogies in the next few chapters); they are inclined therefore to think the earth and indeed the universe vastly younger than the billions of years of age attributed to them by current science.[10] This seems to be a fairly straightforward conflict, and hence part of the answer to our question is that current scientific estimates of the age of the earth and of the universe differ widely (not to say wildly) from scripturally based beliefs on the part of some Christians and other theists (Muslims for example). Of course Christian belief just as such doesn't include the thought that the universe is young; and in fact as far back as Augustine (354–430) serious Christians have doubted that the scriptural days of creation correspond to 24-hour periods of time.[11]

---

10. Creationists often suggest that when God Created the world 6,000–10,000 years ago, he created it in a "mature state," complete with crumbling mountains, fossils, and light apparently travelling from stars millions of light years distant. Here they can appeal to an unlikely ally: in *The Analysis of Mind* (London: Routledge, 1921), p. 159, Bertrand Russell wrote that we can't disprove the proposition that the universe popped into being just five minutes ago, again, complete with apparent memories and other apparent traces of a much longer past.

11. Those Christians who think the world is much younger than current scientific estimates will indeed find a conflict here; they can see it as a superficial conflict as outlined in chapter 6. Concerning Augustine, see *The Literal Meaning of Genesis*, translated and annotated by John Hammond Taylor, S. J., 2 vols. (New York: Newman Press, 1982), vol. 1, chapter 1.

A more important source of conflict has to do with the Christian doctrine of creation, in particular the claim that God has created human beings *in his image*. This requires that God *intended* to create creatures of a certain kind—rational creatures with a moral sense and the capacity to know and love him—and then acted in such a way as to accomplish this intention. This claim is clearly consistent with evolution (ancient earth, the progress thesis, descent with modification, common ancestry), as conservative Christian theologians have pointed out as far back as 1871. Thus, for example, Charles Hodge, the distinguished Princeton theologian, speaking of the design of plants and animals: "If God made them, it makes no difference how He made them, as far as the question of design is concerned, whether at once or by a process of evolution."[12] What is less obvious is that it is also consistent with Darwinism, the view that the diversity of life has come to be by way of natural selection winnowing random genetic mutation. For example, God could have caused the right mutations to arise at the right time; he could have preserved populations from perils of various sorts, and so on; and in this way he could have seen to it that there come to be creatures of the kind he intends.

You might wonder whether *random* genetic mutations could be caused by God: if these mutations are random, aren't they just a matter of chance? But randomness, as construed by contemporary biologists, doesn't have this implication. According to Ernst Mayr, the dean of post-WWII biology, "When it is said that mutation or variation is random, the statement simply means that there is no correlation between the production of new genotypes and the adaptational needs of an organism in a given environment."[13] Elliott Sober, one of the most respected contemporary philosophers of biology,

12. Hodge, *What is Darwinism* (New York: Charles Scribner, 1871).
13. Mayr, *Towards a new Philosophy of Biology: Observations of an Evolutionist* (Cambridge: Harvard University Press, 1988), p. 98.

puts the point a bit more carefully: "There is no *physical mechanism* (either inside organisms or outside of them) that detects which mutations would be beneficial and causes those mutations to occur."[14] But their being random in *that* sense is clearly compatible with their being caused by God.

What is *not* consistent with Christian belief, however, is the claim that this process of evolution is *unguided*—that no personal agent, not even God, has guided, directed, orchestrated, or shaped it. Yet precisely this claim is made by a large number of contemporary scientists and philosophers who write on this topic. There is a veritable choir of extremely distinguished experts insisting that this process is unguided, and indeed insisting that it is a part of contemporary evolutionary theory to assert that it is unguided, so that evolutionary theory as such is incompatible with Christian belief. According to Gould, "Before Darwin, we thought that a benevolent God had created us."[15] After Darwin, though, he says, we realize that "No intervening spirit watches lovingly over the affairs of nature."[16] Gould's sentiments are stated more clearly by the biologist George Gaylord Simpson:

> Although many details remain to be worked out, it is already evident that all the objective phenomena of the history of life can be explained by purely naturalistic or, in a proper sense of the sometimes abused word, materialistic factors. They are readily explicable on the basis of differential reproduction in populations (the main factor in the modern conception of natural selection) and of the mainly random interplay of the known processes of

14. Sober, "Evolution Without Naturalism?" in J. Kvanvig (ed.), *Oxford Studies in Philosophy of Religion*, vol. 3. (New York: Oxford University Press, 2011), p. 192.
15. Gould, *Ever Since Darwin* (New York: Norton, 1977), p. 267.
16. Gould, "In Praise of Charles Darwin," in *Darwin's Legacy* (San Francisco: Harper & Row, 1983), pp. 6–7.

heredity.... Man is the result of a purposeless and natural process that did not have him in mind.[17]

Among the most eloquent and influential spokespersons for this incompatibility claim (the soloists, we might say) are Richard Dawkins in *The Blind Watchmaker* (1986), *River Out of Eden* (1996), *Unweaving the Rainbow* (1998), and *A Devil's Chaplain* (2003), and Daniel Dennett in *Darwin's Dangerous Idea* (1995). Both Dawkins and Dennett assert, loudly and slowly, as it were, that evolution and Christian belief are incompatible. But are they right? Is this claim true? Is there any reason to believe it? Here the best course is to look carefully at what these writers actually say, thus avoiding the danger of attacking straw men. Let's begin with Dawkins.

II DAWKINS

Richard Dawkins has retired from his post as Charles Simonyi Professor of the Public Understanding of Science at Oxford. Dawkins is the world's best known atheist (for what that's worth) and the world's most popular science writer. He is also an extremely *gifted* science writer; his account in *The Blind Watchmaker*, for example, of bats and their ways is a brilliant and fascinating tour de force.[18] In the series of books I just mentioned he states his claim: the enormous variety of the living world has been produced by natural selection winnowing some form of genetic variability—unguided by the hand of God or any other person. Probably his most widely known declaration to that effect is to be found in *The Blind Watchmaker*:

---

17. Simpson, *The Meaning of Evolution* (New Haven: Yale University Press, rev. ed., 1967), pp. 344–45.
18. Dawkins, *The Blind Watchmaker* (New York and London: Norton, 1986).

All appearances to the contrary, the only watchmaker in nature is the blind forces of physics, albeit deployed in a very special way. A true watchmaker has foresight: he designs his cogs and springs, and plans their interconnections, with a future purpose in his mind's eye. Natural selection, the blind, unconscious automatic process which Darwin discovered, and which we now know is the explanation for the existence and apparently purposeful form of all life, has no purpose in mind. It has no mind and no mind's eye. It does not plan for the future. It has no vision, no foresight, no sight at all. If it can be said to play the role of watchmaker in nature, it is the *blind* watchmaker.[19]

The very subtitle of this book trumpets his theme: "Why the evidence of evolution reveals a universe without design." Now it is part of Christian and other theistic belief that God has created human beings, and created them in his own image. Obviously, if Dawkins's claim is true, this claim is false. The latter requires that God intended to create creatures of a certain kind—creatures "in his image"—and then acted in such a way as to see to it that they come into existence. This claim does not require that God *directly* created human beings, or that he didn't do it by way of an evolutionary process, or even that he was especially interested in creating precisely our species (or even you and me). But if he created human beings in his image, then at the least he intended that there be creatures of a certain sort, and acted in such a way as to guarantee that creatures of that sort came to be. Dawkins's claim—that the living world emerged by way of unguided natural selection—is clearly incompatible with this claim. We shall have to look into his reasons. Why does he think that natural selection is blind and unguided? Why does he think that *the evidence of evolution reveals a universe without design*"? How does the evidence of evolution reveal such a thing?

19. Dawkins, *The Blind Watchmaker*, p. 5.

Well, what, exactly, does current evolutionary science claim? That's not entirely easy to say; you can't find an authoritative statement of it emblazoned on the walls of the National Academy of Science or anywhere else; there is considerable diversity of opinion as to what, precisely, are the essentials of contemporary evolutionary theory. Dawkins, for example, apparently thinks once life began, it was more or less inevitable that we would wind up with a living world very much like the one we see. Gould disagreed: he thought that if "the tape were rewound and then let go forward again," chances are we'd get something wholly different. Writers also differ as to how *much* natural selection explains, how much must be explained in other ways, and how much is left unexplained.

For simplicity (and because we are thinking about Dawkins, an enthusiast for natural selection), let's stick with what above I called "Darwinism," the idea that the main or possibly even only mechanism driving the whole process of evolution is natural selection culling random genetic mutation. A Darwinist will think there is a *complete Darwinian history* for every contemporary species, and indeed for every contemporary organism.[20] Start with the population of prokaryotes (e.g., bacteria and blue-green algae) to be found on earth some 3 billion years ago. There is in principle a complete history specifying which genetic mutations occurred with respect to each member of that population, which of these mutations were heritable and adaptive, and which then successfully spread through the population. This history would go on to specify (vagueness aside) when, as a result of this process, the first single-celled eukaryotes (creatures with a proper nucleus) appeared; it would then describe how, in this way, the first new species came to be, the first new genera, the first new phyla, and so on. It would proceed through the Cambrian explosion, specifying in complete

---

20. See Alex Pruss, "How not to Reconcile Evolution and Creation," available on the web at *Philpapers* (http://philpapers.org), 2009.

detail which adaptive and heritable mutations arose at what times and in which creatures, and how they then spread through the population, eventually issuing in that remarkable eruption of life forms. Continuing over the eons, this history would trace in detail the development of all forms of life: the invertebrates, the various forms of vertebrate life including fish, reptiles, birds, and mammals; it would end with a description of all the contemporary forms of life.

This history, if written, would occupy an enormous library: call it the Library of Life. The claim is not, of course, that we are or ever will be in possession of that library. We don't have anything like detailed knowledge of any of the books it contains, or even of any chapters or passages in any of those books. The Darwinian claim is only that (1) there is such a history, (2) there is *good evidence* for current views as to the overall shape of the history, and (3) we have some informed guesses as to how, at a high level of abstraction, some of the transitions occurred: examples would be the sorts of guesses made by Dawkins as to the origin and development of the mammalian eye, or the common suggestion that the bones in the mammalian middle ear developed from the reptilian jawbone.

Now there is nothing here, so far, to suggest that this whole process was unguided; it could have been superintended and orchestrated by God. For all the library says, God could have achieved the results he wanted by causing the right mutations to arise at the right times, letting natural selection do the rest. Another possibility: Thomas Huxley, Darwin's bulldog, was an agnostic (and in fact invented the term); nevertheless he suggested that God could have arranged initial conditions in such a way that the results he wanted would be forthcoming.[21] No

---

21. Huxley as cited in Brooke, *Science and Religion*, p. 36. Clearly this suggestion raises difficult questions about determinism, the chanciness (if any) involved in quantum mechanics, the existence of counterfactuals of chance (that is, propositions specifying what would have happened, if a given chance process had occurred), and so on; some of these questions will be addressed in chapter 3.

doubt there are other ways in which he could have directed and orchestrated the process. Dawkins's claim, of course, is that there is no such intelligent agent guiding the process; *"the evidence of evolution,"* he says, *"reveals a universe without design."* What makes him think this is true? How does he propose to argue for this claim?

Not, naturally enough, by specifying chapter and verse in relevant volumes of the library and showing or even arguing that the processes involved in those transitions were not in fact overseen or guided by such an agent; our powers are a bit slim for that. Instead, he tries to show that it is *possible* that unguided natural selection should have produced all these wonders; it *could be* that they have all come to be just by virtue of unguided natural selection. He does this, first, by attacking arguments for the conclusion that natural selection could *not* have done so. Or rather, he attacks certain kinds of such arguments, ignoring others. Among those he ignores, for example, is John Locke's claim that "it is as impossible to conceive that ever pure incogitative Matter should produce a thinking intelligent Being, as that nothing should of itself produce Matter."[22] Many have concurred with Locke, but Dawkins fails to so much as mention this kind of claim. Nor does he try to show either that there is no such person as God, or that, if there is, it is not possible that he should have somehow set up and directed the whole process.[23] And why should he? After all, he's a biologist and not a philosopher.

Instead, Dawkins tries to refute some of the more specific and specifically biological arguments to the effect that unguided natural

---

22. Locke, *Essay Concerning Human Understanding* IV, x, 10.
23. Although in his later book *The God Delusion* (New York: Bantam, 2006) he offers some sophomoric arguments for the conclusion that it is extremely unlikely that there is such a person as God; see reviews by Thomas Nagel ("The Fear of Religion," *The New Republic*, October, 2006), H. Allen Orr ("A Mission to Convert," *New York Review of Books*, January, 2007), and myself ("The Dawkins Confusion: Naturalism ad Absurdum," *Books and Culture*, March/April, 2007).

selection could not have produced certain of the wonders of the living world—the mammalian eye, for example, or the wing, or the bat's sonar. He argues that the objectors have not made their case. Here he sometimes stumbles; for example, he apparently confuses the question "What good is 5 percent of an eye?" with "What good is 5 percent vision?": "An ancient animal with 5 per cent of an eye," he says, "might indeed have used it for something other than sight, but it seems to me at least as likely that it used it for 5 per cent vision."[24] But not just any old 5 percent of an eye will produce 5 percent vision; indeed there may not be *any* 5 percent of an eye that produces 5 percent vision.

Just for purposes of argument, let's concede that Dawkins succeeds in refuting each of these arguments for impossibility. Clearly that doesn't entail that the impossibility claims are false; it shows only that certain arguments for them are not cogent. The question still remains: *is* it possible that unguided natural selection generate all the stunning marvels of the living world? Dawkins puts this question in the following tripartite fashion:

(3) Is there a continuous series of Xs connecting the modern human eye to a state with no eye at all?

(4) Considering each member of the series of hypothetical Xs connecting the human eye to no eye at all, is it plausible that every one of them was made available by random mutation of its predecessor?

(5) Considering each member of the series of Xs connecting the human eye to no eye at all, is it plausible that every one of them worked sufficiently well that it assisted the survival and reproduction of the animals concerned?[25]

---

24. Dawkins, *The Blind Watchmaker*, p. 81.
25. Dawkins, *The Blind Watchmaker*, pp. 78–9.

Compressing things a bit, we could put the question as follows. Imagine a three-dimensional space—"organic space," as we might call it—where each of the countably infinite points is a possible life form. Then the Big Question is:

> (BQ) Is there a path through organic space connecting, say, some ancient population of unicellular life with the human eye, where each point on the path could plausibly have come from a preceding point by way of a heritable random genetic mutation that was adaptively useful, and that could plausibly then have spread through the appropriate population by way of unguided natural selection?[26]

A couple of comments on (BQ). First, the human eye is just a stand-in for life forms generally; the question is not merely whether the human eye could have developed in this way, but whether *all* the current life forms could have. Second, we must start with an *actual* (not merely possible) population of unicellular life, a population that did in fact exist: the claim is that human beings (and hence the human eye) could have developed via unguided natural selection from some population of unicellular organisms that actually existed. Third, the other life forms on the path—the ones "between" the population of unicellular organisms and human beings—must be possible, but need not be actually existent. (That is, they need not be actually instantiated or exemplified; it's enough if they are possibly instantiated.) Dawkins is really asking whether it is *plausible* that the human eye develop in this way, starting from some population of unicellular organisms. Of course if in fact the eye *did* develop in this way, there would have to be such a path connecting life forms that had existent

---

26. Well, not quite. The relevant pathways through organic space need not be such that each step is a step towards the human eye; there could be brief regressions, feints in irrelevant directions, and so on; the process need not be entirely monotonic, to use Elliott Sober's term.

instantiations. Fourth, the points on the path will have to be temporally indexed, with the temporal distance between a pair of points on the path being sufficient for the relevant mutation to spread through the population in question. That means that the time elapsed from that initial population of unicellular organisms to the appearance of the eye imposes a constraint on the number of points the path in question can contain and the temporal distance between them; the number of points the path contains and the temporal distance between them can be large but is not unlimited.

Finally, and crucially, what is the force of "could plausibly" in "each point along the path is such that it *could plausibly* have come from a preceding point on the path by way of a heritable random genetic mutation?" We're not talking broadly logical possibility, of course; we're not asking whether there is a possible world in which this development takes place. That would be much too weak; to use a Dawkinsian example, there are possible worlds in which the bronze statues in the park (constituted just as they presently are) wave goodbye when you leave. We are instead talking about something like *biological* possibility, and, as Dawkins thinks of biological possibility, it is to be explained in terms of *probability*. A given point on a path could plausibly have come from a preceding point by way of genetic mutation just if it is not too improbable that it do so. It might be possible in the broadly logical sense that a sufficiently complex single mutation take us all the way from a paradigm reptile to a paradigm mammal—possible, but far too unlikely. So the mutations must be reasonably probable, not too improbable, with respect to the previous point. Not too improbable, of course, apart from any special divine aid or special divine action. The mutation in question would have to occur and be caused in the usual way—by way of cosmic radiation, or x-ray, or chemical agent or whatever—but not by way of special divine action. How much improbability is too much? Here one can answer only in the vaguest terms. Dawkins suggests, sensibly enough, that the improbability would have to be much less than that of that statue waving at us as we leave the park.

How does Dawkins answer (BQ), or rather, his tripartite version of it? (3), you recall, was the question "Is there a continuous series of Xs connecting the modern human eye to a state with no eye at all?" His reply: "It seems to me clear that the answer has to be yes, provided only that we allow ourselves a *sufficiently large* series of Xs."[27] No doubt he's right about (3); surely there is such a relevant series. We can see this as follows: consider a particular human eye—one of Dawkins's, for example; assign a number to each cell contained in that eye (as with certain kinds of build-it-yourself toy kits); let the first member of the series be a creature that has cell number 1, the second be one that contains cells number 2 and number 1; the third contain cell number 3 plus cells number 1 and 2, and so on. This won't quite work; for this eye to function, there will also have to be an appropriate brain or part of a brain to which it is connected by an optic nerve. But you get the idea: clearly there is such a series. Of course that by itself doesn't show much; if it's to be relevant, the length of the series will have to be constrained by the time available, and each step in the series will have to be such that it can arise by way of genetic mutation from a previous step. Furthermore (and crucially), each mutation will have to be fitness-conferring (or at least not unduly costly in terms of fitness), so that it's not too improbable that they be preserved by natural selection. This is where his answers to (4) and (5) come in.

Dawkins's answer to (4), (Considering each member of the series of hypothetical Xs connecting the human eye to no eye at all, is it plausible that every one of them was made available by random mutation of its predecessor?): "My feeling is that, provided the difference between neighboring intermediates in our series leading to the eye is *sufficiently*

27. Dawkins, *The Blind Watchmaker*, p. 78.

small, the necessary mutations are almost bound to be forthcoming." Finally question (5): Considering each member of the series of Xs connecting the human eye to no eye at all, is it plausible that every one of them worked sufficiently well that it assisted the survival and reproduction of the animals concerned? As Dawkins notes, some people claim that the obvious answer is "no"; he argues that they are mistaken. These people point to a particular structure or organ and claim that there isn't a Darwinian series for that structure or organ; Dawkins makes suggestions as to how such a series might in fact go.

There are two basic ways in which Dawkins's argument is weak. First, returning to BQ, there is surely no *guarantee* that there is a not-too-improbable path through organic space from some early population of unicellular organisms to human beings, or, for that matter, to fruit flies. It might be, as Michael Behe claims, that some structures simply can't be reached by way of small steps (each advantageous or not too disadvantageous) from preceding life forms.[28] Among his proposed examples: the bacterial cilium, the cascade of electrical activity that occurs when a light sensitive spot is hit by a photon, blood clotting, the mammalian immune system, and the complicated molecular machines to be found in any living cell. Many have rejected Behe's specific arguments here; still, perhaps he's right. (I consider some of Behe's arguments in chapter 7.) Perhaps no matter how small you make the steps, there are life forms that can't be reached from previous forms, except at the cost of astronomical, prohibitive improbability. How could we tell that this isn't so? True, Dawkins says that his feeling is that indeed it isn't so; but how much confidence can we put in feelings and guesses?

So the first weakness in Dawkins's argument is that the premises, his answers to questions (4) and (5) above, are controversial,

---

28. Behe, *Darwin's Black Box* (New York: The Free Press, 1996); *The Edge of Evolution* (New York: The Free Press, 2007).

unsupported, and pretty much guesswork. There is no attempt at the sort of serious calculation that would surely be required for a genuine answer. No doubt such a calculation and hence an answer to those questions is at present far beyond our knowledge and powers; no doubt it would be unreasonable to require such a calculation; still, the fact remains we don't have a serious answer.

But suppose Dawkins's answers to (4) and (5) are correct; the argument is still in trouble. Recall that his answer to question (3) is yes, "provided only that we allow ourselves a *sufficiently large* series"; his answer to (4): "My feeling is that, provided the difference between neighboring intermediates in our series leading to the eye is *sufficiently small*…" But even if he is right about the answers to (3) and (4), it doesn't follow that the whole path is plausibly possible in his sense—that is, it doesn't follow that the path is not astronomically improbable. That is because of the temporal constraint imposed. Suppose there have been multicellular organisms for, say, a billion years. This means that the series can't be arbitrarily long and the distance between the points arbitrarily small.

Dawkins's argument, therefore, is pretty weak. But what about the truth of his conclusion? *Is* there a Darwinian series for the eye, and for the other forms of life? Is Dawkins right? How can we tell? How could we determine a thing like that? Michael Behe is by no means the only biologist who thinks it's at best extremely unlikely that there is such a series; for example, according to the biologist Brian Goodwin,

> It appears that Darwin's theory works for the small-scale aspects of evolution: it can explain the variations and the adaptations with species that produce fine-tuning of varieties to different habitats. The large-scale differences of form between types of organism that are the foundation of biological classification systems seem to require another principle than natural selection operating on small

variation, some process that gives rise to distinctly different forms of organism. This is the problem of emergent order in evolution, the origins of novel structures in organisms, which has always been one of the primary foci of attention in biology.[29]

Others, like Dawkins, think there is such a series.

On this point there is likely to be a difference between theists and nontheists. For the nontheist, undirected evolution is the only game in town, and natural selection seems to be the most plausible mechanism to drive that process. Here is this stunningly intricate world with its enormous diversity and apparent design; from the perspective of naturalism or nontheism, the only way it could have happened is by way of unguided Darwinian evolution; hence it *must* have happened that way; hence there *must* be such a Darwinian series for each current life form. The theist, on the other hand, has a little more freedom here: maybe there is such a series and maybe there isn't; God has created the living world and could have done it in any number of different ways; there doesn't *have* to be any such series. In this way the theist is freer to follow the evidence where it leads.

But the main point here lies in another direction. Dawkins claims that the living world came to be by way of unguided evolution: "the Evidence of Evolution," he says, "Reveals a Universe Without Design." What he actually argues, however, is that there is a Darwinian series for contemporary life forms. As we have seen, this argument is inconclusive; but even if it were air-tight it wouldn't show, of course, that the living world, let alone the entire universe, is without design. At best it would show, given a couple of assumptions, that it is not astronomically improbable that the living world was produced by unguided evolution and hence without design.

29. Goodwin, *How the Leopard Changed its Spots* (Princeton: Princeton University Press, 1994), p. ix.

But the argument form

p is not astronomically improbable

therefore

p

is a bit unprepossessing. I announce to my wife, "I'm getting a $50,000 raise for next year!" Naturally she asks me why I think so. "Because the arguments for its being astronomically improbable fail! For all we know, it's not astronomically improbable!" (Well, maybe it *is* pretty improbable, but you get the idea.) If he's successful, what Dawkins really shows is that the arguments against there being a Darwinian series are not conclusive. What he shows, if he's successful, is that *for all we know* there is such a series, so that for all we know it's possible that the living world came to be in this fashion. We could put it like this: what he shows, at best, is that it's epistemically possible that it's biologically possible that life came to be without design. But that's a little short of what he claims to show.

It is perhaps worth noting and stressing the difference between claim and performance here. Dawkins claims that he will show that the entire living world came to be without design; what he actually argues is only that this is possible and we don't know that it is astronomically improbable; for all we know it's not astronomically improbable. But mere possibility claims are not impressive. To put to better use an example proposed by Bertrand Russell and mentioned by Dawkins in his book *The God Delusion*, it's possible that there is a china teapot orbiting the sun between Earth and Mars, out of reach of our telescopes; this ought not to dispose us favorably to the thought that indeed there is a china teapot orbiting the sun between Earth and Mars.[30] But the same goes for the claim that a certain state of affairs is not astronomically improbable. Perhaps it isn't; but that, so far, gives us no reason whatever to endorse it, and in fact doesn't so much as make it sensible to endorse that claim.

Have I perhaps misinterpreted Dawkins? Some with whom I have discussed his argument have thought that he couldn't possibly have intended an argument as weak as the one I've attributed to him; he must have additional premises in mind. Perhaps they are right; of course it is difficult to consider an argument when one is obliged to guess at its premises. Still, what might be other possibilities? What might Dawkins be thinking? Yehuda Gellman and Dennis Monokroussos have suggested (in personal communication) that perhaps Dawkins intends an argument connected with his claim, made in *The Blind Watchmaker*, that an attempt to explain the stunning variety of life by a hypothesis involving design is misguided in that any being able to create life would itself have to be too complex:

> Organized complexity is the thing that we are having difficulty in explaining. Once we are allowed simply to *postulate* organized complexity, if only the organized complexity of the DNA/protein replicating machine, it is relatively easy to invoke it as a generator of yet more organized complexity. . . . But of course any God capable of intelligently designing something as complex as the DNA/protein machine must have been at least as complex and organized as that machine itself . . . To explain the origin of the DNA/protein machine by invoking a supernatural Designer is to explain precisely nothing, for it leaves unexplained the origin of the Designer.[31]

Design doesn't *explain* organized complexity (says Dawkins); it *presupposes* it, because the designer would have to be as complex as what it creates (designs). Perhaps, therefore, Dawkins means to argue along the following lines: there are really just two explanations of life: unguided Darwinism and an explanation,

---

30. Russell's "Is There a God?" was commissioned by *Illustrated* magazine in 1952, but never published; see Dawkins, *The God Delusion*, p. 52.
31. Dawkins, *The Blind Watchmaker*, p. 140.

guided Darwinism, perhaps, that involves design. But the latter is really no explanation at all. Therefore the only candidate is the former.

Here there are several problems. First, this argument doesn't depend on the facts of biology; it is substantially independent of the latter. Is it likely that Dawkins would be offering an argument of that sort? If so, why would he claim that it is "the Evidence of Evolution" that "Reveals a World Without Design"?

Set that problem aside for the moment; there is another and deeper problem with this argument. Suppose we land on an alien planet orbiting a distant star and discover some machine-like objects that look and work just like a 1941 Allis Chalmers tractor; our leader says "there must be intelligent beings on this planet—look at those tractors." A sophomore philosophy student on the expedition objects: "Hey, hold on a minute! You have explained nothing at all! Any intelligent life that designed those tractors would have to be at least as complex as they are!" No doubt we'd tell him a little learning is a dangerous thing and advise him to take the next rocket ship home and enroll in another philosophy course or two. For of course it is perfectly sensible, in that context, to explain the existence of those tractors in terms of intelligent life, even though (as we can concede for present purposes) that intelligent life would have to be at least as complex as the tractors. The point is we aren't trying to give an *ultimate* explanation of organized complexity, and we aren't trying to explain organized complexity *in general*; we are only trying to explain one particular manifestation of it (those tractors). And (unless you are trying to give an ultimate explanation of organized complexity) it is perfectly proper to explain one manifestation of organized complexity in terms of another. Hence it is not the case, contra Dawkins, that an explanation in terms of divine design is a nonstarter. Such an explanation doesn't constitute an ultimate explanation of organized complexity (if God is complex, nothing could constitute such an explanation); but it is none the worse for that.

A third point: Dawkins argues that "the main thing we want to explain" is "organized complexity." He goes on to say that "the one thing that makes evolution such a neat theory is that it explains how organized complexity can arise out of primeval simplicity," and he faults theism for being unable to explain organized complexity. Now first, in biology we are attempting to describe and explain terrestrial life, not organized complexity generally. And second: *mind* would be an outstanding example of organized complexity, according to Dawkins. Of course it is uncontroversial that if there is such a person as God, he would be a being who thinks and knows; so suppose we take Dawkins to be complaining that theism doesn't offer an explanation of mind. It is perfectly obvious that theists won't be able to give an explanation of mind in general—they won't be able to offer an explanation for the state of affairs consisting in there being at least one mind—because, naturally enough, there *isn't* any explanation of the existence of God. But that is certainly not a point against theism. Explanations come to an end; for theism they come to an end in God. For any other view of the same level of generality they also come to an end. The materialist or physicalist, for example, doesn't have an explanation for the existence of elementary particles or, more generally, contingent physical or material beings; that there are some is, from that perspective, a brute fact. It isn't easy to say precisely what counts as begging the question; but to fault theism for failing to have an ultimate explanation of mind is as good a candidate as any.

Here is a second attempt to reconstrue Dawkins's argument.[32] In *The God Delusion* he argues that the existence of God is monumentally improbable—about as probable as the assembly of a flight-worthy Boeing 747 by a hurricane roaring through a junkyard. Now it is not monumentally improbable, he says, that life should have developed by way of unguided Darwinism. In fact the probability that the stunning complexity of life came to be in that fashion is greater than the probability that there is such a person as God. An explanation involving divine design, therefore, is less probable than the explanation in terms of unguided Darwinism; therefore we should prefer unguided Darwinism to an explanation involving design; but these two are the only viable candidates here; therefore by an inference to the best explanation, we should accept unguided Darwinism.

Clearly a host of considerations clamor for attention here. Concede, for the moment, that unguided Darwinism is more probable than an explanation involving design; does it follow that the former is to be preferred to the latter? There is more to goodness in explanation than the probability of the *explanans*. And how secure is this alleged inference to the best explanation, as an argument form, or, more likely, maxim? If all the explanations are highly unlikely, am I obliged, nonetheless, to pick and endorse one of them? I hear a great roar from the Notre Dame stadium; either the Irish have scored a touchdown, or an extra point, or a field goal, or a safety, or completed a long pass, or made a long run

---

32. Suggested in conversation (but not necessarily endorsed) by Sharon Street.

from scrimmage, or tackled the opposing runner for a loss, or intercepted a pass. Suppose these eight explanations exhaust the field, and suppose the first is slightly more probable than any of the other seven; its probability, on the evidence is .2. Am I obliged to believe that explanation, just because it is more probable than the rest, and even though its probability is much below .5? Whatever happened to agnosticism, withholding belief?

And why think the existence of such a person as God is unlikely in the first place? Dawkins is presumably speaking here of some kind of objective probability, not epistemic probability. Statistical probability hardly seems relevant; presumably, therefore, he's thinking of something like logical probability, something like the proportion of logical space occupied by the possible worlds in which there is such a person as God; his idea is that the more complex something is, the smaller that proportion is. ("God, or any intelligent, decision-taking calculating agent, is complex, which is another way of saying improbable.")[33] But the first thing to note is that according to Dawkins's own definition of complexity, God is *not* complex. According to his definition something is *complex* if it has parts that are "arranged in a way that is unlikely to have arisen by chance alone."[34] Here he's clearly thinking of *material* objects. Setting aside the excesses of mereological universalism, however, one thinks that *immaterial* objects, e.g., numbers, don't have parts. But of course God isn't a material object; strictly speaking, therefore, God has no parts. God is a spirit, an immaterial spiritual being; hence God has no parts at all. *A fortiori* God doesn't have parts arranged in ways unlikely to have arisen by chance. Therefore, given the definition of complexity Dawkins himself proposes, God is not complex.

God has no parts; but isn't God in *some* sense complex? Much ink has been spilled on this topic; but suppose, for the moment, we concede for purposes of argument that God *is* complex. Perhaps we think the more a being knows, the more complex it is; God, being omniscient, would then be highly complex. Perhaps so. But then why does Dawkins just assume that any such being would have to be such that its logical probability was small? Given *materialism* and the idea that the ultimate objects in our universe are the elementary particles of physics, perhaps a being that knew a great deal would be improbable—how

33. Dawkins, *The God Delusion*, p. 109.
34. Dawkins, *The Blind Watchmaker*, p. 7.

could those particles get arranged in such as way as to constitute a being with all that knowledge? But of course we aren't *given* materialism.

So why think God would have to be improbable? According to classical theism, God is of course a being with knowledge—the maximal degree of knowledge—but is also a *necessary* being; it is not so much as possible that there should be no such person as God; God exists in every possible world. If God is a necessary being, if he exists in all possible worlds, then the (objective) probability that he exists, naturally enough, is 1, and the probability that he does not exist is 0. On the classical conception, God is a being who has maximal knowledge, but is also maximally probable. Dawkins doesn't so much as mention this classical conception; he altogether fails to notice that he owes us an argument for the conclusion that this conception is impossible, or anyhow mistaken, so that there is no necessary being with the attributes of God. This version of his argument, therefore, fares no better than the others.

The conclusion to be drawn, I think, is that Dawkins gives us no reason whatever to think that current biological science is in conflict with Christian belief.

Of course Dawkins is not the only thinker to trumpet such conflict. Dawkins together with Daniel Dennett constitute the touchdown twins of current academic atheism: and Dennett follows Dawkins in claiming that evolutionary theory is incompatible with traditional theistic belief.[35] In the next chapter we will see how Dennett develops this theme.

---

35. Although others also vie for that dubious distinction: among them are Sam Harris (*The End of Faith* (New York: Norton, 2004) and Christopher Hitchens (*God Is Not Great* (New York: Hachette Book Group, 2007).

Chapter 2

Evolution and Christian Belief (2)

In the last chapter we considered Richard Dawkins's case for the conclusion that current evolutionary theory is incompatible with Christian (and other theistic) belief. His reasoning was not impressive. Daniel Dennett is the second prominent authority I wish to examine, the other soloist in the choir of voices making that claim. I'll first examine his argument for this conclusion; then I'll turn briefly to arguments by Paul Draper and Philip Kitcher for a similar conclusion.

Dennett's main contribution to this subject is *Darwin's Dangerous Idea*.[1] What is this idea, and why is it dangerous? According to Dennett, "Darwin's dangerous idea" (an idea he himself of course endorses and defends) is really the thought that the living world with all of its beauty and wonder, all of its marvelous and ingenious apparent design, was not created or designed by God or anything at all like God; instead it was produced by natural selection winnowing random genetic mutation, a blind, unconscious, mechanical, algorithmic process, a process, he says, which creates "Design out of Chaos without the aid of Mind": "Here, then, is Darwin's dangerous idea: the algorithmic level *is* the level that best accounts for the speed of the antelope, the wing of the eagle, the shape of the orchid, the diversity of species, and all the other occasions for wonder in the world of nature."[2] (In

---

1. Dennett, *Darwin's Dangerous Idea* (New York: Simon & Shuster, 1995).
2. Dennett, *Darwin's Dangerous Idea*, pp. 50, 59.

Breaking the Spell he adds that the same goes for our moral sense, our religious sensibilities, our artistic strivings, and our interest in and ability to do science.[3]) All of the wonders of the living world have come to be without the help of God or anything at all like God; all of this has happened just by the grace of a mindless natural process. Human beings and all the rest are the outcome of a merely mechanical process; they are not designed or planned for by God (or anyone else). More broadly, the idea is that mind, intelligence, foresight, planning, and design are all latecomers in the universe, themselves created by the unthinking process of natural selection.

Now *why* is Darwin's idea dangerous? Because if we accept it, says Dennett, we are forced to reconsider all our childlike and childish ideas about God, morality, value, the meaning of life, and so on. Why so? Christians and other theists, naturally enough, reject the thought that mind and intelligence, foresight and planning, are latecomers in the universe. They reject this thought because they believe that God, the premier exemplar of mind, has always existed; so *mind* has always existed, and has always been involved in the production and planning of whatever else there is. In fact many theists have thought it *impossible* that mind should be produced just from unthinking matter. In the last chapter I quoted John Locke: "It is as impossible to conceive that ever pure incogitative Matter should produce a thinking intelligent Being, as that nothing should of itself produce Matter."[4] Darwin's dangerous idea is that this notion is not merely not impossible; it's the sober truth of the matter. This idea, then, is inconsistent with any form of theism, and that's what makes it dangerous.

3. Dennett, *Breaking the Spell; Religion as a Natural Phenomenon* (New York: Penguin, 2006).
4. Locke, *Essay Concerning Human Understanding* IV, x, 10.

I DENNETT'S ARGUMENT

How does Dennett propose to argue for this idea? First, he insists that all of life *really has* come about by evolution (and here we are thinking of descent with modification). Indeed, he adds that if you so much as doubt this, you are inexcusably ignorant: "To put it bluntly but fairly, anyone today who doubts that the variety of life on this planet was produced by a process of evolution is simply ignorant— inexcusably ignorant."[5] Note that you don't have to *reject* evolution in order to qualify as inexcusably ignorant: all you have to do is harbor a doubt or two. Perhaps you are a theist; you believe that God created the living world in one way or another; you study the evidence for evolution with great care, but are finally doubtful that God did it that way (you think God might have created certain forms of life directly): according to Dennett, you are then inexcusably ignorant. Here he is stealing a march on Dawkins, who wrote in a 1989 *New York Times* book review that "it is absolutely safe to say that if you meet someone who claims not to believe in evolution, that person is ignorant, stupid or insane (or wicked, but I'd rather not consider that)."[6] At least Dawkins gives skeptics a *choice*: they could be ignorant, *or* stupid, *or* insane or maybe even wicked. Not so for Dennett (he is made of sterner stuff); in fact he plumps for *two* of Dawkins's possibilities: evolutionary skeptics are *both* ignorant *and* wicked (or at least inexcusable). Evolution, apparently, is like the law: ignorance of it is no excuse. Here Dennett and Dawkins remind one of a certain kind of religious personality with which we are all too familiar: if you disagree with them, you are not only wrong, but wicked, and should be punished, if not in this world then certainly in the next.

5. Dennett, *Darwin's Dangerous Idea*, p. 46.
6. Review of Maitland A. Edey and Donald C. Johanson, *Blueprints: Solving the Mystery of Evolution* (Boston: Little Brown, 1989). *New York Times*, April 9, 1989.

Of course Dennett's claim is not merely that all the marvels of contemporary life have been produced by a process of descent with modification; he takes the very considerable step of claiming, further, that the mechanism underlying this process is Darwinian. This mechanism has two parts. First, there is a source of genetic variability: the usual candidate is random genetic mutation. Genetic mutations are allegedly caused by way of copying errors, or vagrant cosmic rays, or chemical agents, or something else; it doesn't really matter. Most of the resulting changes are neutral; a few result in adaptive changes; and some of those adaptive changes are heritable. Perhaps the result is that the descendents of the organism to which the mutation accrues can run (or swim, or fly, or sidle) a bit faster, or see a bit better, or better digest a certain fruit. The other part of the mechanism is natural selection: under the usual conditions of population pressure and scarcity of resources, the descendents of the lucky organism sporting that mutation will tend to survive and reproduce at a greater rate than other members of the population; and eventually the mutation comes to be established as part of the genotype of the species in question. Then the whole process can begin over again. (Of course more than one such process can be under way at a given time.) It is by virtue of countless repetitions of this process, so the claim goes, that the immense variety of creatures in the living world has come to be.

As we've already seen, Dennett maintains that this whole process—the process of descent with modification driven by natural selection winnowing random genetic mutation—is not directed or guided or overseen by any intelligent agent. The whole process has happened without the aid of God or anyone (or anything) at all like God: "An impersonal, unreflective, robotic, mindless little scrap of molecular machinery is the ultimate basis of all the agency, and hence meaning, and hence consciousness, in the universe."[7] Life itself

---

7. Dennett, *Darwin's Dangerous Idea*, p. 203.

originated just by way of the regularities of physics and chemistry (through a sort of extension of natural selection); and undirected natural selection has produced language and mind, including our artistic, moral, religious, and intellectual proclivities.

Now many—theists and others—have found these claims at least extremely doubtful; some have found them preposterous. Is it really so much as possible that language, say, or consciousness, or the ability to compose great music, or prove Gödel's incompleteness theorems, or think up the idea of natural selection should have been produced by mindless processes of this sort? That is an ambitious claim. For example, one of the most striking characteristics of thought is intentionality, *aboutness*. We can think about things of all sorts, some far removed from us: ancient Sparta, the big bang, the angel Gabriel, logical theorems, moral principles, possible worlds, impossible states of affairs, God himself, and much else. Is it really possible that this ability has come about (starting from bacteria, say) just by way of this unguided process? According to Dennett, all of this—mind-boggling or not—is part of Darwin's dangerous idea. That mind and life in all its variety have come to be in this unguided fashion is of course inconsistent with Christian belief, as well as other kinds of theistic belief. For, according to Christians and other theists, God has designed and created the world; he intended that it take a certain form and then caused it to take that form. Further, Dennett claims that all minds have arisen out of matter; that "impersonal, unreflective, robotic, mindless little scrap of molecular machinery" preceded the appearance of mind or mental phenomena.[8] But according to theists, of course, there is a mind that did not arise out of matter. It is mind that comes first; God, the premier instance of mind, has always existed, and has always had knowledge and intentions. God has not arisen from matter or anything else, and does not depend on anything else for his existence.

8. Dennett, *Darwin's Dangerous Idea*, p. 203.

Dennett apparently thinks that Darwin's dangerous idea will come to dominate, and that religious belief is doomed to extinction. While he thinks this is a good thing, he also notes that it is always a bit of a pity to lose part of the biosphere's diversity; he therefore suggests that we should keep a few Baptists and other fundamentalists in something like cultural zoos (no doubt with sizable moats to protect the rest of us right-thinking nonfundamentalists). We should preserve a few Baptists for the sake of posterity—but not, he says, at just any cost. "Save the Baptists," says he, "but not *by all means*. Not if it means tolerating the deliberate misinforming of children about the natural world."[9] Save the Baptists, all right, but only if they promise not to misinform their children by teaching them "that 'Man' is not a product of evolution by natural selection" and other blatantly objectionable views.[10]

Darwin's dangerous idea as set out by Dennett is a paradigm example of naturalism. In this regard it is like Bertrand Russell's famous essay of many years ago, "Why I am not a Christian," except that where Russell appeals to physics, Dennett appeals to biology.[11] Now Dennett's naturalism, like Russell's, is of course inconsistent with theistic religion. But that doesn't automatically make Darwin's idea *dangerous* to theistic religion—theists might just note the inconsistency and, sensibly enough, *reject* the idea. Many propositions are inconsistent with theism (for example, "nothing but turtles exist") but are not a danger to it. Darwin's idea is dangerous to theism only if it is somehow *attractive*, only if there are good reasons for adopting it

9. Dennett, *Darwin's Dangerous Idea*, p. 516; emphasis in original.
10. Dennett, *Darwin's Dangerous Idea*, p. 519. But what if they *do* insist on teaching these heresies to their children? (Baptists will be Baptists, after all.) Will we be obliged to remove Baptist children from their parents' noxious influence? Will we have to put barbed wire around those zoos, maybe check to see if there is room for them in northern Siberia?
11. Russell, *Why I am not a Christian, and Other Essays on Religion and Related Subjects*, ed, with an appendix on the "Bertrand Russell case," by Paul Edwards (New York: Simon and Schuster, 1957). The lecture was first given in 1927 to the National Secular Society, South London Branch, at Battersea Town Hall.

EVOLUTION AND CHRISTIAN BELIEF (2)

and rejecting theism. Why does Dennett think we should *accept* Darwin's dangerous idea? Concede that it is audacious, with it, revolutionary, anti-medieval, quintessentially contemporary, appropriately reverential towards science, and has that nobly stoical hair-shirt quality Russell said he liked in his beliefs: still, why should we believe it? I *think* Dennett means to attempt an answer to this question (and isn't merely preaching to the naturalistic choir).

As far as I can see, Dennett proposes two lines of argument for Darwin's dangerous idea. The first is a reprise of Dawkins: he claims that it is *possible* that all the variety of the biosphere be produced by mindless natural selection: "The theory of natural selection shows how every feature of the world *can* be the product of a blind, unforesightful, nonteleological, ultimately mechanical process of differential reproduction over long periods of time." He also claims that "the power of the theory of natural selection is not the power to prove exactly how (pre)history was, but only the power to prove how it could have been, given what we know about how things are."[12] But does the theory of natural selection really show what Dennett says it does—that every feature of the world, including mind itself "*can* be the product of a blind, unforesightful, nonteleological, ultimately mechanical process of differential reproduction over long periods of time"?

No. Unlike Dawkins, Dennett at least quotes John Locke, who holds it impossible that "pure incogitative matter should produce a thinking intelligent being." Locke believed it impossible in the broadly logical sense that mind should have arisen somehow from "incogitative matter." Supposing, as he did, that matter and mind exhaust the possibilities for concrete beings, he believed it impossible that there should be minds now, but at some earlier time no minds; minds can be produced only by minds. Or by Mind. Locke and other theists

---

12. Dennett, *Darwin's Dangerous Idea*, p. 315, emphasis in original; also p. 319.

agree that mind is a primitive feature of the universe: God (who is part of the universe even if not part of the created universe) has never come into existence; he has always existed; and he has always had intentions, beliefs and aims. Indeed, many theists will add that this is not merely true; it is necessarily true. Contrary to Dennett's suggestion, the neo-Darwinian scientific theory of evolution certainly hasn't shown that Locke is wrong or that God does not exist necessarily; it hasn't even shown that it is possible, in the broadly logical sense, that mind arise from "pure incogitative" matter. It hasn't shown these things because it doesn't so much as address these questions. Like other scientific theories, evolutionary theory does not pronounce on such questions as whether it is logically possible that minds should come to be in a universe which is originally mindless.

Neo-Darwinism hasn't shown that Locke was wrong, and neither has Dennett. His response to Locke is to take Locke's claim as implying that there can't be robots that can actually think—a view, he says, that would "risk hoots of derision today."[13] Well, perhaps in some quarters it would call forth hoots of derision; in others it will receive enthusiastic agreement, and in still others a respectful if uncommitted hearing. But in any event *Argumentum ad Derisionem* is hardly an approved argument form; it will never rank up there with, for example, modus ponens, or even the complex constructive dilemma.

So neither Dennett nor contemporary evolutionary theory shows that possibly, all of the features of our world, including mind, have been produced by unguided natural selection. But assume (contrary to fact, as I see it) that this is in fact possible in the broadly logical sense. If so, is it also *biologically* possible? Biological possibility is a vexed notion. Shall we say that a state of affairs is biologically possible if it is compatible with the biological laws? Or with the conjunction of biological law together with some earlier total state

---

13. Dennett, *Darwin's Dangerous Idea*, p. 27.

of affairs? But *are* there specifically biological laws—that is, biological laws in addition to the laws of physics and chemistry? Or should we instead think (with Dawkins) of biological possibility as simply a matter of less than astronomical improbability? So that it is biologically possible that mind arise from pure incogitative matter if those possible worlds in which it *does* so arise occupy a not-too-negligible volume of logical space? Or if a large enough space is occupied by those worlds in which mind arises from purely incogitative matter and which are like the actual world up to some time *t* at which there are no minds?

No matter. Take biological possibility in any of these ways, and suppose that all of terrestrial life has indeed come to be by way of natural selection. It doesn't follow that life has come to be by way of *unguided* natural selection, and it doesn't even follow that it is *biologically possible* that life has come to be that way. For, of course, it is perfectly possible both that life has come to be by way of *guided* natural selection, and that it could not have come to be by way of *unguided* natural selection. It is perfectly possible that the process of natural selection has been guided and superintended by God, and that it could not have produced our living world without that guidance. Recall the Library of Life in the last chapter: it is perfectly possible that life has developed just as it specifies, that each of the changes it mentions has come to be by virtue of natural selection, and that God has guided and directed the entire process—and that without his guidance life could not have developed at all.[14] The truth of the theory of natural selection, therefore, doesn't for a moment show that all of life has come to be by way of *unguided* natural selection, or even that

---

14. He could do so, for example, by causing the right genetic mutations to arise at the right time, (see chapter 4) or by preserving a genomic feature that isn't fitness-conferring, or in still other ways. He could do so either by "frontloading," i.e., selecting initial conditions he knows will issue, for example, in the mutations he wants, or by causing these mutations at the time they are needed (see chapter 4, part IV for more on these possibilities).

it is biologically possible that it has come to be that way. It is therefore a mistake to say with Dennett that "the theory of natural selection shows how every feature of the world *can* be the product of a blind, unforesightful, nonteleological, ultimately mechanical process of differential reproduction."

As far back as Darwin's day, of course, people have argued that various features of the living world—the *eye* has been a favorite example—could *not* have come about by unguided natural selection.[15] They have claimed either that this is impossible or that it is astronomically improbable. Dennett and other defenders of unguided natural selection try to *refute* these arguments; to show that they do not establish their conclusions. But even if they are successful, what they show is only that these arguments don't succeed; in doing this they do *not* show that unguided evolution *could* have produced these features. If they are right, perhaps the thing to say is that we can't show that unguided natural selection has not produced these wonders (including mind). Given certain assumptions, what the friends of unguided natural selection show (if they are successful) is that we don't know that it is astronomically improbable that unguided natural selection produce all the variety of the living world. Those stories as to how various biological phenomena could have been produced by unguided natural selection could be possible in the sense that we don't know that they are astronomically improbable.

Dennett's claim was that Darwin's dangerous idea is not merely possible, but *true*: that the entire living world *has* been produced by mindless natural selection. Why believe that? What Dennett has so far offered is no more than what Dawkins came up with: *given certain controversial assumptions about logical possibility (for example, that it is possible that mind come to be in a mindless universe), we don't know that*

---

15. Going back to St. George Mivart (1827–1900), a contemporary of Darwin.

Darwin's dangerous idea is astronomically improbable.[16] This argument—that it is not astronomically unlikely that all the variety of life came to be by way of unguided natural selection; therefore that is how it *did* come to be—is no stronger when Dennett gives it than when Dawkins gives it, and we've already seen how weak it is when Dawkins gives it. You've always thought Mother Teresa was a moral hero; someone wanders by and tells you that we don't know that it's not astronomically improbable that she was a complete hypocrite. Would you be impressed? So far, theism doesn't seem much threatened by Darwin's dangerous idea.

So much for Dennett's first line of argument; but he also has a second. If there is no such person as God, then, setting aside a few unlikely possibilities, natural selection is unguided. Dennett's second line of argument, therefore, is for the conclusion that there isn't any such person as God, or at any rate it is irrational to think there is; theism can't be accepted by someone who is thinking straight. How does he propose to argue this point? He repeats several times that believing in an "anthropomorphic" God is childish, or irrational, or anyway obsolete. What he calls an "anthropomorphic" God, furthermore, is precisely what traditional Christians believe in—a God who is a *person*, the sort of being who is capable of knowledge, who has aims and ends, and who can and in fact does act on what he knows in such a way as to try to accomplish those aims. And what, exactly, is the matter with theistic belief? Why does Dennett think such belief is childish or irrational (for informed adults)? As far as I can see, he proceeds as follows. First, he claims that the traditional theistic arguments—the ontological argument, the cosmological arguments, the

---

16. But what about such empirical evidence as the fossil record, the homologies, the relations demonstrated by molecular biology? This is clearly evidence for universal common ancestry and for the proposition that the living world has developed by virtue of a process of descent with modification. It is not, just as such, evidence for the proposition that what drives the whole process is natural selection; *a fortiori*, it is not evidence for the claim that what drives the process is *unguided* natural selection.

argument from (or better, *to*) design—don't work. Next, he assumes that rational belief in God would require broadly scientific evidence and proposes or rather just assumes that there isn't any other source of warrant or rationality for belief in God or for religious beliefs generally.

Dennett mentions only one of the theistic arguments, the design argument, and even there he ignores the work of Richard Swinburne, the preeminent contemporary exponent of the argument, who over a period of at least thirty years or so has produced a powerfully impressive, and highly developed version of this argument.[17] Now Dennett makes quite a show of being serious and forthright where others give in to conventional politeness: "I know it passes in polite company to let people have it both ways and under most circumstances I wholeheartedly cooperate with this benign arrangement. But we're seriously trying to get at the truth here."[18] If we *are* seriously trying to get at the truth, however, it might be good to consider or at least mention the most important contemporary work on the subject.

But suppose Swinburne's arguments are indeed unsuccessful, and add that the same goes for all the other theistic arguments— for example, the moral argument as developed by George Mavrodes and Robert Adams, and the cosmological argument as developed by William Lane Craig, and all the rest.[19] Does it follow that one who believes in God is irrational, unjustified, going contrary to reason, or in some other way deserving of reprimand or abuse or

17. Swinburne, *The Existence of God* (Oxford: Clarendon Press, 1979; new edition 2004).
18. Dennett, *Darwin's Dangerous Idea*, p. 154.
19. See Mavrodes's "Religion and the Queerness of Morality," in Robert Audi and William Wainright, *Rationality, Religious Belief, and Moral Commitment* (Ithaca, N.Y.: Cornell University Press, 1986); Adams's "Moral Arguments for Theistic Belief" in The *Virtue of Faith and other Essays in Philosophical Theology* (Oxford: Oxford University Press); Craig's *The Kalam Cosmological Argument* (London: The Macmillan Press, 1979) and "In Defense of the Kalam Cosmological Argument" in *Faith and Philosophy* 14, no. 2 April 1997; and my "Two Dozen or so Good Theistic Arguments" in Deane-Peter Baker, ed., *Alvin Plantinga* (Cambridge: Cambridge University Press, 2007).

EVOLUTION AND CHRISTIAN BELIEF (2)

disapprobation? No. After all, one of the main lessons to be learned from the history of modern philosophy from Descartes through Hume is that there don't seem to be good arguments for the existence of other minds or selves, or the past, or an external world and much else besides; nevertheless belief in other minds, the past, and an external world is presumably not irrational or in any other way below epistemic par.[20]

Are things different with belief in God? If so, why? What makes the difference? This topic—the question whether rational belief in God requires argument or "scientific evidence"—has been central in philosophy of religion for a long time. Dennett apparently thinks philosophical theologians, some of whom hold that scientific evidence is *not* required for rational religious belief, are thereby committed to flouting rational judgment. He addresses this topic in a truly remarkable passage:

> The philosopher Ronald de Sousa once memorably described philosophical theology as "intellectual tennis without a net," and I readily allow that I have indeed been assuming without comment or question up to now that the net of rational judgment was up. We can lower it if you really want to. It's your serve. Whatever you serve, suppose I rudely return service as follows: "What you say implies that God is a ham sandwich wrapped in tinfoil. That's not much of a God to worship!"[21]

That's a memorable description, all right, particularly if you call to mind the work of such classical philosophical theologians as Thomas Aquinas, John Duns Scotus, and Jonathan Edwards, or such contemporary philosophical theologians as Robert Adams, William Alston,

20. See my *God and Other Minds* (Ithaca, N.Y.: Cornell University Press, 1967), part III.
21. Dennett, *Darwin's Dangerous Idea*, p. 154.

Eleonore Stump, Richard Swinburne, Peter van Inwagen, and Nicholas Wolterstorff, all of whose work, in terms of intellectual rigor and cogency, compares very favorably with that of Dennett (or, for that matter, de Sousa). As a matter of fact this canard is also irrelevant; the question is about the epistemology of religious belief, and in particular whether rational theistic belief requires the presence of cogent theistic argument; it is not about the real or alleged intellectual vices of philosophical theologians.

But what prompts Dennett to bring up his miserable ham sandwich in the first place? What is his point? It's not entirely easy to tell. The topic is the claim on the part of many Christians that *faith* is a source of knowledge or information about the world in addition to reason. Take reason to be the ensemble of such faculties or processes as perception, memory, rational intuition (the source of beliefs about, for example, elementary logic and arithmetic), induction, and the like. Is Dennett claiming that anyone who thinks there is a further source of knowledge or warranted belief in addition to reason would be carrying on as irrationally as Dennett would be if he launched that ham sandwich zinger? It seems so; a bit further down he says: "Think about whether you really want to abandon reason when reason is on your side." Then follows a maudlin little tale about how you are sightseeing in a foreign land, your loved one is killed, and, at the trial, the judge is swayed more strongly by emotional testimonies (from the killer's kinsmen) to the fine character of the accused than by the testimony of eyewitnesses who saw him commit the crime: that would be unreasonable and you wouldn't like it, would you? He goes on:

> Would you be willing to be operated on by a surgeon who tells you that whenever a little voice in him tells him to disregard his medical training he listens to the little voice? I know it passes in polite company to let people have it both ways.... if you think that this common but unspoken understanding about faith is

anything better than socially useful obfuscation to avoid mutual embarrassment and loss of face, then either you have seen much more deeply into this issue than any philosopher has (for none has come up with a good defense for this) or you are kidding yourself.[22]

I'm sorry to say this is about as bad as philosophy (well, apart from the blogosphere) gets; Christian charity, perhaps even good manners might require passing silently by the embarrassing spectacle, eyes averted. As Dennett says, however, we're seriously trying to get at the truth here; the fact is Dennett's way of carrying on is an insulting expression of disdain for those who do serious work in this area, and honesty requires that it be noted as such. (Or perhaps it shows where blind allegiance to ideology can lead.) The question is whether there is a source of rational religious belief going beyond perception, memory, a priori intuition, induction, et cetera. This question has been widely discussed and debated for the last forty years, ever since Dennett was in graduate school.[23] He airily ignores this lively and long lasting research project; instead he just tells absurd stories. Is this because he is ignorant of that work? Or doesn't understand it? Or can't think of any decent arguments against it? Or has decided that the method of true philosophy is inane ridicule and burlesque rather than argument?[24] No matter; whatever the reason, Dennett's ventures into the epistemology of religious belief do not inspire confidence.

---

22. Dennett, *Darwin's Dangerous Idea*, p. 155.
23. See, e.g., Plantinga and Wolterstorff, *Faith and Rationality: Reason and Belief in God* (Notre Dame, Ind.: Notre Dame University Press, 1983) and William Alston, *Perceiving God: The Epistemology of Religious Belief* (Ithaca, N.Y.: Cornell University Press, 1991). See also works by William Abraham, Richard Gale, Richard Swinburne, Eleonore Stump, Peter van Inwagen, and many others.
24. Apparently some of the dreaded "New Atheists" *do* think serious discussion is out of place in this area. Here is Richard Dawkins's suggestion for dealing with those religious people he disagrees with: "We need to go further: go beyond humorous ridicule, sharpen our barbs to

First of all, the fact is contemporary philosophers *have* come up with perfectly sensible defenses of the idea that there can be sources of knowledge in addition to reason; and of course the history of the subject is replete with acute discussions of this topic under the rubric of faith and reason.[25] Naturally these defenses might be mistaken; but to show that they are requires more than a silly story and an airy wave of the hand. Second, Dennett apparently thinks that if there were any sources of information or knowledge in addition to reason, the deliverances of those sources would necessarily go *contrary to* reason ("think about whether you really want to abandon reason"). But that's just a confusion. Christians and other theists typically think they know by faith various truths—for example, the main lines of Christian belief, including incarnation and atonement—that are not among the deliverances of reason. They might also think they know by faith that God created the world. Therefore, if indeed the living world has come to be by way of a process of evolution, then God in some way has superintended or orchestrated or guided this process; thus they would be claiming to know something in addition to what reason delivers—but not, of course, something that goes *contrary to* reason. (As we have seen, there is nothing in current evolutionary science to show or even suggest that God did *not* thus superintend evolution.) They wouldn't be abandoning reason any more than you would be abandoning perception if you relied on memory, rather

---

a point where they really hurt" (comment # 368197 at Richard Dawkins.net, comment 16 Wednesday, April 22, 2009). Fence sitters, he says, "are likely to be swayed by a display of naked contempt. Nobody likes to be laughed at. Nobody wants to be the butt of contempt." Maybe so. Of course some might also find this attempt to replace argument and reason with contumely and contempt less intimidating than mildly amusing. It is more appropriate, however, to view with melancholy the spectacle of discourse in this area lowered to a level beneath that of political discourse at election time, and to feel compassion for those who thus lower it.

25. Among the authors mentioned in footnote 23, see in particular Alston, *Perceiving God*, Plantinga and Wolterstorff, *Faith and Rationality*, and Plantinga, *Warranted Christian Belief* (New York: Oxford University Press, 2000).

than perception, for your views about what you were doing yesterday afternoon. It is no part of reason to insist that there can't be any other source of true or warranted belief; it is perfectly in accord with reason to suppose that there are sources of truth in addition to reason.[26] It looks as if here it is *Dennett* who is conveniently lowering the net a foot or two when he makes his return. (Perhaps a more apt tennis metaphor would have him take a whack at the ball and completely miss it.)

Dennett suggests still a third claim:

> Now if you want to *reason* about faith, and offer a reasoned (and reason responsive) defense of faith as an extra category of belief worthy of special consideration, I'm eager to play.... what I want to see is a reasoned ground for taking faith seriously as a *way of getting to the truth*, and not, say, just as a way people comfort themselves and each other.... But you must not expect me to go along with your defense of faith as a path to truth if at any point you appeal to the very dispensation you are supposedly trying to justify.[27]

Here he seems to assume that if you can't show by *reason* that a given proposed source of truth is in fact reliable, then it is improper to accept the deliverances of that source. This assumption goes back to the Lockean, Enlightenment claim that while there could indeed be such a thing as divine revelation, it would be irrational to accept any particular proposition as divinely revealed, unless you had a good argument from reason for the conclusion that it *was* divinely revealed. This assumption has also been under extensive discussion in contemporary philosophy of religion; perhaps the most impressive work

---

26. Indeed, it isn't even part of reason to claim that there couldn't be a source of truth whose deliverances were (to some degree) *contrary* to the teachings of reason.

27. Dennett, *Darwin's Dangerous Idea*, p. 154.

here (work Dennett ignores) has been done by William Alston, who has cogently argued that this assumption embodies a kind of double standard.[28]

Alston's argument, in rough outline, goes as follows. According to the Lockean assumption, first, there may be warranted (or rational or justified) religious beliefs that go beyond reason in the sense that there are no good rational arguments (no good arguments from perception, memory, rational intuition, et cetera) for them. But second, according to Locke, one can't rationally accept any such belief unless one has a good *rational* argument (an argument from reason) for the conclusion that the belief in question *does* enjoy warrant (or justification or rationality). Alston points out that we don't impose that kind of requirement on other sources of belief or knowledge. Consider, for example, rational intuition, memory, and perception. Can we show by the first or first two that the third is in fact reliable—that is, without relying in any way on the deliverances of the third? Clearly not; rational intuition enables us to know the truths of mathematics and logic, but it can't tell us whether or not perception is reliable. Nor can we show by rational intuition and perception that memory is reliable, nor (of course) by perception and memory that rational intuition is. Nor can we give a decent, noncircular rational argument that reason itself is indeed reliable; in trying to give such an argument, we would of course be *presupposing* that reason is reliable.

Does it follow that there is something irrational in trusting these alleged sources, in accepting their deliverances? Of course not. So why insist that it is irrational to accept religious belief in the absence of an argument for the reliability of the faculty or belief-producing processes that give rise to it? Perhaps it *is* irrational to do that, but surely some argument is needed; one can't simply assume that it is. Why treat the sources of religious belief differently? Is there anything

28. See Alston's *Perceiving God* (Cornell University Press, 1991), p. 234.

EVOLUTION AND CHRISTIAN BELIEF (2)

but arbitrariness in insisting that any alleged source of truth must justify itself at the bar of rational intuition, perception, and memory? Perhaps we have several *different* sources of knowledge about the world, and none can be shown to be reliable using only the others. Once more, arbitrarily lowering the net (or missing the ball).

By way of summary: Quentin Smith, himself a naturalist, deplores the "desecularization" of philosophy over the past quarter century or so. He complains that most naturalist philosophers ordinarily know nothing about contemporary philosophy of religion and pay little heed to it, "the great majority of naturalist philosophers react by publicly ignoring the increasing desecularizing of philosophy (while privately disparaging theism, without really knowing anything about contemporary analytic philosophy of religion) and proceeding to work in their own area of specialization as if theism, the view of approximately one-quarter or one-third of their field, did not exist."[29] Dennett only partially fits this pattern. True, he doesn't know anything about contemporary analytic philosophy of religion, but that doesn't stop him from making public declarations on the subject.[30]

II DRAPER'S ARGUMENT

I've argued so far that evolution and theism, contra Dawkins and Dennett, are compatible: this means, as I am using the term, that there are no obvious truths such that their conjunction with evolution and theism is inconsistent in the broadly logical sense. One might argue, however, that even if this is so, the truth of evolution gives us some reason to reject theism: perhaps evolution constitutes *evidence* against theism. Paul Draper makes just this claim: "I will show that

---

29. Smith, "The Metaphilosophy of Naturalism," *Philo: A Journal of Philosophy* vol. 4, no. 2, p. 196.
30. For further discussion of the bearing of evolutionary science on theistic religion, see Daniel Dennett and Alvin Plantinga, *Science and Religion: Are They Compatible?* (New York: Oxford University Press, 2011).

certain known facts support the hypothesis of naturalism over the hypothesis of theism because we have considerably more reason to expect them to obtain on the assumption that naturalism is true than on the assumption that theism is true."[31] What are these "known facts"? One of them, he says, is evolution: "My position is that evolution is evidence favoring naturalism over theism. There is, in other words, a good *evidential* argument favoring naturalism over theism."[32] The basic idea is that evolution is more likely—at least twice as likely, Draper argues—on naturalism than on theism.

His argument goes as follows. Where "E" is evolution (that is, the proposition that all current forms of terrestrial life have come to be by way of evolution), "T" is theism, and "N" is naturalism, Draper proposes to argue that

(1) $P(E/N)$ is much greater than $P(E/T)$.

From this he infers that if all else is (evidentially) equal, naturalism is more likely than theism. Given that naturalism is incompatible with theism, it follows that theism is unlikely.

Suppose, however, as most theists who have thought about it do think, that theism is noncontingent: necessarily true or necessarily false. If so, (1) doesn't imply that naturalism is more likely than theism; instead (1) obviously entails that theism is true. For if theism is noncontingent and false, then it is necessarily false; the probability of a contingent proposition on a necessary falsehood is 1; hence $P(E/T)$ is 1. But if, as Draper claims, $P(E/N)$ is greater than $P(E/T)$, then $P(E/T)$ is less than 1, hence T is not necessarily false. If T is not necessarily false, however, then (given that it is noncontingent) it is necessarily true. So if theism is noncontingent, and (1) is true, then theism is true, and indeed necessarily true. Draper is of course assuming that theism is contingent; hence his argument

---

31. Paul Draper, "Evolution and the Problem of Evil," in *Philosophy of Religion: An Anthology*, 5th ed., ed. Louis Pojman and Michael Rea (Belmont, California: Thomson Wadsworth, 2008).

32. Draper, "Evolution and the Problem of Evil," p. 208. In this article he also cites, as such known facts, the ways in which pain and pleasure are distributed in our world, and the ways in which pain and pleasure are connected with survival and reproductive success. Here I'll address just the claim mentioned above in the text; in section IV I'll consider Philip Kitcher's claim that the waste, predation, and pain involved in evolution is evidence against theism.

won't be relevant if theism is noncontingent. But let's set this limitation aside and look at his interesting argument.

How does the argument go? Let "S" be the proposition that "some relatively complex living things did not descend from one-celled organisms but rather were independently created by a supernatural person;" then, as Draper points out,

(2) $P(E/N)$ is much greater than $P(E/T)$ if and only if $P(-S/N)$ x $P(E/-S\&N)$ is much greater than $P(-S/T)$ x $P(E/-S\&T)$.[33]

Naturally he proposes to show that $P(E/N)$ is much greater than $P(E/T)$ by showing that $P(-S/N)$ x $P(E/-S\&N)$ is much greater than $P(-S/T)$ x $P(E/-S\&T)$. He proposes to show this by showing (a) that $P(-S/N)$ is much greater than $P(-S/T)$, and by showing (b) that $P(E/-S\&N)$ is *at least as great as* $P(E/-S\&T)$.

Draper argues with respect to (a) that $P(-S/N)$ is at least *twice* $P(-S/T)$. If, as he also argues, $P(E/-S\&N)$ is at least as great as $P(E/-S\&T)$, the consequence is that $P(E/N)$ is at least twice as great as $P(E/T)$; this is sufficient, he apparently thinks, for $P(E/N)$ to be much greater than $P(E/T)$. If his argument is correct, therefore, $P(E/N)$ is at least twice as great as $P(E/T)$.

Suppose this is true: how much does it really show? As he says, *if all else is evidentially equal,* theism is improbable. But of course all else is not evidentially equal. Aren't there are a host of other probabilities in the neighborhood that favor theism at least as heavily? For example, let "L" be "there is life on earth." Given the incredibly difficulties in seeing how life could have come to be just by virtue of the laws of physics, $P(L/N)$ is low. But $P(L/T)$ is not low: it's likely that the God of theism would desire that there be life, and life of various kinds. Hence $P(L/T)$ is much higher, I'd guess orders of magnitude higher, than $P(L/N)$. Similarly, let "I" be "there are intelligent beings"; let "M" be "there are beings with a moral sense"; let "W" be "there are creatures who worship God"; each of $P(I/T)$, $P(M/T)$ and $P(W/T)$ are much greater than $P(I/N)$, $P(M/N)$, and $P(W/N)$. The God of theism would very likely desire that there be creatures who resemble him in being rational and intelligent; he would also, no doubt, desire that there be creatures who have a moral sense, and can tell right from

33. Draper, "Evolution and the Problem of Evil," p. 209.

wrong; and he would also very likely desire that there be creatures who can experience his presence and who are moved to worship by God's greatness and goodness. There will also be many other "known facts" that are more probable on theism than on naturalism. If so, however, the evidence favoring naturalism over theism that Draper cites will be more than counterbalanced by evidence favoring theism over naturalism.

III WHY DO PEOPLE DOUBT EVOLUTION?

As we've seen, Dawkins, Dennett, and the rest of that choir favor us with a *fortissimo* rendition of their claim that current evolutionary theory is incompatible with Christian belief—and, indeed, theistic belief of any sort. As we've also seen, they are mistaken on this point (as on many others). This mistake, however, isn't a merely theoretical error: it has serious practical consequences. Polls reveal that most Americans have grave doubts about the truth of evolution. Only about 25 percent of Americans believe that human beings have descended from ape-like ancestors, whatever they think about the main lines of the whole theory. Many Americans are concerned about the teaching of evolution in the schools and want to add something as a corrective ("intelligent design," perhaps) or they want it taught as a mere "theory" rather than as the sober truth, or they want the objections to it taught, or they want it taught along with "critical thinking."

What accounts for this? Why don't Americans simply accede to the authority of the experts here, and shape their opinions and educational policies accordingly? Kenneth Miller thinks it is because of a "healthy disrespect for authority" on the part of Americans, perhaps going back to frontier days:

> If rebellion and disrespect are indeed part of the American Talent
> for science, then what should we make of the anti-evolutionary

movement? One part of the analysis is clear. The willingness of Americans to reject established authority has played a major role in the way that local activists have managed to push ideas such as scientific creationsim and intelligent design into local schools.[34]

Miller's idea seems to be that Americans tend towards a rugged and self-reliant individualism; they aren't going to let a bunch of pointy-headed intellectuals tell them what to believe. While there may be some truth to this, it can hardly be the whole answer. Americans don't ordinarily reject other basic scientific theses, such as the theory of relativity and quantum mechanics.[35] True; they may not have *heard* much about these theories; but that just raises the question why evolution, as opposed to other central parts of science, is so much in the public consciousness.

The answer, of course, is obvious: it is because of the entanglement of evolution with religion. The vast majority of Americans reject atheism, and hence also naturalism. A solid majority of Americans are Christians, and many more (some 88 or 90 percent, depending on the poll you favor) believe in God. But when that choir of experts repeatedly tell us that evolution is incompatible with belief in God, it's not surprising that many people come to believe that evolution *is* incompatible with belief in God, and is therefore an enemy of religion.[36] After all, those experts are, well, experts. But then it is also not surprising that many Americans are reluctant to have evolution taught to their children in the public schools, the schools they themselves

---

34. Miller, *Only a Theory: Evolution and the Battle for America's Soul* (New York: Viking, 2008), p. 12.

35. Though they do tend to scoff when apprised of such consequences of relativity theory as that the faster you go, the heavier you get, and if you accelerated all the way up to the speed of light, you'd gain an infinite amount of weight.

36. Still another example: until 1997 the National Association of Biology Teachers officially described evolution (on their website) as "an unsupervised, impersonal, unpredictable and natural process."

pay taxes to support.[37] Protestants don't want Catholic doctrine taught in the schools and Christians don't want Islam taught, but the distance between naturalism and Christian belief, either Catholic or Protestant, is vastly greater than the distance between Catholics and Protestants or, for that matter, between Christians and Muslims. Christians, Jews, and Muslims concur on belief in God; naturalism stands in absolute opposition to these theistic religions; and, due in part to those declarations by the "experts," evolution is widely seen as a central pillar in the temple of naturalism. The association of evolution with naturalism is the obvious root of the widespread antipathy to evolution in the United States, and to the teaching of evolution in the public schools.

This antipathy spills over to suspicion of science itself, with a consequent erosion of support for science. As a result, declarations by Dawkins, Dennett, and others have at least two unhappy results. First, their (mistaken) claim that religion and evolution are incompatible damages religious belief, making it look less appealing to people who respect reason and science. But second, it also damages science. That is because it forces many to choose between science and belief in God. Most believers, given the depth and significance of their belief in God, are not going to opt for science; their attitude towards science is likely to be or become one of suspicion and mistrust. Hence these declarations of incompatibility have unhappy consequences for science itself. Perhaps this is not a reason for those who believe these myths to stop promoting them; if that's what they think, that's what they should say. What it does mean, however, is that there is very good reason for exposing them for the myths they are: the damage they do to science.

---

37. It's worth noting that many biology textbooks indeed present evolution as unguided, and hence as incompatible with theistic belief. For a list of such textbooks, see Casey Luskin, "Smelling Blood in the Water" in *God and Evolution; Protestants, Catholics and Jews Explore Darwin's Challenge to Faith*, ed. Jay Richards (Seattle: Discovery Institute Press, 2010), pp. 88–90.

IV KITCHER'S "ENLIGHTENMENT CASE"

Like Dawkins and Dennett, Philip Kitcher thinks evolution creates a problem for theists, believers in God. His *Living With Darwin*, however, is far more responsible and evenhanded than the works of Dawkins and Dennett, but also less venturesome.[38] First, he proposes that those evangelical Christians who rally behind intelligent design "appreciate that the Darwinian picture of life (which goes well beyond current evolutionary science) is at odds with a particular kind of religion, providentialist religion." Providentialist religion is the idea that God "cares for his creatures" and "observes the fall of every sparrow and is especially concerned with humanity."[39] Now how exactly does "the Darwinian picture" cut against such religion? Well, if we think of the Darwinian picture as including the idea that the process of evolution is *unguided*, then of course that picture is completely at odds with providentialist religion. As we have seen, however, current evolutionary science doesn't include the thought that evolution *is* unguided; it quite properly refrains from commenting on that metaphysical or theological issue.

So suppose we ask about current evolutionary science: which parts of it, then, are at odds with providentialist religion as thus characterized? As we saw in chapter 1, section I, we have at least the following: (1) the ancient earth thesis, (2) the descent with modification thesis, (3) the universal common ancestry thesis, (4) the progress thesis, and (5) Darwinism, the thesis that what drives the whole process is (for the most part) natural selection winnowing random genetic mutation. But as we also saw above, none of these seems to cut against providentialist religion. Clearly that sort of religion is compatible (as Augustine already suggested) with the idea that the earth

---

38. Kitcher, *Living With Darwin* (New York: Oxford University Press, 2007).
39. Kitcher, *Living With Darwin*, pp. 122, 123.

is ancient, and indeed as ancient as you please. The same goes for the theses that the diversity of life has come about by virtue of a process of descent with modification and that all creatures are genealogically related. Perhaps these last two are a bit less probable given theism than given naturalism (for the naturalist, these are the only game in town, whereas the theist has other options), but they are certainly not at odds with providentialist religion as such.[40] And the same goes for Darwinism. As we have already noted, God could have created life in all its diversity by way of such a process, guiding it in the direction in which he wants to see it go, by causing the right mutations to arise at the right time, preserving certain populations from extinction, and so on.

Exactly what problem, then, does evolutionary theory pose for providentialist religion? Here Kitcher turns to the traditional problem of evil, claiming that current evolutionary science exacerbates that ancient problem:

> Darwin's account of the history of life greatly enlarges the scale on which suffering takes place. Through millions of years, billions of animals experience vast amounts of pain, supposedly so that, after an enormous number of extinctions of entire species, on the tip of one twig of the evolutionary tree, there may emerge a species with the special properties that make us able to worship the Creator.[41]

But it didn't take Darwin to enable us to see that nature, in Tennyson's phrase (which antedates the publication of *the Origin of Species* by more than a decade), is "red in tooth and claw"; nor does it take Darwin to enable us to see that the earth is old, and that during much

---

40. See chapter 1, section I.
41. Kitcher, *Living With Darwin*, p. 123. For a powerful book-length treatment, see Michael Murray, *Nature Red in Tooth and Claw* (New York: Oxford University Press, 2008).

of its history animals have suffered. So how exactly does evolution exacerbate the problem of evil? Would it be that bit about how the point of the whole process was to produce "a species with the special properties that make us able to worship the Creator"? Kitcher puts it like this:

> When you consider the millions of years in which sentient creatures have suffered, the uncounted number of extended and agonizing deaths, it simply rings hollow to suppose that all this is needed so that, at the very tail end of history, our species can manifest the allegedly transcendent good of free and virtuous action.[42]

Here there are several problems. First, perhaps our species has arisen at the tail end of history. That's the tail end of history *now*, however, and there is little reason to think history will be ending anytime soon; who knows how long our history will be? Second, Kitcher apparently thinks that given evolution, Christians and other theists would have to suppose that the point of the entire process was the production of our species; but why think a thing like that? According to the Bible (Genesis 1:20–26), when God created the living world, he declared it good; he did not add that it was good because it would lead to us human beings. There is nothing in Christian thought to suggest that God created animals in order that human beings might come to be, or that the only value of nonhuman animal creation lies in their relation to humans.

Is the thought that God simply wouldn't use a process of evolution, wasteful and filled with suffering as it is, to bring about any end he had in mind? But this idea ignores too many possibilities. Much in the natural world—just as much in the human world—does indeed

---

42. Kitcher, *Living With Darwin*, p. 127.

seem the sort of thing a loving God would hate. In the case of the human world, we don't think God would choose or approve of genocide, hatred, and a whole list of ills our sorry race is heir to. Believers in God don't think God approves of these things; rather, these atrocities are perpetrated by human beings, and God permits them because he has good reason—one that we may not be able to discern—for permitting them. The same goes for processes in the natural world that cause pain and suffering. Various candidates for these reasons have been suggested.[43]

Here is one that is unlikely to become popular among secularists. God wanted to create a really good world; among all the possible worlds, he wanted to choose one of very great goodness. But what sorts of properties make for a good world? What are the good-making properties for worlds? Many and various: containing rational creatures who live together in harmony, containing happy creatures, containing creatures who know and love God, and many more. Among good-making properties for worlds, however, there is one of special, transcendent importance, and it is a property that according to Christians characterizes our world. For according to the Christian story, God, the almighty first being of the universe and the creator of everything else, was willing to undergo enormous suffering in order to redeem creatures who had turned their backs on him. He created human beings; they rebelled against him and constantly go contrary to his will. Instead of treating them as some Oriental monarch would, he sent his Son, the Word, the second person of the Trinity into the world. The Word became flesh and dwelt among us. He was subjected to ridicule, rejection, and finally the cruel and humiliating death of

---

43. For example, there is Peter van Inwagen's "massive irregularity" defense; see his *The Problem of Evil* (Oxford: Clarendon Press, 2006), Lecture 7. Of course a very great deal has been written about the problem of evil. For a sample, see *A Companion to the Problem of Evil*, ed. Daniel Howard-Snyder and Justin McBrayer (London: Blackwell, forthcoming); *The Problem of Evil*, ed. Robert and Marilyn Adams (New York: Oxford University Press, 1991); *God and the Problem of Evil* (London: Blackwell, 2001).

the cross. Horrifying as that is, Jesus, the Word, the son of God, suffered something vastly more horrifying: abandonment by God, exclusion from his love and affection: "My God, my God, why have you forsaken me?" All this to enable human beings to be reconciled to God, and to achieve eternal life. This overwhelming display of love and mercy is not merely the greatest story ever told; it is the greatest story that *could be* told. No other great-making property of a world can match this one.

If so, however, perhaps all the best possible worlds contain incarnation and atonement, or at any rate atonement.[44] But any world that contains atonement will contain sin and evil and consequent suffering and pain. Furthermore, if the remedy is to be proportionate to the sickness, such a world will contain a great deal of sin and a great deal of suffering and pain. Still further, it may very well contain sin and suffering, not just on the part of human beings but perhaps also on the part of other creatures as well. Indeed, some of these other creatures might be vastly more powerful than human beings, and some of them—Satan and his minions, for example—may have been permitted to play a role in the evolution of life on earth, steering it in the direction of predation, waste and pain.[45] (Some may snort with disdain at this suggestion; it is none the worse for that.)

Not everyone agrees with this theodicy; and perhaps no theodicy we can think of is wholly satisfying. If so, that should not occasion much surprise: our knowledge of God's options in creating the world is a bit limited. Suppose God does have a good reason for permitting sin and evil, pain and suffering: why think we would be the first to know what it is?

44. See my "Supralapsarianism or 'O Felix Culpa'" in *Christian Faith and the Problem of Evil*, ed. Peter van Inwagen (Grand Rapids, Mich.: Eerdmans, 2005).
45. See C. S. Lewis's space trilogy: *Out of the Silent Planet* (London: The Bodley Head, 1938), *Perlandria* (London: The Bodley Head, 1943), and *That Hideous Strength* (London: The Bodley Head, 1945).

The real question here is whether this aspect of our world provides believers in God with a *defeater* for such belief.[46] That, in turn, depends upon the strength of the case *for* theism: why do people accept theism in the first place? Kitcher suggests it is because sacred texts tell them so: "Providentialist Christians reply that they accept a body of background doctrine, which tells them of a powerful, wise, and benevolent Creator. They endorse this doctrine because they believe in the literal truth of certain statements in the Christian Bible."[47] But this gets things backwards. Christians believe the Bible is trustworthy because they believe its ultimate author is God—but they would have to be benighted indeed if they also believed that there is such a person as God because the Bible says so. The sources of theistic belief go much deeper. Christian theology and current science unite in declaring that human beings display a natural tendency to believe in God or something very much like God.[48] According to John Calvin, God has created us with a *"sensus divinitatis,"* a natural tendency to form belief in God; and according to Thomas Aquinas, "To know in a general and confused way that God exists is implanted in us by nature."[49] Of course the vast majority of people around the globe do believe in God or something much like God. This natural inclination might be misleading—just as, I suppose, my natural inclination to believe in other minds, other centers of consciousness, might be misleading—but the point is that believers in God don't accept such belief just because it is written in a book.

Kitcher turns next to what he calls "the Enlightenment case against supernaturalism" of which he sees Darwinism as a part. This

46. See my *Warranted Christian Belief*, chapter 14.
47. Kitcher, *Living With Darwin*, p. 134.
48. See, e.g., Justin Barrett, "Exploring the Natural Foundations of Religion," in *Trends in Cognitive Science*, 2000, vol. 4 and *Why Would Anyone Believe in God* (Alta Mira, 2004); and see chapter 5 in this volume.
49. See the early chapters of Calvin's *Institutes of the Christian Religion*; Plantinga's *Warranted Christian Belief*, chapter 6; and Aquinas's *Summa Theologiae* I, q. 2, a. 1, ad 1.

case consists substantially in three arguments against supernaturalism: the argument from evil, the argument from pluralism, and the argument from historical Biblical criticism. As we've seen, neither Darwin nor Kitcher has much to add to the vast literature on the problem of evil; that discussion remains where it was. The argument from historical Biblical criticism is an argument for the unreliability of the Biblical accounts, for example of the life and death and resurrection of Jesus. We'll look further into this argument in chapter 5; suffice it to say here that in arguing for the unreliability of the gospels and the Pauline letters, Kitcher relies heavily on the claims of the Jesus seminar and *Beyond Belief* by Elaine Pagels.[50] These are interesting and suggestive, but neither is at all mainstream in contemporary Biblical scholarship, and neither represents a consensus or even anything near a majority opinion among contemporary Biblical scholars. And of course showing that the Bible isn't reliable is a very far cry from showing that there aren't any supernatural creatures.

The last element of the Enlightenment case against supernaturalism is the argument from religious pluralism: there are very many different and incompatible supernaturalist doctrines: there is Christianity, to be sure, but also Islam, Judaism, Hinduism, and some forms of Buddhism, not to mention many varieties of African tribal religion and native American religion. Doesn't this cast doubt on the truth of any particular supernaturalist doctrine? As Jean Bodin put it, "each is refuted by all."[51] Well, of course the vast majority of the world's population accept supernaturalism in one form or another; thus the argument from religious pluralism isn't much of an argument against supernaturalism as such and hence doesn't add much to the

---

50. See my *Warranted Christian Belief*, chapter 13; Pagels, *Beyond Belief* (New York: Random House, 2003).
51. Bodin, *Colloquium Heptaplomeres de rerum sublimium arcanis abditis*, written by 1593 but first published in 1857. English translation by Marion Kuntz (Princeton: Princeton University Press, 1975), p. 256.

Enlightenment case against supernaturalism. But what about particular supernaturalist belief—Christianity, or Islam or Judaism, for example? This too is well explored territory, but since I've written on it elsewhere, I won't go into the matter here.[52]

Briefly, however: Kitcher points out, as others before him have, that most believers accept the religion in which they have been brought up. And that can be worrying: if I had been born and brought up in medieval China, for example, I would almost certainly not have been a Christian. Fair enough; and this can induce a certain cosmic vertigo. But doesn't the same go for Kitcher? Suppose *he* had been born in medieval China, or for that matter medieval Europe: in all likelihood, he would not have been skeptical of the supernatural. As I say; this can induce vertigo; but isn't it just part of the human condition? And of course the fact that there are many varieties of supernaturalism can hardly be taken, by itself, to impugn all or even any of these varieties; we have the same problem in, for example, philosophy. Many philosophers disagree with Kitcher on many points including his opinions about supernaturalism; is this in itself much of an argument against his opinions, or against his being perfectly rational in holding them?

The Enlightenment case against supernaturalism, therefore, has little to be said for it; the various strands of this case have been examined at length, and for a very long time, and they have been found wanting. In the present case, furthermore, the Enlightenment case isn't really relevant; we are thinking about the bearing of evolutionary theory on religious belief, but the Enlightenment case against supernaturalism has little to do either with evolution or with science more generally.

In this chapter and the one previous, we have been looking into the claim that current scientific evolutionary theory is incompatible

---

52. See my *Warranted Christian Belief*, chapter 13.

with Christian belief. This claim, as we saw, is false. The scientific theory of evolution as such is not incompatible with Christian belief; what is incompatible with it is the idea that evolution, natural selection, is *unguided*. But that idea isn't part of evolutionary theory as such; it's instead a metaphysical or theological addition. In the next chapter we'll look into another alleged area of conflict: that between science and special divine action.

Chapter 3

Divine Action in the World: The Old Picture

Our topic is alleged conflict between religion and science. In the last two chapters we examined one claim along these lines: the claim that current evolutionary theory is incompatible with Christian belief. This claim, as we saw, has little to be said for it.

We turn now to quite a different allegation of conflict. Religious belief in general and Christian belief in particular is committed to the belief that God *acts in the world*; but this belief is somehow incompatible, so some claim, with contemporary science.

Now Christians do indeed believe that God acts in the world. Most would concur with the Heidelberg Catechism:

> Providence is the almighty and ever present power of God by which he upholds, as with his hand, heaven and earth and all creatures, and so rules them that leaf and blade, rain and drought, fruitful and lean years, food and drink, health and sickness, prosperity and poverty—all things, in fact, come to us not by chance but from his fatherly hand.[1]

Most Christians have concurred, that is, with the thought that God *acts* in the world he has created; and many other theists, Muslims and

1. Question 27.

Jews for example, would agree with this sentiment, even if they are less than enthusiastic about the Heidelberg Catechism.

But why should this be a problem? Here we need a bit of background. According to Christian and theistic views of God, he is a *person*. He is thus a being who has knowledge; he also has affections (he loves some things, hates others); he has ends and aims, and acts on the basis of his knowledge to achieve his ends. Furthermore, God is all-powerful, all-knowing, and wholly good. These properties are essential to him: it isn't possible that he should fail to have them. (Philosophers would state this by saying that he has these properties in every possible world in which he exists.) Still further, God is a necessary being. Philosophers would state this by saying that God exists in every possible world; therefore he has the properties of being all-powerful, all-knowing and wholly good in every possible world. God is therefore a necessarily existent concrete being (and the only necessarily existent concrete being).

Second, God has created our world. He may have done it in many different ways; he may have employed many different means; he may have done it all at once, or in stages; he may have done it relatively recently, or, more likely (given current science) billions of years ago. However he did it, Christians and other theists believe that he has in fact done it. Furthermore, he has created it "out of nothing." This is not, of course, the absurd suggestion that "nothing" names a sort of substance or material or gunk—perhaps extremely thin and gossamer—out of which God fashioned the world; it is instead simply the denial that there was any such pre-existing material out of which God made the world.

Third, God *conserves* the world, sustains it in being. Apart from his sustaining hand, our universe—and if there are other universes, the same goes for them—would disappear like a candle flame in a high wind. Descartes and Jonathan Edwards, indeed, thought of this divine sustenance as a matter of re-creation: at every moment God recreates his world. Maybe so, maybe not. The present point is only that God does indeed sustain his world in being, and, apart from that sustaining, supporting activity, the world would simply fail to exist. Some, including Thomas Aquinas, go even further: every causal transaction that takes place is such that God performs a special act of *concurring* with it; without that divine concurrence, no causal transaction could take place.[2]

Fourth, according to the Heidelberg Catechism (and again, classical theists of all stripes would agree) God so governs the world that whatever happens is to be thought of as "coming from his fatherly hand"; he either causes or permits whatever does in fact happen; none of it is to be thought of as a result of mere chance.[3] And this governing—"ruling," as the Catechism has it—comes in at least two parts. First of all, God governs the world in such a way that it displays regularity and predictability. Day follows night and night follows day; when there is rain and sun, plants grow; bread is good to eat but mud is not; if you drop a rock from a cliff top, it will fall down, not up. It is only because of this regularity that we can build a house, design and manufacture automobiles and aircraft, cure strep throat, raise crops, or pursue scientific projects. Indeed, it is only because of this regularity that we can act in any way at all.

2. Peter van Inwagen suspects this requirement of concurrence is no more than a matter of paying God superfluous metaphysical compliments; why add this to all the rest? One possibility is that conservation is a matter of sustaining a substance in existence, while concurrence is a matter of conserving a particular causal power in the conserved substance. Another possibility, one that no doubt was not foremost in the minds of the medievals, is that concurrence can be useful with respect to the so-called pairing problem: see John Foster, *The Immaterial Self: A Defence of the Cartesian Dualist Conception of the Mind* (London: Routledge, 1991), pp. 163ff; Jaegwon Kim, "Lonely Souls: Causality and Substance Dualism" in *Soul, Body, and Survival,* ed. Kevin Corcoran (Ithaca, N.Y.: Cornell University Press, 2001), pp. 30–43; and my "Materialism and Christian Belief" in *Persons: Divine and Human,* ed. Peter van Inwagen and Dean Zimmerman (Oxford: Clarendon Press, 2007), pp. 130ff.

3. But what is "mere chance"? And is it even possible that something happen by chance in a world created by an all-powerful and all-knowing God?

According to Christian belief, however, it is also true that God sometimes does things differently; he sometimes deviates from the usual way in which he treats the stuff he has made. Examples would be miracles: in the Old Testament, the parting of the Red Sea; in the New Testament, Jesus' changing water into wine, walking on water, restoring a blind man's sight, raising Lazarus, and, towering above all, Jesus himself rising from the dead.

Miracles are not the only examples of God's special action. Most Christians would endorse something like John Calvin's "Internal Witness of the Holy Spirit" and Thomas Aquinas's "Internal Instigation of the Holy Spirit."[4] "The believer," says Aquinas, "has sufficient motive for believing, for he is moved by the authority of divine teaching confirmed by miracles and, what is more, *by the inward instigation of the divine invitation.*"[5] So Aquinas and Calvin concur in the thought that God does something special in enabling Christians to see the truth of the central teachings of the gospel; the Holy Spirit gets them to see the "great truths of the gospel," as Jonathan Edwards calls them. This too would be action beyond creation and conservation, although presumably not miraculous, if only because it is so widespread.

In short, God regularly causes events in the world. Divine action of this sort is action beyond creation and conservation; we could think of it as *special* divine action.

4. See Calvin, *Institutes of the Christian Religion* III, ii, 7; Aquinas, *Summa Theologiae* II-II q. 2, a.9; and see my *Warranted Christian Belief* (New York: Oxford University Press, 2000), chapter 8.

5. *Summa Theologiae* II-II, q. 2, a. 9, reply ob. 3 (my emphasis). According to Aquinas, therefore, faith is produced in human beings by God's action; "for since in assenting to the things of faith a person is raised above his own nature, he has this assent from a supernatural source influencing him; this source is God. The assent of faith, which is its principal act, therefore, has as its cause God, moving us inwardly through grace." *ST* II-II, q. 6, a. 1, *respondeo*.

I THE PROBLEM

Several theologians, curiously enough, have thought there is a serious problem in this neighborhood. In 1961, Langdon Gilkey wrote a widely influential article lamenting the condition of Biblical theology. The problem, as he put it, is that theologians speak the language of divine action in the world, the language of miracle and divine intervention. God has done wonderful things, so they say: he parted the Red Sea so that the children of Israel could pass through on dry ground, he sent them manna in the wilderness; he made the sun stand still. Jesus turned water into wine, fed a multitude with just five loaves and two fish, raised Lazarus from the dead, and was himself raised from the dead. So far so good: where exactly is the problem? The problem, he says, is that modern theologians (Gilkey apparently includes himself) don't really believe that God *did* any of those things—or, indeed, that he did anything at all:

> Thus contemporary theology does not expect, nor does it speak of, wondrous divine events on the surface of natural and historical life. The causal nexus in space and time which the Enlightenment science and philosophy introduced into the Western mind...is also assumed by modern theologians and scholars; since they participate in the modern world of science both intellectually and existentially, they can scarcely do anything else. Now this assumption of a causal order among phenomenal events, and therefore of the authority of the scientific interpretation of observable events, makes a great difference. Suddenly a vast panoply of divine deeds and events recorded in scripture are no longer regarded as having actually happened.... Whatever the Hebrews believed, *we* believe that the biblical people lived in

the same causal continuum of space and time in which we live, and so one in which no divine wonders transpired and no divine voices were heard.[6]

These theologians, says Gilkey, speak the language of divine action, but they don't actually believe that God has acted: thus there is a lamentable hiatus between what they say (at least straightforwardly construed) and what they believe.

Other theologians agree that God does not act in the world. For example, Rudolph Bultmann asserts that:

The historical method includes the presupposition that history is a unity in the sense of a closed continuum of effects in which individual events are connected by the succession of cause and effect. [This continuum, furthermore,] cannot be rent by the interference of supernatural, transcendent powers.[7]

Bultmann apparently believes that no supernatural powers, not even God himself, can interfere with this closed continuum of cause and effect. He seems to endorse something like the Medes and Persians' conception of natural law: God has perhaps created the world and established the way it works; perhaps he has ordained

6. Gilkey, "Cosmology, Ontology and the Travail of Biblical Language," *Journal of Religion* 41 (1961), p. 31. See also, e.g., Gordon Kaufman, "On the Meaning of 'Act of God'," in *God the Problem* (Cambridge: Harvard University Press, 1972), pp. 134–35. Gilkey goes on to say that from this perspective the Bible becomes, not a description of God's mighty acts, but a book of Hebrew interpretation: "the Bible is a book of the acts Hebrews believed God might have done and the words he might have said had he done and said them—but of course we recognize he did not" (p. 33).

In speaking of what "contemporary theology" does or doesn't expect, Gilkey is obviously not speaking for all his contemporaries; there were (and are) many theologians who are vastly less impressed by the Enlightenment picture, some because they see that contemporary science has moved far beyond that picture. See this volume, chapter 4.

7. Bultmann, *Existence and Faith*, ed. Schubert Ogden (New York: Meridian Books, 1960), pp. 291–92.

DIVINE ACTION IN THE WORLD: THE OLD PICTURE

and promulgated the natural laws; but once he has done so, not even he can act in that world.[8] We can add Bultmann's most famous comment: "it is impossible to use electric light and the wireless and to avail ourselves of modern medical and surgical discoveries, and at the same time to believe in the New Testament world of spirits and miracles."[9]

John Macquarrie also agrees:

> The way of understanding miracle that appeals to breaks in the natural order and to supernatural interventions belongs to the mythological outlook and cannot commend itself in a post-mythological climate of thought.... The traditional conception of miracle is irreconcilable with our modern understanding of both science and history. Science proceeds on the assumption that whatever events occur in the world can be accounted for in terms of other events that also belong within the world; and if on some occasions we are unable to give a complete account of some happening...the scientific conviction is that further research will bring to light further factors in the situation, but factors that will turn out to be just as immanent and this-worldly as those already known.[10]

8. Among the members of the court of King Darius, Daniel was the King's favorite, which occasioned jealousy among the other courtiers. They knew that Daniel worshipped the God of Israel; they therefore persuaded King Darius to make it a crime to pray to anyone but King Darius himself (this may not have required excessive effort on their part); the penalty was being thrown into the lion's den. Daniel continued to pray to God; the courtiers pointed this out to Darius, who was greatly distressed at the thought of throwing Daniel into the lion's den. But the courtiers replied "Remember, O king, that according to the law of the Medes and Persians no decree or edict that the king issues can be changed"—not even by the king (Daniel 6:15).
9. Bultmann, *New Testament and Mythology and Other Basic Writings* selected, edited and translated by Schubert Ogden (Philadelphia: Fortress Press, 1984), p. 4.
10. Macquarrie, *Principles of Sacred Theology*, 2nd ed. (New York: Charles Scribner's Sons, 1977), p. 248.

I reported Gilkey as saying that the theologians of whom he speaks don't believe that God does anything at all in the world; but this isn't quite accurate. These theologians don't object to the idea that God creates and sustains the world. Their view is therefore entirely compatible with God's acting in such a way as to preserve it in being. Where they have difficulty is with the claim that God does or has done anything *in addition to* creating the world and sustaining it in existence; creation and preservation, they think (or fear, or suspect) exhaust the divine activity. They have no objection to the thought that God has created the world, and works in it at a general level to preserve and sustain it; their objection is to the idea that God sometimes does something special, something beyond creation and preservation (and concurrence), something like changing water into wine, or feeding five thousand with a few loaves and fishes, or raising someone from the dead. It is *special* divine action that, from their point of view, is the problem. And when they speak of special divine action, they are thinking, among other things, of what are commonly called miracles (those "mighty acts"), and of divine *intervention* in the world. Their idea is that God couldn't or wouldn't do a thing like that. According to Bultmann, a divinely caused miracle or any other special divine action would constitute God's "interfering" in the world; and that, he says, can't happen. Bultmann's idea, shared by the others I mentioned and many others, is what we might call "hand-off theology": God creates the world and upholds it, but for the rest can't or at least doesn't act in it; he steps aside and lets it evolve according to the laws he has set for it.

But what's the problem with special divine action? Why should anyone object to it? Why do these theologians think that the causal continuum "cannot be rent by the interference of supernatural, transcendent powers," that appeal to supernatural activity "cannot commend itself in a post-mythological climate of thought," and that "no wondrous divine events occur on the surface of natural and historical life"? In a word (or two): incompatibility with modern science.

Modern science, they think, shows, or perhaps assumes, or presupposes, that God does not act in that way. As Gilkey puts it, "modern theologians and scholars participate in the world of science," and because they do, they can't help but think of creation as a closed continuum of cause and effect, closed to intervention or interference on the part of beings outside that continuum, including God himself. As he says, "The causal nexus in space and time which the Enlightenment science and philosophy introduced into the Western mind ... is also assumed by modern theologians and scholars; since they participate in the modern world of science both intellectually and existentially, they can scarcely do anything else."[11] The thought seems to be that one who participates in the modern world of science both intellectually and existentially cannot help believing that God (if there is such a person) never acts specially or intervenes in the world. And according to Bultmann, someone who avails herself of modern medicine and the wireless (not to mention, I suppose, television, computers, electric scooters, and smart phones that do everything but mow your lawn) simply can't also believe in the spirit and wonder world of the New Testament.

Clearly, both of these claims deserve to be taken with a grain or two of salt. First, I, personally, have met people—physicists, for example—who participate in the modern world of science intellectually and existentially (if I understand what it is to participate in a world "existentially"), but nevertheless believe that God raised Jesus from the dead, that Jesus fed the five thousand and turned water into wine, that there are miraculous healings, that both angels and even Satan and his minions are active in the world, and so on. (Furthermore, it is likely that many of these physicists have a rather better grasp of the physics of radio transmission—not to mention subsequent developments—than Bultmann and his theological allies.) Indeed, if the

11. Gilkey, "Cosmology, Ontology and the Travail of Biblical Language," p. 291.

relevant polls are to be trusted, some 40 percent of contemporary American scientists believe in a personal God who answers prayers—a percentage that has remained stable since 1916.[12] At the least, Bultmann and Gilkey seem a little optimistic about the extent to which their beliefs are shared—could it be that they are generalizing on the basis of an unrepresentative sample, themselves and their friends, perhaps?[13] And, second, one suspects they underestimate their own powers. If they tried really hard, they could probably stop just assuming the existence of an unbroken causal nexus in the world, a nexus that precludes special divine action, and instead ask themselves whether there is really any reason to think this assumption *true*.

Still, what they claim is that proper respect for modern science implies hands-off theology. And it isn't only theologians who hold this view (of course I don't mean to suggest that *all* or even *most* theologians agree with Bultmann and his friends). According to philosopher Philip Clayton, "Science has created a challenge to theology by its remarkable ability to explain and predict natural phenomena. Any theological system that ignores the picture of the world painted by scientific results is certain to be regarded with suspicion." Well, fair enough; so far no problem. But Clayton goes on:

> Science is often identified with determinism. In a purely deterministic universe there would be no room for God to work in the world except through the sort of miraculous intervention that Hume–and many of his readers–found to be so

---

12. E. J. Larson and L. Witham, "Scientists Still Keeping the Faith," *Nature* 386 (April 3, 1997), pp. 435–36.

13. A less charitable explanation: these theologians suffer from disciplinary low self-esteem, want desperately to be accepted by the rest of the academic world, and thus adopt a more-secular-than-thou attitude. For another less charitable explanation, see my *Warranted Christian Belief*, pp. 404ff.

insupportable. *Thus many, both inside and outside of theology, have abandoned any doctrine of divine action as incompatible with the natural sciences.*[14]

Many scientists would concur. In addition to those dancing on the lunatic fringe such as Richard Dawkins and Peter Atkins, there are perfectly reasonable scientists who reject the idea of special divine action in the world. For example, in 2004 H. Allen Orr wrote a critical review of Richard Dawkins's book *The Devil's Chaplin* in which he suggested that Dawkins was too hard on religion.[15] In a letter to the editor, physiologist Carter Bancroft claimed that religion really was a danger to science because of the miracles religions claim. In his reply, Orr concurred: "It is not that some sects of one religion invoke miracles but that many sects of many religions do. (Moses, after all, parted the waters and Krishna healed the sick.) I agree of course that no sensible scientists can tolerate such exceptionalism with respect to the laws of nature."[16] (Of course, if miracles really do occur, it won't make a whole lot of difference whether scientists, sensible or not, are prepared to tolerate them; it really isn't up to them.)

The problem, then, as these people see it, is this. Science discovers and endorses natural laws; if God did miracles or acted specially in the world, he would have to contravene these laws and miraculously intervene; and that is incompatible with science. Religion and science, therefore, are in conflict, which does not bode well for religion.

But is all this really true?

14. Clayton, *God and Contemporary Science* (Edinburgh: Edinburgh University press, 1997), p. 209; emphasis added.
15. Orr, "A Passion for Evolution," *New York Review of Books*, February 26, 2004.
16. *New York Review of Books*, May 13, 2004.

II THE OLD PICTURE

Bultmann and his friends are evidently thinking in terms of classical science: Newtonian mechanics and the later physics of electricity and magnetism. (Gilkey mentions eighteenth-century science and philosophy.) This is the physics of Newton's laws of motion and gravity, and the physics of electricity and magnetism represented by Maxwell's equations. This is the physics of the great conservation laws, the conservation of momentum, for example (which follows from Newton's third law) and most essentially and most generally, the conservation of energy, especially as developed in the second half of the nineteenth century.[17]

And of course Newtonian mechanics and classical science have been enormously influential. As Alexander Pope put it in his famous epitaph for Newton,

> Nature and nature's law lay hidden in night;
> God said "Let Newton be" and all was light.

But classical science, just by itself, is nowhere nearly sufficient for anti-interventionism or hands-off theology. What's really at issue, rather, is a *Weltanschauung*, a sort of world picture suggested by classical science, endorsed by many influential eighteenth- and nineteenth-century figures, and still accepted by these theologians. Or rather, there are at least two importantly different pictures here.

A. The Newtonian Picture

First, there is the Newtonian picture properly so-called. This picture represents the world (or at any rate the material universe) as a vast

---

17. See, e.g., Y. Elkana, *The Discovery of the Conservation of Energy* (London: Hutchinson, 1974), chapter 2.

machine evolving or operating according to fixed laws: the laws of classical physics. These laws can be thought of as reflecting the very natures of the things God has created, so that (for example) it is part of the very nature of material particles and objects composed of them to attract each other with a force proportional to the product of their masses and inversely proportional to the square of the distance between them. Alternatively, we can think of matter as more tractable, and take the laws to be God's decrees as to how it shall in fact behave. In either case, we consider the universe as a whole—the material universe, anyway—as a collection including material particles and the things made of them, evolving according to the laws of classical mechanics. Theologically, the idea is that the world is a great divine mechanical artifact that runs according to the fixed laws of classical science, the laws prescribed for it by God.[18] The world is mechanical in that the laws of physics are sufficient to describe its behavior; no additional laws—of chemistry or biology, for example—are needed, and if there are such laws, they are reducible (in a sense that never became very clear) to the laws of physics. On this picture, classical physics is in that respect complete. It is worth noting, of course, that it is no part of classical science as such to claim that physics *is* in this sense complete; this is a pious hope, or a philosophical add-on, or both, even if one that is at least rather naturally suggested by the success of physics.

But the Newtonian picture is nowhere nearly sufficient for hands-off theology. First, Newton himself (one hopes) accepted the Newtonian picture, but he didn't accept hands-off theology. He believed that God providentially guides the world. He also believed that God regularly adjusts the orbits of the planets; according to his calculations, their orbits would otherwise spiral off into chaos. More

18. Although not (contrary to Leibniz) what we might call a *strictly* mechanical machine, i.e., a machine where all the forces operate by contact; Newtonian gravity, of course, is a force that acts at a distance.

important, however: according to Newton and classical mechanics, natural laws describe how the world works *when, or provided that the world is a closed (isolated) system, subject to no outside causal influence.*[19] In classical physics, the great conservation laws deduced from Newton's laws are stated for *closed* or *isolated* systems. Thus Sears and Zemanski's standard text *University Physics*: "This is the *principle of* conservation of linear momentum: *When* no resultant external force *acts on a system,* the total momentum of the system remains constant in magnitude and direction." They add that *"the internal energy of an isolated system remains constant.* This is the most general statement of the *principle of conservation of energy."*[20]

These principles, therefore, apply to *isolated* or *closed* systems. If so, however, there is nothing in them to prevent God from changing the velocity or direction of a particle. If he did so, obviously, energy would not be conserved in the system in question; but equally obviously, that system would not be closed, in which case the principle of conservation of energy would not apply to it. Indeed, there is nothing here to prevent God from miraculously parting the Red Sea, or changing water into wine, or bringing someone back to life, or, for

19. See William P. Alston, "God's Action in the World, in *Divine Nature and Human Language* (Ithaca, N.Y.: Cornell University Press, 1989), pp. 211–13, and "Divine Action, Human Freedom, and the Laws of Nature," *Quantum Cosmology and the Laws of Nature; Scientific Perspectives on Divine Action,* ed. by Robert John Russell, Nancey Murphy, and C. J. Isham (Vatican City: Vatican Observatory Publications, and Berkeley: The Center for Theology and the Natural Sciences, 1999), pp. 189–91.

20. Sears and Zemanski, *University Physics* (Boston: Addison-Wesley, 1963), pp. 186, 415 (their emphasis). General relativity presents even more problems for conservation laws taken as objections to special divine action. According to physicist Robert Wald, "In general relativity there exists no meaningful local expression for gravitation stress-energy and thus there is no meaningful local energy conservation law which leads to a statement of energy conservation" (*General Relativity,* Chicago: University of Chicago Press, 1984, p. 70, note 6). Quoted in Robin Collins, "The Energy-Conservation Objection to Mind-body Dualism," *American Philosophical Quarterly* vol. 45, no. 1 (January, 2008), p. 36. Collins explores in satisfying depth the bearing of general relativity on energy conservation.

that matter, creating *ex nihilo* a full-grown horse in the middle of Times Square. It is entirely possible for God to create a full-grown horse in the middle of Times Square without violating the principle of conservation of energy. That is because the systems including the horse would not be closed or isolated. For that very reason, there would be no violation of the principle of conservation of energy, which says only that energy is conserved in closed or causally isolated systems—ones not subject to any outside causal influence. It says nothing at all about conservation of energy in systems that are *not* closed; and, of course, if God created a horse *ex nihilo* in Times Square, no system containing that horse, including the whole of the material universe, would be closed.

Furthermore, it is no part of Newtonian mechanics or classical science generally to declare that the material universe *is* a closed system. You won't find that claim in physics textbooks—naturally enough, because that claim isn't physics, but a theological or metaphysical add-on. (How could this question of the causal closure of the physical universe be addressed by scientific means?)

Classical science, therefore, doesn't assert or include causal closure. The laws, furthermore, describe how things go when the universe is causally closed, subject to no outside causal influence. They don't purport to tell us how things *always* go; they tell us, instead, how things go when no agency outside the universe acts in it. They tell us how things go when the universe (apart from divine conservation) is causally closed. John Mackie (himself no friend of theism) put it like this:

> What we want to do here is to contrast the order of nature with a possible divine or supernatural intervention. The laws of nature, we must say, describe the ways in which the world—including, of course, human beings—works when left to itself, when not interfered with. A miracle occurs when the world is not left to

itself, when something distinct from the natural order as a whole intrudes into it.[21]

If we think of the laws of nature as describing how the universe works when the universe is causally closed (when God isn't acting specially in the world), they would be of the following form:

(LN) When the universe is causally closed (when God is not acting specially in the world), P.

For example, Newton's law of gravity would go as follows:

(G) When the universe is causally closed, any two material objects attract each other with a force proportional to the product of their masses and inversely proportional to the square of the distance between them.

Note that on (LN), the currently canonical account of determinism implies that determinism is false. According to that account, determinism holds just if the natural laws conjoined with the state of the universe at any one time entails the state of the universe at any other time. A bit more exactly: let "L" be the conjunction of the natural laws, and $S(t)$ and $S(t^*)$ be the states of the universe at any times t and t^*: then,

Necessarily, for any t and t^*, if L & $S(t)$, then $S(t^*)$.[22]

21. Mackie, *The Miracle of Theism* (Oxford: Oxford University Press, 1982), pp. 19–20.
22. It is by no means trivial to say just what a physical state of the universe *is*; on pain of triviality, we must suppose at least that a description of the state of the universe at a time t doesn't implicitly refer to or describe the universe or parts of it at some other time t^*. Thus, for example, $S(t)$ couldn't properly include the existence of a person described as the grandmother of someone born at t^* ($t \neq t^*$); nor could $S(t)$ include the laws holding then. Perhaps it would do to take the relevant description as a function assigning to each particle a mass, position and velocity.

(If we wish to accommodate the intuition that it is the past that determines the future, we may add, "such that t precedes t^*.") It is worth noting that if the above account of natural law is correct, determinism so understood is false and indeed necessarily false. For suppose determinism is true. According to (LN), a natural law is of the form

> If the universe (call it "U") is causally closed, then P.

Take the conjunction of the natural laws to be

> If U is causally closed, then P,

where now P is the conjunction of the consequents of all the laws. Let "PAST" denote a specific past state of the universe. Now suppose determinism is true. Then

> (1) (If U is causally closed, then P) and PAST

entails

> F (the future (the actual future)),

that is, (using 'N' to mean 'Necessarily'),

> (2) N (if (1) then F).

(2) is equivalent to

> (3) N [if (if U is causally closed then P) and PAST, then F],

that is,

> (4) N [if (either U is not causally closed or P) and PAST, then F],

that is,

(5) N {if [(PAST and P) or (PAST and U is not causally closed)] then F}.

(5) is of the form

N if (p or q) then r;

but then each of p and q entail r; hence

(6) N [if (PAST and P) then F] and N[if (PAST and U is not causally closed) then F].

But the right hand conjunct of (6) is obviously false: clearly there is a possible world that (i) shares its past with the actual world, (ii) is not causally closed (because, perhaps, God acts specially in it) and (iii) does not share its future with the actual world. Therefore determinism, which entails (6), is false. Indeed, given the usual view that propositions of the form *necessarily p* are noncontingent, either necessarily true or necessarily false, (6) is necessarily false; hence determinism, which entails it, is also necessarily false.

Mackie's suggestion seems a good description of the laws of nature, and certainly fits nicely with the Newtonian picture.[23] So thought of, the natural laws offer no threat to special divine action. Miracles are often thought to be problematic, in that God, if he were to perform a miracle, would be involved in "breaking," going contrary to, abrogating, suspending, a natural law. But given this conception of law, if God were to perform a miracle, it wouldn't at all involve contravening a natural law. That is because, obviously, any occasion on which God performs a miracle is an occasion when the universe is not causally closed; and the laws say nothing about what happens

---

23. Taken as descriptive of the natural world. Theists also think of the laws prescriptively, as something like rules as prescribed for the world by God, who at creation says something like "Let it be that energy is conserved in causally closed systems!"

when the universe is not causally closed. Indeed, on this conception it isn't even possible that God break a law of nature.[24] For to break a law, he would have to act specially in the world; yet any time at which he acted specially in the world would be a time at which the universe is not causally closed; hence no law applies to the circumstance in question and hence no law gets broken.

Objection: why can't we just as well say that the law is P itself, rather than what (LN) says it is? Why can't we say that Newton's law is just the result of deleting that proviso "when the universe is causally closed" from the above formulation of it? And then wouldn't divine action have to involve breaking a law, in which case there really is conflict between classical science and special divine action?

Reply: we can certainly think of laws like that if we wish; it's a free country. If we do, however, then classical science as such doesn't imply that the laws as ordinarily thought of—Newton's law, for example—are actually *true*; it doesn't imply that they are exceptionless generalizations. What classical science does imply is that these laws hold when the material universe is causally closed; but again, it is no part of classical science to assert that the material universe *is* causally closed. So taking laws this way, special divine action would indeed be "breaking" a law, but it would be no part of classical science to assert that the laws are not broken. Once again there would be no conflict between science and divine special action, including miracles.

What we've seen so far is that classical science doesn't entail either determinism or that the universe is in fact causally closed. It is therefore entirely consistent with special divine action in the world, including miracles. Hands-off theologians can't properly point to

24. Is there any conception of law on which it *is* possible that God "break" a law of nature? David Hume and David Lewis think of a law as an exceptionless generalization, one that (according to Lewis) displays a best combination of simplicity and strength; but then any generalization that gets "broken" wasn't a law after all. If laws are exceptionless generalizations, then it isn't possible for anyone, including God, to break what is in fact a law; what is not ruled out is the possibility of acting in such a way that a proposition which is in fact a law, would not have been one. The whole idea of breaking natural law seems to arise from an unhappy (if historically explicable) analogy between the moral law promulgated by God and the natural laws he ordains for his creation.

science—not even to eighteenth- and nineteenth-century classical science—as a reason for their opposition to divine intervention. What actually guides their thought is not classical science as such, but classical science plus a gratuitous metaphysical or theological addition—one that has no scientific credentials and goes contrary to classical Christianity.

B. The Laplacean Picture

The Newtonian picture isn't sufficient for hands-off theology; so what is it that guides the thought of these hands-off theologians? The Laplacean picture. Here the classic statement, naturally enough, is by Pierre Laplace:

> We ought then to regard the present state of the universe as the effect of its previous state and as the cause of the one which is to follow. Given for one instant a mind which could comprehend all the forces by which nature is animated and the respective situations of the beings that compose it—a mind sufficiently vast to subject these data to analysis—it would embrace in the same formula the movements of the greatest bodies of the universe and those of the lightest atom; for it, nothing would be uncertain and the future, as the past, would be present to its eyes.[25]

Note that this great mind would have to have quite remarkable powers of computation: the classical three-body problem—the problem of giving an analytical solution for the equations of motion for three bodies—has not so far been solved, let alone the classical n-body problem for large n. Note also that this demon (as she has

---

25. Laplace, *A Philosophical Essay on Probabilities*, tr. F. W. Truscott and E. L. Emory (New York: Dover, [1812] 1951), p. 4.

come to be called) would have to know the initial conditions with enormous—indeed, perfect—accuracy:

> In a game of billiards suppose that, after the first shot, the balls are sent in a continuous series of collisions, that there are a very large number of balls, and the collisions occur with a negligible loss of energy. If the average distance between the balls is ten times their radius, then it can be shown that an error of one in the 1000th decimal place in the angle of the first impact means that all predictability is lost after 1000 collisions.[26]

What, exactly, must be added to the Newtonian picture to get the Laplacean picture? Determinism plus *the causal closure of the physical universe*.[27] Although this addition is not at all implied by the physics (as I said, it's a philosophical or theological assumption), it was and is widely accepted, and indeed so widely accepted that it is often completely overlooked in contexts where it is crucial.[28] That the universe is indeed closed, once more, is not testified to by classical science nor a consequence of it. In touting the prowess of his calculating demon, Laplace was just *assuming* that God couldn't or wouldn't act specially.

26. Arthur Peacocke, "God's Interaction with the World," *Chaos and Complexity*, ed. Robert John Russell, Nancey Murphy and Arthur Peacocke (Vatican City: Vatican Observatory, and Berkeley: the Center for Theology and the Natural Sciences, second edition, 2000), p. 267. Peacocke refers, in this connection, to Michael Berry, "Breaking the Paradigms of Classical Physics from Within," 1983 Cercy Symposium *Logique et Théorie des Catastrophes*.
27. You might think causal closure, for Newtonian mechanics, implies determinism. That is because causal closure together with the conjunction of the laws taken as above, i.e., with the prefix "When God is not acting specially" is substantially equivalent to the conjunction of the laws with that prefix omitted; and the result is ordinarily taken to be a deterministic theory. This isn't exactly right, however; in his *Primer on Determinism* (Dordrect and Boston: D. Reidel, 1986) John Earman shows that there are some special circumstances that violate determinism in Newtonian mechanics. Since these circumstances are extremely special (for example, space invader systems of particles that, coming from infinity, enter an empty space), I'll proceed as if causal closure does imply determinism.
28. See, for example, David Papineau, "The Rise of Physicalism" in *Physicalism and its Discontents* (Cambridge: Cambridge University press, 2001), pp. 15, 17.

(He was also assuming that the laws of physics are *deterministic* or non-probabilistic and *complete*, in the sense that they apply at every time to every configuration of particles.) He wasn't getting this idea out of the physics, even though it has been widely accepted and often thought to be somehow enforced by classical science. And it is this Laplacean picture that guides the thought of the hands-off theologians. If it is true, as Gilkey suggests, that these theologians, like Martin Luther, can do no other, then it is the Laplacean picture that has them so firmly in its grip.

It is also the Laplacean picture—the laws of classical science plus the causal closure of the physical universe—that leaves no room for divine action in the world. Recall that the laws are of the form

(LN) When the universe is causally closed (when God is not acting specially in the world), P.

The Laplacean demon assumes that the universe is causally closed. But then she assumes that the antecedents of the laws are satisfied, and therefore she assumes, for each of the natural laws, that its consequent is true. Given the consequents of the laws and the state of the universe at any one time (and given that the laws of nature are complete and deterministic), the state of the universe at any other time is a necessary consequence. Hence, given the laws God originally sets for the universe together with causal closure and the state of the universe at any one time, she can simply deduce the state of the universe at any other time.

And this would leave no room for special divine action. If God ever acted specially, that Laplacean demon would be unable to make those calculations. If God acted specially, there would be a time t such that the state of the universe at t doesn't follow from the consequents of the laws together with the state of the universe at any other time. Therefore, if the demon tried to calculate what happens at t by using the laws and what happens at some other time t^*, she would get the wrong answer. (Of course it also follows directly from causal closure alone that God doesn't act specially in the world.) This picture (think of it as a proposition) does not entail that God *cannot* act specially in the world. Even if the physical universe is causally closed, it isn't a necessary truth that it is, and presumably God, being omnipotent, could act specially in it if he saw fit. What the picture entails is only that as a matter of fact he *does not* act specially.

This picture also has an important implication for human freedom. For if the universe is causally closed, the consequents of the laws together with $S(t)$ (where t is, let's say, a million years ago and $S(t)$ is the state of the universe at t) entail the current state of the universe, $S_{(just\ now)}$. So suppose $S_{(just\ now)}$ includes my going to the kitchen for a drink. If so, and if the Laplacean picture is correct, it was not within my power to refrain from getting a drink then. For it would have been within my power to refrain from going to the kitchen then only if it had been within my power, then, to perform some action A (where refraining counts as an action) such that if I had performed A, then either the consequents of the natural laws would have been different from what in fact they are, or $S(t)$ would have been different from what *it* was, or the physical universe would not have been causally closed. It would have been within my power to avoid that action only if either the laws, or the state of the universe a million years ago, or the causal closure of the universe were within my power—only if I could have done something such that if I *had* done that thing, then either the physical universe would not have been causally closed, or else either the laws or that state of the universe would have been different from what in fact they are. It seems likely that none of these things is within my power. Therefore it is plausible to think that my action of going to the kitchen for a drink was not a free action.[29] Hence the Laplacean picture implies (or strongly suggests) that no human actions are free.[30]

Whether determinism is incompatible with human freedom depends on the nature of the laws. If the laws are no more than Humean descriptive generalizations, if they merely record what actually happens, then there is no reason to think that determinism *is* incompatible with human freedom. For consider some law L that bears on what I do: perhaps L together with other things entails that I will raise my hand at t. If L is no more than a complex descriptive generalization, then it describes a situation that includes, among other things, my raising my hand at t. But so far this is entirely compatible with my having the power to refrain from raising my hand at t; the mere fact that I *do* raise my hand then doesn't imply that I wasn't able to refrain from raising it then. (Of course if I had refrained from raising my hand, L would have been false and hence would not have been a law.) The same goes for a conception of laws like that of David Lewis: a set of exceptionless generalizations that is maximal with respect to a combination of strength and simplicity. Here (as in the previous case) laws would supervene on particular matters of fact. And on this conception of law, as in the previous case, it is entirely possible that I have the power to refrain from performing an action A such that the laws together with the state of the universe

---

29. Here I assume that the ability to do otherwise is a necessary condition of free action. For the canonical version of the argument that freedom is incompatible with determinism, see Peter van Inwagen's "Consequence Argument" in *An Essay on Free Will* (Oxford: Clarendon Press, 1983).

30. It isn't only hands-off theology that we owe to the Laplacean picture; it is also (anachronism aside) partly responsible for the critical philosophy of Immanuel Kant. If the material universe is a closed system, there is no room for free human action. The material universe, of course, includes human bodies; and it is this picture of the material universe, including our own bodies, going its own merry way, each preceding state of it sufficient for the succeeding state, with no room in it for free human action, that absorbed Kant's attention.

Of course Kant tried to solve the problem by a sort of radical segregation: causal closure reigns supreme in the phenomenal world; the noumenal realm, however, somehow permits or involves or underwrites human freedom. The details (and indeed the main lines) are a bit baroque and more than a bit obscure; what is of present interest, though, is that Kant's problem was set by his endorsing the Laplacean picture. It is also worth noting that in his case, as in the case of the hands-off theologians, it isn't at all the physics or the classical science as such that sets the problem: the difficulty really arises from the assumption of the causal closure of the physical.

at some time *t* entail that I perform *A*. Again, if I were to do so, then some proposition *L* that is in fact a law, would not have enjoyed lawhood, because it would not have been an exceptionless generalization. (Laplace, of course, was thinking of those laws as the laws of classical science; and presumably it is not within the power of any human being so to act that a proposition that is in fact a law of physics would not have been a law of physics.)

Although the Laplacean picture implies that human beings are not free; it's worth noting that the same definitely does not go for the Newtonian picture. Just as the Newtonian picture leaves room for divine action in the world, so it also leaves room for human free action. What is crucial here is that the Newtonian picture does not imply that the material universe is causally closed; but then, just as it is compatible with the Newtonian picture that *God* act specially in the world, so it is compatible with that picture *that human beings* act freely in the world. For suppose—along with Plato, Augustine, and Descartes and many of our contemporaries—that human beings resemble God in being immaterial selves or substances.[31] Then just as God, who is an immaterial being, can act in the hard, heavy, massy physical universe, so too, perhaps, can human beings; God could confer on them the power to cause changes in the physical universe. Perhaps my willing to move my arm causes neurophysiological events in my brain, which in turn cause my arm to move. Classical physics and the Newtonian picture, therefore, unlike the Laplacean picture, do not imply either that human beings cannot act freely or that God does not act specially in the world.

Laplace's picture is accurate only if the universe is closed: only if God doesn't act specially in the world. We could think of the Laplacean

---

31. See (among many others) Richard Swinburne, *The Evolution of the Soul* (Oxford: Oxford University Press, 1997), Foster, *The Immaterial Self*, and my "Against Materialism," *Faith and Philosophy* 23:1 (January 2006), pp. 3–32, and "Materialism and Christian Belief" (above, footnote 2, p. 67).

picture as the Newtonian picture plus closure. This Laplacean picture, clearly enough, is the one guiding the thought of Bultmann, Macquarrie, Gilkey, et al. There is interesting irony, here, in the fact that these theologians, in the name of being scientific and up to date (and who wants to be thought unscientific, or obsolete?), urge on us an understanding of classical science that goes well beyond what classical science actually propounds (and, as we'll see in the next chapter, they also urge on us a picture of the world that is scientifically out of date by many decades).

As we have seen, however, classical science doesn't assert or include Laplacean determinism. The laws don't tell us how things always go; they tell us how they go when the relevant system is causally closed, subject to no outside causal influence. In classical science, therefore, there is no objection to special divine action (or for that matter to human free action, dualistically conceived). As we have also seen, to get such an objection, we must add that the universe is causally closed, which is not itself part of classical science. Accordingly, classical science is perfectly consistent with special divine action, including miracles. So far, therefore, we haven't found a religion/science conflict; what we have is only a conflict between religion—Christian belief, for example—and a particular metaphysics according to which the universe is causally closed.

Of course we have been thinking about *classical* science. What happens if we turn to contemporary science, in particular quantum mechanics? Will we find conflict there? That's the subject for chapter 4.

The New Picture

In chapter 3 we saw that many theologians, scientists, and philosophers hold that special divine action in the world—causing a miracle, for example—is incompatible with science. I argued that this claim together with the hands-off theology to which it gave rise is no doubt popular, but it suffers from a common if unhappy condition: it is wholly mistaken. That is, it is mistaken with respect to classical science, the physics of Newtonian mechanics, and of electricity and magnetism. It is the Laplacean picture that is incompatible with special divine action, but the Laplacean picture with its causal closure of the physical universe is really a piece of metaphysics unsupported by classical science. As everyone knows, however, the old Laplacean (and Newtonian) scientific picture has been superseded—by two large-scale, indeed stunning revisions. First, there is relativity theory, both special and general; second, and crucial for our purposes, there is quantum mechanics; both have been with us since the second or third decade of the twentieth century. As I noted above, there is an interesting irony in these theologians urging the deterministic, Laplacean picture, when that picture is no part of the classical science to which they solemnly pledge fealty. There is a further irony: the classical science they so eagerly meant to accommodate was well out of date at the time they were eagerly accommodating it. In this chapter I'll argue that quantum mechanics offers even less of a problem for divine special action than classical science, even though the latter doesn't offer much of a problem.

I QUANTUM MECHANICS

So what about current science, in particular quantum mechanics (QM)?[1] How does it stand with respect to the question of special divine action in the world? This is not the place to outline the essentials of QM, even if that were within my powers; let me just recommend "Distilling Metaphysics from Quantum Physics" by Tim Maudlin.[2] Still, a few remarks about it are essential to the current project. QM is characterized by several substantial departures from classical physics; of these, only *indeterminism* is relevant to our present concerns. Classical mechanics is deterministic in the following sense. Suppose you are given an initial configuration of a material system—that is, a system of particles together with their positions, masses and velocities—at a time t. Now consider any time t^* future with respect to t; if the system is causally closed, there is just one outcome consistent with classical mechanics. It may be impossible to calculate the outcome—indeed, as mentioned above, we don't have analytic solutions for the "n-body problem" where n is greater than 2; nevertheless, for any t^* only one outcome is permitted by classical mechanics.[3]

Things are very different for QM. The Schrödinger equation for a system S—a system of particles, for example—associates a wave

---

1. For present purposes I suggest we understand quantum mechanics *realistically*: that is, take the theory as an effort to describe the world (as opposed, e.g., to an attempt to come up with a theory that is empirically adequate, whether or not true). This is a nontrivial suggestion; given the weird, fitful, intermittent, shadowy, evanescent, nature of the quantum world, antirealism of the sort proposed by Bas van Fraassen is certainly attractive. See, e.g., his *The Scientific Image* (Oxford: Clarendon Press, 1980).

2. Maudlin, *Oxford Handbook of Metaphysics*, ed. Dean Zimmerman and Michael Loux (Oxford: Oxford University Press, 2003), p. 461. Maudlin gives a particularly clear and cogent explanation of the essentials of quantum mechanics and the relation between the quantum mechanical formalism and its interpretations.

3. So, at any rate, the usual story goes. Not all is well with this story, however; there are certain exceptions. See the caveat in footnote 27 of the last chapter.

function with S; in essence, for any future time t, the wave function assigns a complex number to each of the many configurations possible for S at t. This wave function is used (via "Born's Rule") to assign a certain probability to each possible configuration c for S at t: the probability of finding S in c at t. The point, here, is that (in contrast with classical mechanics) we don't get a prediction of a unique configuration for the system at t, but only a distribution of probabilities across many possible outcomes. Given a quantum mechanical system, therefore, QM doesn't say which configuration will *in fact* result from the initial conditions; instead, it assigns a spectrum of probabilities to the possible outcomes. If our system consists in a single particle, for example, QM doesn't tell us where that particle will be found at a subsequent time t^*, but (via Born's Rule) only gives us probabilities for its location then.[4] (Strictly speaking, it could be anywhere, although of course for most locations the probability of its being there then will be infinitesimal.)

QM as such, therefore, does not support the Laplacean picture: many different positions for that particle at t^* are consistent with the laws of QM together with its position at t; for a system of particles, many different configurations at t^* are consistent with the laws together with its configuration at t. Hence not even someone as talented as Laplace's demon (chapter 3, section IIB) could predict the physical condition of the universe at future times, even if she is given the laws along with a maximally determinate description of the

---

4. Things are complicated by the fact that there are interpretations of or, better, approaches to QM that are said to be deterministic; the best known of these is Bohmian mechanics. Since Bohmian mechanics is empirically equivalent to QM *simpliciter*, it is also indeterministic in the same sense as QM *simpliciter*: it predicts, not specific outcomes, but statistical patterns of probabilities. But it is deterministic in another sense, in that it postulates a further law (the "guiding equation") that together with the Schrödinger equation for the universe and the initial configuration of mass/energy at the beginning of the universe (and given causal closure of the physical) completely determines its subsequent states. Of course that initial configuration isn't available to us.

universe at t. It is this indeterminism that has led people to say that, according to QM, it is possible (however unlikely) that all the particles in my body (and hence my body itself) be on one side of a wall at t, and at t^* as close as you please to t, these particles (and hence my body) be on the other side of that wall. In the same vein, so we are told, QM permits the equestrian statue of Robert E. Lee in Richmond, Virginia, to leap from its pedestal and gallop off into the distance, waving its hat and bellowing the rebel yell.

We saw earlier (chapter 3, section IIA) that the classical laws of mechanics and conservation of energy come with an implicit proviso: they apply *when the relevant system (the universe, for example) is causally closed*. The same proviso holds, substantially, in the case of QM: the laws apply to causally closed systems. But even if we ignore this proviso, special divine action, including miracles, is by no means incompatible with QM.[5] That is because (again) QM doesn't determine a specific outcome for a given set of initial conditions, but instead merely assigns probabilities to the possible outcomes. This means that, even apart from that proviso, QM doesn't constrain special divine action in anything like the way classical deterministic mechanics does.

Clearly QM doesn't prohibit divine providential action and answers to prayer; what about such stunning miracles as walking on water, raising the dead, changing water into wine, parting the Red Sea, miraculous healings, and so on? Here, since I am not a quantum mechanic, I am reduced to arguing from authority. According to the expert opinion to which I have had access, some of these (parting the Red Sea, miraculous healings) are unproblematically compatible with QM. On other miracles, however—for example, raising the dead, and transmutation, as with changing water into wine—there seems

---

5. We could put this more exactly as follows. Let L be the conjunction of the consequents of the laws; L is not incompatible with special divine action.

to be substantial difference of opinion among the experts. Little analysis of these kinds of cases has been published; but some of the experts I've talked with—Katherine Brading, Craig Lent, Bas van Fraassen—think it implausible that QM is compatible with these miracles. Others, for example John Earman and Bradley Monton, think QM is compatible with them. Thus Earman:

> If we try to define a miracle as an event that is incompatible with (what we presume, on the basis of the best evidence, to be) laws of nature, then it seems that water changing to wine, a dead man coming back to life, etc. are not miracles because they are not incompatible with QM. But QM does say that they are very, very improbable.[6]

And according to Monton,

> For what it's worth, I think that all the miracles are pretty unproblematically compatible with the GRW theory. The wave function for each particle is spread throughout an unbounded region of the universe, at every time (except perhaps momentary instants of time). This means that for each particle, there is at most a finite region where it couldn't be localized by a GRW hit. (For some (probably even most) particles, they could be localized anywhere.) So for changing water into wine, it's not a big deal—you've got a bunch of individual particles (electrons, protons, etc.) that are composing the water, and they can all have GRW hits such that their positions are redistributed to the locations that would be appropriate for them to compose wine. Since there's at most a finite region of the universe where these particles can't show up, and there's no reason to expect the finite

6. Personal communication from John Earman, August 9, 2007.

regions for the different particles to overlap in any special way, the particles can all appear in the positions appropriate for them to compose wine.[7]

Monton is speaking of the Ghirardi-Rimini-Weber (GRW) approach to quantum mechanics (discussed in more detail later in this chapter); presumably a similar point would apply to the classical Copenhagen interpretation. So the first thing to see here is this: it is far from clear that QM, even bracketing the proviso according to which the laws apply to closed systems, is incompatible with miracles. And if what happens in the physical world at the macroscopic level supervenes on or is determined by what happens at the microlevel—the quantum level—then if miracles are compatible with the laws of quantum mechanics, they will also be compatible with any macroscopic laws.

On the "new picture," therefore—the picture presented by QM—there is no question that special divine action is consistent with science; and even the most stunning miracles are not clearly inconsistent with the laws promulgated by science. One might therefore expect that the whole concern about special divine action would disappear. If one did, however, one would be sadly disappointed. The fact is many philosophers, theologians and scientists—thinkers who are wholly aware of the QM revolution—still apparently find a problem with miracles and special divine action generally. Rudolph Bultmann, Langdon Gilkey, John Macquarrie, and their friends rejected divine intervention in the name of an eighteenth-century picture of science; many contemporary writers on religion and science also reject divine intervention—not, now, by appealing to outmoded science, but for other more obscure reasons. I shall argue two points: first, that their reasons for rejecting intervention are no more cogent than those of Gilkey and others. And second, I'll argue that,

---

7. Personal communication from Bradley Monton, August 8, 2007.

given contemporary quantum physics, there isn't any sensible way to say what intervention *is*, let alone find something in science with which it is incompatible.

II WHAT IS THE PROBLEM WITH "INTERVENTION"?

First, however, we need a representative sample of contemporary thinkers in this area who reject intervention. An excellent exhibit is "the Divine Action Project" (DAP), a multi-year series of conferences and publications that began in 1988.[8] So far these conferences have resulted in five or six books of essays involving some fifty or more authors—scientists, theologians, philosophers—including many of the most prominent writers in the field: Ian Barbour, John Polkinghorne, Arthur Peacocke, Robert Russell, Thomas Tracy, Nancey Murphy, Philip Clayton, and many others. This is certainly a serious and impressive attempt to come to grips with the topic of divine action in the world. Nearly all of these authors believe that a satisfactory account of God's action in the world would have to be *noninterventionistic* (and to begin with, let's suppose we have a good idea as to what intervention is). It would be fair to say, I think, that the main problem for the project is to find an account of divine action in the world—action beyond creation and conservation— that doesn't involve God's intervening in the world. Thus the late Arthur Peacocke, one of the most prominent members of this project, comments as follows on a certain proposal for divine action, a proposal according to which God's special action would be undetectable:

8. I take the name from Wesley Wildman, "The Divine Action Project, 1988–2003," *Theology and Science* vol. 2, no. 1, April 2004.

God would then be conceived as acting, as it were, 'within' the flexibility we find in these (to us) unpredictable situations in a way that could never be detected by us. Such a mode of divine action would never be inconsistent with our scientific knowledge of the situation..... God would have to be conceived of as actually manipulating micro-events (at the atomic, molecular, and according to some, quantum levels) in these initiating fluctuations on the natural world in order to produce the results at the macroscopic level which God wills.

But such a conception of God's action...would then be no different in principle from that of God *intervening* in the order of nature with all the problems that that evokes for a rationally coherent belief in God as the creator of that order. The only difference...would be that...God's intervention would always be hidden from us.[9]

What *are* the problems evoked "for a rationally coherent belief in God as the creator of that order"? Why should we expect God to avoid intervention? Philip Clayton, one of the authors in this group, puts it as follows: "the real problem here, apparently, is that it is very difficult to come up with an idea of divine action in the world in which such action would not constitute 'breaking natural law' or 'breaking physical law.'"[10] But can this be right? As we've seen, it is extremely hard to "break"

9. Peacocke, "God's Interaction with the World," in *Chaos and Complexity: Scientific Perspectives on Divine Action*, ed. Robert John Russell, Nancey Murphy, and Arthur Peacocke (Vatican City State: Vatican Observatory Publications, and Berkeley: The Center for Theology and the Natural Sciences, 2000), pp. 277–78. Elsewhere he adds that, "So we have to accept the interplay of chance and laws as the node of God's creativity. It seems to me to be more consistent with the fundamental creativity of reality than the belief—stemming from a Newtonian, mechanistic, determinist view of the universe with a wholly transcendent God as the great lawgiver—that God intervenes in the natural nexus for the good or ill of individuals or society" ("Chance and Law" in *Chaos and Complexity*, p. 142).

10. Clayton, *God and Contemporary Science* (Edinburgh: Edinburgh University Press, 1997), pp. 195, 203, 206.

quantum mechanical laws—even with the "when the universe is causally closed" proviso deleted. And in any event the whole notion of
"breaking" a natural law seems confused, as I argued earlier. Wesley
Wildman proposes a more promising problem for intervention:

> The DAP project tried to be sensitive to issues of theological
> consistency. For example, the idea of God sustaining nature and
> its law-like regularities with one hand while miraculously inter-
> vening, abrogating or ignoring those regularities with the other
> hand struck most members as dangerously close to outright con-
> tradiction. Most participants certainly felt that God would not
> create an orderly world in which it was impossible for the creator
> to act without violating the created structures of order.[11]

According to George Ellis, another prominent member of this group,

> Nevertheless it seems probable that fixed laws of behavior of
> matter, independent of interference by a Creator or any other
> agency, is a requisite basis of existence of independent beings
> able to exercise free will, for they make possible meaningful com-
> plex organized activity without outside interference (physical
> laws providing a determinate frame within which definite local
> causal relations are possible). Thus we envisage the Creator
> choosing such a framework for the universe (thus giving up all
> the other possibilities allowed by the power available to him,
> such as the power to directly intervene in events by overruling
> the laws of physics from time to time).[12]

---

11. Wildman, "The Divine Action Project," p. 38.
12. Ellis, "The Theology of the Anthropic Principle," *Quantum Cosmology and the Laws of Nature*, ed. Robert John Russell, Nancey Murphy, and C. J. Isham (Vatican City: Vatican Observatory Publications and Berkeley: The Center for Theology and the Natural Science, 1999), p. 384.

Elsewhere Ellis goes on:

> The problem of allowing miraculous intervention, to turn water into wine, to heal the sick, to raise the dead ... is that this involves either a suspension or alteration of the natural order. Thus the question arises as to why this happens so seldom. If this is allowed at all to achieve some good, why is it not allowed all the time, to assuage my toothache as well as the evils of Auschwitz?[13]

He adds that what we need, in order to understand divine action of this sort, is a criterion:

> What one would like here—if one is to make sense of the idea of miracles—is some kind of rock-solid criterion of choice underlying such decisions to act in a miraculous manner, for if there is the necessity to hold to these laws during times of the persecutions and Hitler's Final Solution, during famines and floods, in order that morality be possible, then how can it be that sometimes this iron necessity can fade away and allow turning water to wine or the raising of Lazarus?[14]

Finally, Nicholas Saunders explains why Philip Hefner, another member of the group, objects to intervention: "He feels it challenges the concepts of divine faithfulness and self-consistency: how can God uphold the laws of nature with one hand, whilst simultaneously overriding them by performing miracles with the other?"[15]

So how shall we understand these objections to intervention? What exactly (or even approximately) is the problem? I'm not quite

13. Ellis, "Ordinary and Extraordinary Divine Action" in *Chaos and Complexity*, p. 383.
14. Ellis, "Ordinary and Extraordinary Divine Action," p. 384.
15. Saunders, *Divine Action and Modern Science* (Cambridge: Cambridge University Press, 2002), p. 48.

sure, but the authors quoted seem to see essentially three problems; I'll say just a bit about each. First, there is that connection with the problem of evil noted by Ellis: "The problem of allowing miraculous intervention," he says, is that if God intervenes some of the time—for example, raising Jesus from the dead, parting the Red Sea—why doesn't he intervene more often, "to assuage my toothache as well as the evils of Auschwitz?"[16] I begin with a small protest: Ellis speaks of the "problem of allowing miraculous intervention." But of course that isn't actually a problem for us (or anyone else); it isn't up to us whether or not to allow miraculous intervention. God will intervene, miraculously or otherwise, if and when he sees fit.

What Ellis means, of course, is that we can't *sensibly suppose* that God intervenes unless we have "some kind of rock-solid criterion of choice underlying such decisions to act in a miraculous manner"— that is, unless we have a rock-solid criterion saying when God would intervene and when he wouldn't. Surely that's demanding too much? God will intervene (if that's the right word) when he has a good reason for doing so; but why suppose we human beings would be in a position to know when he does and when he doesn't? Perhaps we are in a position like the Biblical Job; what happened to him was a result of mysterious transactions among beings some of whom were wholly unknown to him. Couldn't something similar hold for us? True; perhaps we can't say what God's reason is for intervening (if that's the right word) in raising Lazarus from the dead and not intervening at Auschwitz; but why should that incline us to think he never

16. Ellis, "Ordinary and Extraordinary Divine Action," p. 384. This objection is widely shared. In the course of a defense of deism, Maurice Wiles responds to the testimony of Christians claiming to benefit from divine intervention: "In many cases the nature of such claimed interventions seems trivial when set in the context of Auschwitz and Hiroshima, which no providential action prevented." "Divine Action: Some Moral Considerations" in *The God Who Acts*, ed. Thomas Tracy (University Park: Pennsylvania State University Press, 1994), p. 22.

intervenes at all? It's not as if, if he has such a reason, we'd be the first to know. His options and possibilities are far beyond our ken; his ways are "past finding out"; we can hardly expect to come up with a "rock-solid criterion" underlying God's decisions to act.[17]

Second, Ellis suggests that "fixed laws of behavior of matter, independent of interference by a Creator or any other agency, is a requisite basis of existence of independent beings able to exercise free will." The idea seems to be that if the creator "interfered" in the workings of the world, we couldn't exercise free will.[18] Again, first a protest. "Interfering" is clearly pejorative: one who interferes, meddles in something where he has no business, and should therefore be ashamed of himself.[19] But God is the creator and sustainer of the world; it's really his world. So how could he be "interfering" or "meddling" by acting in it? What Ellis means, I take it, is that if God (often?) intervened in our world, we wouldn't be able to make sensible decisions as to what to do. What's at issue here is not so much freedom; Ellis's point, I take it, is that if God constantly intervened, the regularities we must rely on in deciding how to act would be absent. (If God often and unaccountably turned automobiles into small elephants, for example, it would be much more difficult to drive to the grocery store.)

Is Ellis right? First, what counts with respect to the possibility of intelligent free action isn't really the absence of divine intervention; it is rather *regularity* and *predictability*. (Predictability by the free creatures in question.) Intelligent free action would not be possible in a world without regularity and predictability, even if God never

---

17. Compare St. Paul: "How unsearchable are his judgments and how inscrutable his ways!" *Romans* 11:33.

18. Some make the same suggestion about science: scientific investigation, they say, would be impossible if God intervened in the world.

19. Note its occurrence also in the quotations from Bultmann, p. 72; Mackie (pp. 81–82) uses the word "intrusion."

intervened in it; such action *would* be possible in a world in which God often intervened, provided he did so in a regular and predictable way. Suppose, for example, that God always performed a miraculous healing whenever a witch doctor did a certain dance: this might enhance rather than compromise intelligent free action.

For purposes of argument, however, let's temporarily assume that divine intervention always introduces irregularity. Still, isn't it much too strong to suppose that if God sometimes intervenes in the world, intelligent free action just wouldn't be possible? What's required for free action is that there be enough regularity for us to know or sensibly conjecture—at least for the most part and with reasonably high probability—what will happen if we freely choose to take a given action. Ric is rock climbing; he's half way up a vertical 150-foot face, ten feet above his last protection, and it looks as if it's another ten feet to the next protection point; so if he fell just before reaching that point, he'd drop at least 40 feet before the rope stopped him. (In fact more, because of slack in the system, rope stretch, possible inattention on the part of his belayer, et cetera.) To decide whether to carry on or retreat, he must be able to form a decent opinion as to how likely it is that he will fall there, and on what will happen if he does fall there: will he hit a ledge on the way down? Will his top protection pull out, so that he'll plunge still farther? If he has no answer at all to these questions, he can't make a sensible decision as to whether to back off.

For him to be able to make a sensible decision, however, it isn't required that God never intervene in the world's workings. Suppose Ric thinks someone has been miraculously healed or even raised from the dead: that obviously doesn't mean that he can't make a sensible decision here. More to the point, suppose he thinks God sometimes intervenes in situations like the one he is in, perhaps causing a piece of protection to hold that would otherwise have failed: again, his so thinking in no way means that he can't make a sensible decision.

Here Ric is acting under uncertainty, and the best he can do is an educated guess. But even in cases where we are very sure what will happen, sensible free action does not require that God never intervene. Ric reaches the top; the fastest way down would be to jump; he's not tempted, though, because he knows a 150-foot fall would kill or injure him. Now suppose he also believes that God occasionally intervenes, causing someone who takes such a fall to survive unhurt; that still won't tempt him to jump. All that's required for purposeful free action is reasonable confidence in substantial regularity in the neighborhood of the proposed action. And that's certainly compatible with God's sometimes intervening.[20]

The third objection—what we might call "the divine consistency objection"—is apparently the one most widely urged by the members of the Divine Action Project. Paul Tillich, himself no member of the DAP, puts it in engaging if Delphic form: "Miracles cannot be interpreted in terms of supranatural interference in natural processes. If such an interpretation were true, the manifestation of the ground of being would destroy the structure of being; God would be split within himself."[21] As we saw above, Wildman speaks of "theological consistency" and "coming dangerously close to outright contradiction" in this connection, and (according to Nicholas Saunders), Philip Hefner objects to intervention because he believes that it "challenges the concepts of divine faithfulness and self-consistency." Peacocke suggests that God's intervening in the order of nature creates problems for a rationally coherent belief in God as the creator of that order; and several of the members of DAP concur in the question "how can God

---

20. The same goes with respect to science and technology. Surely the occasional miraculous cure of cancer, for example, wouldn't make it impossible to seek a more ordinary cure for the disease.

21. Tillich, *Systematic Theology* (London: Nisbet, 1953), vol. 1, p. 129; quoted in William Alston's "God's Action in the World," in *Evolution and Creation*, ed. Ernan McMullin (Notre Dame: University of Notre Dame Press), p. 209.

uphold the laws of nature with one hand, whilst simultaneously over-riding them by performing miracles with the other?"[22]

Now the members of the DAP, unlike Bultmann and the hands-off theologians, are of course perfectly aware of the quantum revolution, perfectly well aware of the ways in which quantum science has under-mined Laplacean determinism. Nevertheless, they still seem to display a decided list in the Laplacean direction: Clayton speaks of God's "breaking" natural laws, and Saunders, just quoted, speaks of "overriding" the laws of nature by performing miracles. As I argued earlier, however, it's exceedingly difficult to see how God could over-ride or "break" natural laws by miraculous healings or raising someone from the dead; under the new picture it's doubtful that these things are precluded by quantum mechanical laws, even if we set aside the proviso according to which these laws apply only to closed systems. How, then, are we to understand this consistency problem? The pic-ture seems to be that of God's establishing a world with certain regu-larities, and then occasionally acting contrary to those regularities. He creates and governs the world in such a way that water ordinarily doesn't change into wine, people don't typically walk on water, and dead people usually don't come back to life. Indeed, these things hardly ever happen. But then, very occasionally, God acts in a way that goes contrary to those regularities: Jesus turns water into wine, walks on water, raises Lazarus from the dead and is himself raised from the dead on the third day. And this is thought to be *inconsistent*: God doesn't always act in the relevantly same way: he doesn't always treat the stuff he has made in the same way.

Here the objection, obviously, is theological. It has nothing to do with science. The idea is that God simply wouldn't do such a thing; this sort of action is inconsistent with his unfathomable augustness and unsurpassable greatness. As the late Ernan McMullin put it,

22. Saunders, *Divine Action and Modern Science*, p. 48.

The Creator whose powers are gradually revealed in these texts [Genesis, Job, Isaiah, Psalms] is omnipotent and all-wise, far beyond the reach of human reckoning. His Providence extends to all His creatures; they are all part of His single plan, only a fragment of which we know, and that darkly. Would such a being be likely to "intervene" in the cosmic process, that is, deal in two different manners with it?[23]

Intervening, so the claim goes, would make God fall into inconsistency—not the sort of inconsistency involved in asserting inconsistent propositions, but the kind involved in, for example, sometimes treating one of your spouse's peccadilloes with patience and good humor and other times under relevantly similar circumstances responding with tight-lipped annoyance. The problem, here, would be something like caprice or arbitrariness; there is something arbitrary and whimsical in "dealing in two different manners" with the cosmic process.

This of course is a very large subject; obviously I don't have the space to treat it with the care it deserves. Still, what, exactly, is wrong with the idea that God should intervene (again, supposing we knew what intervention is)? The suggestion is that God would display a sort of arbitrary inconsistency if he sometimes acted contrary to the regularities he has established for his world. But is this really true? There would be arbitrariness and inconsistency only if God had no special reason for acting contrary to the usual regularities; but of course he might very well have such reasons. This is obvious for the case of raising Jesus from the dead: God intends to mark the special status accruing to Jesus by this mighty act of raising him from the dead.

23. McMullin, "Evolution and Special Creation," *Zygon* vol. 28, no. 3 (September 1993), p. 324. Note that McMullin doesn't object to "intervention" and miracles in *Heilsgeschichte* (salvation history); he's talking just about *Naturgeschichte* (the history of the natural world).

In other cases too, however, he might have reasons for "dealing in two different manners" with his cosmos; how could we be even reasonably sure that he doesn't? Perhaps he aims to establish basic regularities, thus making science and free intelligent action possible for his creatures. But perhaps he also has good reason for sometimes acting contrary to those regularities: to mark special occasions, for example, or to make clear his love or his power, or to authorize what someone says, or to guide history in a certain direction. Why should any of this be in any way incompatible with his unsurpassable greatness?

Well, many seem to think of God as like a classical artist, one who prizes economy, restraint, discipline. Thus Michael Murray, explaining the views of Leibniz and Malebranche:

> There is something grand, beautiful, and artful about a universe which contains within it everything that is necessary in order for it to bring about the results God intends for it. God could cause every event that we see in the natural world directly. But a powerful and rational designer would... display his power and reason far more manifestly in a universe which is itself a machine-making machine. A universe which achieves the ends God has for it in this self-contained fashion does as much to express the glory of its creator as do the end-products of the creative process.[24]

Perhaps; but also, perhaps God is more like a romantic artist; perhaps he revels in glorious variety, riotous creativity, overflowing fecundity, uproarious activity. (Why else would he create a million species of beetles?) Perhaps he is also very much a hands-on God, constantly

---

24. Murray, *Nature Red in Tooth and Claw; Theism and the Problem of Animal Suffering* (New York: Oxford University Press, 2008), p. 146.

active in history, leading, guiding, persuading and redeeming his people, blessing them with "the Internal Witness of the Holy Spirit"
(Calvin) or "the Internal Instigation of the Holy Spirit" (Aquinas)
and conferring upon them the gift of faith.[25] No doubt he is active in
still other ways.[26] None of this so much as begins to compromise his
greatness and majesty, his august and unsurpassable character.

III WHAT *IS* INTERVENTION?

The reasons for supposing God couldn't or wouldn't intervene in his
creation are weak. But now we must face a more poignant question:
what, from the point of view of the new picture, *is* intervention? Can
we so much as say what it consists in?

We can say what it is on the classical picture, at least approximately. Of
course, we can't characterize an intervention as an action that causes an event E
which is contrary to a natural law. That is because, as you will recall, the form of
a natural law is

> (LN) When the universe is causally closed (when God is not acting
> specially in the world), P;

but if and when God intervenes, the universe is not then causally closed, so that
the proviso of the proposed law is not satisfied.[27] Nor can we say that an intervention is a divine act producing an event that would not have occurred but for
that act: any act of conservation meets that condition, and conservation is not a
case of intervention.

25. See Calvin, *Institutes of the Christian Religion* III, ii, 7; Aquinas, *Summa Theologiae* II-II q. 2,
   a. 9; and see my *Warranted Christian Belief* (New York: Oxford University Press, 2000),
   chapter 8.
26. See section IV of this chapter.
27. And even if we thought of a law as the result of deleting the antecedent from (LN), taking
   a law to be an exceptionless generalization, it still wouldn't be possible for God to act in a
   way contrary to a natural law (although it would be possible for him to act in such a way as
   to falsify a proposition that would have been a natural law but for that act).

Suppose we look in a different direction. Returning to (LN), delete the antecedents from all the laws, conjoin the resulting propositions, and use "L" as the name for that conjunction. On the deterministic Laplacean picture, as we've seen, $S(t)$, the physical state of the universe at any time t, conjoined with L, entails $S(t^*)$ for any (later) time t^*. Let's make a couple of simplifying assumptions: suppose the material universe has a beginning at a time t_0, suppose it evolves according to L, suppose no intervention occurs at t_0, suppose no two interventions occur at exactly the same time, and suppose there are at most countably many interventions.[28] Then an intervention will have occurred at the first time t^* such that

$$S(t_0)L$$

does not entail

$$S(t^*).$$

More generally, we can let t be *any* time, not just that hypothetical first moment; let t^* be the first time after t such that $S(t^*)$ is not entailed by $S(t_0)$ & L: an intervention will have occurred at t^*.[29]

Of course this still doesn't tell us what an intervention *is*. As an effort in that direction, we might try saying that an intervention is an action (divine, demonic, angelic, human) that causes an event E to occur at a time t, such that for some t^* prior to t, $S(t^*)$ & L doesn't entail that E occurs at t. The idea is that God, for example, causes an event E to occur at t, such that at some earlier time t^*, Laplace's demon could not have predicted that E would occur at t (even if she knew both L and the total physical state $S(t^*)$). Sadly enough, however, this won't quite do the trick. For suppose God intervenes in this sense at t: say he

28. Indeed, how *could* an intervention occur at t_0? What occurs at t_0 would be the initial conditions, and presumably the initial conditions would simply be a result of the initial divine creative act, in which case the action resulting in the initial conditions would not be an action that goes beyond creation and conservation.

29. The unduly scrupulous might object that while there is a time t^* after t such that $S(t)\&L$ does not entail $S(t^*)$, perhaps there is no first such time: perhaps the interval in question is open. I leave to them the project of making the necessary repairs.

creates a full-grown horse *ex nihilo*, so that E is the coming-to-be of this horse. Let t^* be an earlier time such that $S(t^*)$ doesn't entail that E occurs at t. Now consider some time t^{**} later than t and suppose God performs a noninterventionist act of preserving or sustaining that horse at t^{**}. This act causes an event E^* consisting in the horse's existing at t^{**}; $S(t^*)$ & L clearly doesn't entail that E^* occurs. So on our definition, this act of sustaining counts as an intervention. But it shouldn't.

We might try the following: stipulate that where E results from an intervention at t, for every earlier time t^*, $S(t^*)$ & L does not entail that E occurs at t. The definition thus goes as follows:

> (INT) An act A (divine, demonic, angelic, human) is an intervention just if A causes an event E to occur at a time t, where there is an interval of times bounded above by t such that for every time t^* in that interval, $S(t^*)$ & L doesn't entail that E occurs at t.[30]

(INT) looks as if it will work for the classical context; we can therefore say for the classical context what an intervention is. But (INT) won't work in the QM context. We can see this as follows. Suppose, once more, we delete the antecedents of the laws, conjoin the resulting propositions, and call that conjunction "L": according to quantum mechanical indeterminacy, $S(t^*)$ & L, for a given time t, will not (except under extremely unusual conditions) entail $S(t^*)$ for other times t^*. Hence (INT) as it stands will count every divine act of conservation as an intervention—which means, of course, that it won't do. Given the indeterminism of quantum mechanics, nothing like (INT) is available. So what would an intervention be? (INT) won't work for the New Picture, but what else can we come up with?

The aim of most of the DAP members, apparently, is to come up with an account of special divine action—action beyond creation

---

30. As Luke Van Horn pointed out (personal communication), this (arguably) isn't exactly right: what if God simultaneously suppresses some natural cause of an event, and then specially causes that event himself? That would seem to be a case of special divine action, but it wouldn't qualify as such on (INT).

and conservation—that doesn't entail or involve intervention. Several of the DAP authors apparently hold that intervention requires "violating the laws," "setting aside natural law," or "overriding" those laws; but how could God set aside or override the probabilistic laws of quantum mechanics in performing those miraculous acts?[31] What would intervention be, in the context of the new picture, involving QM?

One fairly common thought—perhaps more like a sort of assumption than an actual proposal as to the nature of intervention—is that an intervention occurs when God performs an action, the consequence of which is an event that would not have occurred had God not performed that action:

(1) God intervenes if and only if he performs an action A, thereby causing a state of affairs that would not have occurred if God had not performed A.

As it stands, this can't be right: in any act of conservation God causes a state of affairs that would not have occurred had he not performed that act. If God conserves you in existence, your continuing to exist is a state of affairs that would not have occurred (been actual) if he had not so acted. But conservation is not intervention.

---

31. On "violating the laws" see Robert Russell, "Divine Action and Quantum Mechanics" in *Quantum Mechanics: Scientific Perspectives on Divine Action*, ed. Robert John Russell, Philip Clayton, Kirk Wegter-McNelly, and John Polkinghorne (Vatican City: Vatican Observatory Publications, and Berkeley: Center for Theology and the Natural Sciences, 2001), p. 295 and Wesley Wildman, "The Divine Action Project," p. 50. On "setting aside natural law" see Philip Clayton, "Wildman's Kantian Skepticism: a Rubicon for the Divine Action Debate," *Theology and Science* 2, 2 (October, 2004), p. 187. On "overriding" those laws see Thomas Tracy, "Scientific Perspectives on Divine Action? Mapping the Options," *Theology and Science* 2, 2 (October, 2004), p. 197.

Another possibility, therefore, would be:

(2) God intervenes if and only if he performs an action A thereby causing an event E that (a) goes beyond conservation and creation, and (b) is such that if he had not performed A, E would not have occurred.

This won't work either. For what would be the difference between intervention, so construed, and special divine action? The project is to find a conception of special divine action—divine action that goes beyond conservation and creation—that doesn't involve intervention; if (2) is true, however, every case of special divine action will *automatically* be a case of intervention—thus making the whole project of trying to find a conception of special divine action that doesn't involve intervention look a little unlikely.

So what is divine intervention? Wildman speaks more vaguely of "violating the created structure of order":

> Most participants certainly felt that God would not create an orderly world in which it was impossible for the creator to act without violating the created structures of order.... A noninterventionist special divine act is in accord with created structures of order and regularity within nature, while an interventionist special divine act involves abrogating, suspending, or ignoring created structures of order and regularity within nature.[32]

William Stoeger adds that he believes that all the DAP participants agree with this definition.[33] What are these created structures of order and regularity? Presumably they aren't the natural laws as

---

32. Wildman, "The Divine Action Project," p. 38.
33. "The Divine Action Project: Reflections on the Compatibilism/Incompatibilism Divide," *Theology and Science* 2, 2 (October, 2004), p. 194.

disclosed in QM—once again, God's performing a miracle wouldn't violate them. So what are they?

IV INTERVENTION AND DIVINE ACTION AT THE QUANTUM LEVEL

Perhaps there is a way around this problem. Members of the DAP don't or can't say what intervention is; even so, it may be possible to specify a way God can act specially in the world that avoids the objections they bring against intervention. The chief objection, the heart of the matter, is two-fold. First, there is that concern with intervention as somehow going against the natures of the things God has created. And second, there is that alleged "inconsistency": as McMullin puts it with admirable succinctness, for God to intervene is for him to "deal in two different manners" with the cosmos he has created. The idea is that typically, God does nothing special; he just conserves the world and allows it to develop or evolve according to the laws he has established for it, or he permits it to develop in accord with the natures of the entities it contains, or he treats the stuff he has made in the same way. Once in a while, however, he steps in and does something special; and it is that contrast between his ordinary dealings with the world, and the way in which he deals with it on special occasions, that is the cause for complaint.

Now as I've argued, neither of these objections is at all clear or clearly accurate. Furthermore, it isn't easy to see what is problematic about God treating what he has made differently on different occasions: might he not have a good reason for doing so? Still there may be a way in which God can act specially in the world, and do so in a manner that accommodates those concerns; then even if we don't know what intervention is, we could still specify a mode of divine action that isn't subject to those objections. Even if we can't say whether or not that mode of action is interventionistic, we can still see that it isn't subject to the objections brought against intervention, whatever exactly intervention is.

In 1958 William Pollard suggested that God *acts at the quantum level*; several members of the DAP have taken up, examined and developed his suggestion.[34] All of these authors focus on the conventional Copenhagen interpretation. God can cause quantum events, and, because the laws are merely statistical, do so without "suspending" those laws. This action on his part can perhaps be amplified—by chaotic effects or in other ways—to the macroscopic level; in this way, perhaps, God can cause dramatic effects at the level of everyday life, and do so without falling into intervention.

John Polkinghorne notes a problem with this suggestion. First, the above authors speak of quantum *events*. On the Copenhagen interpretation, the only events for which indeterminism holds are those mysterious *measurements*. But then, says Polkinghorne,

> There is a particular difficulty in using quantum indeterminacy to describe divine action. Conventional quantum theory contains much continuity and determinism in addition to its well-known discontinuities and indeterminacies. The latter refer, not to all quantum behavior, but only to those particular events which qualify, by the irreversible registration of their effects in the macro-world, to be described as measurements. In between the measurements the continuous determinism of the Schrödinger

34. Pollard, *Chance and Providence* (New York: Scribner, 1958); see also Robert Russell, "Quantum Physics in Philosophical and Theological Perspective," *Physics, Philosophy and Theology: A Common Quest for Understanding*, ed. Russell, William Stoeger, and George Coyne (Vatican City: Vatican Observatory, 1988), pp. 343ff., and "Divine Action and Quantum Mechanics: a Fresh Assessment," *Quantum Mechanics*, pp. 293ff.; Nancey Murphy, "Divine Action in the Natural Order: Buridan's Ass and Schrödinger's Cat," *Chaos and Complexity*, pp. 325ff.; Thomas Tracy, "Particular Providence," *Chaos and Complexity*, pp. 315–22, and "Creation, Providence, and Quantum Chance," *Quantum Mechanics*, 235ff. See also the pieces by Philip Clayton and George Ellis in *Quantum Mechanics*.

equation applies. Occasions of measurement only occur from time to time, and a God who acted through being their determinator would also only be acting from time to time. Such an episodic account of providential agency does not seem altogether satisfactory theologically.[35]

Measurements are mysterious, and have been variously interpreted; but given (as on the Copenhagen interpretation) that they occur thus episodically, Polkinghorne's stricture seems accurate.

The Copenhagen interpretation is a *collapse* interpretation; but there are other collapse approaches. For example, there are spontaneous collapse theories, including in particular the Ghirardi-Rimini-Weber (GRW) approach.[36] On these collapse approaches, collapses are not restricted to measurements; they occur spontaneously, and at a regular rate. One of the main motivations here is to help with the location problem: on the standard Copenhagen interpretation, objects, including macroscopic objects, don't seem to *have* a location when their location isn't being measured or detected; this can seem at the least embarrassing. On the GRW interpretation, however, "it follows that a macroscopic [system] undergoes a localization every 10^{-7} seconds."[37] Puzzles remain: won't it be true that a macroscopic system, my body, for example, is only intermittently located, even if located 10 million times a second?[38]

35. Polkinghorne, "The Metaphysics of Divine Action," *Chaos and Complexity*, pp. 152–53.
36. G. C. Ghirardi, A. Rimini, and T. Weber, "Unified dynamics of microscopic and macroscopic systems," *Physical Review D*, 34 (1986), pp. 470ff.; see also G. C. Ghirardi, "Collapse Theories," *The Stanford Encyclopedia of Philosophy* (Fall 2007 edition), ed. Edward N. Zalta, available at http://plato.stanford.edu/archives/fall2007/entries/qm-collapse/.
37. Ghirardi, "Collapse Theories."
38. There is also the so-called "counting problem" for collapse theories proposed by Peter Lewis ("Quantum Mechanics, Orthogonality, and Counting," *The British Journal for the Philosophy of Science*, 48, pp. 313ff.): the problem alleged is that each of a large number of marbles may be in a box, while it is false that all the marbles are in the box. For a resolution, see Bradley Monton, "The Problem of Ontology for Spontaneous Collapse Theories," *Studies in History and Philosophy of Modern Science*, 2004.

At any rate there seems to be substantially less offense to common opinion, here, than on the classical Copenhagen interpretation.

On this approach we could think of the *nature* of a system as dictating that collapses occur at the regular rate they in fact display. What is presently of significance, however, is that on these approaches there is no cause for a given collapse to go to the particular value (the particular position, for example) or eigenstate to which in fact it goes. That is, there is no *physical* cause; there is nothing in the previous physical state of the world that causes a given collapse to go to the particular eigenstate to which it *does* go. But of course this state of affairs might very well have a *non*physical cause. It's wholly in accord with these theories that, for any collapse and the resulting eigenstate, it is *God* who causes *that* state to result. Perhaps, then, all collapse-outcomes (as we might call them) are caused by God.[39] If so, then between collapses, a system evolves according to the Schrödinger equation; but when a collapse occurs, it is divine agency that causes the specific collapse-outcome that ensues. On this view of God's special action—call it "divine collapse-causation" ("DCC")—God is *always* acting specially, that is, always acting in ways that go beyond creation and conservation, thus obviating the problem alleged to lie in his sometimes treating the world in hands-off fashion but other times in a hands-on way.

Furthermore, if, as one assumes, the macroscopic physical world supervenes on the microscopic, God could thus control what happens at the macroscopic level by causing the right microscopic collapse-outcomes. In this way God can exercise providential guidance over cosmic history; he might in this way guide the course of evolutionary history by causing the right mutations to arise at the right time and preserving the forms of life that lead to the results he intends. In this way he might also guide human history. He could do this without in any way "violating" the created natures of the things he has created. For on

39. But see p. 119.

this suggestion, it is in the nature of physical systems to evolve between collapses according to the Schrödinger equation; it also is in their nature to undergo periodic collapses; but it is not part of their nature to collapse to any particular eigenstate. Hence, in causing a system to collapse to a particular eigenstate, God need not constrain it against its nature. From the point of view of the objections to intervention, the beauty of DCC is three-fold: first, God is always and constantly engaging in special action; second, DCC shows how God can seamlessly integrate the regularity and predictability in our world necessary for free action with the occasional miraculous event; and third, it shows how all this can happen without any divine "violation" or interruption of the created order. Hence it eludes those objections to intervention.

Another objection: "Isn't it part of the very nature of such a system to collapse in such a way as not to violate the probabilities assigned by Born's Rule? And wouldn't God's causing the collapses in fact violate those probabilities? Wouldn't there have to be something like a divine statistical footprint, if God caused those collapses?" This objection rests on false assumptions. Consider the collapses that occur at a given time or during a given period—one second, let's say. Each collapse will be to a specific eigenstate of some observable; call the conjunction of all those specific eigenstates a "superconfiguration." Any particular superconfiguration for a given moment or period will presumably be monumentally improbable. Now the objector seems to think we can somehow see or know, if only vaguely, that if God causes the collapses, the probabilistic pattern of the superconfigurations would be detectably different from the actual pattern of those superconfigurations. But why think so? Specifying any particular superconfiguration would be a bit beyond our powers (impressive though they be); the same goes in spades for specifying probabilistic patterns of superconfigurations; and the same goes for determining how these would or wouldn't be different if the collapses were divinely caused. Look at it from this angle: suppose God *has* in fact caused all the collapses; how could one argue that some probabilistic pattern of superconfigurations must be different from what it otherwise would have been?[40]

But what about miracles? What about the parting of the Red Sea, changing water into wine, raising Lazarus from the dead? Most crucially, what about the resurrection of Jesus? Miracles are a mixed lot: some are unproblematically compatible with QM, but, as we saw above, about others (changing water into wine, for example) the experts disagree. However, even if all the usual suspects are in fact compatible with QM in the sense that their occurrence is not flatly inconsistent with the latter, there is another way in which some could be incompatible with it. Perhaps some of the suggested miracles, while not flatly excluded by QM, are so improbable (given QM) that they wouldn't be expected to occur in a period 10^{10} times the age of the universe. Such a miracle, if it were to occur (and if we were to think of QM as universally applicable), would *disconfirm* QM; it would be evidence against QM, and in that sense would be incompatible with it.

Of course it is far from obvious that miracles *are* incompatible with QM in either of these ways; finding a problem with them out of deference to QM seems premature, if not wholly quixotic. Still, suppose certain miracles are incompatible with QM in one or another of these ways. Would that produce a problem for supposing that those miracles have actually occurred? I think not. Of course we can't think about natural laws as we did with respect to the "old picture." There we followed John Mackie in the supposition that natural laws describe the material universe as it behaves when it is causally closed; on DCC, however, God is constantly acting specially in the world and the material universe is never causally closed. Therefore we must content ourselves with something vaguer. On those occasions where God's

40. In *Divine Action and Modern Science*, Saunders raises further objections to the thought that God acts at the quantum level; these objections are nicely dealt with in Thomas Tracy's review of the book: "Divine Action and Modern Science," *Notre Dame Philosophical Reviews*, October 9, 2003 (available online at http://ndpr.nd.edu/reviews.cfm).

action results in states of affairs incompatible with QM in either of the above two ways, God is treating his world differently from the way in which he ordinarily treats it; but the laws of nature, including QM, should be thought of as descriptions of the material universe when God is not treating what he has made in a special way. Here (as often) it's not at all easy to say just what constitutes a *special* way of treating the world, but we do have an intuitive sense for the idea.

Objection: "But doesn't this result in divine determinism, perhaps even occasionalism, in that God really causes whatever happens at the macro-level?" Here still another virtue of DCC comes into view. Just as it could be that God causes collapse-outcomes and does so freely, so it could be that we human beings, dualistically conceived, do the same thing. Suppose human beings, as the vast bulk of the Christian tradition has supposed, resemble God in being immaterial souls or selves, immaterial substances—with this difference: in their case but not in his, selves intimately connected with a particular physical body.[41] Suppose, further, God has endowed human selves (and perhaps other agents as well) with the power to act freely, freely cause events in the physical world. In the case of human beings, this power could be the power to cause events in their brains and hence in their bodies, thus enabling them to act freely in the world. And suppose, still further, the specific proximate events human beings can cause are quantum collapse-outcomes. The thought would be that

41. Current objections to dualistic interactionism are vastly overrated; see my "Against Materialism," *Faith and Philosophy* 23:1 (January 2006) and "Materialism and Christian Belief" in *Persons: Divine and Human*, ed. Peter van Inwagen and Dean Zimmerman (Oxford: Clarendon Press, 2007), especially pp. 120–36. One objection often raised to dualistic interactionism is that it would violate the principle of the conservation of energy. The main answer here is the same as that to the above objections to divine action in the world: this principle is stated for closed systems; but any physical system (a brain, e.g.) in which an immaterial substance caused a change would obviously not be a closed system. (It's also worth noting, however, that spontaneous collapse theories reject the principle of conservation of energy; energy is not conserved when a GRW collapse happens. See Bradley Monton, "The Problem of Ontology for Spontaneous Collapse Theories.")

God's action constitutes a theater or setting for free actions on the part of human beings and other persons—principalities, powers, angels, Satan and his minions, whatever. God sets the stage for such free action by causing a world of regularity and predictability; but he causes only some of the collapse-outcomes, leaving it to free persons to cause the rest.[42] If so, our action in the world (though of course vastly smaller in scope) resembles divine action in the world; this would be still another locus of the *imago dei*. Here we see a pleasing unity of divine and human free action, as well as a more specific suggestion as to what mechanism these actions actually involve.

Of course questions remain. DCC is tied to a particular version of QM; what happens if that version gets jettisoned? Indeed, what happens if QM itself gets jettisoned or seriously revised? After all, there is deep conflict between QM and general relativity; who knows what will happen here? First: if Christian belief is true, the warrant for belief in special divine action doesn't come from quantum mechanics or current science or indeed any science at all; these beliefs have their own independent source of warrant.[43] That means that in case of conflict between Christian belief and current science, it isn't automatically current science that has more warrant or positive epistemic status; perhaps the warrant enjoyed by Christian belief is greater than that enjoyed by the conflicting scientific belief. Of course there could be defeaters for these Christian beliefs; but as we've seen, current science (at least as far as we've explored the matter) provides no such defeaters, and the theological objections proposed seem weak *in excelsis*.

---

42. This suggestion as to the mechanism of free human action works much better for dualism than for the materialism that, sadly enough, is becoming more common among Christian thinkers. In my view this is less a limitation of the suggestion than another strike against materialism, which is in any event implausible from a Christian perspective; see the preceding footnote.

43. See my *Warranted Christian Belief* (New York: Oxford University Press, 2000), part III, especially chapters 8 and 9.

What we should think of special divine action, therefore, doesn't depend on QM or versions thereof, or on current science more generally. Indeed, what we should think of current science can quite properly depend, in part, on theology. For example, science has not spoken with a single voice about the question whether the universe has a beginning: first the idea was that it did, but then the steady state theory triumphed, but then big bang cosmology achieved ascendancy, but now there are straws in the wind suggesting a reversion to the thought that the universe is without a beginning. The sensible religious believer is not obliged to trim her sails to the current scientific breeze on this topic, revising her belief on the topic every time science changes its mind; if the most satisfactory Christian (or theistic) theology endorses the idea that the universe did indeed have a beginning, the believer has a perfect right to accept that thought. Something similar goes for the Christian believer and special divine action.

But where Christian or theistic belief and current science can fit nicely together, as with DCC, so much the better; and if one of the current versions of QM fits better with such belief than the others, that's a perfectly proper reason to accept that version. True, this version may not win out in the long run (and the same goes for QM itself); so the acceptance in question (as of QM itself) must be provisional. Who knows what the future will bring? But we can say at least the following: at *this* point, given *this* evidence, this is how things look. And that's as much as can be said for any scientific theory.

V A COUPLE OF OTHER ALLEGED CONFLICTS

What we've seen is that there is nothing in science, under either the old or the new picture, that conflicts with or even calls into question special divine action, including miracles. By way of conclusion, I'd like to mention a couple of other allegations of conflict between science and religion—I don't have the space to do them justice, but I can at least say how my reply to them might go. Some people claim that science, taken as a whole, somehow supports or underwrites a naturalistic view of the universe, one in which there is no such person as God or any other supernatural beings. Indeed, this way of looking at the world is sometimes called the scientific worldview, or, following Peter Unger, "scientiphicalism."[44] But calling your view "scientific" doesn't make it so, anymore than naming your son "Jack Armstrong" guarantees that he will have mighty biceps. And how is science supposed to support naturalism? Neither quantum mechanics nor general relativity has any connection with naturalism, and, as we saw in the first couple of chapters, the same goes for evolution. So where, in science, is this support supposed to come from? In addition, the fact is there is deep conflict between science and naturalism, as I'll argue in chapter 10.

A second suggestion may be thought of as a special case of the first. John Worrall claims that there is a deep difference between religion and science—one that does not redound to the credit of religion.[45] According to Worrall, there is a profound contrast between what we might call the *epistemic styles* of religion and science. The scientist, says Worrall, holds her beliefs tentatively, dispassionately, only on the basis of evidence, and is always looking for a better hypothesis, one that is better supported by the evidence. The religious believer, on the other hand, typically holds his beliefs dogmatically: he is unwilling to consider the evidence and often holds his beliefs with a

44. Unger, "Free Will and Scientiphicalism," *Philosophy and Phenomenological Research*, vol. 65, issue 1 (July, 2002), p. 1. In Unger's mind, as in mine, there is no intrinsic connection between science and scientiphicalism.
45. Worrall, "Why Science Discredits Religion" in *Contemporary Debates in Philosophy of Religion*, ed. M. Peterson and R. Van Arragon (Oxford: Blackwell, 2000).

degree of firmness out of proportion to their support by the evidence; he is unwilling to look for a better hypothesis.

Of course it is well known that the way scientists hold their beliefs is often anything but tentative and dispassionate. For example, here is Werner Heisenberg on a discussion between Niels Bohr and Erwin Schrödinger:

> Bohr, who was otherwise most considerate and amiable in his dealings with people, now appeared to me almost as an unrelenting fanatic, who was not prepared to make a single concession to his discussion partner.... It will hardly be possible to convey the intensity of passion with which the discussions were concluded on both sides, or the deep-rooted convictions which one could perceive equally with Bohr and with Schrödinger in every spoken sentence.[46]

Not exactly tentative and dispassionate. As is also well-known, scientists sometimes hang on to their scientific hypotheses in the teeth of the evidence. As a matter of fact, that may be a good thing, since it improves the chances of the theory's getting a good run for its money; and indeed sometimes the initial evidence is against a good theory.

For the moment, however, suppose there is the difference Worrall says there is. That difference indicates a science/religion conflict only if *science* tells us that beliefs in all the areas of our epistemic life ought to be formed and held in the same way as scientific beliefs typically are.[47] But of course that isn't a scientific claim at all; it is

46. Heisenberg, *Physics and Beyond* (New York: Harper and Row, 1971), pp. 73–76.
47. Just for the sake of completeness: I'm taking it for granted that science doesn't tell us that all beliefs should be held the way religious beliefs are, and that religion doesn't tell us either that all beliefs should be held the way scientific beliefs are held, or that all beliefs should be held the way religious beliefs are held.

rather a normative epistemological claim, and a quixotic one at that. There are all sorts of beliefs we don't accept on the basis of evidence and don't accept tentatively; and in all sorts of cases we do not constantly look for better alternatives. We don't accept elementary mathematical and logical beliefs in that way, or beliefs of the sort *it seems to me I see something red*, or *I am not the only thing that exists*, or *my cognitive faculties are reliable*, or such beliefs as *there has been a past, there are other persons*, and *there is an external world*; and all this is, epistemically speaking, perfectly proper. It is *scientific hypotheses* which (for the most part) ought to be accepted in the way Worrall celebrates; but of course not nearly all of our beliefs are scientific hypotheses. In particular, religious beliefs are not. Maybe a few people accept religious beliefs strictly on the basis of what they take the evidence to be; perhaps, for example, this was true of Anthony Flew.[48] But for most of us, our religious beliefs are not like scientific hypotheses; and we are none the worse, epistemically speaking, for that. According to Paul Feyerabend, "Scientists are not content with running their own playpens in accordance with what they regard as the rules of the scientific method; they want to universalize those rules, they want them to become part of society at large."[49] As applied to scientists generally, this is certainly overblown; but it does seem to apply to some science enthusiasts.

We began part I of this book by considering claims to the effect that contemporary evolutionary theory is incompatible with Christian belief (see chapters 1 and 2). I concluded that this conflict is vastly exaggerated; there is conflict between *unguided evolution* and Christian belief, but it is no part of contemporary evolutionary theory to declare that evolution is indeed unguided. We then turned to a

48. See Anthony Flew and Roy Varghese, *There is a God: How the World's Most Notorious Atheist Changed His Mind* (New York: Harper and Collins, 2007).
49. Feyerabend, *Against Method* (London: New Left Books, 1975), p. 220.

second alleged locus of conflict: special divine action in the world (chapters 3 and 4). We noted that many theologians, philosophers and scientists object to the thought that God acts specially in the world. At least some of their objections have to do with science: special divine action, they say, goes contrary, somehow, to science. As we've seen, however, none of these objections is even remotely cogent; there is nothing in current or classical science inconsistent with special divine action in the world.

So far, therefore, we have found no conflict between Christian or theistic belief and current science. But there are other areas of science, and in some of them theories clearly inconsistent with Christian belief are proposed. Do these theories, supposing they achieved the status of scientific orthodoxy, offer a defeater for Christian belief? Or is this conflict merely superficial? In part II of the book we'll explore this question, beginning, in the next chapter, with some theories from evolutionary psychology.

PART II

SUPERFICIAL CONFLICT

Chapter 5

Evolutionary Psychology
and Scripture Scholarship

In part I we examined some alleged conflicts between science and religion, in particular between science and theistic belief. First, there was the claim that there is conflict between theistic belief and contemporary evolutionary theory; and second, the claim that science somehow refutes or casts doubt upon the idea, common to the theistic religions, that God acts specially in the world. These claims turned out to be wholly mistaken. There is no conflict between theistic belief and evolutionary theory, including the thought that all of life has come to be by way of natural selection operating on random genetic mutation. According to theistic religion, God has created the world and created human beings in his image. It is perfectly possible, however, that he did so by employing, guiding, and directing the process of genetic variation and natural selection. He may not in fact have done it in that fashion; perhaps you think it rather unlikely that he did it that way. Still, he certainly could have. Of course there *is* conflict between the widely accepted idea that natural selection, or evolution more generally, is *unguided*; but that claim, though widely accepted, is no part of current science. It is instead a metaphysical or theological add-on; an assumption that in no way enjoys the authority of science.

Nor is there conflict between contemporary science—physics, for example—and the thought that God acts specially in the world. True, many have claimed that there is conflict between Newtonian physics and special divine action. They have ignored the fact that Newtonian laws are stated for *causally closed* systems, but obviously no system in which God acts specially would be a closed system; hence God's special action would not go contrary to the laws of Newtonian physics. And with the advent of quantum mechanics it has become harder yet to find conflict between special divine action and current physics.

There are other areas of science, however, where the appearance of conflict is matched by reality. I'm thinking in particular of *evolutionary psychology* and *scientific scripture scholarship*—historical Biblical criticism, as it is sometimes called. You may think that historical Biblical criticism and evolutionary psychology have little in common. Perhaps so; still, they are alike in a couple of ways crucial to our inquiry. First, in each of these areas we find claims and assertions incompatible with theistic or Christian belief; here there really is conflict. But second, I call this conflict "superficial," and in chapter 6 I will explains why. Very briefly, however: even though Christians are committed to a high view of science, and even if these disciplines do constitute science or good science (a state of affairs that is by no means self-evident), these developments in evolutionary psychology and historical Biblical criticism don't offer, or even threaten to offer, *defeaters* for Christian or theistic belief. Hence there is conflict, but it is merely superficial.

I EVOLUTIONARY PSYCHOLOGY

Those who accept Darwinism, as one might expect, often try to explain various features of contemporary organisms in Darwinian terms. One way to do this is to show how the trait in question does or did contribute to the reproductive fitness of the organisms in question. Why do tigers have stripes? Because they provide camouflage, which, given the tiger's lifestyle, is fitness-enhancing. Or perhaps the trait in question is not itself adaptive, doesn't itself contribute to fitness, but is genetically associated with traits that do. As a special case, perhaps the trait in question is a spandrel, a trait that isn't itself fitness-enhancing, but is a consequence of traits that are.[1] Such explanations sometimes seem plausible, at least within limits: if you think the organisms in question arose by virtue of natural selection, then this seems a fairly sensible way in which to try to explain at least some of their traits.

As one might expect, this sort of explanation has been extended to human beings as well; one enterprise of giving such explanations is sociobiology, or, as it is now called, evolutionary psychology. Sociobiology burst upon the scene in 1975 with the publication of E. O. Wilson's *Sociobiology: The New Synthesis*. Wilson's work provoked pointed criticism. Some claimed it tended to dismiss rape and other violence as merely a part of our evolutionary heritage; others claimed it was deeply sexist; still others declared it bad science. Work along these lines is now called "evolutionary psychology"; we need not enter the controversy as to whether evolutionary psychology is a successor discipline to sociobiology, or just the same thing renamed to deflect criticism. Either way, evolutionary psychology has been growing, and is rapidly becoming an established part of academic psychology.

In essence, evolutionary psychology is an attempt to explain important human traits and behaviors in terms of the evolutionary origin of the human species. The heart and soul of this project is the effort to explain distinctive human traits—our art, humor, play, love, sexual behavior,

---

1. Stephen Jay Gould and Richard Lewontin: "Spandrels—the tapering triangular spaces formed by the intersection of two rounded arches at right angles—are necessary architectural byproducts of mounting a dome on rounded arches." "The Spandrels of San Marco and the Panglossian Paradigm: a Critique of the Adaptionist Program" (London: *Proceedings of the Royal Society*, B 205, 1979), p. 581.

poetry, sense of adventure, love of stories, our music, our morality, and our religion itself—in terms of adaptive advantages accruing to our hunter-gatherer ancestors back there on the plains of Serengeti.

Some of this can be a pretty tall order. Take our love of beauty, for example: here it isn't easy to see what an evolutionary explanation would look like. (Of course it is always possible to declare a trait a spandrel.) There is the glorious beauty and grandeur of mountains— Mt. Baker, for example, or Mt. Shuksan, or the Grand Teton, or any of a hundred more. There is the splendor of a craggy ocean shore, but also of a tiny highly articulate flower. Alan Shepard, the first American in space, gasped at the sheer beauty of the earth as seen from space. It is hard to see how a capacity to find marvelous beauty in such things would be of adaptive use to our hunter-gatherer ancestors. And of course there is Mozart, and Bach. Perhaps we can see how love of something like heavy metal rock could be adaptively useful, possibly like the martial airs that encourage troops going into battle. But Mozart's Ave Verum Corpus? Bach's B-minor Mass?

Harvard evolutionary psychologist Steven Pinker once told a gathering of musicologists why music had rated only eleven pages of his 660-page *How the Mind Works:* "He told the musicologists why the topic did not merit more attention: music was 'useless' in terms of human evolution and development. He dismissed it as 'auditory cheesecake,' a trivial amusement that 'just happens to tickle several important parts of the brain in a highly pleasurable way, as cheesecake tickles the palate.'"[2] Anthropologist Steven Mither defends music against this charge of being useless: music does too have evolutionary significance, he said, because it is connected with walking and marching and other rhythmical activities.[3] It's a little startling to

2. Pinker, *How the Mind Works* (New York: Penguin, 1997). Pinker's statement as reported by Rodney Clapp in *The Christian Century*, February 10, 2009, p. 45.
3. Mither, *The Singing Neanderthals* (London: Weidenfeld and Nicolson, 2005).

see something as deep, powerful, and significant as music denigrated or defended in those terms. Is an activity important only if it has played a prominent role in our evolution, enabling our ancestors to survive and reproduce? What about physics, mathematics, philosophy, and evolutionary biology itself: do (did) they have evolutionary significance? After all, it is only the occasional assistant professor of mathematics or logic that needs to be able to prove Gödel's theorem in order to survive and reproduce. Indeed, given the nerdness factor, undue interest in such things would have been counterproductive in the Pleistocene. What prehistoric woman would be interested in some guy who prefers thinking about set theory to hunting?

Evolutionary psychology is extremely popular, at present, and growing in popularity. As I said, it is becoming an established part of academic psychology; it is also gaining purchase in more popular culture. Just about every other issue of *The New York Review of Books* carries a review of still another book intended to interpret ourselves to ourselves along these lines. A recent high (or maybe low) point is a book in which a new understanding of *religion* is proposed. At a certain stage in our evolutionary history, so the claim goes, we human beings made the transition from being prey to being predators. Naturally that occasioned great joy, and religion arose as a celebration of that happy moment! Granted, that sounds a little far-fetched: wouldn't we have needed the consolations of religion even more when we were still prey? Still, that was the claim. Some of these projects, therefore, are a little hard to take seriously, but others are both intellectually challenging and adorned with all the trappings of serious science, complete with mathematics, models, the fitting of models to data, and the sort of stiff, impersonal literary style in which science is properly written.

Even a cursory glance at the literature shows that many theories from this area of science seem, at least on first inspection, to be deeply problematic from a Christian perspective. According to Michael Ruse and E. O. Wilson, "ethics is an illusion fobbed off on us by our own genes to get us to co-operate; thus morality ultimately seems to be about self-interest."[4] They also claim that "humans function better if they are deceived by their genes into thinking there is a disinterested objective morality binding upon them, which we should obey."[5] Why so? Individuals with our moral intuitions will be likely to cooperate with each other; groups with our moral intuitions will therefore do better, from the point of view of survival and reproduction, than groups that lack those intuitions.[6] What has been selected for, then, are people with a penchant for forming a twofold belief on this head. First, they have the sense that there really is such a thing as objective obligation, a categorical *ought* that holds, whatever your goals or aims, whatever you or anyone thinks or desires. And second, they think that among these obligations is something like the golden rule: treat others (or at least others in your group) as you yourself would like to be treated. We are thus inclined to think that this injunction is an objective and categorical requirement of morality. According to Ruse and Wilson, however, our thinking this is no more than a trick played on us by our genes to get us to cooperate: in fact there aren't any such objective moral obligations or requirements.

Consider an example. Herbert Simon's article "A Mechanism for Social Selection and Successful Altruism" is concerned with the problem of altruistic behavior—that is, behavior that promotes the fitness of someone else at the expense of the altruist's own fitness.[7]

---

4. Ruse and Wilson, "The Evolution of Ethics," in *Religion and the Natural Sciences: The Range of Engagement*, ed. James Huchingson (San Diego: Harcourt Brace, 1993), p. 310.

5. Ruse and Wilson, "Moral Philosophy as Applied Science," *Philosophy* 61, 1986, p. 179.

6. There has been controversy about whether the notion of group selection is viable; for a spirited and convincing argument that it is, see Elliott Sober and David Sloan Wilson, *Unto Others: The Evolution and Psychology of Unselfish Behavior* (Cambridge: Harvard University Press, 1998).

7. Simon, *Science* vol. 250 (December, 1990) pp. 1665ff. Simon won a Nobel Prize in economics, but later became professor of computer studies and psychology at Carnegie-Mellon University in Pittsburgh.

Why, asks Simon, do people like Mother Teresa, or the Scottish missionary Eric Liddel, or the Little Sisters of the Poor, or the Jesuit missionaries of the seventeenth century—why do these people do the things that they do? Why do they devote their time and energy and indeed their entire lives to the welfare of other people? Of course it isn't only the great saints of the world that display this impulse; most of us do so to one degree or another. Most of us give money to help feed and clothe people we have never met; we may support missionaries in foreign countries; we try, perhaps in feckless and fumbling ways, to do what we can to help the widow and orphan. Now how, asks Simon, can we account for this kind of behavior? Given our evolutionary origin in natural selection, a rational, properly functioning human being could be expected to act or try to act in such a way as to increase her personal fitness—that is, to act so as to increase the probability that her genes will be widely disseminated in the next and subsequent generation, thus doing well in the evolutionary derby.[8] A paradigm of rational behavior, so conceived, was reported in 1991: "Cecil B. Jacobson, an infertility specialist [in Alexandria, Virginia], was accused of using his own sperm to impregnate his patients; he may have fathered as many as 75 children, a prosecutor said Friday."[9] Unlike Jacobson, however, such people as Mother Teresa and Thomas Aquinas cheerfully ignore the short or long term fate of their genes. What is the explanation of this behavior?

This behavior, says Simon, is to be explained at the individual level in terms of two mechanisms: "docility" and "bounded rationality":

Docile persons tend to learn and believe what they perceive others in the society want them to learn and believe. Thus the

---

8. More simply, says Simon, "Fitness simply means expected number of progeny" (p. 1665).
9. *The South Bend Tribune*, December 21, 1991.

content of what is learned will not be fully screened for its contribution to personal fitness.

Because of bounded rationality, the docile individual will often be unable to distinguish socially prescribed behavior that contributes to fitness from altruistic behavior. In fact, docility will reduce the inclination to evaluate independently the contributions of behavior to fitness.....By virtue of bounded rationality, the docile person cannot acquire the personally advantageous learning that provides the increment, d, of fitness without acquiring also the altruistic behaviors that cost the decrement, c.[10]

The idea is that a Mother Teresa or a Thomas Aquinas display "bounded rationality"; they are unable to distinguish socially prescribed behavior that contributes to fitness from altruistic behavior (socially prescribed behavior which does not). As a result they fail to acquire the personally advantageous learning that provides that increment d of fitness without, sadly enough, suffering that decrement c exacted by altruistic behavior. They acquiesce unthinkingly in what society tells them is the right way to behave; and they aren't quite up to making their own independent evaluation of the likely bearing of such behavior on the fate of their genes. If they *did* make such an independent evaluation (and were rational enough to avoid silly mistakes), they would presumably see that this sort of behavior does not contribute to personal fitness, drop it like a hot potato, and get right to work on their expected number of progeny. From a Christian perspective, obviously, this explanation of the behavior of Mother Teresa and other altruists is wildly off the mark—not even close enough to be a miss.

10. That is (in Simon's sense), behavior that exacts a cost in terms of the agent's fitness. "A Mechanism for Social Selection and Successful Altruism," pp. 1666–67.

II EVOLUTIONARY PSYCHOLOGY AND RELIGION

I suppose the place to look for the most overt conflict would be the accounts of religion itself that are proffered by the scientific study of religion, including evolutionary psychology and cognitive science. Of course many of these theories of religion are incompatible with each other: according to some, religion is adaptive, but according to others it is nonadaptive or even maladaptive (a malignant virus, as Richard Dawkins seems to think); according to some, religion arises by way of group selection, but according to others group selection is impossible. Still, there is no dearth of examples of proclamations that conflict with religious belief (not to mention with each other). For example, Steven Pinker asks: "How does religion fit into 'a mind that one might have thought was designed to reject the palpably not true?" and states that "religion is a desperate measure that people resort to when the stakes are high and they have exhausted the usual techniques for the causation of success—medicines, strategies, courtship, and, in the case of the weather, nothing." He goes on, resurrecting the old canard about how religion is the result of crafty priests and credulous parishioners: "I have alluded to one possibility: the demand for miracles creates a market that would-be priests compete in, and they can succeed by exploiting people's dependence on experts. I trust such experts as dentists and doctors; that same trust would have made me submit to medical quackery a century ago and to a witch doctor's charms millennia ago."[11]

This is perhaps more a declaration of personal dislike for religion than a scientific or semi-scientific pronouncement, but there are many others. Rodney Stark proposed a theory according to which religion is a kind of spandrel of rational thought, an attempt to acquire nonexistent goods—eternal life, a right relationship with

11. Pinker, *How the Mind Works*, pp. 554, 556, 557.

God, salvation, remission of sins—by negotiating with nonexistent supernatural beings.[12] The idea is that rational thought, that is, means/ends or cost/benefit thinking, comes to be in the usual evolutionary way. But having the capacity for such thought inevitably carries with it the capacity to pursue nonexistent goals, like the pot of gold at the end of the rainbow, or the ones connected with religion. Taken neat, this theory is clearly incompatible with Christian belief, according to which at least some of the supernatural beings and some of the goods mentioned do indeed exist. Another example: David Sloan Wilson (not to be confused with E. O. Wilson) suggests that religion is essentially a means of social control employing or involving fictitious belief.[13] Again, taken neat, this is incompatible with Christian belief.

Among the most important writers on the scientific study of religion would be Pascal Boyer, Scott Atran, and Justin Barrett ; there is also a popular presentation of some of this material in Daniel Dennett's *Breaking the Spell*.[14] Like the early Stark, Boyer takes religion to be a kind of spandrel: it is a consequence or side effect of having the sort of brain we actually have. That we have that sort of brain is to be explained in the usual way, in terms of its contribution

12. The views of the "old" Rodney Stark must be carefully distinguished from those of the "new," which are vastly more friendly to religion: see, e.g., (with Roger Finke) *The Churching of America* (New Brunswick: Rutgers University Press, 1992), *The Rise Of Christianity* (Princeton: Princeton University Press, 1996), and *Discovering God* (New York: Harper Collins, 2007). As David Sloan Wilson puts it, "[For Stark] Religion is envisioned as an economic exchange between people and imagined supernatural agents for goods that are scarce (e.g., rain during a drought) or impossible (e.g. immortal life) to obtain in the real world" (*Darwin's Cathedral: Evolution, Religion, and the Nature of Society*, Chicago: University of Chicago Press, 2002, p. 52). Stark has since rejected this theory.

13. *Darwin's Cathedral: Evolution, Religion, and the Nature of Society*. I'll say more about Wilson's theory later.

14. Boyer, *Religion Explained* (New York: Basic, 2001); Atran, *In Gods We Trust* (Oxford: Oxford University press, 2002); see also Todd Tremlin, *Minds and Gods* (Oxford: Oxford University Press, 2006), and D. Jason Slone, *Theological Incorrectness: Why Religious People Believe What They Shouldn't* (New York: Oxford University Press, 2004); Barrett, "Exploring the Natural Foundations of Religion," in *Trends in Cognitive Sciences*, vol. 4, 2000, pp. 29–34; and Dennett, *Breaking the Spell* (New York: Penguin Books, 2006).

to fitness; but given such a brain, according to Boyer, the development of religion naturally occurs. In essence, he thinks, religion is a whole family of cognitive phenomena involving "counterintuitive" beings (beings who act in ways counter to our ordinary categories): for example, religion often involves beings who can act in the world without being visible. This out-of-the-ordinary counterintuitive character of the beings in question attracts attention and makes them memorable. However they must be *minimally* counterintuitive; too much departure from the ordinary makes them both hard to take seriously and hard to remember. A box of Kleenex that is secretly the ruler of the world, for example, is *too* counterintuitive; a religion of which this was the central feature probably wouldn't thrive.

Atran endorses several features of Boyer's theory and adds more: according to him "religion is (1) a community's costly and hard-to-fake commitment (2) to a counterfactual and counterintuitive world of supernatural agents (3) who master people's existential anxieties such as death and deception."[15] According to Atran, therefore, not just any old counterfactual and counterintuitive idea will make a religion (a whistling teakettle orbiting the sun, for example, won't fill the bill); the ideas have to involve supernatural *agents*. And not just any old remarkable agent will fill the bill either (Mickey Mouse, he says, will not); the agents have to address and assuage people's existential anxieties. So why is it that human beings are religious? Like Boyer, Atran believes that while our minds have come to be and have been developed by natural selection, religion itself isn't adaptive, but is a byproduct of our cognitive architecture:

> Religion is materially expensive and unrelentingly counterfactual and even counterintuitive. Religious practice is costly in terms of material sacrifice (at least one's prayer time), emotional

15. Atran, *In Gods We Trust*, p. 4.

expenditure (inciting fears and hopes) and cognitive effort (maintaining both factual and counterintuitive networks of belief).[16]

Now some writers seem to think that in coming up with a suggestion as to the evolutionary origin of religion, they are in some way discrediting it.[17] Apart from that gratuitous "counterfactual," however, there is nothing in Boyer or Atran that is inconsistent with theistic or Christian belief (although both seem at best extremely skeptical of such belief). Describing the origin of religious belief and the cognitive mechanisms involved does nothing, so far, to impugn its truth.[18] No one thinks describing the mechanisms involved in perception impugns the truth of perceptual beliefs; why should one think things are different with respect to religion? According to Christian belief, God has created us in such a way that we can know and be in fellowship with him. He could have done this in many ways; for example, he could have brought it about that our cognitive faculties evolve by natural selection, and evolve in such a way that it is natural for us to form beliefs about the supernatural in general and God himself in particular. Finding a "natural" origin for religion in no way discredits it.[19]

---

16. Atran, *In Gods We Trust*, p. 4.
17. For example, according to Jesse Bering, director of the Institute of Cognition and Culture, Queens University, Belfast, who apparently believes that with his research, "we've got God by the throat and I'm not going to stop until one of us is dead" ("The God Fossil," *Broward Palm Beach New Times*, March 9, 2006). (Do you suppose God is trembling in the face of this threat?)
18. Many writers seem not to grasp this obvious fact. The same goes for suggestions as to what components and dynamics of the brain underlie religious experience, as in Michael Persinger, "The sensed presence within experimental settings: Implications for the male and female concept of self," *Journal of Psychology: Interdisciplinary and Applied* 137:1 (2003). Suppose centers for perception were identified in the brain, and suppose artificial stimulation of these centers could cause experiences as of seeing a tree; would this cast doubt upon our perception of trees?
19. See Kelly Clark and Justin Barrett, "Reformed Epistemology and the Cognitive Science of Religion." *Faith and Philosophy* 28 (2010), pp. 174–89.

A more promising line of criticism: it might be suggested that the cognitive mechanisms giving rise to religious belief, as opposed to those involved in, for example, perception, are prone to substantial error. The central such suggested mechanism is called an "agency detection device." Such a device, so the thought goes, would probably deliver many false positives; Stewart Guthrie dubs this device "the Hypersensitive Agency Detection Device" (HADD).[20] This device is hypersensitive, he says, because, while little is lost by a false positive, a false negative can be catastrophic. You glimpse a tiger apparently looking at you from a distance of fifty yards; failure to see it as an agent (looking for lunch, perhaps) can be disastrous. By comparison, attributing agency to trees or clouds or the moon is mistaken, but much more benign. ("Better safe than sorry" shows up in nearly all these accounts.)

But of course the fact that belief in supernatural agents arises from HADD (if indeed that is a fact) doesn't even tend to show that such belief is among the false positives; that same device is also responsible for many true beliefs, for example, the belief that there are other minds, other people.[21] Presumably no one would argue that belief in other minds is dubious or irrational or intellectually second rate on the grounds that it has been produced by an agent detection device that sometimes produces false positives. So merely finding or positing a source of religious belief, as with HADD, does nothing to discredit such belief, and neither does pointing out that the source in question delivers false positives.[22] So far we don't have conflict.

20. Guthrie, *Faces in the Clouds: A New Theory of Religion* (New York: Oxford University Press, 1993).
21. See Justin Barrett, "Is the Spell Really Broken?" *Theology and Science*, vol. 5, no. 1, March 2007, p. 69.
22. But wouldn't this at least show that religious beliefs lack *warrant*, that property enough of which is what separates knowledge from mere true belief? (See my *Warranted Christian Belief* (New York: Oxford University Press, 2000), chapter 5.) Not just as such; after all, even if belief in other minds originates in HADD, we do presumably know that there are other people. What counts here is not the global reliability of the faculty or cognitive mechanism in question, but its reliability in the relevant circumstances.

Consider the early Stark proposal—that religion is a spandrel of rational thought and is devoted to the pursuit of nonexistent goods by way of negotiation with nonexistent supernatural agents. This proposal is inconsistent with Christian thought or commitment just because it declares these goods and agents nonexistent. But wouldn't there be another theory, perhaps just as good and even empirically equivalent to Stark's, that was noncommittal on the existence or nonexistence of these goods? And anyway, would one really want to say that it was part of *science*—part of a scientific theory—to declare these goods nonexistent? Suppose I propose as a theory the conjunction of Newton's laws and atheism: have I succeeded in producing a scientific theory inconsistent with theism? Hardly. So delete the offending bit from Stark's theory and call the result "Stark-minus": would Stark-minus be inconsistent with Christian belief? Stark-minus is something like the claim that (a) religion involves the pursuit of certain kinds of ends or goods—salvation, eternal life, and the like—by way of negotiating with alleged supernatural beings, and (b) that it arises as a kind of byproduct or spandrel of the evolution of the capacity for rational thought. Is *that* theory incompatible with Christian thought? Not obviously.

Or consider Wilson and Ruse. According to their theory, there is really no such thing as objective moral obligation, but it is adaptive for people to think that there is. So think about (Wilson and Ruse)-minus, which is the theory that results from theirs when we delete the bit according to which in reality there is no such thing as objective moral obligation. The resulting theory says only that morality—that is, belief in an objective obligation to treat others the way we would like them to treat us, together with the resulting tendency to behave in accordance with this belief to at least some extent—the theory says only that this phenomenon is adaptive at the group level and has become ubiquitous among human beings by way of group selection. Is that incompatible with Christian belief? Again, not obviously; it adds little to the obvious claim that morality is a civil good, a claim going back to ancient Rome. (Of course it does add the thesis that morality has come to be by way of group selection; perhaps you don't think that's a small addition.) Similarly for Wilson-minus, the theory that results from David Sloan Wilson's theory by deleting the idea that the beliefs involved in religion are fictitious. Wilson-minus, fundamentally, is the theory that religion arises or at least becomes ubiquitous among human beings by way of group selection, because it is a useful form of social control that involves beliefs of a certain kind. (Thus it pays the same compliment to religion that (Wilson and Ruse)-minus pays to morality.) Is this theory incompatible with Christian belief? Again, not obviously. Or consider Atran: he says that religion is "counterfactual," by which I take it he means that religious beliefs are (always? typically?) false. Atran-minus would be the result of deleting the claim that religious belief is false from the rest of his theory: is Atran-minus incompatible with Christian belief? Once more, not obviously.

These theories, therefore, do conflict with religion, but in a merely superficial way. They conflict with religion in the way in which a theory that results from conjoining Newtonian physics with atheism does: that theory conflicts with religion, all right, but it certainly doesn't constitute a serious religion-science conflict.

Here we should briefly pause to ask the following question: what, exactly, *is* a religion/science conflict? As we saw in chapter one, a religion might be itself inconsistent: then of course it will be inconsistent with any scientific theory, but this would be an uninteresting religion/science conflict. Suppose there is a scientific theory that is inconsistent with theistic belief but only a very few scientists endorse it: would that be an example of science/religion conflict? Or does a genuine science/religion conflict require that the theory in question be widely accepted among scientists? But is even that sufficient? What about general relativity and contemporary quantum mechanics? As they stand, they are incompatible with each other; physicists have been trying to develop a theory of quantum gravity to replace them, but so far have been unsuccessful (although some people look to string theory and its sucessors as a promising source of reconciliation). The deliverances of current science, therefore, contain a contradiction. General relativity and quantum mechanics are inconsistent with each other; hence their conjunction is inconsistent with any religious belief; each is widely accepted among scientists; do we therefore have a religion/science conflict? If so, it would be, again, at best an uninteresting conflict.

So not just any case of explicit religion/science inconsistency is a genuine case of religion/science conflict. Furthermore, conflict can happen in several different ways. For example, a scientific theory might not be explicitly inconsistent with Christian belief, but inconsistent with Christian belief together with propositions that can't sensibly be rejected. A theory might be formally consistent with Christian belief, but still be massively improbable with respect to a set of beliefs or a noetic structure more or less like that of most contemporary Christians, or most contemporary Christians in the Western world (and for that matter, most Christians in the non-Western world). Such Christians will typically believe some propositions F by way of faith, and other propositions R because they are or seem to be deliverances of reason (including memory, perception, rational intuition and so on). A given theory might not be improbable with respect to F and also not improbable with respect to R, but massively improbable with respect to the conjunction of F with R, and hence with respect to a noetic structure that contains both F and R. Such a theory might be so unlikely with respect to such a noetic structure that it wouldn't be a real candidate for belief. An example would be a theory entailing that if human beings have come to be by way of natural selection culling genetic variability, then no rational human being knowingly sacrifices her reproductive prospects in favor of advancing someone else's welfare. This isn't incompatible with F, and perhaps also not incompatible with the deliverances of reason. However, a Christian will think the consequent massively improbable, and might (by virtue of reason) be inclined to accept the antecedent. This theory, then, would be incompatible with the noetic structures of such Christians, even if not logically inconsistent with Christian belief as such. There are still other forms of conflict, as I'll argue later in this chapter.[23]

23. Of course there are conflicts between science and particular religious beliefs that are not part of Christian belief as such: belief in a universal flood, a very young earth, etc.

To look more deeply into this question of conflict or compatibility between Christian belief and these theories from evolutionary psychology, suppose we examine one of them more carefully: David Sloan Wilson's theory of religion.[24] This theory is a so-called "functional interpretation" of religion. Both terms deserve comment. First, Wilson explicitly says many times that his theory is an *interpretation* of religion. This is a bit surprising: one wouldn't think of Newton's laws, for example, or special relativity as interpretations of something or other. What is involved in the theory's being an interpretation? *Understanding* of one sort or another, presumably; the thought is that once you see religion as having the function ascribed to it in the theory, then you understand it, or understand it more deeply. You understand why there is such a thing as religion, why religions arise and persist, and what they are *for*—what their function or purpose is. In the particular case of Wilson's theory, the idea is that religions play an important role in group selection. "Many features of religion, such as the nature of supernatural agents and their relationships with humans, can be explained as adaptations designed to enable human groups to function as adaptive units."[25] (A crucial difference between his theory and those of Atran and Boyer, therefore, is that according to the latter religious belief isn't in fact adaptive.) He aims to "see if the detailed properties of Calvin's Church can be interpreted as adaptation to its environment," and he summarizes his theory as follows:

> I claim that a knowledge of the details [of Calvin's Geneva] clearly supports a group-level functional interpretation of Calvinism. Calvinism is an interlocking system with a purpose:

---

24. Wilson, *Darwin's Cathedral*, pp. 48ff. See also Robert A. Hinde, *Why Gods Persist* (London: Routledge, 1999), pp. 553ff.

25. Wilson, *Darwin's Cathedral*, p. 51.

to unify and coordinate a population of people to achieve a common set of goals by collective action. The goals may be difficult to define precisely, but they certainly included what Durkheim referred to as secular utility—the basic goods and services that all people need and want, inside and outside of religion.[26]

The thought is that Calvinism is an interlocking system with a purpose: "to unify and coordinate a population of people to achieve a common set of goals by collective action." This sounds a bit as if he thinks of Calvinism as a project or activity that people undertake in order to achieve a common set of goals, these goals including at least that secular utility of which he speaks. If this were what he means, he would be wrong: Calvin and the other Calvinists weren't (and aren't) embracing Calvinism in order to achieve some kind of secular utility. In fact it is doubtful that Calvinism, or Roman Catholicism, or Christianity or for that matter Judaism or Islam are (wholly) intentional activities in that way at all. Are they human activities undertaken in order to achieve a goal? What is the purpose or aim of being a Calvinist? What is the purpose or aim of believing in God? Well, what is the purpose or aim of believing in other people, or believing that there has been a past? The right answer, one thinks, is that believing in God, like believing in the past or in other people, typically doesn't have any purpose or aim at all. It isn't that you believe in God or other people in order to achieve some end or other. You might as well ask me what my purpose or aim is in believing that I live in Michigan or that $7+5 = 12$. In one sense these are intentional activities; but they are not undertaken in order to achieve some end or other.

You may reply that there is more to Christianity in general and Calvinism in particular than holding beliefs. This is certainly true:

26. Wilson, *Darwin's Cathedral*, pp. 91, 118.

there is also love of God, and prayer, and worship, and ritual, cere-
mony and liturgy, for example. These are activities one intentionally
undertakes. But again, it's not clear that there is some *purpose* for the
sake of which one undertakes to love God: you love God because he
is attractive, such as to attract or compel love. Christians pray because
it seems the right thing to do, or because they are instructed to pray,
and how to pray, by Jesus Christ. The same holds for worship. When
worship is going properly it isn't something done in order to achieve
some end outside itself: it is much more spontaneous and immediate
than that, and you participate just because it seems right and appropriate. (Of course you *might* engage in worship to please your parents
or spouse or children: but then in a case like that it *isn't* going properly.) This is a complex subject, and now is not the time to go into it.
What is clear, however, is that there isn't any goal or purpose or end
involved, typically, in accepting the central tenets of Calvinism or
Christianity, and even if there is a purpose or goal or end involved in
worship and prayer, it most certainly is not the achievement of the
secular goods Wilson mentions.

But Wilson isn't really proposing that Calvinists themselves
engage in the practice of Calvinism in order to achieve those goals.
This practice has goals, all right, but they aren't the goals or purposes
of the people engaged in the practice. It is rather that the aims or goals
are provided, somehow, by evolution. And of course it isn't that these
aims or goals are those of evolution, or natural selection; as Wilson is
thinking of it, those processes don't have any aims or goals at all and
aren't aiming at the actualization of some state of affairs. Still, the idea
is that some of the structures and processes that result from natural
selection do have purposes, purposes they acquire from their roles in
maximizing fitness. The ultimate purpose of the heart, he no doubt
thinks, is to enhance or maximize fitness; its proximate purpose is to
pump blood (and pump it in a certain way), and the idea is that it ful-
fills the former purpose by fulfilling that latter. The proximate purpose

of the immune system is to overcome disease; this purpose is in the service of its ultimate purpose of maximizing fitness. Whether one can really speak of purpose and proper function for organs such as the heart or liver or brain absent a designer and outside the context of theism is of course a matter of dispute; I say you can't.[27] But this isn't the place to enter that discussion.

So let's suppose that a heart or a liver, and also an activity like a religion can have a purpose conferred upon it by natural selection, even if God is not orchestrating and guiding that process. According to Wilson, the purpose of a religion, at least in the case of Calvinism, is "to unify and coordinate a population of people." That isn't a purpose endorsed by those who practice the religion; still, he thinks, that is its purpose. Here it is instructive to compare Wilson's views on religion with those of that great master of suspicion, Sigmund Freud. On Freud's view, religion (and here he's thinking especially of theistic religions) is an illusion, in his technical sense. This sense is not such as to entail the falsehood of theistic belief, although in fact Freud thinks theism is false: there is no such person as God. Still, illusions have their uses and indeed their functions. The function or purpose of religious belief is really to enable believers to carry on in this cold and hostile or at any rate indifferent world in which we find ourselves. The idea is that theistic belief arises from a psychological mechanism Freud calls "wish-fulfillment"; the wish in this case is father, not to the deed, but to the belief.[28] Nature rises up against us, cold, pitiless, implacable, blind to our needs and desires. She delivers hurt, fear, pain, anxiety, suffering; and in the end she demands our death. Paralyzed and appalled, we invent (unconsciously, of course) a father in heaven who exceeds our earthly fathers as much in goodness and

27. See chapter 11 of my *Warrant and Proper Function* (New York: Oxford University Press, 1993).
28. And in such a way that it (or its deliverances) rather resembles Calvin's *sensus divinitatis*; see *Moses and Monotheism*, pp. 167ff.

benevolence as in power and knowledge. The alternative would be to sink into depression, stupor, paralysis, and finally death.

This illusion enables us to carry on and survive: therefore it contributes to our fitness. Is this Freudian claim incompatible with Christian belief? Could I accept Christian belief and also accept Freud's explanation or account of it? Well, maybe. For it is at least possible that God gets us to be aware of him by way of a mechanism like wish-fulfillment. According to Augustine, "Our hearts are restless till they rest in you, O God." But then it might be that one way God induces awareness of himself in us is through a process of wish-fulfillment: we want so much to be in God's presence, we want so very much to feel his love, to know that we are loved by the first being of the universe, that we simply come to believe this. I don't say that's in fact the way things go; I say only that it is possible and not incompatible with Christian belief.

There is more to Freud's account, however, than just the idea that we come to believe in God by way of wish-fulfillment; if that were all he thinks, there would be no reason to call theistic belief an *illusion*. What more does Freud say here? That this process of wish-fulfillment isn't *reality oriented*, as we might say; it is this that makes theistic belief an illusion. We human beings display a large number of belief-producing processes or faculties or mechanisms. There is perception, memory, a priori intuition, credulity, induction, and much else. We ordinarily think these faculties or processes are aimed at the production of true belief: that is what they are *for*, and that is their purpose or function. There are some cognitive processes, however, that are not aimed at the production of true belief, but at some other desideratum. Someone may remember a painful experience as less painful than it actually was. According to John 16:21, "a woman giving birth to a child has pain because her time has come; but when her baby is born she forgets the anguish because of her joy that a child is born into the world." You may continue to believe in your friend's honesty long after evidence and cool, objective judgment would have dictated a reluctant change of mind. I may believe that I will recover from a dread disease much more strongly than is warranted by the statistics of which I am aware. A mountain climber, faced with a life or death situation, might believe more strongly than his evidence warrants that he can leap the crevasse before him.

In all of these cases, there is no cognitive dysfunction or failure to function properly; but the processes in question don't seem to have as their functions the production of true beliefs. Rather, they produce beliefs that in the context are useful in one way or another. And exactly this is the way things stand with Freud's explanation: an essential part of his account of theistic belief is that it is not produced by truth-aimed cognitive processes, but by a process with a different sort of function. At this point the Christian or any serious theist will disagree with him. The serious theist will think that God has created us in such a way that we come to know him; and the function of the cognitive processes, whatever they are, that ordinarily produce belief in God in us is to provide us with true belief. So even if she agrees with Freud that theistic belief arises from wish-fulfillment, she will think that this particular instance of wish-fulfillment is truth-aimed; it is God's way of getting us to see that he is in fact present and in fact cares for us. At this point she will have to disagree with Freud.

Something similar goes for David Sloan Wilson. He holds that the purpose or function of Calvinism and Christianity generally is to enhance fitness; a group with a religion of that sort will do well in competition with groups without any such religion (or anything similar). And specifically religious *belief* plays an important role here. The role of such belief is not to reflect reality, he says, but to play a part in the production of what religion produces. As he says: "our challenge is to interpret the concept of God and his relationship with people as an elaborate belief system designed to motivate the behaviors listed."

In a very interesting passage Wilson proposes that religious belief isn't reality oriented, but, unlike Freud (and most of those who write on the scientific study of religion), goes on to defend it. The passage is worth quoting in full:

> In the first place, much religious belief is not detached from reality.... Rather, it is intimately connected to reality by motivating behaviors that are adaptive in the real world—an awesome achievement when we appreciate the complexity that is required to become connected in this practical sense. It is true that many religious beliefs are false as literal description of the real world, but this merely forces us to recognize two forms of realism: a factual realism based on literal correspondence and a practical realism based on behavioral adaptiveness.
>
> In the second place, much religious belief does not represent a form of mental weakness but rather the healthy functioning of the biologically and culturally well-adapted mind.... Adaptation is the gold standard against which rationality must be judged, along with all other forms of thought. Evolutionary biologists should be especially quick to grasp this point because they appreciate that the well-adapted mind is ultimately an organ of survival and reproduction.... factual realists detached from practical reality were not among our ancestors.[29]

This account of religion, then, is like Freud's in that, like Freud, Wilson sees the cognitive processes that produce religious belief as not aimed at the production of true belief, but at belief that is adaptive by way of motivating those adaptive behaviors. Religious belief in general and Christian and Calvinistic belief in particular originate in

---

29. Wilson, *Darwin's Cathedral*, p. 228.

belief-producing processes that are aimed, not at the production of true belief, but at the production of belief that will motivate that behavior. And here someone who accepts Christian belief will be forced to demur, just as with Freud. For if Christian belief is in fact true, as, naturally enough, the Christian will think, it will be produced in us by cognitive processes that God has designed with the end in view of enabling us to see the truth of "the great things of the Gospel" (as Jonathan Edwards calls them). She will no doubt think that these processes typically involve what Calvin calls "the internal witness (or testimony) of the Holy Spirit" and what Aquinas calls "the internal instigation of the Holy Spirit." And these processes, so the Christian thinks, will then be truth-aimed: they are aimed at enabling us to form these true beliefs about what God has done and about the way of salvation. So there is indeed a conflict between Wilson's theory of religion and Christian belief.[30]

III HISTORICAL BIBLICAL CRITICISM

A. Traditional Biblical Commentary

We turn now to a second area of conflict between Christian belief and science: historical Biblical criticism (HBC, as I'll call it). There are striking parallels, in this regard, between HBC and evolutionary psychology.[31] To see some of these parallels, we must begin with traditional Biblical commentary. Now classical Christians take the Bible

---

30. Tom Crisp points out (private communication) that (again, as with Freud) there is no incompatibility between religious belief and the thought that it arises in the way Wilson says it does. Clearly God, if he chose, could use the process of group selection to bring it that people are aware of him and in a position to worship him.

31. Here I can be brief; for a much fuller account of HBC, see chapter 12 of my *Warranted Christian Belief.*

to be authoritative in one way or another. That is because they think of the Bible as a special word from the Lord; as they see it, God is the principal and ultimate author of the Bible. Of course the Bible is also a library, each of its books has a human author. But God has used these authors in such a way that what they write has the divine stamp of approval; hence the Bible—the whole Bible—is divinely inspired in such a way that its principal author is God. The Bible is a library, but it is also like a single book in that it has a single principal author. This is the source and warrant for the proposal that we can "interpret scripture with scripture"; if we find a certain obscurity in one of the epistles of Paul, for example, we can look for light, not just elsewhere in that epistle or to other writings of Paul, but also to the epistles of John and the Gospels. And the chief function of the Bible is to disclose to mankind God's gospel—the good news of salvation through the life and death and resurrection of Jesus Christ, himself both a human being but also the divine son of God, the second person of the trinity.

Now what the Lord teaches is of course trustworthy; therefore this entire book, so Christians think, is authoritative. Many questions arise: just how does this work? Just how does this inspiration happen? Just how can it be said that the Bible is divine discourse?[32] This is not the place to enter those discussions. But even if the entire Bible is a word from the Lord, many parts of it are at best difficult to understand. It isn't always easy to tell what the Lord is teaching in a given passage. What he is teaching is certainly true and to be accepted; but it may be hard indeed to see what he *is* teaching. In Colossians 1:24, for example, we read: "Now I rejoice in what was suffered for you, and I fill up in my flesh what is still lacking in regard to Christ's afflictions, for the sake of his body which is the church." But what could be

---

32. See Nicholas Wolterstorff, *Divine Discourse: Philosophical Reflections on the Claim that God Speaks* (Cambridge: Cambridge University Press, 1995).

lacking in Christ's afflictions, Christ's sacrifice? Isn't his sacrifice completely sufficient? How could it be otherwise? So how can we understand the passage in question, which seems to suggest that there was something lacking in Christ's sacrifice?

Traditional Biblical commentary tries to answer questions like this. And the roll call of those who have engaged in this project is most impressive: the church fathers, Augustine, Aquinas, Calvin with his twenty-some volumes of commentary, Luther, and of course many more. This enterprise is characterized by the assumption I mentioned just above: that God is the principal author of all of the books of the Bible and that it is therefore authoritative. It's important to see, furthermore, that those who engage in this enterprise also accept and take for granted, in the project, the main lines of Christian belief. Here there may be a bit of diversity; a Roman Catholic commentator will not take for granted precisely what a Protestant commentator does, but the agreement will be much more extensive than the disagreement. The aim is to discover what God is teaching in a given passage, and to do so in the light of these assumptions; the aim is not to determine whether what is taught is true, or plausible, or well supported by arguments. In Kant scholarship, for example, one tries to figure out what Kant means in a given passage—the Antinomies, or the transcendental deduction of the categories, or maybe more broadly how to understand the whole picture presented by one of the critiques. Having accomplished this task (at least to one's own satisfaction), one quite properly goes on to ask whether Kant's views are true or plausible, or whether he has made a good case for them. This last step is not appropriate in traditional Biblical commentary. Once you have established, as you think, what God is teaching in a given passage, what he is proposing for our belief, that settles the matter. You do not go on to ask whether it is true, or plausible, or whether a good case for it has been made. God is not required to make a case.

B. Historical Biblical Criticism

HBC (also called "higher criticism," "historical criticism," and "historical critical Biblical scholarship") is a very different kettle of fish. This is an Enlightenment project, going back at least to Spinoza, who declared that "the rule for [Biblical] interpretation should be nothing but the natural light of reason which is common to all—not any supernatural light nor any external authority."[33] In pursuing this project, one doesn't assume that the Bible is specially inspired by God, or that it contains anything like specifically divine discourse. Nor does one assume the main lines of Christian belief—that Jesus Christ is the divine son of God, for example, or that he arose from the dead, or that his suffering and death is in some way an atonement for human sin. Instead, you prescind from all of these theological beliefs; you bracket them; you set them aside for the purposes of the inquiry in question. Thus Jon Levenson:

> Historical critics thus rightly insist that the tribunal before which interpretations are argued cannot be confessional or 'dogmatic'; the arguments offered must be historically valid, able, that is, to compel the assent of *historians* whatever their religion or lack thereof, whatever their backgrounds, spiritual experiences, or personal beliefs, and without privileging any claim of revelation.[34]

Raymond Brown adds that HBC is "scientific biblical criticism"; it yields "factual results"; he intends his own contributions to be

33. *Theologico-Political Tractate*, 14.
34. Levenson, "The Hebrew Bible, the Old Testament, and Historical Criticism" in *The Hebrew Bible, the Old Testament, and Historical Criticism: Jews and Christians in Biblical Studies*, ed. Jon Levenson (Louisville: Westminster/John Knox Press, 1993), p. 109. An earlier version of this essay was published under the same title in *Hebrew Bible or Old Testament? Studying the Bible in Judaism and Christianity*, ed. John Collins and Roger Brooks (Notre Dame: University of Notre Dame Press, 1990).

"scientifically respectable," and practitioners of HBC investigate the scriptures with "scientific exactitude."[35]

The point here is precisely this effort to be *scientific*. Traditional Biblical commentary is not scientific, so the claim goes, exactly because it proceeds on the basis of the assumptions I mentioned above; HBC, therefore, eschews these assumptions in its effort to be scientific. We could also put it like this: traditional Biblical commentary depends on *faith*. The assumptions mentioned above, that is, the main lines of Christian belief including the thought that the Bible is divine discourse, are deliverances of faith; they are not deliverances of reason. Take reason to include the cognitive faculties that are employed in everyday life and ordinary history and science: perception, testimony, reason taken in the sense of a priori intuition together with deductive and probabilistic reasoning, Thomas Reid's sympathy, by which we discern the thoughts and feelings of another, and so on; in its inquiries, HBC restricts itself to propositions that are delivered by these sources of belief, explicitly excluding any that are known or believed by faith and not solely by reason.[36]

For a long time there has been a good deal of tension between HBC and traditional Christians. In *Das Leben Jesu*, an early manifesto of HBC, David Strauss declares, "Nay, if we would be candid

35. Brown, *The Virginal Conception and Bodily Resurrection of Jesus* (New York: Paulist Press, 1973), pp. 9, 11, 18–19.
36. But what if the main lines of the Christian gospel can in fact be arrived at by reason alone, by virtue of arguments—probabilistic argument—that employ only premises that are deliverances of reason? This is the position of Richard Swinburne, who is the most distinguished contemporary proponent of this view. Among his many works, see, for example, *The Existence of God* (Oxford: Clarendon Press, 2nd edition 2004), *Was Jesus God?* (Oxford: Oxford University Press, 2008), and *Revelation* (Oxford: Clarendon Press, 2007). If you think this is how things stand, then you could proceed just as traditional Biblical commentators do, while also claiming that what you do depends only on premises that are among the deliverances of reason, so that your enterprise, though indistinguishable in terms of results from traditional Biblical commentary, is nonetheless science. It's fair to say, I think, that HBC presupposes that this idea—that the main lines of Christian belief can be established by reason alone—is mistaken (and indeed this idea is not widely accepted).

with ourselves, that which was once sacred history for the Christian believer is, for the enlightened portion of our contemporaries, only fable."[37] To leap to the present, according to Luke Timothy Johnson:

> The Historical Jesus researchers insist that the "real Jesus" must be found in the facts of his life before his death. The resurrection is, when considered at all, seen in terms of visionary experience, or as a continuation of an "empowerment" that began before Jesus' death. Whether made explicit or not, the operative premise is that there is no "real Jesus" after his death.[38]

Sometimes those who engage in HBC wind up very far indeed from classical Christianity. Thus according to G. A. Wells, our name "Jesus," as it turns up in the Bible, doesn't trace back to anyone at all; it is like the name "Santa Claus."[39] So there wasn't any such person as Jesus. John Allegro agrees that there was no such person as Jesus of Nazareth.[40] Still, the name "Christ" is not empty. Christianity, he says, began as a hoax designed to fool the Romans and preserve the cult of a certain hallucinogenic mushroom (*Aminita muscaria*), and, he thinks, the name "Christ" is really a name of that mushroom. As engaging an idea as any is to be found in Thomas Sheehan's *The First Coming*: Jesus, while neither merely legendary, nor actually a mushroom, was in fact an atheist, the first Christian atheist![41] And even if

37. Straus, *Das Leben Jesu* (1835), tr. Marian Evans as *The Life of Jesus Critically Examined* (New York: Calvin Blanchardd, 1860).
38. Johnson, *The Real Jesus: The Misguided Quest for the Historical Jesus and the Truth of the Traditional Gospels* (San Francisco: HarperCollins 1996), p. 144.
39. Wells, "The Historicity of Jesus," in *Jesus in History and Myth*, ed. R. Joseph Hoffman and Gerald A. Larue (Buffalo: Prometheus Books, 1986), pp. 27ff.
40. Allegro, *The Sacred Mushroom and the Cross* (Garden City: Doubleday, 1970).
41. Sheehan, *The First Coming* (New York: Harper and Row), p. 197; see my review "Sheehan's Shenanigans" in *The Analytic Theist: an Alvin Plantinga Reader*, ed. James Sennett (Grand Rapids: Eerdmans, 1998).

we set aside such ludicrous excess, Van Harvey seems to be right: "So far as the biblical historian is concerned,...there is scarcely a popularly held traditional belief about Jesus that is not regarded with considerable skepticism."[42]

Accordingly, some of those who engage in HBC come to conclusions wholly at variance with traditional or classical Christian belief. Many of these scripture scholars practice what we could call Troeltschian HBC, so called because of allegiance to principles enunciated by Ernst Troeltsch.[43] These principles can be understood in more than one way, but taken the way his scripture scholarship followers understand him, they imply that proper scripture scholarship proceeds on the assumption that God never does anything specially; in particular there are no miracles, and God neither raised Jesus from the dead nor specially inspired the Biblical authors.[44] In connection with the claim that special divine action is incompatible with modern science, I quoted Rudolf Bultmann:

> The historical method includes the presupposition that history is a unity in the sense of a closed continuum of effects in which individual events are connected by the succession of cause and effect. This continuum, furthermore, cannot be rent by the interference of supernatural, transcendent powers.[45]

42. Van Harvey, "New Testament Scholarship and Christian Belief," in *Jesus in History and Myth* ed. R. Joseph Hoffman and Gerald A. Larue (Buffalo: Prometheus Books, 1986), p. 193.

43. See especially his "Über historische und dogmatische Methode in der Theologie" in *Gesammelte Schriften* (Tubingen: Mohr, 1913), vol. 2, pp. 729–53, and his article "Historiography" in James Hastings, *Encyclopedia of Religion and Ethics*.

44. For an account and endorsement of Troeltsch's principles, see John Collins, "Is Critical Biblical Theology Possible?" in *The Hebrew Bible and its Interpreters*, ed. William Henry Propp, Baruch Halpern, and David Freedman (Winona Lake, Ind.: Eisenbrauns, 1990), p. 2. For much more detail on Troeltschian HBC, see my *Warranted Christian Belief*, pp. 390–95.

45. Bultmann, *Existence and Faith*, ed. Schubert Ogden (New York: Meridian Books, 1960), pp. 291–92. For more recent expressions of the same opinion, see John Macquarrie,

This applies equally to scripture scholarship: one who employs the historical method Bultmann is endorsing will not think of the Bible as in any way specially inspired by God.

But there are at least two kinds of HBC, at least two ideas as to what "scientific" biblical scholarship requires. A second kind of HBC, Duhemian HBC, takes as guiding principle, not that God never does anything special, but that the proper procedure, in scripture scholarship, is to use as evidence only what would be acceptable to everyone (or nearly everyone) who is party to the project.[46] For example, according to E. P. Sanders, the idea is to rely only on "evidence on which everyone can agree."[47] A prime example of Duhemian scripture scholarship is John Meier's fantasy of "an unpapal conclave" of Jewish, Catholic, Protestant and agnostic scholars, locked in the basement of the Harvard Divinity School library until they come to consensus on what historical methods can show about the life and mission of Jesus.[48] The Duhemian scripture scholar won't take for granted any theological, religious, or metaphysical assumptions that aren't accepted by everyone in the relevant community.[49] She won't

Principles of Christian Theology, 2nd ed. (New York: Charles Scribner's Sons, 1977), p. 248; Langdon Gilkey, "Cosmology, Ontology, and the Travail of Biblical Language" in *God's Activity in the World: the Contemporary Problem*, ed. Owen C. Thomas (Chico, Calif: Scholars Press, 1983), p. 31; and John Collins, "Is Critical Biblical Theology Possible?"

46. Named for Pierre Duhem, who argued (in response to Abel Rey) that metaphysics shouldn't enter the texture of physics; if it did, the sorts of disagreements that characterize metaphysics would also break out in physics. See the appendix to Duhem's *The Aim and Structure of Physical Theory*, tr. Philip P. Wiener, foreword by Prince Louis de Broglie (Princeton: Princeton University Press, [1906] 1954). The appendix is entitled "Physics of a Believer" and is a reprint of Duhem's reply to Rey; it was originally published in the *Annales de Philosophie Chrétienne* Vol I (October and November) 1905, pp. 44ff. and 133ff.

47. Sanders, *Jesus and Judaism* (Philadelphia: Fortress Press, 1985), p. 5.

48. Meier, *A Marginal Jew: Rethinking the Historical Jesus vol. 1* (New York: Doubleday, 1991), p. 1.

49. Of course it may be difficult to specify the relevant community. Suppose I am a scripture scholar at a denominational seminary: what is my relevant community? Scripture scholars of any sort, all over the world? Scripture scholars in my own denomination? In western academia? The people, academics or not, in my denomination? Christians generally? The first thing to see here is that our scripture scholar clearly belongs to many different communities, and may accordingly be involved in several different scholarly projects.

assume either that God is the principal author of the Bible or that the main lines of the Christian story are in fact true; these are not accepted by all who are party to the discussion. She won't take it for granted that Jesus rose from the dead, or that any other miracle has occurred, or even that miracles are possible; there are those party to the discussion that reject these claims. On the other hand, of course, Duhemian scripture scholarship can't take it for granted that Christ did *not* rise from the dead or that *no* miracles have occurred, or that miracles are *im*possible.

Those who practice Duhemian HBC don't ordinarily propose views in conflict with classical Christian belief. What they ordinarily propose as the most that can be said, however, is, from the standpoint of Christian belief, monumentally minimal. Thus A. E. Harvey proposes the following as beyond reasonable doubt from everyone's point of view:

> that Jesus was known in both Galilee and Jerusalem, that he was a teacher, that he carried out cures of various illnesses, particularly demon-possession and that these were widely regarded as miraculous; that he was involved in controversy with fellow Jews over questions of the law of Moses: and that he was crucified in the governorship of Pontius Pilate.[50]

Another example: John Meier's *A Marginal Jew: Rethinking the Historical Jesus* is absolutely monumental; it is magnificently thorough and thoroughly judicious, discussing and sifting an amazing range of evidence about the life of Jesus. But about all that emerges from Meier's painstaking work is that Jesus was a prophet, proclaiming an eschatological message from God; he performed powerful deeds, signs and wonders that announce God's kingdom, and also ratify his message. Here, as with Harvey, there are no miracles; there

---

50. Harvey, *Jesus and the Constraints of History* (Philadelphia: Westminster Press, 1982), p. 6.

is no resurrection, and certainly nothing to suggest that Jesus was the incarnate second person of the Trinity or even that he was son of God in any unique sense.

Obviously, then, there is conflict between Christian belief and some of the theories or "results" from HBC as well as from evolutionary psychology. And the next question is this: suppose you are a classical Christian, accepting, for example, the whole of the Apostle's Creed. Suppose you are also, as I believe Christians should be, wholly enthusiastic about science; you believe that it is a magnificent display of the image of God in which humanity has been created. Still further, suppose you see both evolutionary psychology and HBC as proper science. How then should you think about the negative results coming from these scientific enterprises? In particular, do they provide or constitute *defeaters* for the beliefs with which they are in conflict? That is, do they give you a good reason to reject those beliefs, or at any rate hold them less firmly? In the next chapter we'll address that question.

Chapter 6

Defeaters?

In the last chapter we saw that some scientific theories or claims—theories or claims taken from evolutionary psychology and historical Biblical criticism—do indeed conflict with Christian (and Muslim and Jewish) belief. Evolutionary psychologists have come up with a number of theories that are wholly incompatible with Christian beliefs: theories purporting to explain altruism in terms of unusual docility and limited rationality, morality as an illusion fobbed off on us by our genes, and religion itself as involving belief that is false, even if, according to some of these theories, adaptive. According to certain theories from historical Biblical criticism, furthermore, the Bible is just another ancient book; Jesus didn't rise from the dead; miracles don't and have not occurred. Of course questions can be raised about whether these disciplines are really science, or good science; but let's set those questions aside for the moment, assuming, perhaps contrary to fact, that they are.[1] There is also the following question: suppose there is just one theory—from evolutionary psychology, for example—that is inconsistent with Christian belief, and suppose just a few scientists accept or believe or propose it: does that by itself constitute a science/religion conflict? How widely accepted must such a theory be, in order to constitute a science/religion conflict? Again, we can set this question aside, in particular since evolutionary psychology contains many widely accepted theories and claims that (at least as they

---

1. For an examination of this question with respect to some of the early claims of sociobiology or evolutionary psychology, see Philip Kitcher's *Vaulting Ambition* (Cambridge: The MIT Press, 1987).

stand) are in conflict with Christian belief. And let's call scientific theories incompatible with Christian belief Simonian science, in honor of Herbert Simon and his theory of altruism (see chapter 5).

Our next question: suppose you are a classical Christian; you accept the main lines of the Christian story—incarnation, resurrection, atonement, the work of the Holy Spirit, and so on. Suppose (as is appropriate for Christians) you are also enthusiastic about science. You are profoundly impressed by the sheer intellectual power and marvelous intellectual energy and insight that has gone into modern physics, starting, say, with Newton; you are also impressed by the deep and revealing insights gained by microbiology over the last fifty years or so. You therefore take modern science to be a magnificent display of the image of God in us human beings. Then what should you think about scientific theories incompatible with Christian belief? Should the existence of these theories induce intellectual disquiet, cognitive dissonance? To put the matter less metaphorically, does the existence of such theories give you a *defeater* for those beliefs with which they are incompatible? For example, in the last chapter we saw that according to David Sloan Wilson's theory, religious belief is produced in those who display it by cognitive processes not aimed at the production of true beliefs; assuming this is good science, should it give me a defeater for my belief that the processes that produce Christian belief are indeed aimed at the production of true belief? Similarly, some scripture scholars who aspire to be scientific produce theories according to which either Jesus did not arise from the dead, or at any rate it is vastly improbable that he did: does this give me a defeater for my belief that he did indeed so arise?

I DEFEATERS AND THEIR NATURE

The answer, in a word, is no. To see why, we must descend (or maybe it's ascend) into a bit of epistemology; in particular we must say something about defeaters and defeat. Here's a classic example of a defeater for a belief. I look into a pasture and see what looks like a sheep: I form the belief that I see a sheep. Then you come along; I know that you are the owner of the pasture and an honest man. You tell me that while there are no sheep in the pasture, you have a sheepdog that looks like a sheep from this distance. Now I have a defeater for my belief that I see a sheep in the pasture; if I am rational, I will no longer believe that I see a sheep there. Another example: I've always believed that there are no cacti in Michigan's Upper Peninsula. On a hike through the Porcupine Mountains I come across a fine specimen of prickly pear. This gives me a defeater for my belief that there are no cacti in the Upper Peninsula. In these two cases, I learn that the defeated belief is false; defeaters of this kind are called *rebutting* defeaters.

In other cases I don't learn that the belief is false, but instead lose my reason for holding the belief: *undercutting* defeaters, as they are called. For example, I see someone emerge from the house across the street and form the belief that Paul is emerging from his house; you then tell me that Paul's twin brother Peter arrived last night, is staying with Paul, and is indistinguishable from Paul by everyone except their wives. Then I should no longer believe that it is Paul who emerged from the house. Still, I won't believe that it *isn't* Paul either; instead I will withhold the belief that it's Paul: I'll be agnostic as to whether or not it is he. Another example: my guidebook says there are no cacti in the Upper Peninsula of Michigan; but then I learn that this guidebook is notoriously unreliable. I lose my reason for holding the belief, and will no longer hold it. However I also won't form the belief that there *are* cacti there; I'll be agnostic on that question.

One more point about defeaters: whether a belief B is a defeater for another belief B* depends on what else I believe. I believe there is a sheep in the field; you tell me there aren't any sheep there, although there is a sheepdog that looks like a sheep from this distance. If

I already believe that you are the owner of the field, an honest man, and would know if there are sheep there, I will have a defeater for my belief that I see a sheep. On the other hand, if I already believe that you are a contrarian and love to contradict people just for the fun of it, and that anyway you aren't in any position to know whether there is a sheep in that field, I won't acquire a defeater for the belief. (The same goes if I happen, oddly enough, to believe that I and I alone know that dogs are really sheep in disguise.) Another example: I believe that the surface of the moon contains no aircraft, but then I read in the *National Enquirer* that a complete World War II B17 bomber was found there. If I believe the *National Enquirer* is wholly reliable, I will now have a defeater for my original belief; if I believe that this magazine is a typical tabloid, so that its reporting an item as news doesn't make it likely that the item is true, then I won't have such a defeater.

Rationality defeaters must be distinguished from *warrant* defeaters (where warrant is the quality that distinguishes knowledge from mere true belief), circumstances that result in my belief's failing to have warrant in a state of affairs where it would otherwise have it. Another classic example, this one to illustrate warrant defeat: I am driving through southern Wisconsin, see what looks like and in fact is a barn, and form the belief "now that's a fine barn!" In an effort to mask their poverty, however, the natives have erected a large number of barn facades (four times the number of real barns), fake barns that look just like the real thing from the highway. As it happens, I am looking at a real barn. Nevertheless my belief that it *is* a barn, it seems, lacks warrant; it is only by virtue of the sheerest good luck that I form this belief with respect to a real barn. There is no failure of proper function here; nothing in the situation suggests that I am not carrying on in a perfectly rational fashion in forming that belief. But clearly enough the belief, though true, has little warrant for me; at any rate it doesn't have enough to constitute knowledge.

All rationality defeaters are warrant defeaters; the converse, of course, doesn't hold. A rationality defeater, furthermore, will be a belief (or an experience); a warrant defeater need not be, but will ordinarily be just some feature of the environment, as in the barn case above. One need not be aware of warrant defeaters, and in the typical case of warrant defeaters that are not also rationality defeaters, one is not aware of them; a rationality defeater, however, is ordinarily a belief of which one is in fact aware. Finally, if you come to know about a situation that constitutes a warrant defeater for a belief you hold, then (typically) you also have a rationality defeater for that belief.[2]

II EVIDENCE BASE

The second notion we need is that of an *evidence base*. My evidence base is the set of beliefs I use, or to which I appeal, in conducting an inquiry. Suppose I am a detective investigating a murder. Someone floats the hypothesis that the butler did it. I happen to know, however, that the butler was in Cleveland, three hundred miles away at the time of the murder; this belief is part of my evidence base. I will then reject the hypothesis that the butler did it. Alternatively, I may know that the butler is seventy years old and was a mile from the scene of the crime six minutes before the time of the crime, with no automobile, bicycle, horse, or other means of transportation in addition to his own two feet. I also know that only a very small proportion of seventy-year-old men can run a mile in six minutes. Then I won't simply rule out the hypothesis that the butler did it, but I will assign it (initially, at any rate) a low probability. My car won't start; among the hypotheses that might present themselves is the thought that it is inhabited by an evil spirit who is out to cause me inconvenience and frustration. But if I believe or think it very likely that evil spirits never inhabit automobiles, then I will assign that hypothesis a very low probability and will not pursue it further as a live option. A Brazilian tribesman, on the other hand, might think it

---

2. For a masterful account of defeaters and their ways, see chapter six of Michael Bergmann's *Justification Without Awareness* (New York: Oxford University Press, 2006).

much more likely that evil spirits should do such things, and might therefore assign this hypothesis much greater probability.

One of the main functions of one's evidence base, therefore, is that of evaluating possible hypotheses, evaluating them as plausible and probable or implausible and improbable. Some hypotheses, like the one that an evil spirit is inhabiting my automobile, will (given my background knowledge or evidence base) be very unlikely, perhaps so unlikely as not to be worth thinking about at all. Another hypothesis that might suggest itself is that my car has been hit by an errant but powerful cosmic ray, which somehow disabled it. Again, not at all likely. Other hypotheses will be assigned a much higher initial probability—that the car is out of gas, for example, or that the spark plugs are dirty, or that the fuel pump has failed. It is important to see in this connection that the evidence base of a Christian theist will include theism, belief in God and also the main lines of the Christian faith; therefore it will assign a high probability to hypotheses probable with respect to the Christian faith.[3]

III METHODOLOGICAL NATURALISM

Our aim, as you recall, is to address the following question. Suppose you are a serious Christian and you come to recognize that Simonian science endorses conclusions incompatible with certain Christian beliefs; and suppose you also hold science in high regard. Do you, as a result, acquire a defeater for those beliefs? To address this question properly, we need one more notion: *methodological naturalism*.

As we noted in the last chapter, many evolutionary psychologists and many scripture scholars come up with hypotheses and theories

---

3. Of course that there are several versions of the Christian faith, and I don't mean to suggest that every Christian's evidence base will include the same religious beliefs.

incompatible with Christian belief and with theism more generally. Now why do they do so? Why do evolutionary psychologists come up with theories according to which morality is an illusion foisted on us by our genes, or the goods Christians seek are nonexistent, or the beliefs they hold are fictitious or...? Why do they come up with theories according to which religious belief is not produced by truth-aimed cognitive processes? Have they discovered, somehow, that Christian belief is in fact false? Why do some practitioners of historical Biblical criticism propose theories according to which Jesus did no miracles and did not rise from the dead? Well, one answer is that at least some of those who propose these theories are themselves naturalists; they therefore think religious belief in general and Christian belief in particular is false, and theorize accordingly. But a wholly different kind of reason may also be in play. Consider the fact that many who practice historical Biblical criticism themselves personally accept the whole range of Christian belief, but separate their personal beliefs (as they might put it) from their scripture scholarship; in working at scripture scholarship, they prescind from their theological beliefs; they bracket them, set them aside. Why would they do that? Because they believe an effort to be scientific requires this separation or dissociation. Their thought is that scientific investigation requires thus setting aside theological belief. They accept the *methodological naturalism* (MN) that is widely thought to characterize science.

What is MN? First, MN is not to be confused with philosophical or ontological naturalism, according to which there is no such person as God or anything at all like God; there is no supernatural realm at all. The methodological naturalist doesn't necessarily subscribe to ontological naturalism. MN is a proposed condition or constraint on proper science, or the proper practice of science, not a statement about the nature of the universe. (Of course if philosophical naturalism were known to be true, then MN would presumably be the sensible way to proceed in science.) Thus Eugenie Scott, executive director of the National Center for Science Education: "Science neither denies or opposes the supernatural, but ignores the supernatural for methodological reasons."[4] And the thought is that any activity, in order to qualify as science, must be characterized by MN. Ernan McMullin put it like this:

> But, of course, methodological naturalism does not restrict our study of nature; it just lays down which sort of study qualifies as *scientific*. If someone wants to pursue another approach to nature—and there are many others—the methodological naturalist has no reason to object. Scientists *have* to proceed in this way; the methodology of natural science gives no purchase on the claim that a particular event or type of event is to be explained by invoking God's creative action directly.[5]

More generally, the idea is that in science we should proceed as if the supernatural is not given: in science, we can't properly appeal to God's creative activity, but we also can't appeal to angels or demons. For example, if there were a sudden outbreak of irrational behavior in Washington, D.C., we couldn't as scientists properly attribute it to an influx of demon possession there. MN also plays a crucial role in the controversy over intelligent design and the questions whether it should be taught or discussed in schools. In the famous Dover trial of 2005, Judge John Jones explains why intelligent design, as he sees it, doesn't count as science:

> We find that ID fails on three different levels, any one of which is sufficient to preclude a determination that ID is science. They

4. Scott, "Darwin Prosecuted: Review of Johnson's *Darwin on Trial*" *Creation Evolution Journal* vol. 13, no. 12 (1993).
5. McMullin, "Plantinga's Defense of Special Creation," *Christian Scholar's Review xxxi:* 1 (September 1991), p. 56.

are: (1) ID violates the centuries-old ground rules of science by invoking and permitting supernatural causation; (2) the argument of irreducible complexity, central to ID, employs the same flawed and illogical contrived dualism that doomed creation science in the 1980's; and (3) ID's negative attacks on evolution have been refuted by the scientific community.[6]

You may think (2) and (3) are pretty flimsy grounds on the basis of which to declare something not science. If you did, you'd be right: obviously many scientific arguments have employed flawed arguments, and many scientific claims and theories have been refuted by the scientific community. A flawed argument might be bad science, and a refuted theory or claim would presumably be rejected by the scientific community; it certainly doesn't follow that they aren't science at all. It is criterion (1) of Jones's decision that is presently relevant, however. He says "ID violates the centuries-old ground rules of science by invoking and permitting supernatural causation." Here he is clearly embracing MN as a necessary condition of science; that centuries-old ground rule ID violates is the idea that science, proper science as opposed to pseudoscience of various sorts, can't invoke the supernatural. A discourse that invokes the supernatural is thereby excluded from science. (Of course a scientific discourse can refer to *beliefs about* the supernatural, as with David Sloan Wilson's theory of Calvinism discussed in chapter 5.)

Suppose we try to state MN a bit more exactly. First, following Bas van Fraassen, we note that for any scientific theory, there is its *data set* or *data model*; roughly speaking we can think of this as the data or phenomena that are to be explained by the theory in question.[7] The data

6. Jones, *Kitzmiller, et al. v. Dover Area School District, et al.*; Jones, *Kitzmiller v. Dover Memorandum Opinion* 2005, p. 64.
7. Van Fraassen, *The Empirical Stance* (New Haven: Yale University Press, 2004).

must be presented or stated in terms of certain parameters or categories; it could include, for example, the results of certain experiments, but will not (ordinarily) include alleged information described as hearsay. According to MN, furthermore, the data model of a proper scientific theory will not invoke God or other supernatural agents, or employ what one knows or thinks one knows by way of revelation. Thus the data model of a proper theory could include the proposition that there has been a sudden outbreak of weird and irrational activity in Washington, D.C., but it couldn't include the proposition that there has been an outbreak of demon possession there.

Secondly, there will also be constraints on the theory itself. Now the theory can properly employ categories or parameters not permitted by the data model. For example, the data might include a deep depression in a Siberian forest; the theory but not the data might posit a meteorite that struck there. (Of course in another context the meteorite and its effects might be part of the data.) But according to MN the parameters for a scientific theory are not to include reference to God or any other supernatural agents (although, again, they can refer to beliefs about the supernatural); and the theory, like the data set, also can't employ what one knows or thinks one knows by way of revelation. Suppose your data set includes that recent outbreak of irrational behavior in Washington, D.C.: MN says you can't try to account for that data by a theory according to which there has recently been increased demonic activity there.

Still further (and this is important for our present inquiry) MN also imposes a constraint on the evidence base of any scientific inquiry. This evidence base will include mathematics and logic, relevant current science, various common sense beliefs and propositions (for example, that there is an external world, and that the world has existed for a long time), and perhaps also maxims outlining proper scientific procedure. The evidence base, as we saw above, functions in various ways. For example, in any given context there are of course a vast number of possible scientific theories, most of which don't rate a second (or even a first) thought; others are a bit more sensible, but too implausible or improbable to take seriously. It is the evidence base that determines the initial plausibility or probability of a proposed scientific theory. Now I said above that the evidence base of a Christian theist will include (among much else) belief in God as well as belief in incarnation and atonement. According to MN, however, those propositions can't be part of the evidence base of a scientific inquiry. The evidence base of a scientific inquiry will not contain propositions obviously entailing the existence of God (or other supernatural beings); nor will it include propositions one knows or thinks one knows by way of revelation. Hence rejecting, for example, Herbert Simon's theory of altruism because it is massively improbable with respect to a Christian evidence base would presumably not be proper science—not, at least, if proper science involves methodological naturalism.

Now we began by asking whether Simonian science—science that comes to conclusions incompatible with Christian belief—gives the Christian a defeater for the beliefs it contradicts. The important point to see, with respect to that question, is this: the scientific evidence base, the evidence base from which current science is conducted, does *not* include the belief that there is such a person as God; it does not include incarnation, resurrection, atonement. And this means that the scientific evidence base is importantly different from a Christian evidence base. The Christian's evidence base includes belief in God as well as belief in the main lines of the Christian faith; the former doesn't include these things.

Indeed, the scientific evidence base may include the *denials* of these beliefs. In chapter 5 we noted that there are at least two varieties of historical Biblical criticism: one of them takes it as given, as part of the evidence base in question, that there aren't any miracles, that God never acts specially in the world, and that it is not the case that the Bible is in some special way divine discourse, or a revelation from

God. Simonian science of this sort incorporates the denials of crucial elements of the Christian faith in its evidence base. But there is also another kind of HBC, one where neither the beliefs in question nor their denials are part of the evidence base. Thus there are at least two kinds of MN, corresponding to these two kinds of HBC—strong MN and weak MN. According to weak MN, a scientific evidence base will not include the proposition that there is such a person as God, or any other supernatural being; nor, of course, will it include the main lines of the Christian faith. Strong MN goes further; it adds the *denials* of at least some of these beliefs to the evidence base. Weak MN includes neither these beliefs nor their denials; strong MN includes their denials.

IV IS SIMONIAN SCIENCE A DEFEATER FOR CHRISTIAN BELIEF?

Contemporary science, science as it is currently practiced, is characterized by MN, either weak or strong. So of course Simonian science—science that produces theories incompatible with Christian belief—is characterized by MN of either the strong or the weak sort. Suppose it's the strong sort. Then the relevant point is that the evidence base of the inquiry in question includes the denial of central Christian (and indeed) theistic beliefs. If so, however, the fact that this inquiry comes to conclusions incompatible with Christian belief would be neither surprising, nor—for Christians—an occasion for consternation or dismay. It would certainly not constitute a defeater for Christian belief. As an example, consider Troeltschian HBC (chapter 5): it takes as part of its evidence base that God never acts in special ways and that there aren't any miracles. But then the mere fact that those who engage in this enterprise come to the conclusion that there aren't any miracles—that, say, Jesus did not arise from the dead—is certainly no surprise: how could they come to any other conclusion? And the fact that they come to this conclusion, furthermore, is obviously not a defeater for the Christian belief that Jesus did rise from the dead—that conclusion is a simple consequence of the evidence base they start with. Their coming to that conclusion from that starting point is surely no reason to give up or moderate belief in the resurrection of Jesus; it does not constitute a defeater for that belief.

Suppose, on the other hand, that what is involved in Simonian science is weak MN. Then the important thing to see is that the evidence base of Simonian science, as of science generally, is only a part, a subset, as they say, of the Christian believer's evidence base. That latter includes the beliefs to be found in the evidence base of Simonian science, but it also includes more. It includes belief in God, and also belief in "the great things of the gospel." And that means that Simonian science doesn't as such provide the Christian theist with a defeater for those of her beliefs incompatible with Simonian science.[8] For what the success of Simonian science really shows is something like this: that with respect to its evidence base, its conclusions are probable, or sensible, or approvable as science or as good science. What it shows with respect to the Christian's evidence base, therefore, is that from the perspective of *part* of that evidence base—the part coinciding with the scientific evidence base—the Simonian conclusions are probable, or sensible, or approvable, or constitute good science. Therefore what it shows is that with respect to *part* of her evidence base, some of her beliefs are improbable or unlikely.

That need not give her a defeater for those beliefs. For it can easily happen that I come to see that one of my beliefs is unlikely with

---

8. Of course there *could be* defeaters embedded in a piece of Simonian science discourse; my claim is only that Simonian science doesn't automatically, just as such, provide a defeater for the Christian beliefs with which it is incompatible.

respect to part of my evidence base, without thereby incurring a defeater for that belief. You tell me you saw me at the mall yesterday; I remember that I wasn't there at all, but spent the entire afternoon in my office, thinking about evolutionary psychology. Then with respect to part of my evidence base—a part that includes your telling me that you saw me at the mall—it is unlikely that I was in my office all afternoon; but that fact doesn't give me a defeater for my belief that that's where I was. My knowledge of your telling me that you saw me at the mall doesn't constitute a defeater for my belief that I wasn't there.

Another example: imagine a group of whimsical physicists who try to see how much of physics would be left if we refused to employ, in the development of physics, anything we know by way of memory. Perhaps something could be done along these lines, but it would be a poor, paltry, truncated, trifling thing. Suppose further that general relativity turned out to be dubious and unlikely from this point of view. And now consider physicists who do physics from the usual scientific evidence base, and furthermore believe the results: would they get a defeater for General Relativity upon learning that it was unlikely from the perspective of truncated physics? Surely not. They would note, as a reasonably interesting fact, that there was indeed a conflict: the best way to think about the subject matter of physics from the standpoint of the *truncated* evidence base is incompatible with the best way to think about that subject matter from the perspective of the *whole* scientific evidence base. But of course they take the perspective of the whole scientific evidence base to be normative; it is the right perspective from which to view the matter. As a result, their knowledge of the way things look from that truncated base doesn't give them a defeater for the beliefs appropriate with respect to the whole scientific base.

One final example: consider someone convicted of a crime he knows he didn't commit. So suppose I am accused of a crime— slashing your tires again, for example. At the trial my department chairman—a man of impeccable probity—claims to have seen me lurking around your car at the time the crime occurred; I am also known to resent you (in part because of your article in the department newsletter claiming that in church I slyly withdraw money from the collection plate under the guise of contributing). I had means, motive and opportunity; furthermore there have been other such sordid episodes in my past; the evidence against me convinces the jury. However, *I* recall very clearly spending the entire afternoon skiing in Love Creek County Park, twenty miles away, when the offense occurred; the fact is I *know* that I didn't commit that crime. Now in a way I have no quarrel with the jury. Given what they know, they came to the right conclusion—or rather, they came to a conclusion that was right in one sense but wrong in another. They came to a conclusion that was very probable, perhaps beyond reasonable doubt, given what they knew. Unfortunately that conclusion was false. I have no quarrel with them; but does their coming to that conclusion—does my standing convicted of the crime—give me a defeater for my belief that I didn't commit it? Should I give up the belief that I didn't do it? I should think not.[9] And the reason is that I have a source of knowledge or warranted belief they don't: I *remember* that I didn't commit that crime.

I submit that the same goes for Simonian science and Christian belief. The evidence base for Simonian science (given weak MN) is part of the Christian's evidence base, but only part of it. Hence the fact that Simonian science comes to conclusions incompatible with Christian belief doesn't provide the believer with a defeater for her belief. For the Christian, Simonian science is like truncated physics.

---

9. Of course there *could* be such a preponderance of evidence as to convince me that my memory has been playing me tricks—for example, if several independent witnesses claimed they *saw* me slash your tires, the security camera in the parking lot clearly shows me slashing away, etc. The point is only that it is possible that the right conclusion for the jury to come to, given their evidence, might be a conclusion I know to be false. (Think of people—some on death row—convicted of crimes they know they didn't commit.)

Concede that from the point of view of the evidence base of Simonian science, constrained as it is by weak MN, Simonian science is indeed the way to go (and of course perhaps it isn't): this need not give the Christian a defeater for those of her beliefs contradicted by Simonian science; for the evidence base of the latter is only part of her evidence base.

V FAITH AND REASON

What we have here is really a special case of a topic long discussed in the history of Christian thought: the so-called problem of faith and reason. According to classical Christian belief, there are two sources of knowledge or rational opinion: faith and reason. Reason includes such faculties as perception, a priori intuition (whereby one knows truths of mathematics and truths of logic), memory, testimony (whereby one can learn from others), induction (whereby one can learn from experience) and perhaps others, such as Thomas Reid's sympathy, whereby we know of the thoughts and feeling of other people. Perhaps there is also a moral sense, whereby we know something of what is right and wrong; perhaps there are still others. These faculties or sources of belief/knowledge are part of our created cognitive nature; every properly functioning human being has them. Of course there are substantial individual differences with respect to the acuity of the faculty in question: for example, what may be child's play for the gifted mathematician may be beyond the reach of the rest of us, and some people display an unusual ability to discern the thoughts and feelings of others.

Faith, on the other hand, is a wholly different kettle of fish: according to the Christian tradition (including both Thomas Aquinas and John Calvin), faith is a special gift from God, not part of our ordinary epistemic equipment. Faith is a source of belief, a source that goes beyond the faculties included in reason. It is not that the deliverances of faith are to be contrasted with *knowledge*; according to John Calvin, faith "is a firm and certain *knowledge* of God's benevolence towards us."[10] So a proposition I believe by faith can (at least according to followers of Calvin) nonetheless be something I know. But even if faith is a source of knowledge, it is still a source of knowledge distinct from reason. Of course it could be that a given proposition can be known both by faith and by reason; perhaps one of the deliverances of faith—for example, that Jesus arose from the dead—can also be shown to be very probable with respect to what one knows by way of reason.[11] Indeed, perhaps this item of faith can be *known* by way of reason. But there are many of the deliverances of faith such that it is at least plausible to think that they cannot be known by way of reason.[12]

This is not so far, of course, to say that there is *conflict* between faith and reason. Maybe there is and maybe there isn't; but the mere fact that the deliverances of faith include propositions not among the deliverances of reason doesn't show that there is such a conflict. In the same way, my knowing by way of testimony something that I don't and can't know by way of perception doesn't show that there is a conflict between perception and testimony. You tell me you have a headache; I can't learn this from perception; I therefore learn something by way of testimony that I couldn't learn from perception; it doesn't follow that there is conflict between the two. I remember where I was yesterday; I can't determine that by way of a priori intuition; it doesn't follow that there is conflict between memory and a priori intuition.

10. Calvin, ed. John T. McNeill and tr. by Ford Lewis Battles (Philadelphia: the Westminster Press, [1559] 1960). *Institutes* III, ii, 7, p. 551. My emphasis.
11. See some of the many attempts to give arguments from reason (taken as including history) for Jesus' resurrection—e.g., N. T. Wright, Willliam Lane Craig, Stephen Davis, Gary Habermas, Timothy and Lydia McGrew, Richard Swinburne, and many others.
12. For a much fuller account of faith and its relation to reason, see my *Warranted Christian Belief* (New York: Oxford University Press, 2000), chapter 8.

In other cases, however, there can be what we might call *weak* conflict. Consider again the case where I'm falsely accused of slashing your tires: I have the same evidence as the jurors for the proposition that I committed the crime (the testimony of the witnesses, my previous predilection for criminal behavior, et cetera), but I also remember that I was elsewhere at the time. In this case, therefore, with respect to the deliverances of the faculties involved in my apprehending the evidence the jurors have, the right thing to think is that I committed the crime; but my memory tells me differently. So here there is conflict between the deliverances of memory, on the one hand; and, on the other, the deliverances of testimony and whatever other faculties are involved in my (and the jurors) acquiring the evidence for my having committed the crime. But this is a *weak* conflict. That is because my acquiring the evidence for my having committed the crime (the same evidence as the jurors have for that proposition) doesn't give me a defeater for my belief, based on memory, that in fact I didn't commit the crime. It doesn't give me a reason to give up that belief, or even to hold it less firmly.

Of course there *could be* a strong conflict here; it could be that the testimony of others was sufficiently strong to give me a defeater. If several unimpeachable witnesses claim to have seen me slashing your tires, I may have to conclude that my memory was somehow playing me tricks; rationality may require my giving up the belief that I was innocent. How *much* evidence of that sort would be required to give me a defeater? That's a question without an answer; much would depend on the reliability of the witnesses, the question what I know or believe about whether my memory had ever before failed me in such drastic fashion, and so on. The point is only that sufficient evidence of that sort could give me a defeater for my belief that I was innocent, and where that does in fact happen, what we have is a strong conflict between memory and these other sources of belief.

Now return to Simonian science and Christian belief, and let's suppose the scientific evidence base here is constrained by weak MN. Given this evidence base and the current state of evolutionary science, perhaps the right thing to think is that human beings have indeed come to be by way of a process of evolution driven by natural selection working on random genetic mutation. Given that idea, and, as weak MN requires, setting aside the Christian claim that God has created human beings in his image, it might be that the most plausible thing to think, as with David Wilson, is that the mechanisms that produce religious belief in us are not truth aimed; they are not aimed at the production of beliefs that are true, but rather at the production of beliefs that conduce to some other end, such as securing the benefits of cooperation. Suppose that is the right thing to think from this point of view (I don't say that it is): do I thereby get a defeater for my belief that in fact these mechanisms *are* truth-aimed? Clearly not. My evidence base contains the belief that God has created human beings in his image. I now learn that, given an evidence base that *doesn't* contain that belief, the right thing to believe is that those mechanisms are not truth-aimed; but of course that doesn't give me any reason at all to amend or reject my belief that in fact they are truth-aimed. It does not give me a defeater for that belief, or for the belief that God has created human beings with something like the *sensus divinitatis* of which John Calvin speaks, or the natural but confused knowledge of God of which Aquinas speaks. More generally, the fact that scientists come up with views like Wilson's does not, just as such, offer a defeater for Christian belief. The conflict in question is superficial.

Is there even a superficial conflict? What, exactly, does science assert here, or more exactly, what does a scientist who proposes a Wilsonian claim assert? Or still more exactly, what is it that a scientist is entitled to assert here, assuming that in fact he has done everything properly? Is he asserting that in fact belief in God is not reality oriented? Or is he asserting something more like a conditional: from the scientific evidence base, this is the best way to look at the matter? This is the theory that has the best scientific credentials?

Given the scientific evidence base and the current evidence, this theory is the most acceptable, rational, sensible, warranted, or whatever? Analogy: you think you have an appointment with your hairdresser for Thursday; you call up to confirm it; the receptionist claims your appointment is for Friday; you protest, saying you are sure it is for Thursday (and Friday you'll be out of town); she replies as follows: "well, all I can say is that the record here says it's Friday." She retreats from the claim that it is Friday to the claim that from a certain perspective it is clearly Friday.

There is some reason to think something similar goes on in the case of Simonian science. Consider again work in the scientific study of religion: the more careful books in this area begin by saying they aren't addressing such questions as whether or not Christianity or theism is in fact true; they are instead simply engaging in an effort to see what there is to say about religion from a scientific perspective. Thus Scott Atran:

> Religious beliefs and practices involve the very same cognitive and affective structures as nonreligious beliefs and practices—and no others—but in (more or less) systematically distinctive ways. From an evolutionary standpoint, these structures are, at least proximately, no different in origin and kind from the genetic instincts and mechanical processes that govern the life of other animals. Religious explanations of religion may or may not accept this account of proximate causes, but no faith-based account considers it to be the *whole* story. I do not intend to refute such nonscientific explanations of religion, nor do I pretend that they are morally worthless or intellectually unjustified. The chosen scientific perspective of this book is simply blind to them and can elucidate nothing about them—so far as I can see.[13]

The suggestion is that there is such a thing as a scientific perspective, and that Atran's book is written from that perspective; as such, says Atran, the book says nothing about the truth or falsehood of religious belief, because the scientific perspective is "blind" to these things. Atran isn't claiming that his conclusions

---

13. Atran, *In Gods We Trust: The Evolutionary Landscape of Religion* (New York: Oxford University Press, 2002), p. 4.

are in fact correct, but rather that they are correct (or plausible or promising) from that "chosen scientific perspective." Atran thinks his conclusions are correct, given the scientific evidence base and the current evidence. Whether these conclusions are also correct just as such will depend, among other things, upon whether the scientific perspective is, in this area, the right perspective and whether the scientific evidence base is the right evidence base. (Of course it might be the right evidence base in one area but not in another.) The Christian theist will think that it isn't the right evidence base, because it is at best incomplete; it fails to include important elements of the Christian's evidence base. But then the fact that competent work from the scientific perspective comes up with claims inconsistent with Christian belief isn't, just as such anyway, a defeater for those beliefs; the scientific evidence base of the latter is only part of the Christian's evidence base.

VI CAN RELIGIOUS BELIEFS BE DEFEATED?

But isn't this just a recipe for intellectual irresponsibility, for hanging on to beliefs in the teeth of the evidence? Can't a Christian always say something like the above, no matter what proposed defeater presents itself? "Perhaps B (the proposed defeatee) is improbable or unlikely with respect to part of what I believe," she says, "but it is certainly not improbable with respect to the totality of what I believe, that totality including, of course, B itself." No, certainly not. If that were proper procedure, every prospective defeater could be turned aside and defeat would be impossible. The believer could always just say that his evidence base includes the challenged belief, and is therefore probable with respect to that evidence base (because entailed by it). But the fact is defeat is not impossible; it sometimes happens that I *do* acquire a defeater for a belief B I hold by learning that B is improbable on some proper subset of my evidence base.

For example: according to Isaiah 41:9, God says, "I took you from the ends of the earth, from its farthest corners I called you. I said, 'You are my servant'; I have chosen you and have not rejected you." Now suppose that, on the basis of this text, I've always believed R, the proposition that the earth is a rectangular solid with edges and corners (I have never encountered any of the evidence for the earth's being round). Won't I acquire a defeater for this belief when confronted with the scientific evidence against it—photographs of the earth from space, for example? The same goes for someone who holds pre-Copernican beliefs on the basis of such a text as "The earth stands fast; it shall not be moved" (Psalm 104:5). But then what is the difference? Why is there a defeater in these cases, but not in the case of Simonian science? How is it that you get a defeater in some cases of this sort, but not in others? What makes the difference?

Here's an unhelpful answer: the one case conforms to the definition of rationality defeat, and the other one doesn't. In the case of Simonian science, I learn that such science comes to conclusions inconsistent with Christian belief, and I also believe that Simonian science is good science; nevertheless I can rationally continue to hold Christian beliefs (although of course I can't also accept those conclusions of Simonian science inconsistent with them). But I can't rationally continue to believe R, once I see those photographs and realize that in fact they are photographs.[14] *That's* the difference.

Right; but can't we do a little better than that? Think about the case where I believe, on the basis of that text from the Bible, that

(N) The earth is the stationary center of the universe.

Now this scientific evidence (those photographs) against this proposition shows up; I begin to think about it. My acceptance of

14. Of course there is still the relativity of defeat to noetic structure; there are some noetic structures with respect to which those beliefs would not be a defeater for the belief that R. For example, I might believe, for some reason, that space is pervaded by an ether-like substance that causes photographs of cubical objects to appear spherical, or I might believe that the camera in question had the unusual property (sort of like a fisheye lens) of photographing cubes in such a way that they look like spheres.

184

(N) is based on the Bible, which I think is a revelation from God. And of course I am prepared to believe whatever the Lord teaches; what he teaches is nonnegotiable. But it isn't always easy to determine just what he *does* teach in a given passage; might it not be, with respect to this passage, that the message endorsed by God is not (N) but something else?[15] What is my reason for thinking that (N) is indeed what the Lord is teaching in this passage?

On thinking the matter over, I see that my reasons for thinking (or assuming) this are pretty flimsy. I consult the Hebrew text: it's not at all clear that what's being taught has anything to do with whether the earth is the unmoved center of the universe. Other translations go like this: "You set the earth on its foundations so that it shall never be shaken" (New Revised Standard) and "He established the earth upon its foundation, so that it will not totter forever and ever" (New American Standard Bible). These don't even suggest anti-Copernicanism; the earth won't totter and it won't shake, but not much follows about the difference between Copernicus and Ptolemy. What is clearly being taught is that the Lord has established the natural order, and that he is faithful and reliable; this includes the fact that the physical universe goes on in a certain regular way, a way that can be relied upon, so that planning and intentional action are possible for God's creatures. But it is certainly far from clear that what is being taught has to do with the issue between Ptolemy and Copernicus. On the other hand, the evidence for Copernicanism looks solid (well, maybe it didn't look so solid in the seventeenth century, but by now it surely does). So which has the greater warrant for me: the thought that in the verse God is teaching anti-Copernicanism, or the thought, based on the evidence, that the earth is not the center of things? Pretty clearly it's the latter. In this way I can indeed acquire a defeater for a belief I held on the basis of scriptural teaching; part of what

15. See chapter 5, section IIIA.

I come to see is that the belief in question isn't really scriptural teaching. Hence in this way I learn something important about the Bible—something about the intended teaching of a given passage—by way of scientific investigation.

My present point is that in some cases one can indeed acquire a defeater for a belief held on the basis of the Bible; I can come to see that what the Bible teaches isn't what I thought it was. I argued that Simonian science doesn't give a Christian a defeater for the beliefs with which it is incompatible, because the evidential basis of science is just part of the Christian evidential basis; my point here is that this doesn't imply that a Christian can never get a defeater for one of his religious beliefs.

VII THE REDUCTION TEST

Can we go further? Can we come up with a nontrivial test for determining when we get a defeater? Consider some Christian belief incompatible with some bit of Simonian science, for example,

> (B) Mother Teresa was perfectly rational in behaving in that altruistic manner.

Now I learn

> (A) Simonian science is successful science and implies the denial of (B).

Do I thereby acquire a defeater for (B)? Say that my evidence base is EB_{me}; add A to EB_{me}. The right question, perhaps, is this: is (B) epistemically improbable or unlikely with respect to that new evidence base? If it is, perhaps, we have a defeater; if not, not. Of course (B) might initially be a member of EB_{me}, in which case it will certainly not be improbable with respect to it. But if that were sufficient for (A)'s not being a defeater of (B), no member of the evidence base could ever be defeated by a new discovery; and that can't be right. So let's delete (B) from EB_{me}. Call the result of deleting (B) from my evidence base "EB_{me} reduced with respect to (B)": "EB_{me}-(B)" for short. The idea—call it "the reduction test for defeat"—is that (A) is a defeater for (B) just if (B) is relatively improbable—epistemically improbable—with respect to EB_{me}-(B).

Of course it won't work to delete only (B) from EB_{me}—we must also delete conjunctions that include (B)—for example, the conjunction of (B) with $2+1 = 3$. We must also delete all the beliefs in EB_{me} that entail (B)—for example, beliefs of the sort *(If R then (B)) and R*. Still further, we shall also have to deal with pairs of beliefs that entail (B), since it might be that I hold a pair of beliefs that together entail B but do not happen to believe their conjunction. (Maybe I've never thought of them together.) Should we delete one member of each such pair? But here we run into a problem: in general there will be no unique way of following this procedure, and different ways of following it can yield significantly different results. So let's resort to the vague way out (vagueness is all the rage these days): let's say that EB_{me}-(B) is any subset of EB_{me} that doesn't entail (B) and is otherwise maximally similar to EB_{me}. Now: could we say the following: could we say that I have a defeater for (B) if and only if (B) is epistemically unlikely with respect to EB_{me}-(B), i.e., if and only if (A) and (B) satisfy the reduction test for defeat?

Well, this test gives the right result in the present cases. First, consider our question about Simonian science and Christian belief. (B) is the proposition that Mother Teresa was perfectly rational in behaving in that altruistic fashion and (B), we are assuming, is incompatible with Simonian science. To apply the proposed criterion, we must ask whether (B) is epistemically improbable (henceforth I'll suppress the "epistemically") with respect to EB_{me}-(B)—where of course EB_{me}-(B) includes (A), the proposition that Simonian science is successful science. The answer, I should think, is that (B) is not improbable with respect to EB_{me}-(B). For that body of beliefs includes the empirical evidence, whatever exactly it is, appealed to by the Simonian, but also the proposition that we human beings have been created by God and created in his image, along with the rest of the main lines of the Christian story. With respect to *that* body of propositions, it is not likely that if Mother Teresa had been more rational, smarter, she would have acted so as to increase her reproductive fitness rather than live altruistically. But then (B), the proposed defeatee, is not improbable on that evidence basis. Hence, on the proposed reduction test, the fact that

Simonian science is more likely than not with respect to the scientific evidence base does not give the Christian theist a defeater for what she thinks about Mother Teresa.

Now compare the case of the person who first believes the earth is a rectangular solid on the basis of the Biblical verse I mentioned above, and then acquires the evidence, including photographs, that the earth is spherical. Consider her new evidence base reduced with respect to the proposed defeatee—that is, the proposition that the earth has corners. With respect to this reduced evidence base, the proposition that the earth has no corners is very likely. For that reduced evidence base contains or includes all of our reasons for supposing that in fact the earth doesn't have corners. And what does it include on the other side—that is, what does it include by way of support for the belief that the earth has corners? Only what would be, presumably, the rather tentative thought that in the passage in question, God was intending to teach us that the earth has corners. But clearly there are other perfectly plausible ways of construing that passage. On balance, therefore, she will conclude that in fact that is not what the passage in question is intended to teach. Hence in this case, unlike the case of Simonian science, the reduced evidence base provides evidence, indeed powerful evidence, against the proposed defeatee, and the proposed defeatee is improbable with respect to the reduced evidence base.

So the reduction test gives the right result in the present case. But it can't be right in general. Perhaps it states a necessary condition of rationality defeat: perhaps, wherever I get a defeater for a belief (B) by way of acquiring a new belief (A), B will be relatively improbable with respect to EB_{me}-(B). But this condition is nowhere nearly sufficient for defeat. And the reason is of the first importance. For it might be, clearly enough, that (B) has a lot of warrant on its own, *intrinsic* warrant, warrant it doesn't get from the other members of EB_{me} or indeed any other propositions; (B) may be *basic* with respect to warrant. But then the fact that it is unlikely with respect to EB_{me}-(B) doesn't show for a moment that the belief isn't perfectly rational. This is easily illustrated by the example (above, pp. 176ff) where I am falsely accused of slashing your tires. There is strong evidence against me; however, I clearly recall spending the entire afternoon skiing in Love Creek County Park. My belief that I was skiing there then isn't based on argument or inference from other propositions (I don't note, for example, that I feel a little tired, that my ski boots are damp, and that there is a map of Love Creek in my parka pocket, concluding that the best explanation of these phenomena is that I was skiing there).

So consider EB_{me}-P, my evidence base diminished with respect to P, the proposition that I didn't slash your tires. With respect to EB_{me}-P, P is epistemically improbable; after all, I have the same evidence as everyone else for the denial of P, and everyone else is quite properly (if mistakenly) convinced that I did slash your tires. Still, I certainly don't have a defeater, here, for my belief that I didn't do it. And the reason, of course, is that P has for me a source of warrant independent of the rest of my beliefs: I *remember* it. In a case like this, whether I have a defeater for the belief P in question will depend, on the one hand, upon the strength of the intrinsic warrant enjoyed by P, and, on the other, the strength of the evidence against P from EB_{me}-P. Very often the intrinsic warrant will be the stronger (husband *in flagrante delicto* to wife: "Who are you going to believe—me or your lying eyes?"). But it isn't automatically the case, of course, that the intrinsic warrant of P overcomes the evidence from EB_{me}-P; if the latter is strong enough I may have to conclude that the source of the apparent warrant of P is deceiving me. If the department chairman, assorted grad students, and the chaired professor most distinguished for probity and judiciousness unite in declaring that they *saw* me slash those tires, I may have to conclude that my memory has let me down; perhaps I have repressed the whole unpleasant episode.

It is clear, therefore, that Simonian science doesn't (automatically, anyway) constitute a defeater for the Christian beliefs with which it is incompatible. The Christian can think of Simonian science as specifying how things look from a given perspective, how they look given a particular evidence base, an evidence base that includes only a part of the Christian evidence base. The mere existence of Simonian science—science that comes to conclusions incompatible with tenets of the Christian faith—has no tendency to produce a defeater for those tenets. Of course it is theoretically possible, as I said above, that a defeater for Christian belief should arise in the course of work at Simonian science; as far as I know, however, this hasn't happened. The conclusion to draw is that there is indeed conflict between science and Christian belief in this area, but the conflict is merely superficial, of no deep significance. There is conflict, of a sort, but it shouldn't occasion any concern for Christians.

Simonian science specifies how things look from a given perspective or evidence base, a perspective characterized by methodological naturalism. It may be of considerable interest to see how things look from that evidence base. But shouldn't the Christian also want to know how the phenomena in question look from the standpoint of the Christian evidence base? Shouldn't she, perhaps in addition to pursuing scientific study of those phenomena from the conventional scientific perspective, also want to study it from the perspective of her own evidence base? Would such study fail to be science? Shouldn't the Christian community engage in Christian science—not in the sense of following Mary Baker Eddy, but in the sense of engaging in empirical study unconstrained by methodological naturalism? These are excellent questions. Excellent as they are, however, addressing them here would take us on a side track, too far from the main line of argument.[16] To return to the main line: so far I've argued that there is no conflict between Christian belief and evolution; nor is the claim that God acts specially in the world in conflict with science. I've gone on to argue that there is indeed conflict between Christian belief and certain areas of evolutionary psychology and historical Biblical criticism; this conflict, however is superficial. So much for conflict; I turn next to concord between Christian belief and science.

16. I have addressed them in a preliminary way in "Science: Augustinian or Duhemian?" *Faith and Philosophy* (July, 1996), "Christian Philosophy at the End of the 20th Century," in *Christian Philosophy at the Close of the Twentieth Century*, ed. Bert Balk and Sander Griffioen (1995), and "On Christian Scholarship," in *The Challenge and Promise of a Catholic University*, ed Theodore Hesburgh (Notre Dame, Ind.: University of Notre Dame Press, 1994); I hope to address them at greater length elsewhere.

PART III

CONCORD

Chapter 7

Fine-Tuning

This most beautiful system of the sun, planets and comets, could only proceed from the counsel and dominion of an intelligent and powerful Being..... This Being governs all things, not as the soul of the world, but as Lord over all.

—Isaac Newton[1]

So far we have seen that there is indeed conflict between Christian belief and at least some purported scientific theories, in particular in the areas of evolutionary psychology and historical Biblical scholarship. I went on to argue, however, that—due to the difference between Christian and scientific evidence bases—this conflict is superficial; it doesn't as such tend to provide a defeater for Christian belief. It is now time to turn to concord. Now one sort of concord would be illustrated by support for theistic belief offered by science. I've argued that science doesn't conflict with Christian belief: can we go further, and say science offers positive support for it? That is the question for the next couple of chapters. How could science do a thing like that? One way would be as follows: scientific discoveries provide premises for good arguments for the existence of God. And indeed two kinds of arguments of this sort have been suggested, both connected in one way

---

1. The General Scholium to Isaac Newton's Philosophiae Naturalis *Principia Mathematica*, published for the first time as an appendix to the 2nd (1713) edition of the *Principia*.

or another with intelligent design. First, there are the "fine-tuning" arguments for theism; scientific discoveries in physics and astronomy about the structure of the universe offer the premises for a theistic argument. Secondly, there are arguments from biology, arguments involving the nature and character of the living beings our world displays. This chapter will examine fine-tuning arguments. The next will do the same for those biological arguments, and go on to propose and examine a different way in which these phenomena could support theism.

I FINE-TUNING

In the epigraph at the beginning of this chapter, Isaac Newton, often said to be the greatest scientist the world has so far produced, proposes that "this most beautiful system of the sun, planets and comets, could only proceed from the counsel and dominion of an intelligent and powerful being." Going back to the late sixties and early seventies of the 20th century and continuing to the present, there has been a remarkable burst of support for Newton's suggestion, starting from the so-called fine-tuning in cosmology. Astrophysicists and others have noted that several of the basic physical constants—the velocity of light, the strength of the gravitational force, and of the strong and weak nuclear forces—must fall within very narrow limits if intelligent life of our kind is to develop.

Thus Brandon Carr and Martin Rees:

> The basic features of galaxies, stars, planets and the everyday world are essentially determined by a few microphysical constants and by the effects of gravitation.... several aspects of our Universe—some of which seem to be prerequisites for the

evolution of any form of life—depend rather delicately on apparent 'coincidences' among the physical constants.[2]

For example, if the force of gravity were even slightly stronger, all stars would be blue giants; if even slightly weaker, all would be red dwarfs; in neither case could life have developed.[3] The same goes for the weak and strong nuclear forces; if either had been even slightly different, life, at any rate life even remotely similar to the sort we have, could probably not have developed.

Even more interesting in this connection is the so-called *flatness* problem: the existence of life also seems to depend very delicately upon the rate at which the universe is expanding. Thus Stephen Hawking says that "reduction of the rate of expansion by one part in 10^{12} at the time when the temperature of the Universe was 10^{10} K would have resulted in the Universe starting to recollapse when its radius was only $1/3000$ of the present value and the temperature was still 10,000 deg"—much too warm for comfort.[4] Hawking concludes that life is possible only because the universe is expanding at just the rate required to avoid recollapse. At an earlier time, the fine-tuning had to be even more remarkable:

We know that there has to have been a very close balance between the competing effect of explosive expansion and gravitational contraction which, at the very earliest epoch about which we can even pretend to speak (called the Planck time, 10^{-43}

2. Carr and Rees, "The Anthropic Principle and the Structure of the Physical World" (*Nature*, 1979), p. 605.
3. Brandon Carter, "Large Number Coincidences and the Anthropic Principle in Cosmology," in M. S. Longair, ed, *Confrontation of Cosmological Theories with Observational Data*, 1979, p. 72. Carter concludes that if the strength of gravity were even slightly different, habitable planets would not exist.
4. Hawking, "The Anisotropy of the Universe at Large Times" in *Confrontation of Cosmological Theories with Observational Data*, p. 285.

sec. after the big bang), would have corresponded to the incredible degree of accuracy represented by a deviation in their ratio from unity by only one part in 10 to the sixtieth.[5]

These are striking facts. One sympathizes with Paul Davies: "the fact that these relations are necessary for our existence is one of the most fascinating discoveries of modern science."[6]

Then in 1986 John Barrow and Frank Tipler's big book *The Anthropic Cosmological Principle* emerged from the press, provoking a veritable flood of books and articles on fine-tuning.[7] One reaction to these apparently enormous coincidences is to claim that none of this ought to be seen as requiring explanation: after all, no matter how things had been, it would have been exceedingly improbable that they be that particular way. Appropriately taken, this point is perhaps right; but how is it relevant? We are playing poker; each time I deal I get four aces and one wild card; you get suspicious; I try to allay your suspicions by pointing out that my getting these cards each time I deal is no less probable than any other equally specific distribution over the relevant

5. John Polkinghorne, *Science and Creation: The Search for Understanding* (Boston: New Science Library; New York: Random House, 1989), p. 22.
6. Davies, P. C. W., *The Accidental Universe* (Cambridge: Cambridge University Press, 1982). Davies adds that
   All this prompts the question of why, from the infinite range of possible values that nature could have selected for the fundamental constants, and from the infinite variety of initial conditions that could have characterized the primeval universe, the actual values and conditions conspire to produce the particular range of very special features that we observe. For clearly the universe is a very special place: exceedingly uniform on a large scale, yet not so precisely uniform that galaxies could not form; ... an expansion rate tuned to the energy content to unbelievable accuracy; values for the strengths of its forces that permit nuclei to exist, yet do not burn up all the cosmic hydrogen, and many more apparent accidents of fortune (p. 111).
7. Among the most prominent: John Leslie, *Universes* (New York: Routledge, 1989), and Martin Rees, *Just Six Numbers: The Deep Forces that Shape the Universe* (New York: Basic, 2000).

number of deals. Would that explanation play in Dodge City, or Tombstone?[8]

Another reaction is to see them as substantiating the theistic claim that the universe has been created by a personal God and as offering the material for a properly restrained theistic argument: the fine-tuning argument (FTA).[9] In addition to the relatively informal expositions of such arguments by John Polkinghorne and others, there are a number of recent and fuller expositions: for example, Roger White's "Fine-Tuning and Multiple Universes," William Lane Craig's "Design and the Anthropic Fine-Tuning of the Universe," Richard Swinburne's "Argument from the Fine-Tuning of the Universe" and "The Argument to God from Fine-Tuning Reassessed," and Robin Collins's "A Scientific Argument for the Existence of God: the Fine-Tuning Design Argument" along with his "The Teleological Argument: an Exploration of the Fine-Tuning of the Universe" (perhaps the deepest and most technically competent presentation of the argument).[10]

8. It is easy to see why this distribution is likely to end in gunfire: the probability of that distribution is much greater on the hypothesis that I am cheating than on the hypothesis that the cards have been dealt fairly; by Bayes theorem it therefore follows that the probability of my cheating given this distribution is much greater than on other distributions. The same goes for the fine-tuning arguments: the probability of fine-tuning on the proposition that God has created the universe is much greater than on the proposition that the universe has not been created; consequently the probability of God's having created the universe is greater on fine-tuning than on other distributions of values over those constants.

9. E.g., see Polkinghorne, *Science and Creation*, p. 23.

10. White, "Fine-Tuning and Multiple Universes," *Nous* 34 (2000); Craig, "Design and the anthropic fine-tuning of the Universe" in Neil Manson, ed., *God and Design: The Teleological Argument and Modern Science* (London: Routledge, 2003); Swinburne, "Argument from the fine-tuning of the Universe" in John Leslie, ed., *Physical Cosmology and Philosophy* (New York: Macmillan, 1990) and "The Argument to God from Fine-Tuning Reassessed" in Manson, ed., *God and Design*; Collins, "A Scientific Argument for the Existence of God: The Fine-Tuning Design Argument" in *Reason for the Hope Within*, ed. Michael Murray (Grand Rapids: Eerdmans, 1999) and "The Teleological Argument: an Exploration of the Fine-Tuning of the Universe" in *The Blackwell Companion to Natural Theology*, ed. William Lane Craig and J. P. Moreland (New York: Wiley, 2009).

In a detailed and technically informed piece, Collins points out that many of
the claims made for a given example of fine-tuning are at best problematic (for
example, a line of reasoning involving the effect of an increase in the strength of
the strong nuclear force endorsed by several prominent writers, and a claim about
gravity proposed by Martin Rees).[11] He also notes that in several important cases,
we have solid evidence only for "one-sided" fine-tuning. Two-sided fine-tuning
occurs when the value of a parameter (the strength of gravity, for example) falls
within a life-permitting range, and the life-permitting range is small compared to
the total range within which that parameter could fall. One-sided fine-tuning
occurs when we know one edge of the life-permitting range, but don't know the
other, and the actual value of the parameter in question is close to the known
edge; Collins argues that one-sided fine-turning will do about as well as two-sided.
He then presents six detailed and, as far as present knowledge goes, solid examples of fine-tuning, which he explains in illuminating detail. These involve the
cosmological constants, the strong and electromagnetic forces, carbon production in stars, the proton/neutron difference, the weak force, and gravity.[12] The
degree of fine-tuning in these cases ranges from 1 part in 10 to one part in 10^{53}.

We may think of these cases in terms of a set of dials: here we have six dials
that must be tuned (in order for life to be permitted). In the most moderate case,
the dial has to be tuned to a value somewhere in a range that is one-tenth the
total range; in the most exacting case, the dial has to be tuned, with incredible
precision, to a point in a range that is 10^{53} of the total range. If we think of these
cases of fine-tuning in terms of probability, then the probability on chance that
the first dial will be properly tuned is about .1, and that of the second 10^{53}.
Assuming the values of these parameters are independent of each other, the fine-
tuning is of course multiplicative: the probability (on chance) that all six of the
dials will be tuned to life-permitting widths is less than 10^{-100}. Now of course
these figures are not totally secure, and they are also just approximations. Also,
it isn't known that the values of these parameters *are* independent. On the other
hand, there are many more proposed examples of fine-tuning, some of them
with numerical values attached, and others merely qualitative.[13] On balance, the

11. "Evidence for Fine-Tuning" in Manson, pp. 191–192.
12. Collins, "Evidence for Fine Tuning," pp. 180–83.
13. See Michael Denton, *Nature's Destiny: How the Laws of Biology Reveal Purpose in the Universe* (New York: The Free Press, 1998).

sensible conclusion seems to be that there is indeed an enormous amount of fine-tuning, although the precise amount isn't known, and it is possible to quarrel with many of the specific examples proposed.

So several of the cosmological constants are fine-tuned; how do we turn this into an argument for theism? The basic idea is that such fine-tuning is not at all surprising or improbable on theism: God presumably would want there to be life, and indeed intelligent life with which (whom) to communicate and share love. Of course this life could take many different forms (indeed, perhaps it *has* taken many forms). But it doesn't seem at all improbable that God would want to create life, both human life and life of other sorts; and if he wanted to create human life in a universe at all like ours, he would have been obliged to fine-tune the constants. On the other hand, on the atheistic hypothesis according to which these constants have their values by chance (that is, those values are not the result of anyone's choice or intention) it is exceedingly improbable that they would be fine-tuned for life. This seems to offer support for theism: given theism, fine-tuning is not at all improbable; given atheism, it is; therefore theism is to be preferred to atheism.

II OBJECTIONS

A. The Anthropic Objection

Naturally enough there are objections to the FTA; I'll consider four. One of the most interesting begins with the *anthropic principle*, which is exceedingly hard to understand and comes in several varieties but (in the version that makes most sense) points out that a necessary condition of anyone observing these values of the constants is that those constants have very nearly the values they *do* have.[14] We are here to observe these constants only because they have the values they do have; if the universe were not fine-tuned, we wouldn't be here to note that fact.[15] This seems right, but how is it an objection to the FTA? It is still puzzling that these values should have been just as they are, and it still seems that this fact cries out for explanation. It's no explanation to point out that these constants have to be fine-tuned for us to observe that they are fine-tuned—anymore than I can "explain" the fact that God decided to create me (instead of passing me over in favor of someone else) by pointing out that if God had not thus decided, I wouldn't be here to raise the question. According to Elliott Sober, the anthropic criticism is the "standard criticism" of the FTA; but exactly how do we get an objection to the FTA out of the fact that it's impossible that we should have observed that the universe is not fine-tuned?[16]

The problem is supposed to be that with respect to our evidence here (that the universe is fine-tuned) there is an "observational selection effect" (OSE): we are arguing that the universe is fine-tuned, but it isn't possible that we should observe that it is *not* fine-tuned. We could not have failed to have the evidence we do in fact have; we could not instead have observed that the universe is *not* fine-tuned; and this fact is supposed to invalidate the argument.

Many arguments that involve an observational selection effect are clearly mistaken. So, for example, suppose I propose a straightforward inductive argument for the conclusion that all amoebae are within one inch of a microscope. I point out that all *observed* amoebae have been

14. Martin Gardner distinguishes the Weak Anthropic Principle (WAP), the Strong Anthropic Principle (SAP), the Future Anthropic Principle (FAP), the Participatory Anthropic Principle (PAP), and the Completely Ridiculous Anthropic Principle; see his "WAP, SAP, FAP and PAP," *New York Review of Books,* May 8, 1986.
15. See, e.g., Richard Dawkins in *The God Delusion* (New York: Bantam, 2006), chapter 4.
16. Sober, "Absence of Evidence and Evidence of Absence: Evidential Transitivity in Connection with Fossils, Fishing, Fine-tuning and Firing-squads," *Philosophical Studies,* vol. 143, no. 1.

within one inch of a microscope; reasoning in the ordinary inductive way, I conclude that *all* amoebae are within one inch of a microscope. Here there is an obvious OSE: even if there were amoebae that were not within an inch of a microscope, I wouldn't be able to observe them. As a result, my sample class (amoebae I have observed) is such that it couldn't have contained a counterexample to my conclusion even if there were one; there is excellent reason, therefore, to doubt that the sample class is representative; and this ruins the argument. Similarly for the inductive argument for idealism, the idea that there aren't any unobserved physical objects. All observed physical objects have been observed (naturally enough); therefore probably all physical objects are observed, and there aren't any unobserved physical objects.

These arguments are obviously crazy, and the craziness results from the OSE they involve. But the FTA isn't of the same form. These crazy arguments are efforts to determine the composition of a certain class of objects: what proportion of amoebae are within an inch of a microscope? What proportion of physical objects have been observed? The method of sampling involved, however, guarantees that the sample will contain a certain proportion of amoebae with the property of being observed (in this case, 100 percent) no matter what the composition of the whole class of amoebae. The FTA isn't an argument of this form, however. To be of the same form, the argument would have to go as follows:

All observed universes are fine-tuned.

Therefore,

Probably all universes are fine-tuned.

That would be crazy in the same way as the above two arguments: but of course the FTA doesn't at all proceed in that fashion.

Clearly not all arguments with an OSE lurking in the neighborhood are bad arguments. For example, it might be important for some medical procedure to know whether or not I am sometimes awake at 3:00 A.M.; I can observe that I am awake at 3:00 A.M. and infer that I am sometimes awake then, but I can't observe that I am not awake then. Still, there is nothing wrong with the argument

I observe that I am awake and it is 3:00 A.M.

Therefore

I am sometimes awake at 3:00 A.M.

Arguments involving OSEs aren't always bad arguments; why think the FTA is? Elliott Sober and others sometimes start by comparing FTA with arguments that involve an OSE and do seem to be seriously defective.[17] A particularly popular argument has been proposed by Arthur Eddington.[18] Suppose you are netting fish in a lake. Your net is pretty coarse-grained: it will only catch fish that are more than ten inches long. You then note that all the fish you catch are more than ten inches long. You consider two hypotheses: H1, according to which all the fish in the lake are more than ten inches long, and H2, according to which only half of the fish are more than ten inches long. The probability of your observation—that is, that all the fish you've caught are more than ten inches long—is greater on H1 than on H2; but you would certainly be rash if you thought this really confirms H1 over H2, or that it gave you a good reason to endorse H1. Given your net, you'd wind up with

---

17. See Sober's "The Design Argument" in Manson, and "Absence of Evidence and Evidence of Absence: Evidential Transitivity in connection with Fossils, Fishing, Fine-Tuning, and Firing Squads."
18. Eddington, *The Philosophy of Physical Science* (Cambridge: Cambridge University Press, 1939).

fish more than ten inches long no matter what the proportion of such fish in the lake. This argument for the superiority of H1 to H2 is pretty clearly fishy, and defective just because it involves an OSE.

But is the FTA like this argument? Opponents of the anthropic objection propose that the FTA is more like the firing squad argument.[19] Here the scenario goes as follows: I am convicted of high treason and sentenced to be shot. I am put up against the wall; eight sharpshooters fifteen feet away take aim and shoot, each shooting eight times. Oddly enough, they all miss; I emerge from this experience shaken, but unscathed. I then compare two hypotheses: H3, that the sharpshooters intentionally missed, and H4, that the sharpshooters intended to shoot me. I note that my evidence, that I am unharmed, is much more likely on H3 than it is on H4, and I conclude that H3 is to be preferred to H4. Here we also have an OSE; it would not be possible (we may suppose) for me to observe that I had been fatally shot. But my argument for the superiority of H3 to H4 certainly looks entirely right and proper. So our question is: which of these two arguments is the FTA more like?

I say it's much more like the firing squad argument. Let's suppose there are (or could be) many universes (see pp. 210ff); use "alpha" as a name of the universe we find ourselves in, the universe that is comprised by everything that is spatiotemporally related to us. What we observe is

O Alpha is fine-tuned.

We have the following two hypotheses:

D: Alpha has been designed by some powerful and intelligent being,

19. Due to Leslie, *Universes*.

and

C: Alpha has come to be by way of some chance process that does not involve an intelligent designer.

We note that O is more likely on D than on C; we then conclude that with respect to this evidence, D is to be preferred to C.

Granted: we could not have existed if alpha had not been fine-tuned; hence we could not have observed that alpha is not fine-tuned; but how is that so much as relevant? The problem with the fishing argument is that I am arguing for a particular proportion of ten-inch fish by examining my sample, which, given my means of choosing it, is bound to contain only members that support the hypothesis in question. But in the fine-tuning case, I am certainly not trying to arrive at an estimate of the proportion of fine-tuned universes among universes generally. If I were, my procedure would certainly be fallacious; but that's not at all what I am doing. Instead, I am getting some information about alpha (nevermind that I couldn't have got information about any other universe, if there are other universes); and then I reason about alpha, concluding that D is to be preferred to C. There seems to be no problem there. Return to Eddington's fishing example, and suppose my net is bound to capture exactly one fish, one that is ten inches long. I then compare two hypotheses:

H_1 this fish had parents that were about 10 inches long

and

H_2 this fish had parents that were about 1 inch long.

My observing that the fish is ten inches long is much more probable on H_1 than on H_2; H_1 is therefore to be preferred to H_2 (with respect to this observation). This argument seems perfectly proper; the fact that I couldn't have caught a fish of a different size seems wholly irrelevant. The same goes for the fine-tuning argument.

B. Is the Relevant Probability Space Normalizable?

Lydia McGrew, Timothy McGrew, and Eric Vestrup propose a formal objection to the FTA; there is, they claim, no coherent way to state the argument.[20] Why not? We are talking about various parameters—the strength of the gravitational force, the weak and strong nuclear forces, the rate of expansion of the universe—that can take on various values. But it looks as if there are no logical limits to the values these parameters could take on:

> In each case, the field of possible values for the parameters appears to be an interval of real numbers unbounded at least in the upward direction. There is no *logical* restriction on the strength of the strong nuclear force, the speed of light, or the other parameters in the upward direction. We can represent their possible values as the values of a real variable in the half open interval [0, infinity].[21]

Now there are several parameters involved here, and in principle we must consider various sets of assignments of values to the whole ensemble of parameters; the idea, of course, is that some of these sets are life-permitting but others are not. In the interests of simplicity, however, we can pretend there is just one parameter, which is apparently fine-tuned. The thought is that it could (by chance) have assumed any positive value (its value could have been any positive real number you please); but it does in fact assume a value in a small life-permitting range. That it does so is much more likely on theism than on chance; hence this fine-tuning is evidence, of one degree of strength or another, for theism.

Well then, what is the objection?

20. McGrew et al., "Probabilities and the Fine-tuning Argument: A Skeptical View," in Manson, *God and Design*, p. 200.
21. McGrew et al., "Probabilities and the Fine-tuning Argument," p. 201.

The critical point is that the Euclidean measure function described above is not normalizable. If we assume every value of every variable to be as likely as every other—more precisely, if we assume that, for each variable, every small interval of radius e on R has the same measure as every other—there is no way to "add up" the regions of R so as to make them sum to one.[22]

But, they go on to say,

Probabilities make sense only if the sum of the logically possible disjoint alternatives adds up to one—if there is, to put the point more colloquially, some sense that attaches to the idea that the various possibilities can be put together to make up 100 percent of the probability space. But if we carve an infinite space up into equal finite-sized regions, we have infinitely many of them; and if we try to assign them each some fixed positive probability, however small, the sum of these is infinite.[23]

By way of illustration, consider flying donkeys. For each natural number n, it is logically possible, I suppose, that there be exactly n flying donkeys. Now suppose we think that for any numbers n and m, it is as likely (apart from evidence) that there be n flying donkeys as m; in order to avoid unseemly discrimination, therefore, we want to assign the same probability to each proposition of the form *there are exactly n flying donkeys*. Call this *non-discrimination*: each proposition is to get the same probability. Suppose we also assume (as McGrew et al. apparently do, although they don't mention it) *countable additivity*: the idea that for a countable set of mutually exclusive alternatives, the probability of any disjunction of the alternatives is equal to the sum of the probabilities of the disjuncts. Then obviously we can't assign the same non-zero probability to each of these propositions, there being infinitely many of them; if we did, their sum would be infinite, rather than one. On the other hand, if we assign a probability of zero to each, then, while we honor non-discrimination and countable additivity, the probability space in

22. McGrew et al., "Probabilities and the Fine-tuning Argument," p. 203.
23. McGrew et al., "Probabilities and the Fine-tuning Argument," p. 203.

question isn't normalizable; given countable additivity, the (infinite) sum of the probabilities assigned to those propositions is zero, not one.

The point is we can't have each of non-discrimination, countable additivity, and normalizability when assigning probabilities to these propositions. We can have countable additivity and normalizability if we are willing to violate nondiscrimination: we could assign probabilities in accord with some series that sums to one (for example, a probability of 1/2 to the first proposition, 1/4 to the second, 1/8 to the third, and so on). We can have non-discrimination and countable additivity if we are willing to forgo normalizability; for example, we could assign each a probability of zero, and their countable sum also a probability of zero (not an attractive possibility). We can have non-discrimination and normalizability if we are willing to fiddle with additivity: for example, we could assign each proposition zero probability but assign their infinite disjunction a probability of one. What we can't have is all three.

In the same way, if we consider any particular physical parameter—the velocity of light, for example—and if we respect non-discrimination by holding that for any natural numbers n and m, the velocity of light is as likely to be within one mile per second of n as of m, then we can't respect both countable additivity and normalizability. This means, according to McGrew et al., that the fine-tuning arguments involve a fundamental incoherence. For suppose that in order for life to be permitted, the velocity of light must be within a mile or two per second of its actual value: one couldn't properly erect a fine-tuning argument on that fact by arguing that it is much more probable that the velocity of light fall within that narrow range on theism than on chance. That is because if we respect non-discrimination and countable additivity, then the relevant probability measure isn't normalizable. There is no (logical) upper limit on the velocity of light; hence its velocity in any units could be any positive real number. Hence the interval within which its velocity could fall is infinite. Any way of dividing up that interval into equal subintervals will result in infinitely many subintervals. But then there is no way of assigning probabilities to those subintervals in such a way that the sum (given countable additivity) of the probabilities assigned is equal to 1: if any nonzero probability is assigned to each, the sum of those probabilities will be infinite, but if a probability of zero is assigned to each, the sum of the probabilities will be zero. A genuine probability measure, however, must be additive and normalizable. Hence no FTA involves a genuine probability measure; therefore FTAs are incoherent.

So say McGrew et al. I think we can see, however, that their objection is clearly defective: it proves too much. Imagine the night sky displaying the words: "I am the Lord God, and I created the universe." These words, a heavenly sign, as it were, are visible from any part of the globe at night; upon investigation they appear to be a cosmic structure with dimensions one light year by twenty light years, about forty light years distant from us. Following Collins, Swinburne, and others, one might offer an argument for theism based on this phenomenon: it is much more likely that there be such a phenomenon given theism than given chance.

But not if the McGrew et al. objection is a good one. For think about the parameters involved here—confine consideration to the length of the structure. Not just any length will be "message-permitting." Holding its distance constant, if the structure is too short, it won't be visible to us. But the same goes if it is too long—for example, if it is so long that we can see only a minute and uninterpretable portion of one of the letters. Therefore there is a "message permitting" band such that the length of this structure must fall within that band for it to function as a message. What are the logical constraints on the length of this structure? None; for any number n, it is logically possible that this structure be n light years long. (You might object that our universe is, or is at least at present thought to be, finite in extent; that, however, is a contingent rather than a logically necessary fact.) But if the structure can be any length whatever, this parameter, like those involved in the FTA, can fall anywhere in an infinite interval. This means that if we honor non-discrimination, the relevant probability measure isn't normalizable: we can't assign the same positive probability to each proposition of the form *the message is n light years long* in such a way that these probabilities sum to 1. Hence the McGrew claim implies that a design argument based on the existence of this message can't be coherently stated. But surely it can be; the fact is it would be powerfully persuasive. The objection is too strong in that it eliminates arguments that are clearly successful.

Nevertheless, the McGrew objection is certainly based on genuine intuitions. Suppose we have finitely many mutually exclusive and jointly exhaustive equi-probable possibilities: the relevant measure will assign each possibility the same probability; it will be additive; and the probabilities of these possibilities will sum to 1. We have non-discrimination, normalizability, and additivity. There are fifty-two cards in the deck; in a random draw, each card has the same probability (1/52) of being selected; the sum of these probabilities is 1. But things go awry when we move to infinite magnitudes. Suppose we have an infinite deck of cards: now we run into the difficulty noted above: we can no longer assign each card the same probability of being drawn in such a way that these probabilities sum, given countable additivity, to 1. As before, if we assign the same finite probability to each, the sum of these probabilities will be infinite; if we assign zero probability, the sum of the probabilities will be zero. We can't have all of non-discrimination, countable additivity and normalizability. We can preserve normalizability by asserting that the probability (given a drawing) that one or another of the cards will be drawn is 1, while the probability with respect to each card that it will be drawn is zero; but then of course we lose (countable) additivity. Or we can preserve countable additivity by assigning probabilities to the various cards in accord with some series that sums to 1: assign the first card a probability of 1/2, the second 1/4, and so on. But then we lose non-discrimination: we are not assigning them the same probability. We can also preserve countable additivity by assigning each of them together with their (infinite) disjunction a probability of zero: but then of course we lose normalizability.

Formally similar problems arise when we try to understand and generalize to the infinite case, our homely notions of length, area, and volume. Probability theory is a branch of measure theory, which grew out of attempts to deal satisfactorily with these geometrical notions. The history of measure theory is the history of attempts to come to an account of measure that deals properly with sets of infinite magnitude and is also intuitively satisfactory.[24] As it turns out, no wholly satisfactory account is possible. Thus H. L. Royden:

> Ideally, we should like m (the measure) to have the following properties: that m is defined for every set of real numbers, that the measure of an interval is its length, that the measure is countably additive, and that it is translation invariant. Unfortunately, as we shall see ... it is impossible to construct a set function having all of these properties.[25]

24. See Bas van Fraassen's *Laws and Symmetries* (Oxford: Oxford University Press, 1989), pp. 325–31 for a brief but instructive account (with further references) of this history.

25. Royden, *Real Analysis* (New York: Macmillan, 1968), pp. 53–54.

These problems with probability and infinite magnitudes arise at a more basic level. Suppose we think about logical probability in terms of possible worlds. Clearly, if there are only finitely many possible worlds, there's no problem: the logical probability of a proposition A will be the proportion of A worlds; the conditional probability of a proposition A on a proposition B will be the proportion of A worlds among B worlds, that is, the quotient of the number of worlds in which both A and B are true by the number of worlds in which B holds. If there are infinitely many possible worlds, however, there will be infinitely many mutually exclusive propositions (for any possible world W, for example, there will be the proposition that W is actual). And now problems rear their ugly heads. For example, suppose propositions form a countable set; each of the possible worlds is presumably as likely (on no contingent evidence) to be actual as any other; but (given countable additivity) clearly it won't be possible to assign each proposition of the form W *is actual* the same nonzero probability in such a way that these probabilities sum to 1.[26] And of course problems are only exacerbated if there are more than countably many possible worlds. Here as elsewhere infinity presents serious problems. One possibility, obviously, is to follow Leopold Kronecker and a host of finitary mathematicians and stoutly declare that there aren't any actual infinities. There may be quantities that approach infinity as a limit, but there aren't and couldn't be any actually infinite quantities. Given the various paradoxes of infinity (for example, Hilbert's hotel), this has a certain ring of sense. Whether it is actually true, however, is of course a monumentally contentious question.

With respect to our current topic, the McGrew et al. objection to the FTA: if we don't reject infinite magnitudes, perhaps the most sensible way to proceed is to give up countable additivity. The velocity of light could fall within each of infinitely many mutually exclusive and jointly exhaustive small intervals; the

---

26. It's not obvious that propositions form a set at all: for any set S of propositions, there is presumably the proposition that S is distinct from the Taj Mahal; but then the set of propositions (supposing there is one) will be as large in cardinality as its power set; and this conflicts with the theorem of ordinary set theories to the effect that the power set of a set S always exceeds S in cardinality. It is also far from obvious that if propositions form a set, they form a countable set: if there are actual infinities at all, it seems likely that there are uncountably many possible worlds. You are h inches tall; for any real number r in some interval centering on h, there is a possible world in which you are r inches tall.

probability that it falls within any particular one of these intervals is zero, but of course the probability that it falls within one or another of them is one. This seems to fit well with intuition, or at any rate as well or better than any other proposed solution. For example, suppose space is in fact infinite, and suppose it is divided into infinitely many mutually exclusive and jointly exhaustive cubes one cubic mile in volume. Suppose you know that exactly one of them contains a golden sphere of radius one-half mile. You will of course assign a probability of one to the proposition that one of them contains that golden sphere; but you won't assign any finite probability to the proposition, with respect to any particular cube, that it contains that sphere. No matter what the odds, you won't place a bet on the proposition, with respect to any particular cube, that it contains the sphere.[27]

But surely it is not the right remedy to follow McGrew et al. in accepting infinitary mathematics while refusing to countenance probabilistic arguments where the values of the quantities in question fall into intervals that are unbounded. With respect to the FTA, we can sensibly think of the matter as follows. Let C be the comparison range for the value of some parameter P—the strength of gravity, for example—and let L be the life-permitting range of values for P. The larger the ratio between C and L, the greater the fine-tuning of P. Say that P is fine-tuned to degree d (where d is a positive integer greater than 1) if C/L is greater than or equal to d. As C goes to infinity (given L finite), so does the degree to which P is fine-tuned; add that if C is actually infinite, P is maximally fine-tuned. McGrew et al. and others point out ("the coarse-tuning argument") that if we follow this course, we'll have to take any parameter with an infinite comparison range but a finite life-permitting range as maximally fine-tuned—even if the finite life-permitting range is very large; they propose this as a *reductio* of fine-tuning arguments with infinite comparison ranges. But better to reverse the argument: these coarse-tuning arguments are also good arguments, despite our initial distrust; this is just one more area where our intuitions get severely bent when we think about infinite magnitudes.

27. For a similar example, see Collins, "The Teleological Argument," in *The Blackwell Companion to Natural Theology*, ed. William Lane Craig and J. P. Moreland (London: Blackwell, 2009), p. 250.

C. Many Universes?

One of the most interesting responses to the FTA goes as follows: perhaps there are very many, even infinitely many different universes or worlds; the physical constants and other parameters take on different values in different worlds, so that very many (perhaps all possible) different sets of such values get exemplified in one world or another. If so, however, it's likely or inevitable that in some worlds these parameters take on values permitting life, and of course we would find ourselves in such a world. There are several ways to develop this thought. According to the inflationary "multiverse" suggestion, for example, in the very early history of the universe, an enormous number of subuniverses formed, these subuniverses displaying different values for those parameters. Another suggestion (surprisingly similar to the ancient stoics "palingenesia"): there is an eternal cycle of "big bangs," with subsequent expansion to a certain limit and then subsequent contraction to a "big crunch" at which those cosmological values are arbitrarily reset.[28] Under either scenario, it isn't at all surprising that in one or another of the resulting universes, the values of the physical constants are such as to be life-permitting. (Nor is it at all surprising that the universe in which we find ourselves has life-permitting values: how could we find ourselves in any other sort?) But then the FTA fails: if there are all those other universes, it is very likely that at least one of them should be fine-tuned, and of course we could only find ourselves in one that *is* fine-tuned.

What are these alternative universes supposed to be like; what sort of beast are they? First, we aren't talking about possible worlds in the usual philosopher's sense. On the most common way of thinking about possible worlds, they are abstract objects—maximal possible

28. See Daniel Dennett, *Darwin's Dangerous Idea* (Simon & Schuster, 1995), p. 179.

states of affairs, or propositions, perhaps.[29] The many universes of the many worlds objection are not, of course, abstract; they are not like propositions or states of affairs; they are concrete objects (or perhaps heaps of concrete objects). They are therefore much more like the possible worlds of David Lewis—spatiotemporally maximal concrete objects (that is, concrete objects that are spatiotemporally related only to themselves and their parts).[30] On the big bang/big crunch scenario, the many universes of the many worlds objection, like Lewis worlds, are also related, spatiotemporally, only to themselves and their parts.[31] On the inflationary scenarios, the universes may be spatiotemporally related to each other in that they form a branching structure, so that any two such universes share an initial segment. But of course the main thing to see here is that these universes are concrete, not abstract.

Here is one response to this many-worlds objection. True, given many universes displaying different sets of parameters, the probability that *one or another* of them will be fine-tuned, display a life-permitting set of parameters, is high. Perhaps it is as high as the probability that our universe, the one we find ourselves in, is fine-tuned, given theism. But how does that affect the probability that *our* universe, *this particular* universe is fine-tuned? Return to the Old West: I'm playing poker, and every time I deal, I get four aces and a wild card. The third time this happens, Tex jumps up, knocks over the table, draws his sixgun, and accuses me of cheating. My reply: "Waal, shore, Tex, I *know* it's a leetle

29. See, e.g., my *The Nature of Necessity* (Oxford: Clarendon Press, 1974).
30. Lewis, *On the Plurality of Worlds* (Oxford: Wiley Blackwell, 1986). They differ from Lewis worlds, however, in that, first, Lewis posits many more worlds—at least 2 to the power of the continuum—and second, for any kind of object (a donkey or a flea, for example) there is a Lewisian possible world that is an object of that kind. So some Lewis worlds are fleas, and others are donkeys.
31. Although those are usually thought of as occurring, not simultaneously, but in some kind of temporal order; the nature of the time in which they are thus related is not ordinarily discussed.

mite suspicious that every time I deal I git four aces and a wild card, but have you considered the following? Possibly there is an infinite succession of universes, so that for any possible distribution of possible poker hands, there is a universe in which that possibility is realized; we just happen to find ourselves in one where someone like me always deals himself only aces and wild cards without ever cheating. So put up that shootin' arn and set down'n shet yore yap, ya dumb galoot." Tex probably won't be satisfied; this multi-game hypothesis, even if true, is irrelevant. No doubt *someone* in one of those enormously many poker games deals himself all the aces and a wild card without cheating; but the probability that *I* (as opposed to someone or other) am honestly dealing in that magnificently self-serving way is very low. (In the same way, it is not probable that *I* will live to be 110 years old, although it is very likely that *someone or other* will.) It is vastly more likely that I am cheating; how can we blame Tex for opening fire? And doesn't the same go for the many-worlds objection to FTA? The fact, if it is a fact, that there are enormously many universes has no bearing on the probability (on atheism) that *this* universe is fine-tuned for life; that remains very low.

But suppose theism is true, and that there are very many universes: doesn't that mean that the probability that this universe is fine-tuned for life is small, perhaps as small as its probability on the atheistic many-universe hypothesis? After all, while it makes good sense to suppose God would want there to be life and indeed intelligent life, why think he would be especially interested in there being life in this particular universe?[32] I think there is a reasonably good reply here. Ever since the sixteenth century, many believers in God have supposed that the universe is teeming with life; if so, it is unlikely that Earth is the only place where God has created life. If theism is true and there is only one universe, the chances are

32. See White, "Fine-Tuning and Multiple Universes," *Nous* 34.

that intelligent life is to be found in many places in that universe. But in the same way, if theism is true and there are many universes, the chances are that a significant proportion of those universes contain life. So the sensible thing to think is that if theism is true and there are many universes, the proportion of universes that contain life is fairly high—much higher than the proportion of universes that contain life if the atheistic many-universe hypothesis is true. If so, the probability, with respect to any particular universe that it is fine-tuned, is greater given the theistic many-universe hypothesis than given the atheistic many-universe hypothesis. Hence the objection fails.

I said above that on the many-worlds hypothesis, it is likely that *some world or other* is fine-tuned for life, but no more likely that *this* world is thus fine-tuned: that remains as unlikely as ever. That response seems right in the above Old West poker scenario; but does it also work with those many other universes? Maybe not. As Neil Manson puts it,

> the "This Universe" objection helps itself to some non-obvious metaphysical assumptions, the most important of which is that the Universe could have taken different values for its free parameters.... whether the values of its free parameters are among the essential properties of a universe will depend, we think, on what a given multiverse theory says a universe is.[33]

The suggestion is that perhaps *our* universe *couldn't have had* different values for its parameters.[34] Let a, b, c, and d be the values displayed by the strength of the four fundamental forces in our universe: the suggestion is that our universe has essentially the property of being such that the strength of those four forces is a,

33. Manson, *God and Design*, p. 21.
34. "Our universe": this term is to rigidly denote the universe in which in fact we find ourselves. It is not to be taken as a definite description, e.g., as "the universe in which we find ourselves." It is therefore logically possible that we fail to exist in our universe; the sentence "we do not exist in our universe" does not express the same proposition as "we do not exist in the universe in which we find ourselves."

b, c, and d. In every possible world in which this universe exists, it is such that those forces display these values. This very universe could perhaps have been different in many ways: there are possible worlds, perhaps, in which it contains more or fewer stars, or more or fewer horses; but none in which it displays different values for those parameters. But then the probability that *this* universe should be fine-tuned for life is 1, and is 1 on any hypothesis—chance, design, whatever you like.

Is it plausible or reasonable to claim that this universe has these properties essentially? An important question, obviously, is one Manson raises: what sort of thing *are* these universes? A prior question: are these universes *things*—that is, substances—at all? We talk as if there are such things as heaps or piles of sand; but it is also plausible to think there really aren't any such things. There are (as we may suppose for purposes of argument) grains of sand; but it is not obvious that a multitude of grains of sand located close to each other combine to make up still another thing in addition to those grains of sand, namely a heap of them. In the same way, perhaps a universe is just an assemblage, a pile or heap of other things—stars and planets, or living things, or atoms, or elementary particles. So are there any such things as universes? Or is talk involving "universes" just a *façon de parler*, to be paraphrased into sentences that aren't even ostensibly about universes, but about things of other sorts—elementary particles, for example?

It would be nice if we didn't have to settle this difficult question in order to evaluate the multiverse objection. And perhaps we don't. For suppose there really aren't any such things as universes, but only (say) elementary particles and things composed of them—animals, for example. Then what would it mean to say that our universe has the property of being such that the strengths of those four forces are a, b, c, and d? Presumably that those elementary particles spatio-temporally related to us, and whatever is made of them, have the relevant properties. And to say that a universe has these properties *essentially* would just be to say that those elementary particles have these properties essentially. We can then restate the objection (to the "this universe" objection to the multiverse objection to the FTA): the elementary particles that are spatiotemporally related to those that are, say, parts of our body, have the above properties essentially. And then we can also restate our question: is it reasonable or plausible to hold that those elementary particles do have those properties essentially?

To begin with, we certainly don't *see* any impossibility in these particles' being such that the four forces display somewhat different strengths. There is certainly no contradiction there, and it does not seem that there is incoherence or impossibility in the broadly logical sense. Of course it is important, here, to distinguish carefully between *failing to see that there is an impossibility* and *seeing that there is no impossibility.* Our knowledge or grasp of such esoterica as quarks and gluons is pretty insubstantial; our failure to see that certain properties are essential to them is probably not of great significance. Our intuitions about elementary particles are faint and probably not worth a lot; they are too far from the areas where we have experience, too far from the areas where we can think to some purpose.

Still, we have stronger and more reliable intuitions about some of the things these particles compose—trees and animals, for example. And here it certainly seems that these things could exist even if the parameters in question had slightly different values. Aren't there possible worlds that are just like the actual world except that the law of gravity isn't inversely proportional to r^2, but to $r^{2o...o1}$? Isn't it possible in the broadly logical sense that you and I (more exactly, our bodies) should have existed even if the law of gravity had been different in that minute way? It certainly seems so.[35]

So how do things stand with the "essential properties" objection to the "this universe objection" to the "multiverse objection to the fine-tuning argument" (whew!)? It's clearly not a strong objection. The multiverse objection, recall, goes like this: it could be that there is no designer, but there are very many different universes, with the values of the parameters set at random or by chance; among them would be our universe, where the parameters are life-permitting. Given that there is this whole vast ensemble of universes, the probability that at least one of them is fine-tuned would be high; and (it is suggested) this is a good

35. But isn't it the whole point of fine-tuning to claim that living things such as trees and animals and you and I could not have existed, had these parameters had even minutely different values? First, the claim is not that life requires the precise values the constants do in fact display; for each of the constants there is a life-permitting *range* of values. Second, and more important, the claim is not that life *logically* requires that the constants fall into that range, i.e., that it is logically impossible that life arise when those values fall outside that range. The claim is much weaker: *given the laws (or regularities) that do in fact obtain,* those values must fall within those ranges if there is to be life.

counter to the FTA. The rejoinder: though it is indeed true that given many universes, the probability is high that at least one of them is fine-tuned, the same can't be said for the probability that *our* universe is fine-tuned; that probability remains what it was on the atheistic single-universe hypothesis. The counter-rejoinder from the opponents of the FTA: perhaps our universe could not have had values for its free parameters different from the ones it does have: it has those values *essentially*, in which case the probability that it is fined-tuned on any hypothesis is very high, indeed, 1. And the proper response to that is that there is certainly no reason at all to think that if there are many universes, they will have essentially the property of displaying the values, for those parameters, that they do in fact display. There isn't any reason at all to accept this essential properties objection.

Of course at this point the opponent of the FTA is not obliged to assert that our universe *is* essentially fine-tuned. It is enough if this is possible—that is, epistemically possible. It is enough if, for all we know, there are many different universes, and they have essentially the values for the four forces they do in fact display, or at any rate are such that those of them that are fine-tuned are essentially fine-tuned, or more weakly yet, that our universe is essentially fine-tuned. Is this epistemically possible? Is it true for all we know? Well, I doubt that we *know* that it is false. Of course to require that we know that it is false is to set the bar very high—with respect to arguments like this, we can seldom claim that we *know* that their premises are true (or for that matter false). It does seem that it is *epistemically unlikely* that our universe is essentially fine-tuned; after all, the whole discussion began with the fact that its being fine-tuned seems to be an enormous and fortuitous coincidence. And that means, I think, that the FTA survives this objection in reasonably good shape. The FTA is far from conclusive; it is epistemically probable, though by no means epistemically certain, that our universe could have failed to be fine-tuned; therefore the probability that it *is* fine-tuned, given the atheistic many-universe hypothesis, is low, much lower than on the hypothesis of theism. So far the FTA survives—bloody, perhaps, but unbowed.[36]

---

36. For a more complete evaluation of the FTA coming to a similar conclusion, see Collins, "The Teleological Argument."

D. Can We Come Up with the Relevant Probabilities?

There is still another objection to the FTA, one requiring a little stage setting. There are fundamentally three ways the FTA can be stated, three forms it can take. First, it can be thought of as an inference to the best explanation. The best explanation of the fine-tuning of our universe is theism; alternatively, theism is a better explanation of fine-tuning than any atheistic explanation; and that means that, at least with respect to the phenomenon of fine-tuning, theism is to be preferred to atheism. (Of course there may be other phenomena such that atheism explains *them* better than theism.)

Second, the argument can be stated in terms of Bayes' theorem, a theorem of the probability calculus, which tells us that the probability of a hypothesis H on evidence E is equal to the probability of H times the probability of E given H, divided by the probability of E. As specified to the case in hand:

$$P(T/F) = \frac{P(T) \times P(F/T)}{P(F)}$$

where T is theism and F is the proposition that our universe is fine-tuned. $P(T)$ and $P(F)$ are the *antecedent* probabilities of theism and fine-tuning. The antecedent probability of theism, we may say, is the probability of theism before the evidence of fine-tuning is taken into account; the antecedent probability of fine-tuning is its probability prior to our discovery that the universe is indeed fine-tuned for life.[37] The idea would be to compare the probability of theism, given fine-tuning, with the probability of the atheistic hypothesis, given fine-

---

37. There are problems with the notion of antecedent probabilities in this context (in particular, the problem of old evidence: see Bradley Monton, "God, Fine-tuning and the Problem of Old Evidence," *British Journal for the Philosophy of Science* (June 2006, 57 (2), 405 ff), but they don't essentially affect the line of argument we're pursuing.

tuning; and the thought would be that the former is greater than the latter. This would suggest that with respect to the evidence of fine-tuning, theism is to be preferred to atheism. That's the second way to take the FTA.

A third way: some philosophers, for example Elliott Sober, object to this way of stating the argument, claiming that those antecedent probabilities are too hard to discover—or perhaps too subjective, in that different people will make very different estimates of them. They therefore propose a "likelihood" version of the argument. In Bayes' theorem, the second term in the numerator (in the above example, "$P(F/T)$") is called the *likelihood*; in the likelihood version of the argument, we make no references to antecedent probabilities, but think only about the likelihoods. We compare the probability of fine-tuning given theism with the probability of fine-tuning given the atheistic hypothesis: $P(F/T)$ vs. $P(F/A)$. If the former is greater than the latter, then, again with respect to the evidence of fine-tuning, theism is to be preferred to atheism. We could put it like this: if fine-tuning is more to be expected given theism than given atheism, then the existence of fine-tuning confirms theism over atheism. The likelihood version of the FTA, therefore, claims that $P(F/T)$ is greater than $P(F/A)$, in which case theism is to be preferred to atheism, at least with respect to fine-tuning.

Now we can turn to the objection. Suppose we think about the likelihood version of the FTA: we are to compare $P(F/T)$ with $P(F/A)$. But can we make a sensible estimate of $P(F/T)$? Elliott Sober thinks not:

The problem is to say how probable it is, for example, that the vertebrate eye would have features F1,...Fn if the eye were produced by an intelligent designer..... The problem is that the design hypothesis confers a probability on the observation only when it is supplemented with further assumptions about what the Designer's goals and abilities would be if He existed.[38]

Sober is not thinking about the God of theism, here, but more broadly about a designer of some sort or other. Still, his problem can also be raised with respect to God. God is transcendent; his ways are not our ways; his purposes are inscrutable; can we really say how probable it is that God would create the vertebrate eye, or, more relevantly, would fine-tune the universe? Do we know enough about God to say what this probability is, even within very wide limits? Sober thinks not. If so, we can't sensibly claim that $P(F/T)$ is greater than $P(F/A)$.

But why can't we just add to theism those further assumptions Sober speaks of? Why not revise the theistic FTA by adding some further propositions to the hypothesis? For example, we could take the hypothesis to be, not just as

T There is such a person as God,

but as the proposition that

T* There is such a person as God and he wants there to be life;

$P(F/T^*)$ would certainly seem to be greater than $P(F/A)$.

That looks good, except that two can play at this game. Why can't the atheist, in response, beef up A to

A* There is no such person as God and the universe has a powerful intrinsic impulse towards the existence of life?

38. Sober, "The Design Argument," in Manson, p. 109.

$P(F/T^*)$ isn't obviously greater than $P(F/A^*)$. But the theist can then respond by replacing T^* with

T^{**} There is such a person as God, and he really, really wants there to be intelligent life of the sort requiring fine-tuning.

Of course the atheist can respond with an A^{**} on which fine-tuning is even more probable. What we get here is a sort of arms race in which each side can produce a series of hypotheses on which F is ever more probable; indeed, each can finally produce a hypothesis on which the probability of F is 1. You might think that these hypotheses become more and more improbable; but on the likelihood version of the argument, we don't take the prior probabilities of the hypotheses into account; hence in thinking about the likelihood version of the FTA, we can't raise this as an objection to the arms race. On the likelihood version of the argument, how can we determine which hypotheses are to be compared, i.e., how can we determine which are the right ones with respect to which to estimate the probability of fine-tuning? On the Bayes theoretic version of the FTA, it is the prior probabilities that perform that function; but on the likelihoods version we have to ignore them.

What this arms race problem really shows is that the FTA is pretty anemic if stated in the likelihood version. Sadly enough, something similar holds for the Bayes theoretic version. Here, of course, we do take the antecedent probabilities into account. But how do we figure out the antecedent probability of theism? What is the probability of theism, prior to the consideration of the evidence, if any, afforded by fine-tuning? There are serious problems in determining this. First, there is the problem with the modal status of theism. According to classical theism, God is a necessary being; he exists in every possible world; the probability of theism is therefore 1, and 1 on any evidence. Of course the atheist will think the probability of classical theism is 0;

if the proposition that there is such a person as God, conceived as a necessary being, is false, then it is necessarily false, in which case its probability is 0, and 0 on any evidence.

Suppose we turn from objective probability to epistemic probability, or from classical theism to a version in which theism is, if true, contingently true: we still have problems. The theist will assign a high probability here; the atheist a low probability; others a probability somewhere between these extremes; still others won't find themselves able to assign any probability at all to the proposition. So to whom is this argument addressed? It may possibly add a bit of confirmation for the theist; for the atheist it may slightly raise the probability of theism.[39] Perhaps the argument can carry the most weight with those who are prepared to assign a probability to theism, but one that is neither extremely high nor extremely low (provided they see their way past the many-worlds objection); perhaps it can sensibly be expected to cause them to modify their estimates of the probability of theism. It is fairly clear, however, that FTA, taken this way—that is, taken as involving antecedent probabilities—offers at best modest support for theism. Of course modest support is still support, and it is not to be disdained.

The third way in which the FTA can be construed is as an inference to the best explanation. We should note that inference to the best explanation isn't really *inference*: you aren't compelled by some rule of inference to accept a bad explanation of some phenomenon, even if that explanation is the best one you can think of. Suppose

---

39. See Bradley Monton, *Seeking God in Science: an Atheist Defends Intelligent Design* (Peterborough: Broadview Press, 2009). Monton is an atheist, and says that the FTA slightly raises the probability of theism, for him, but only slightly. On the other hand, see Antony Flew, *There Is a God: How the World's Most Notorious Atheist Changed His Mind* (New York: Harper, 2007). On the strength of scientific arguments for theism, in particular biological arguments, but also the argument from fine-tuning, the late Antony Flew renounced his atheism in favor of some form of deism.

there are six candidates; suppose the most probable among them has a probability of .2. Even if that explanation is the best one, you will quite properly refuse to accept it as the truth of the matter. And this points to a problem with the FTA construed as something like an inference to the best explanation; substantially the same problem that afflicts it construed Bayesianly. Part of what makes an explanation good or bad is its probability. My car won't start. A Brazilian tribesman might think it quite likely that it is inhabited by a malicious spirit who is out to give me trouble (or at least minor annoyances). That explanation doesn't commend itself to me, however—mainly because I think it very unlikely. Upon walking past the Notre Dame Stadium on a Saturday afternoon, we hear a roar from the crowd. I suggest the explanation is that there is a football game there with thousands of fans present and a small plane has just flown over, dropping many $1000 bills. That would certainly explain the roar, all right, but you very sensibly refuse to accept it because there are other, more probable explanations. So we are back at the antecedent probability of theism: whether theism is a good explanation of the phenomena depends in part on the antecedent probability of theism. And this will be no easier to fix in this case than in the case of the FTA taken Bayesianly.

The right conclusion, I think, is that the FTA offers some slight support for theism. It does offer support, but only mild support. Granted: this is not a very exciting conclusion, not nearly as exciting as the conclusion that the argument is extremely powerful, or the conclusion that it is wholly worthless. It does, however, have the virtue of being correct. In the next chapter we'll consider a different and more promising approach to the phenomena to which the FTA appeals.

Chapter 8

Design Discourse

I MICHAEL BEHE AND BIOLOGICAL ARGUMENTS

In the last chapter, we thought about cosmological fine-tuning arguments for the conclusion that our world has been designed.

There are biological arguments for the same conclusion. Chief among these are Michael Behe's. In *Darwin's Black Box* he created quite a stir by arguing that there are a number of structures and phenomena at the molecular level that display "irreducible complexity."[1] Behe then describes a number of molecular structures that, he says, are "irreducibly complex" in his sense: among them are the bacterial flagellum, the cilia employed by several kinds of cells for motion and other functions, the incredibly complex cascade of biochemical reactions and events that occur in vision, blood clotting, the transport of materials within cells, and the immune system. He doesn't say merely that there are such systems: he explains them in considerable and illuminating detail.

What exactly is irreducible complexity? According to Behe, "By *irreducibly complex* I mean a single system composed of several well-matched, interacting parts that contribute to the basic function, wherein the removal of any one of the parts causes the system to effectively cease functioning."[2]

---

1. Behe, *Darwin's Black Box: The Biochemical Challenge to Evolution* (New York: Simon and Schuster, 1996).
2. Behe, *Darwin's Black Box*, p. 39.

As an example, consider his account of the biochemistry of human vision, in particular the astounding series of events that take place at the molecular level when a photon strikes the retina. What happens is a stunning, multifarious concatenation of interconnected biochemical reactions and events. These are related in such a way that if any of them doesn't occur, or doesn't function properly, vision won't happen.[3]

According to Behe, there is no way in which this whole complex system could have evolved (from simpler systems, by way of the small, incremental steps required by a Darwinian explanation). That is because the system is irreducibly complex. And the significance of irreducible complexity is this:

> An irreducibly complex system cannot be produced directly (that is, by continuously improving the initial function, which continues to work by the same mechanism) by slight, successive modifications of a precursor system, because any precursor to an irreducibly complex system that is missing a part is by definition nonfunctional.[4]

Irreducibly complex structures and phenomena, therefore, can't have come to be, he says, by gradual, step-by step Darwinian evolution. These systems, then, present what Behe calls a Lilliputian challenge to (unguided) Darwinism; if he is right, he might also have said they present a Gargantuan challenge.

What is peculiarly interesting about his account of the biochemistry of vision is that the adequacy of Darwinian explanations of the eye has been a subject of dispute and controversy ever since Darwin's day. A great deal was known about the anatomy of the eye in the

---

3. Behe, *Darwin's Black Box*, pp. 18–22.
4. *Darwin's Black Box*, p. 39. Elsewhere Behe seems to suggest, not that such systems *cannot* be produced directly, but that it is prohibitively improbable that they should be so produced.

nineteenth century. It was known that the pupil is an adjustable shutter that closes down to let in the right amount of light to permit vision in bright sunlight, but also opens up in dim light. The lens focuses light in a sharp image on the retina; the lens is also adjustable; the ciliary muscle causes it to relax or contract in order to accommodate both near and distant vision; and the density of the lens changes over its surface to correct for chromatic aberration, thus permitting color vision. St. George Mivart, for example, pointed out as early as 1871 that there is a problem here for Darwinian explanations. Such explanations proceed in terms of natural selection operating on a source of genetic variation such as so-called random genetic variation. Obviously the various components of the eye must all work together to enable vision; so all these different parts would have to evolve in tandem. But an improvement to the lens (a step on the way to the present function of the lens) wouldn't automatically permit better vision, and in fact may interfere with it.

The problem, then, is to conceive of a series of steps through "design space" where (1) the first point is occupied by a design with no more than a light sensitive spot, as we find with certain relatively primitive animals; (2) each point (except the first) represents a design arising by way of heritable genetic variation (the main candidate is random genetic mutation) from the previous point; (3) divine or other guidance or causality is not involved in the transition from any point to the next; (4) each point is an adaptive step forward with respect to the previous point, or else a consequence, by way of spandrel or pliotropy, of a design that is such a step forward; (5) each point is not overwhelmingly improbable with respect to the previous point; and (6) the last point is occupied by (correlated with) the design of the human eye.[5]

---

5. A spandrel is a characteristic not itself adaptive developed as a side effect of an adaptive trait. Pleiotropy occurs when a single gene influences multiple traits; such a gene might be selected for by virtue of one of these traits, but nonetheless induce changes with respect to other of them. See also footnote 26 in chapter 1.

Naturally it isn't required that the Darwinist come up with the actual sequence of design plans here, or a sequence which could have been that actual sequence; what is required for a satisfying evolutionary account of the eye is perhaps more like a reasonably detailed specification of some important stages along the way. Darwin attempted to meet the challenge by pointing to a series of other animal eyes varying in complexity from a simple light sensitive spot, a patch of photoreceptors as in certain jellyfish, through cupped eyes (that is, a patch of photoreceptors at the bottom of a kind of cup, thus registering the direction from which the incident light is coming) as in marine limpets, and primitive eyes with a lens, as in marine snails. It's hard to say what exactly *is* required, and it is equally hard to say whether Darwinists have discharged their obligation to make the requisite specifications. Due to long familiarity, however, most people seem to have become accustomed to the problem, and tend for the most part to ignore it. (Of course similar problems beset proposed Darwinian accounts of other anatomical features and structures.)

Behe claims something stronger than just that Darwinian accounts of the structures he describes—vision, cilia, flagella, cellular transport, and so on—are extremely *difficult* to find. Sometimes, at least, he claims that there *aren't* any Darwinian accounts of any of these structures, and, by virtue of their irreducible complexity, there *won't be* any; such accounts can't possibly be given. What he proposes as an alternative, notoriously, is intelligent design.[6]

Not everyone is pleased. We are in the neighborhood of cultural conflicts ("culture wars") where feelings run high; the level of vitriol, vituperation and contempt heaped on Behe's unsuspecting head is really quite remarkable. There are screams of hysterical anguish, frenzied denunciations, accusations of treason (how could an actual scientist say things like this?), charges of deceit, duplicity, deviousness,

6. Behe, *Darwin's Black Box*, chapters 3–6 and pp. 192ff.

tergiversation, pusillanimity, and other indications of less than total agreement.[7] One is reminded of the medieval philosopher Peter Damian, who said that those who held a certain position (oddly enough, one different from his own) are contemptible, not worthy of a reply, and should instead be branded. Many of those who comment on Behe seem to think along similar lines. These screeds are not of course the sort of thing to which one can give an argumentative reply: they aren't so much arguments as brickbats.

Fortunately there are less hysterical replies to Behe's arguments. One of the best is by Paul Draper.[8] According to Draper, Behe fails to show that the systems he says are irreducibly complex are in fact irreducibly complex (that is, such that if they missed any of their parts, they couldn't function at all); some biochemists, Draper points out, have argued that they are not. Perhaps some of these systems could function, even if not as well, in the absence of one or more of their parts. There is also difficulty, here, about what constitutes a *part*: couldn't some of these systems function perfectly well in the absence of a molecule or two? So Behe's book doesn't really deliver what he says it will—at any rate he doesn't show that these systems are irreducibly complex in the sense he specifies. "A careful reading of the second part of his book," says Draper, "reveals that he rarely even claims (let alone proves) that all of the parts of the systems he discusses are required for those systems to function."[9] In a subsequent

---

7. "Despite Dr. Behe's training as a scientist, he has been brought up in a religious milieu, where answers by instant gratification are the norm"; his view is "silly, lazy, ignorant and intellectually abominable"; he deserts reason, instead "invoking that first resort of the intellectually challenged (that is, God)." Peter Atkins, review of *Darwin's Black Box*. Available at http://infidels.org/library/modern/peter_atkins/behe.html. Some of the reaction to Behe's work on the part of the scientific community—rivaling, as it does, the irrationality of extremist political discourse—would make a fascinating case-study in the sociology of science.

8. Draper, "Irreducible Complexity and Darwinian Gradualism: a Reply to Michael J. Behe," *Faith and Philosophy* 22 (2002), pp. 3–21.

9. Draper, "Irreducible Complexity," p. 12.

paper, Draper reports, Behe changes his definition of irreducible complexity to accommodate the above difficulties:

> This response presupposes a new definition of irreducible complexity, one that implies that a system is irreducibly complex even if it has working parts that are not essential for it to function, so long as it has (at least two) interacting and closely matched parts which are essential. Given this definition, it would seem that the biochemical systems Behe discusses are indeed irreducibly complex.[10]

Behe argues that there are no direct Darwinian routes to these complex phenomena. Draper points out however, that even if there aren't any direct Darwinian routes to these systems, there may still be various *indirect* Darwinian routes to them:

> The sort of route I have in mind occurs when an irreducibly complex and irreducibly specific system S that serves function F evolves from a precursor S* that shares many of S's parts but serves a different function F*. Notice that parts that S and S* share and that are required for F need not be required for F* even if they contribute to F*, and parts that are irreducibly specific relative to F may be only reducibly specific relative to F*. Thus, both the parts of S* and their specificity may have been gradually produced by a direct evolutionary path. Then one or more additional parts are added to S*, resulting in a change of function from F* to F. And relative to F, the parts and their specificity, which had not been essential for F*, are now essential.[11]

10. Draper, "Irreducible Complexity," p. 15.
11. Draper, "Irreducible Complexity," p. 20.

Finally, Draper ingeniously argues that Behe hasn't even shown that direct routes to the systems he discusses are impossible. It's important to note that the possibilities Draper suggests are merely abstract possibilities. Draper doesn't argue or even venture the opinion that in fact there are routes of these kinds that are not prohibitively improbable; he simply points out that Behe has not eliminated them. And of course this is quite proper, inasmuch as Draper is doing no more than evaluating Behe's argument. All he is trying to show is that Behe's conclusion doesn't deductively follow from his premises. Draper's conclusion:

> Since my objections concerning both complicated and simple direct routes establish only conceptual possibilities rather than probabilities, I believe Behe's most promising reply to these objections would be to admit the possibility of direct routes to irreducible complexity, but claim that, like indirect routes, they are very unlikely to produce the specific biochemical systems on which Behe builds his case. Of course, it would not be enough for Behe simply to *claim* that direct routes to these systems are very unlikely; he would need to argue for that claim. And it is an open question whether or not a good argument is available.[12]

As far as I can make out, Draper is right: Behe's argument, taken as Draper takes it, is by no means airtight. Behe has not demonstrated that there are irreducibly complex systems such that it is impossible or even monumentally improbable that they have evolved in a Darwinian fashion—although he has certainly provided Darwinians with a highly significant challenge. We have some of the same problems as with the fine-tuning argument of the last chapter: we don't have a good way to ascertain the probability of these irreducibly

12. Draper, "Irreducible Complexity," p. 26.

complex systems, given the Chance hypothesis, and we also don't have a good way to evaluate the probability of these phenomena, given an intelligent designer.

Behe fluttered the dovecotes again with his book *The Edge of Evolution*.[13] Like *Darwin's Black Box*, *Edge* argues that there are structures at the molecular level of life that could not have been produced by (unguided) natural selection. His argument is serious and quantitative, and is one of the few serious and quantitative arguments in this area. Consider the living cell, both prokaryotic and eukaryotic, with its stupefying complexity and its multitude of elaborately complex protein machines. According to Bruce Alberts, president emeritus of the National Academy of Sciences and no friend of Intelligent Design,

> as it turns out, we can walk and we can talk because the chemistry that makes life possible is much more elaborate and sophisticated than anything we students had ever considered. Proteins make up most of the dry mass of a cell. But instead of a cell dominated by randomly colliding individual protein molecules, we now know that nearly every major process in a cell is carried out by assemblies of 10 or more protein molecules. And, as it carries out its biological functions, each of these protein assemblies interacts with several other large complexes of proteins. Indeed, the entire cell can be viewed as a factory that contains an elaborate network of interlocking assembly lines, each of which is composed of a set of large protein machines.[14]

Behe argues that natural selection (and again, I believe he means *unguided* natural selection) is very probably incapable of producing these

13. Behe, *The Edge of Evolution: The Search for the Limits of Darwinism* (New York: The Free Press, 2007).
14. Alberts, "The Cell as a Collection of Protein Machines: Preparing the Next Generation of Molecular Biologists," *Cell*, (1998) 92(3): 291–94.

protein machines. His argument is quantitative and empirical rather than a priori; its centerpiece is the saga of the malaria parasite, *Plasmodium falciperum*, and its long trench warfare with the human genome.

I won't go into his argument here, but the brief overview, in Behe's own words, is as follows:

> In its battle with poison-wielding humans, the malaria genome has... been terribly scarred. In the past half century a number of genes have been broken or altered to fend off drugs such as chloroquine.... Has the war with humanity caused malaria to evolve any new cellular protein-protein interactions? No. A survey of all known malarial evolutionary responses to human drugs includes *no* novel protein-protein interactions.
>
> Since widespread drug treatments first appeared about fifty years ago, more than 10^{20}, a hundred billion billion, malarial cells have been born in infested regions. It thus appears that the likelihood of the development of a new, useful, specific protein-protein interaction is less than one in 10^{20}.[15]

Behe goes on to argue that we get roughly the same results from an examination of the AIDS virus and its battle with the various drugs employed to combat it; here too there have been roughly 10^{20} examples of this virus over the past several decades, during which it has been assaulted by the drugs used to combat it, but in this case too, no new protein-protein interaction sites have arisen. But if it takes 10^{20} organisms to develop one new protein-protein interaction site, then a mutation issuing in two new (simultaneous) protein-protein interaction sites will require 10^{40} organisms.[16] Estimates of the total number

15. Behe, *The Edge of Evolution*, p. 136.
16. "Simultaneous": the thought is that if they didn't develop simultaneously, the first mutation would be selected against and disappear before the second showed up.

of organisms that have so far come to be in the history of Earth put that number at less than 10^{40}. But then, so the thinking goes, it will be improbable that unguided natural selection should produce three protein-protein interaction sites in the history of Earth, and enormously improbable that it should produce the large protein machines involving assemblies of 10 or more proteins of which Alberts speaks.

Reviews of *The Edge of Evolution* by mainstream biologists have been predictably hostile.[17] But again, the high proportion of vitriol, invective, mockery, ridicule, and name-calling makes it hard to trust these reviews. In addition, the reviewers seem to suffer from an inability to pay attention to what Behe actually says. For example, Dawkins and Jerry Coyne both point out that artificial selection over the last few millennia has produced very different breeds of dogs, as if this somehow counted against Behe's thesis. But of course it doesn't; these different breeds of dogs do not involve new protein-protein interaction sites. Behe sets the "edge of evolution" at the level of orders, families, and genera; unguided evolution, he thinks, could produce new species, and therefore could certainly produce new varieties of the same species, as with dogs.[18] A stronger criticism is that Behe's sample may be biased; *P. falciperum* and the HIV virus involve host-parasite interaction, and perhaps what holds for host-parasite interaction doesn't hold generally. Perhaps; to see whether this is in fact so will of course require further empirical work. Still another criticism: where two or more new protein-protein interaction sites are required, perhaps one of these appears, and is in some way adaptive, so that it persists until the other also appears.

But suppose, just for purposes of argument, that the criticisms are ineffective. How shall we think of Behe's argument? The conclusion

---

17. See, e.g., reviews by Sean Carroll (*Science*, June, 2007), Jerry Coyne "The Great Mutator," (*The New Republic*, June, 2007), and Richard Dawkins, "Inferior Design" (*New York Times Sunday Book Review*, July 1, 2007).
18. Behe, *The Edge of Evolution*, p. 218.

of the argument is that the living cell, with all its protein machines, is the product of intelligent design. How does the argument go? One possibility: the main alternative to intelligent design is unguided evolution, but the probability that unguided evolution should produce these protein machines is so low that we must conclude that it is false. Is this right? Not clearly. First, exceedingly improbable things do happen, and happen all the time. Consider a deal in a hand of bridge. If you distribute the fifty-two cards into four groups of thirteen cards each, there are some 10^{28} possible combinations. Therefore the probability that the cards should be dealt just as they are dealt is in the neighborhood of 10^{-28}. So consider a rubber of bridge that takes four deals: the probability that the cards should be dealt precisely as they are, for those four deals, is about 10^{-112}. At any given time, there are certainly at least 1000 rubbers of bridge being played in living rooms and rest homes around the world; the probability that the cards should be dealt just as they are dealt for those rubbers will be about $10^{-112,000}$. That is an overwhelmingly small probability; yet the thing happens. What is the probability that unguided evolution should produce these protein machines? Is it less than $10^{-112,000}$? How can we tell? We don't have anything like the means of making the relevant calculations.

Well, should we instead compare P(protein machines/unguided evolution), the probability of the existence of these protein machines given unguided evolution, with P(protein machines/intelligent designer), the probability of the existence of these protein machines given the existence of an intelligent designer? Here, again, the problem is that we don't have a very good grasp of either of those probabilities. Surely P(protein machines/unguided evolution) is low; but it is hard *in excelsis* to say *how* low. P(protein machines/intelligent designer) is also really hard to determine. Suppose there is an intelligent designer: how likely is it that he or she (or it) would design and cause to come to be just *these* protein machines? *Intelligent designer* as a description is so generic that it is hard to make much of a guess here. As Behe puts it,

> I strongly emphasize that it is not an argument for the existence of a benevolent God..... Thus, while I argue for design, the question of the identity of the designer is left open. Possible candidates for the role of designer include: the God of Christianity; an angel–fallen or not; Plato's demiurge; some mystical new-age force; space aliens from Alpha Centauri; time travelers; or some utterly unknown intelligent being.[19]

An intelligent designer that really hated life, or proteins, or protein machines, would be very unlikely to design protein machines; one that really liked protein machines would probably design some. But an intelligent designer just as such—I don't think we can make any very good guesses here. It is therefore exceedingly difficult to compare P(protein machines/unguided evolution) with P(protein machines/intelligent designer). My guess is that the latter is greater than the former; this isn't just obvious, however, and it is unclear that the difference in probability is sufficient to constitute serious support for the existence of an intelligent designer.

II *PERCEIVING* DESIGN?

In this chapter and the last we have been thinking about fine-tuning arguments for design, and Behe's biological arguments for design. We

---

19. Behe, "The Modern Intelligent Design Hypothesis," in Neil Manson *God and Design* (London and New York: Routledge, 2003), p. 277. It's worth noting, in this connection, that the probability of these protein machines given the existence of *God* (as theists think of him) seems to be considerably higher than the probability given just a generic intelligent designer.

have been calling them, naturally enough, "arguments." But perhaps
there is a better way to think about what is going on here. You are hik-
ing up Ptarmigan Ridge towards Mt. Baker in the North Cascades;
your partner points out a mountain goat on a crag about two hundred
yards distant. She thus gets you to form a belief—that there is a
mountain goat there. But of course she doesn't do so by giving you an
argument (you are appeared to in such and such a way; most of the
time when someone *S* is appeared to that way there is a mountain
goat about two hundred yards distant in the direction *S* is looking).
Perhaps what is going on in the arguments like Behe's, as well as the
fine-tuning arguments of the last chapter, can be better thought of
as like what is going on in this sort of case, where it is *perception*
(or something like it) rather than argument that is involved.[20]

Fine-tuning and Behe-type arguments are ordinarily thought of
as contemporary versions of a venerable theistic argument, the
so-called "argument from design" (although a better name would be
"argument *for* design" or *to* design). Design arguments go back to the
"fifth way" of Thomas Aquinas and can also be found in the ancient
world.[21] A particularly well known (and often cited) version is due to
William Paley (1743–1805):

In crossing a heath, suppose I pitched my foot against a *stone*, and
were asked how the stone came to be there, I might possibly
answer, that, for anything I knew to the contrary, it had lain there
for ever; nor would it perhaps be very easy to show the absurdity
of this answer. But suppose I had found a *watch* upon the ground,

20. This suggestion is explored in detail by Del Ratzsch in his "Perceiving Design" in *God and Design*, pp. 124ff, to which I am heavily indebted in what follows. In this connection, see also *Design Arguments Within a Reidian Epistemology*, Ph.D. dissertation by John Mullen, Notre Dame, 2004.
21. Aquinas, *Summa Theologiae* I, q. 2, a. 3. In the ancient world see for example Diogenes; G. S. Kirk and J. E. Raven, *The Presocratic Philosophers: A Critical history with a Selection of Texts* (Cambridge: Cambridge University Press, 1957), p. 433.

and it should be inquired how the watch happened to be in that place, I should hardly think of the answer which I had before given, that, for any thing I knew the watch might have always been there. Yet why should not this answer serve for the watch as well as for the stone? Why is it not as admissible in the second case as in the first? For this reason, and for no other, namely, that, when we come to inspect the watch, we perceive (what we could not discover in the stone) that its several parts are framed and put together for a purpose.[22]

Paley goes on to describe in more detail what we perceive, citing the intricacy of the design of the parts, the precision with which the various parts fit together to accomplish their function, the dependence of each part on others, and the like. He then claims that the same holds with respect to various features of the organic world: here too, he proposes, we can perceive design.

Every indication of contrivance, every manifestation of design, which existed in the watch, exists in the works of nature; with the difference, on the side of nature, of being greater and more, and that in a degree which exceeds all computation. I mean that the contrivances of nature surpass the contrivances of art, in the complexity, subtlety, and curiosity of the mechanism; and still more, if possible, do they go beyond them in number and variety; yet, in a multitude of cases, are not less evidently mechanical, not less evidently contrivances, not less evidently accommodated to their end, or suited to their office, than are the most perfect productions of human ingenuity.[23]

22. Paley, *Natural Theology: or, Evidences of the Existence and Attributes of the Deity*, 12th ed. (London: J. Faulder, 1809), pp. 1–2.
23. Paley, *Natural Theology*, pp. 17–18.

Paley devotes special attention to the eye, which he compares in detail to a telescope.

Now there are several ways in which this argument can be taken. Hume, for example, in his famous criticism of the argument in his *Dialogues Concerning Natural Religion*, sometimes seems to take it as an argument from analogy: the "contrivances of nature" resemble the contrivances of human beings; the latter are designed; therefore probably the former are too. At other times Hume seems to construe it as a straightforward inductive argument: all the things that exhibit "that curious adaptation of means to ends" which are such that we have been able to determine whether they are the product of design, *are* the product of design: therefore probably all things that exhibit that feature are the product of design; the contrivances of nature exhibit that feature; therefore probably they are the product of design.[24] It can also be formulated as a so-called inference to the best explanation; roughly speaking, the argument taken this way claims that design, perhaps divine design, is the best explanation for various features—in particular biological systems—of the natural world. Paul Draper understands it this way, and states it as follows:

1. Some natural systems (e.g., the human eye) are mechanically ordered (i.e., they exhibit the same sort of order as watches and other machines produced by human beings).

2. Intelligent design is a very good explanation of mechanical order.

3. No other explanation (or no equally good explanation) of mechanical order is available.

4. Every instance of mechanical order has an explanation.

24. For an examination of Hume's criticism of the argument, see Elliott Sober, *Philosophy of Biology* (Boulder, Colo.: Westview Press, 1993), pp. 34–35.

So,

    5. Some natural systems were (probably) designed.[25]

There are still other ways of putting the argument. In the last chapter we saw that fine-tuning arguments can be stated in Bayesian fashion, as employing antecedent probabilities, but also as likelihood arguments, which eschew antecedent probabilities; Paley's argument too can be stated these two ways.

III DESIGN *ARGUMENT* VS. DESIGN *DISCOURSE*

Taken any of these ways, however, what we have is a discursive argument, something with premises and a conclusion. But there is a wholly different way of thinking about this alleged argument. To appreciate this different way, suppose we make a brief detour. Consider our knowledge of other persons, in particular our knowledge of their mental states. I sometimes know of another that she is bored, resentful, or euphoric, that she believes that Berlin, Michigan is smaller than Berlin, Germany, that she intends to go to graduate school, believes in God, accepts Darwinism, and the like. How do I know these things? One traditional suggestion is that I know them by way of inference or argument of some kind. Perhaps I know about others by way of an analogical argument (note the connection with Paley's argument taken as an analogical argument): when I'm in a certain mental state, for example, pain, I behave in a certain way— writhing and screaming, perhaps.[26] I see someone else, more exactly

---

25. "Irreducible Complexity and Darwinian Gradualism: a Reply to Michael J. Behe," *Faith and Philosophy* 19:1 (2002), pp. 3, 8–9. Elliott Sober (*Philosophy of Biology*, p. 30) understands it the same way.

26. See my *God and Other Minds: A Study of the Rational Justification of Belief in God* (Ithaca, N.Y.: Cornell University Press, 1967, 1990), chapters 4 and 8.

another human body, writhing and screaming, and conclude that there is a self connected with that body, a self that is in pain. Alternatively, perhaps the argument is an inference to the best explanation; the best explanation I can think of for the bodily phenomena I perceive is that the body is animated by a mind with the mental properties in question.

The fact is, though, we don't come to believe these things in those ways. As Thomas Reid puts it,

> No man thinks of asking himself what reason he has to believe that his neighbour is a living creature. He would be not a little surprised if another person should ask him so absurd a question; and perhaps could not give any reason which would not equally prove a watch or a puppet to be a living creature.
>
> But, though you should satisfy him of the weakness of the reasons he gives for his belief, you cannot make him in the least doubtful. This belief stands upon another foundation than that of reasoning; and therefore, whether a man can give good reasons for it or not, it is not in his power to shake it off.[27]

Surely Reid is right? We don't in fact come to hold these beliefs by way of argument. I look at Paul and say to myself "Oh, oh, he's furious again—what have I done this time?" thus forming the belief that he is furious again. Do I form this belief by way of a quick but tacit induction, or an application of an analogical argument from premises involving the proposition that he looks a certain way, and when *I* look that way I am ordinarily furious? Clearly not. First, it seems that I don't ordinarily form any belief (any explicit belief, anyway) at all as

27. Reid, *Essays on the Intellectual Powers of Man* (1785) in *Inquiry and Essays,* ed. Ronald Beanblossom and Keith Lehrer (Indianapolis: Hackett Publishing Co., 1983), VI, 5, pp. 278–79. See also my *God and Other Minds* and *Warrant and Proper Function* (New York: Oxford University Press, 1993), chapter 4.

to how Paul is looking: I move directly to the view that he is furious. Perhaps I *could* form such a belief: but typically I don't. I don't form a belief about how Paul looks and sounds ("his brow is knit; his eyes are narrowed to slits; his mouth is wide open; loud noises of such and such timber and pitch emanate therefrom"). And even if I did form such a belief, it would be far too crude to play the role of a premise in a decent analogical argument: any such description would fail to distinguish the way he looks from a thousand other ways which do not warrant the belief that he is furious.

Further, I sometimes ascribe to others emotions I have seldom if ever experienced myself; I could hardly do this on the basis of simple analogical reasoning from correlations between behavior and mental states in my own case. Moreover, much of the relevant behavior is such that I *can't* observe it in my own case: facial expression, for example, is extremely important, and I typically can't observe what sort of facial expressions I am presenting to the world. Of course we have mirrors; but our ancestors, prior to the advent of mirrors, no doubt sometimes knew that someone else was angry or in pain.[28] And we ourselves form these beliefs without adverting to mirrors; how many of us carry a mirror, or (when in the grip of strong emotion) remember to consult it in order to establish correlations between mental states and facial expressions?

No doubt we come to beliefs about the mental states of others on the basis, somehow, of perception of their behavior: but not by way of an analogical or inductive inference from what we have observed

28. Reid goes on:
That many operations of the mind have their natural signs in the countenance, voice and gesture, I suppose every man will admit..... The only question is, whether we understand the signification of those signs, by the constitution of our nature, by a kind of natural perception similar to the perceptions of sense; or whether we gradually learn the signification of such signs from experience, as we learn that smoke is a sign of fire..... It seems to me incredible, that the notions men have of the expressions of features, voice, and gesture, are entirely the fruit of experience. *Essays*, VI, 5, pp. 278–79.

about the connection between those bodily states and those mental states in our own case; if we did, our beliefs would not be well-founded and would certainly not constitute knowledge.[29] Small children apparently form beliefs about the mental states of their parents long before they come to the age at which they make inductive inferences. The capacity for this sort of belief formation is not something one gains by inductive learning; it is instead part of our native and original cognitive equipment.[30] We might put it by saying that we form beliefs of this sort in the basic way, not on the evidential basis of other beliefs, other propositions we believe. That is to say, we don't form these beliefs on the basis of inference. It is rather that we are hard-wired, as they say, to form these beliefs in certain experiential circumstances.

This account of belief formation is not, of course, restricted to beliefs about other minds. The same goes for beliefs about the past. I remember what I had for breakfast: Irish oatmeal; and of course I take it that my having breakfast was in the past. I don't form this belief—that it was in the *past* that I had breakfast—on the basis of any arguments: I simply remember it, which automatically involves the idea of the past, and automatically refers the event in question to the past. Indeed, it is exceedingly hard to see how I *could* acquire the thought that there are past events by way of an argument. What would be the premises? The same goes for perception: I look out the window and form the belief that the trees in my backyard are turning green. I don't ordinarily form this belief on the basis of an inference (the

---

29. See my *Warrant and Proper Function*, pp. 65–71.

30. Indeed, tiny babies, presumably at an age at which they form little by way of beliefs of any sort, respond to human-face-like figures differently than to figures made of the same parts but scrambled: "It also appears that some of the capacity to establish spatial relations is manifested by the visual system from a very early age. For example, infants of 1–15 weeks of age are reported to respond preferentially to schematic face-like figures, and to prefer normally arranged face figures over 'scrambled' face patterns (Fantz, 1961)." Shimon Ullman, "Visual Routines" in *Visual Cognition*, ed. Steven Pinker (Cambridge: The MIT Press, 1985), p. 99. The reference to Fantz is to R. L. Fantz, "The Origin of Form Perception," *Scientific American* 204 (5), pp. 66–72.

trees look as if they are turning green; usually, when things look that way they *are* turning green; therefore . . .). Instead, I form this belief in the basic way; I have been forming perceptual beliefs in this way ever since I was a small child, and the same, I daresay, goes for you.

How we form these beliefs is important along several different dimensions, but it is particularly relevant to the question how much warrant, or justification, or positive epistemic status the beliefs in question have. Based on a tenuous analogical inference or a speculative explanatory conjecture, these beliefs wouldn't have anything like the degree of warrant or positive epistemic status they actually do have; this basis wouldn't warrant anything like the degree of confidence we actually invest in them. They would then be more like risky conjectures or guesses than beliefs that are solidly grounded and can indeed constitute knowledge. On the other hand, if they are formed in the basic way, then they might very well constitute knowledge. For suppose (as seems to me to be true) that a belief *B* has *warrant*, that property or quantity enough of which is what distinguishes mere true belief from knowledge, just if *B* is formed by cognitive faculties functioning properly in the sort of environment for which we were designed (by God or evolution) according to a design plan successfully aimed at the production of true beliefs.[31] Then if these beliefs about external objects, or the past, or the mental states of others are formed in the basic way, they could certainly constitute knowledge. And this is so even if there aren't any very good arguments for them. This sort of belief formation is not a result of movement from one set of beliefs (premises) to another (conclusion), but from a set of circumstances (being appeared to a certain way, for example) to a belief.

Now suppose we return to Paley's so-called design argument. Hume takes such arguments to be inductive or analogical; Draper

---

31. See my *Warrant and Proper Function*, chapters 1 and 2.

takes Paley's version to be an argument to the best explanation. But there is a quite different way of interpreting it: this so-called design inference isn't a matter of inference or argument at all. I encounter something that looks designed and form the belief that it is designed: perhaps this isn't a matter of argument at all (anymore than in the case of perception or other minds). In many cases, so the thought goes, the belief that something or other is a product of design is not formed by way of inference, but in the basic way; what goes on here is to be understood as more like *perception* than like *inference*.[32]

Paley himself suggests something along these lines: "When we come to inspect the watch," he says, "we perceive—what we could not discover in the stone—that its several parts are framed and put together for a purpose."[33] We *perceive* this, he says: we don't *argue* to this conclusion, or infer it. William Whewell (1794–1866) makes a similar proposal: "When we collect design and purpose from the arrangements of the universe, we do not arrive at our conclusion by a train of deductive reasoning, but by the conviction which such combinations as we perceive, immediately and directly impress upon the mind."[34] We don't arrive at the conclusion by a train of deductive reason; rather there is an immediate and direct impression. Whewell speaks of "deductive reason" here; no doubt he wasn't thinking of deductive arguments in particular, but of arguments more generally, whatever their form. Indeed, Darwin himself sometimes seems to acquiesce in the same conclusion. The Duke of Argyle recounts a conversation he had with Darwin a year before Darwin died:

> I said to Mr. Darwin with reference to some of his own remarkable works on the *Fertilisation of Orchids*, ... and various other

32. Again, here I am heavily indebted to Del Ratzsch; see "Perceiving Design."
33. Paley, *Natural Theology*, pp. 1–2.
34. Whewell, *Astronomy and General Physics: Considered with Reference to Natural Theology* (London: William Pickering, 1834); quoted in Ratzsch, "Perceiving Design," p. 125.

observations he made of the wonderful contrivances for certain purposes in nature—I said it was impossible to look at these without seeing that they were the effect and the expression of Mind. I shall never forget Mr. Darwin's answer. He looked at me very hard and said, "Well, that often comes over me with overwhelming force; but at other times" and he shook his head vaguely, adding "it seems to go away."[35]

This idea comes over him "with overwhelming force": that sounds more like something in the neighborhood of perception than the result of an argument.

This is a sensible (perhaps even compelling) way to understand Paley.[36] Taking him this way, we should no longer think of what he writes in these chapters as the provision of an argument, whether inductive, or analogical, or an inference to the best explanation, or whatever. But then what *is* he doing? At least two things. Sometimes he is calling attention to the sorts of beliefs we do in fact find ourselves forming, or inclined to form: "When we come to inspect the watch," he says, "we perceive—what we could not discover in the stone—that its several parts are framed and put together for a purpose."[37] In this context he then asks us to note or remember that there is that same movement of the mind in the case of "the contrivances of nature."[38] Other times what he seems to be doing can perhaps be described as putting us in the sorts of situations in which design beliefs are in fact

35. George Douglas Campbell, Eighth Duke of Argyll, "What is Science?" in *Good Words* 1885; quoted in Ratzsch, "Perceiving Design," p. 124.
36. I say this is a good way to understand Paley, but my aim here is not to contribute to Paley scholarship. I mean to explore this thought as a suggestion as to how best to understand design.
37. Paley, *Natural Theology*, p. 2.
38. See chapter 5 on HADD, that alleged hypersensitive agency detector device. Perhaps what Paley asks us to note is another special case of HADD. Of course that doesn't in the least compromise this "movement of the mind," or suggest that it is misleading or unreliable; see pp. 141.

formed, as when he describes the exquisite and enormously articulate structure of the eye, with its many parts that fit together in such a way that they cannot function without each other:

> Knowing as we do what an eye comprehends, namely, that it should have consisted, first, of a series of transparent lenses—very different, even in their substance, from the opaque materials of which the rest of the body is, in general at least, composed, and with which the whole of its surface, this single portion of it excepted, is covered: secondly, of a black cloth or canvas—the only membrane in the body which is black—spread out behind these lenses, so as to receive the image formed by pencils of light transmitted through them; and placed at the precise geometrical distance at which, and at which alone, a distinct image could be formed, namely, at the concourse of the refracted rays: thirdly, of a large nerve communicating between this membrane and the brain; without which, the action of light upon the membrane, however modified by the organ, would be lost to the purposes of sensation.[39]

Construed in this way, Paley is not proposing an argument; he is instead directing our attention to the way we are inclined to form design beliefs in certain circumstances, and trying to get us into those circumstances by describing in detail what those "contrivances of nature" are like; he is trying to get us to recall design beliefs, and put us in situations in which we form design beliefs. What should we call this activity? There is no familiar name; I'll just speak of design *discourse* as opposed to a design argument.

Now the fact is, of course, that Paley wasn't thinking of this distinction between design arguments and design discourses, and plumping for the latter. What he says sometimes sounds like a design

---

39. Paley, *Natural Theology*, p. 2.

argument (often like an argument from analogy) and other times like a design discourse. We need not try to decide which interpretation fits Paley better; that doesn't really matter for my purposes. What I mean to stress, here, is that there are these two possibilities: there are non-argumentative design discourses as well as design arguments. Note further that the recognition of non-argumentative design discourses fits in well with the way in which we typically form beliefs about other minds. Indeed, insofar as design entails mental states on the part of some other person (the designer), the belief that a given object has been designed *is* a mental state-ascribing belief. If our other beliefs about minds, the mental states of others, are formed in that basic way, it is not implausible to suppose that the same goes for this sort of belief. The idea would be, therefore, that when you are on that walk with Paley and encounter a watch, you don't make an *inference* to the thought that this object is designed; instead, upon examining the object, you form the belief in that immediate or basic way. The same goes if you are on a voyage of space exploration, land on some planet which has an earth-like atmosphere, but about which nothing or next to nothing is known, and come across an object that looks more or less like a 1929 Model T Ford. You would certainly see this object as designed; you would not engage in probabilistic arguments about how likely it is that there should be an object like that that was not designed. You might also encounter something that was obviously designed, but such that you had no idea what its function was; you don't have to know what the function is in order to perceive that it has been designed by a conscious, intelligent agent.

IV THE DIFFERENCE IT MAKES

"Well," you say, "perhaps we could think of these situations where we form design beliefs along the above lines, but so what? Why should that be of any particular interest?" I think it *is* of interest, and in fact of very considerable interest. First, the suggestion is that you come to form design beliefs, at least on some occasions, in the basic way. If so, the belief in question can have warrant or positive epistemic status, indeed, a great deal of warrant or positive epistemic status for you, even if you don't know of any good argument from other beliefs for the belief in question—even, indeed, if there *aren't* any good arguments of that sort. As we've seen, this is how it goes with our beliefs about the mental states of others; but the same goes for our perceptual beliefs.[40] The same also goes for our beliefs about the past; as Bertrand Russell pointed out, it is consistent with our evidence that the world, complete with its crumbling mountains, wrinkled faces, and apparent memories, popped into existence five minutes ago.[41] In all of these cases, it is exceedingly hard to find good arguments for the conclusions in question; but surely you often do know such things as that the flowers in the backyard are blooming, or that Martha is thinking about what to make for supper, or that you went for a walk earlier this afternoon. Perhaps the same goes for design beliefs; perhaps one can't find a way of formulating much of an argument for the conclusion that hearts, for example, are designed, even though the belief to that effect, formed upon seeing how they are constructed and how they work, has a good deal of warrant.

Secondly, there is a difference here in the way in which the beliefs in question can be criticized, or refuted. Beliefs formed in the basic

---

40. The dialectic of modern philosophy from Descartes to Hume overwhelmingly supports the idea that there are no good (noncircular) arguments for the existence of an external world. See William P. Alston's landmark book, *The Reliability of Sense Perception* (Ithica: Cornell University Press, 1993). What is the connection between *perceiving* that something is designed, and *seeing* that thing *as* designed? I'm inclined to think that many cases of perceiving that a thing x has property P are cases of seeing x as having P. Perceiving that the thing before me has such and such shape and color doesn't, perhaps, involve seeing it *as* shaped and colored; perceiving that it is a tractor, however, does involve seeing it as a tractor.

41. Russell, *The Analysis of Mind;* see also my *Warrant and Proper Function,* chapter 3.

way are not, of course, immune to criticism. To return to an example from chapter 6, I look into a field, see what looks like a sheep, and form the belief that there is a sheep in the field. You, whom I know to be the owner of the field, come along and tell me there are no sheep in that field, although the field is frequented by a dog which from this distance is visually indistinguishable from a sheep. Then I have a *defeater* for my belief, even though that belief was formed in the basic way.[42] Another example: I believe on the basis of my guidebook that King's College in Old Aberdeen, Scotland, was founded in 1595. I form this belief in the basic way; I don't reason as follows: this is a reputable guidebook; reputable guidebooks are usually right when they give the date of a College's founding; therefore.... But then I learn that this particular guidebook is unreliable in most of what it says about Scottish universities; this gives me a defeater for that belief about the foundation of King's College, and I will no longer hold it.

A belief formed on the basis of an argument, however, can be criticized in a different way as well. When you (properly) form a belief on the basis of argument, what typically happens is that warrant or positive epistemic status is transferred from the premise belief(s) to the conclusion. Consider, for example, Euclid's *reductio ad absurdum* argument for the proposition that there is no greatest prime. Suppose there is a greatest prime and call it n; now multiply together n and all the prime numbers smaller than n and add 1: call this number p. Clearly p is not evenly divisible by n or any prime smaller than n; hence p is either prime or evenly divisible by a prime greater than n; either way there is a prime greater than n; hence n is not the greatest prime after all. Suppose I form my belief that there is no greatest prime on the basis of this argument. If my belief has warrant, it acquires warrant by way of warrant-transfer from the premises, for example the premise that if a set S includes only primes, then the product of all those primes plus 1 will not be evenly divisible

42. See chapter 6 in this volume, section I.

by any member of S. A belief formed in that way, as the conclusion of an argument, can be criticized in terms of the cogency of the argument. We can ask whether the argument is valid, i.e., whether the conclusion really follows from the premises; we can also ask whether the premises are true; we can also ask whether the argument is circular, or begs the question, or is in some other way dialectically deficient. None of these sorts of criticism is relevant to beliefs formed in the basic way. And this makes an important difference with respect to our discussion of modes of forming design beliefs.

Turning back to Paley, as we saw, we can construe him either as giving a design argument, or as giving a design discourse. Now in what way can such a discourse fail: how can a design discourse be shown to be unsuccessful? Well, of course one way would be to show, somehow, that the design discourse fails to produce any tendency to form the relevant design belief. But there is also another way. A basic belief can be subject to defeaters: one way, therefore to argue that a design discourse is unsuccessful would be to show that the design belief formed in this way is in fact subject to defeat. This would be a matter of producing a defeater for the design belief—that is, getting a person who holds a certain design belief to accept another belief D such that she can't sensibly continue to hold the design belief, as long as she holds the defeating belief D. In this case, what would do the trick is a belief such that once you held *that* belief, you could no longer accept the conclusion of Paley's design discourse— for example, that the eye has been designed by an intelligent and powerful being. Such a defeater could take two forms.

On the one hand, you might become convinced that as a matter of fact the eye was *not* designed, but came to be in some other way. Then you would have a *rebutting* defeater: you come to believe a proposition that you see is incompatible with the proposed defeatee.[43]

---

43. See chapter 6, section I.

That's the sort of defeater I acquire in the example above about the dog I mistake for a sheep; based on your testimony, I acquire the belief that there are no sheep in that field. On the other hand, I might acquire an *undercutting* defeater. This would happen, roughly, if I come to believe something that undercuts or nullifies or negates my reason for the proposed defeatee. For example, you might have told me not that there were no sheep in that field, but only that a dog who is a sheep lookalike often frequents the field. Then my reason for thinking there is a sheep there would be undercut, and I'd no longer believe that proposition. Still, I would not form the belief that there *weren't* any sheep in that field: what I saw could have been a sheep even if that dog is in the neighborhood (and also, perhaps there were sheep in parts of the field I couldn't see). It's worth noting that undercutting defeaters come in degrees: rather than bringing it about that I can no longer rationally hold the belief in question, they can bring it about that I can no longer rationally hold that belief as *firmly* as I did. For example, Mic and Martha tell me they saw you at the party; I believe, naturally enough, that you were at the party; then Mic tells me he didn't see you there, but was just relying on Martha's testimony. This partially undercuts my reason for thinking you were there; I may continue to believe that you were, but I will believe this less firmly.

Now Darwin is often credited with having *refuted* Paley's argument. Translated into the present context, this would be the claim that Darwin has provided a defeater for the design beliefs to which Paley calls our attention. How would that go? Some writers seem to believe that Darwin, or current evolutionary science, has provided a *rebutting* defeater: they believe that evolutionary science has shown that as a matter of fact eyes and other biological structures have *not*, in point of sober truth, been designed. As we saw in chapter 1, Richard Dawkins believes contemporary evolutionary science "reveals a universe without design"; and in chapter 2, we saw that Daniel Dennett apparently thinks current evolutionary science includes the claim that this process is unguided. If either of these were correct, and if current evolutionary science is successful, then current evolutionary science would have provided a rebutting defeater for design beliefs. Current evolutionary science would have given us sufficient reason to believe the *denials* of these design beliefs—that is, sufficient reason to believe that these biological structures have *not* been designed. As we also saw Dawkins's argument for this conclusion, however, is unsound *in excelsis*; and Dennett, for his part, simply assumes without argument that current evolutionary theory includes the proposition that the process of evolution has not been guided (by God or anyone else), despite the fact that this proposition looks much more like a metaphysical or theological add-on than a part of the scientific theory as such.

What current Darwinian evolutionary theory shows, if successful, is that the living world with all its apparently designed structures has come to be by way of natural selection operating on something like random genetic mutation. Well, suppose they did come to be in this way. Would that show that Paley's design beliefs—for example, that the human eye was designed—was mistaken? Of course not. As we saw earlier, God (or other beings he has created) could have planned, superintended, and guided this process. Indeed, he (or they) could have been more intimately involved in it: he could have *caused* the relevant genetic mutations. God might have caused the right mutations to arise in the right circumstances in such a way as to bring it about that there exists organisms of a type he intends; the organisms resulting from this kind of evolution would be designed, but also a product of natural selection working on random genetic mutation.[44] So even if (contrary to fact) either Darwin or more recent biology were to have actually shown that the biological structures in

---

44. For the biological sense of "random," see chapter 1, section I.

question *have* come to be by way of these Darwinian mechanisms, it wouldn't follow that they have not been designed; therefore they do not provide a rebutting defeater for Paley design beliefs or a problem for Paley's design discourse.[45] To provide a rebutting defeater here, Darwinian science would have to show that the biological phenomena in question have been produced by *unguided* Darwinian evolution. But (naturally enough) they haven't shown that evolution *is* unguided by God or any other intelligent agent; that wouldn't be the sort of thing, one supposes, within the capability of empirical science.

Does Darwinism provide an *undercutting* defeater for the design belief? How would it do a thing like that? Perhaps as follows: "It was Darwin's greatest accomplishment to show that the complex organization and functionality of living beings can be explained as the result of a natural process, natural selection, without any need to resort to a Creator or other external agent."[46] Putting this another way, Darwinian science could perhaps show that it is *possible* that the structures and traits in question have come to be by way of unguided evolution. It wouldn't be necessary to show that they actually *did* come to be by way of unguided evolution; it would suffice to show that it *could have* happened that way. So the idea would be to show that the eye, for example, could have come to be by Darwinian evolution, unguided by the hand of deity (or other intelligent agents). Of course bare *logical possibility* is not enough: it is logically possible that the horse, say, sprang into being from the unicellular level (bacteria, perhaps) in one magnificent leap. What the Darwinian has to show, to provide a

45. Of course cases of what look like suboptimal design (human knees, backs, the blind spot in the human eye) might provided partial defeaters for the belief that it is *God*—wholly good, powerful, knowledgeable—that has done (all) the designing; this wouldn't affect the belief that these things have been designed.
46. Francisco Ayala, "Intelligent Design: The Original Version" in *Theology and Science* 1:1 (April 2003), pp. 17, 18, 22.

defeater, is an unguided evolutionary path which is not *prohibitively improbable*. Have Darwinians actually accomplished this? Have they shown, for example, that it is not prohibitively improbable that the mammalian eye has developed in this way from a light sensitive spot?

They have *not* shown this. The typical procedure, one adopted by Darwin himself, is to point to the various sorts of eyes displayed by living things, lining them up in a series of apparently increasing adaptive complexity, with the mammalian eye at the top of the series. But that of course doesn't actually show that it is biologically possible—that is, not prohibitively improbable—that later members of the series developed by Darwinian means from earlier members. To put it in terms of the scheme developed on p. 225, it has not been shown that there is a path through "design space" where (1) the first point is occupied by a design with no more than a light sensitive spot, as with certain relatively primitive animals, (2) each point (except the first) represents a design arising by way of heritable genetic variation (the main candidate is random genetic mutation) from the previous point, (3) each point is an adaptive step forward with respect to the previous point, or else a consequence, by way of spandrel or pleiotropy, of a design that is such a step forward, (4) each point is not prohibitively improbable with respect to the previous point, and (5) the last point is occupied by (correlated with) the design of the human eye. Of course this hasn't been demonstrated at all. (What perhaps has been, if not demonstrated, at least shown to be reasonably plausible, is that *for all we know* there is such a series: no one has succeeded in showing that there *isn't* any such series.[47]) Not only don't we know that there is such a path, we don't even know how to go about determining whether or not there are such paths through design space. It's simply not known how to make the relevant calculations; judgments

47. See chapter 1, section II.

as to whether there are or aren't any such pathways are very much seat of the pants, tenuous, hard to support, and, apparently, responsive to and coordinated with one's metaphysical or theological views.

So *does* current evolutionary science give us a defeater for Paley design beliefs with respect to the eye? The sensible thing to think, here, is that we have a *partial* undercutting defeater for those beliefs (formed in that way).[48] As we saw earlier, undercutting defeaters come in degrees. Evolutionary biologists present considerations designed to show how it could be that these structures have arisen by way of unguided Darwinian processes; they give us some reason to believe that this is possible. These considerations, when you first become aware of them, should *somewhat reduce* your confidence that these structures have been designed. How much should your confidence be reduced? That will depend upon several factors, including in particular what the rest of your belief structure is like— what else you believe, and how firmly you believe it. There is no general answer to the question "How much?"

We can see that the same ideas apply with respect to the fine-tuning consideration of chapter 7. Suppose we take those appeals to fine-tuning as the basis for arguments for design. Then various proposed objections—the anthropic objection, the normalizability objection, the many-worlds objection, the problem with ascertaining the relevant probabilities—seem to be reasonably plausible, even if not ultimately decisive.[49] But if we take them as design discourse rather than argument, then none of these objections (with the possible exception of the third) is even relevant.

48. Of course one might believe on altogether different grounds that the eye has been designed—one might have other grounds, e.g., for thinking there is such a person as God, who has created and thus designed the world and the various biological organisms it contains.

49. In chapter 7, I proposed an example to show that the normalizability objection is misguided; I should add here that this example is perhaps better construed as design discourse than as a design argument.

Now return to Behe. I concluded above that Behe's arguments in *Darwin's Black Box* and *The Edge of Evolution*, taken as discursive *arguments*, are by no means airtight. But suppose we take what Behe says, not as an argument, not as a discursive structure with premises and conclusion, but as a design discourse in the way we were thinking of Paley's argument. Sometimes Behe himself seems to think this way: "There is an elephant in the roomful of scientists who are trying to explain the development of life. The elephant is labeled 'intelligent design.'"[50] This sounds as if Behe thinks that upon becoming acquainted with the structures he mentions, one is subject to a powerful inclination to believe that they are designed. These complex structures—the cilia, flagella, structures involved in blood clotting, and so on of *Darwin's Black Box* and the molecular machines of *The Edge of Evolution*—these complex and beautifully tailored structures certainly *appear* to be designed. There is that great complexity joined to simplicity; there is that precise tailoring of the various parts to each other, a tailoring necessary to their performing their function at all; these things give all the appearances of devices that have been designed to produce a certain result. Indeed, we ordinarily think of them in that fashion; we speak of them as *functioning properly* or *working properly*, or *healthy*; we also speak of them as *defective*, as *unhealthy*, as *needing repair*, all of which fits in naturally with the supposition that they have been designed. These structures look as if they have been designed, and it takes considerable training and effort to resist that belief. Thus Sir Francis Crick, himself very far from a friend of divine design: "Biologists must constantly keep in mind that what they see was not designed, but rather evolved."[51] Clearly the reason they must constantly keep this in mind is that the structures they deal with look for all the world as if they *were* designed.

---

50. Behe, *Darwin's Black Box*, p. 193.
51. Crick, *What Mad Pursuit: a Personal View of Scientific Discovery* (New York: Basic, 1988), p. 138. (One imagines biologists gritting their teeth and repeating to themselves, "They aren't designed; they aren't designed; they....")

Has contemporary Darwinian biology provided undercutting defeaters for Behe design beliefs, beliefs that those cellular structures have been designed? Here the answer is clearly "no." When Behe wrote *Darwin's Black Box*, he claimed there were no Darwinian accounts of the structures he mentioned: the bacterial flagellum, blood clotting, etc. With respect to the bacterial flagellum, it is true that since Behe wrote, several structures simpler than the flagellum have since been discovered to have functions other than locomotion, and on the basis of these discoveries evolutionary pathways have in fact been proposed. In the words of biologist Jeffrey Schloss, however, "at present nothing is firmly accepted; there are debates over (a) whether the actual phylogenetic history of the structures is concordant with their being precursors to as opposed to mere degradations of the flagellum, (b) even if they're precursors, whether we have a sufficient number of these structures to support a plausible evolutionary pathway, and (c) whether a single path is adequate for the diversity we see in bacterial flagella." If so, however, these proposals don't constitute defeaters for the relevant design beliefs. Those ardent devotees of natural selection who proclaim that contemporary Darwinian science has completely explained the apparent design in the biological realm, and in fact thus completely explained it away, are mistaken about the entire molecular level.

If this is true, then there aren't any defeaters, either rebutting or undercutting, for Behe design beliefs. So the real significance of Behe's work, as I see it, is not that he has produced incontrovertible arguments for the conclusion that these systems have been designed; it is rather that he has produced several design discourses, several sets of circumstances in which design perception occurs, for which in fact there aren't any defeaters. The difference, of course, is this: pointing to deficiencies and holes in Behe taken as producing an argument, as Draper (for example) skillfully does, fails to show that there are defeaters for Behe design beliefs.

But then what overall conclusion should we draw about these design discourses? I said we have partial defeaters for the design discourses at the level of gross anatomy; we have partial defeaters for design beliefs having to do with the eye, with the structure of limbs, and the like. We don't have any such defeaters for Behe design beliefs at the molecular and cellular level. How should we put this together? Should we go with those who assimilate the latter to the former, arguing that if we just wait awhile (after all, molecular biology and biochemistry have been with us only since the 1950s or so), there will be plausible Darwinian explanations for them, just as there are (as they think) for structures at the gross anatomical level? Or should we go with partisans of design, who point out that it isn't at all clear that there are defeaters at the gross anatomical level, and it *is* clear that there aren't any at the cellular level, so that on balance the design conclusion is the stronger?

Here, I think, the friends of design have the better of the argument; the partisans of Darwinism are tugging the laboring oar. True, there are reasonably plausible Darwinian explanations at the anatomical level for many structures and systems; that fact should perhaps reduce the confidence with which one forms design beliefs at the cellular level. So we can say that here too we have a partial defeater. But (in my judgment) it is an *extremely* partial defeater. So the right conclusion, as it seems to me, is that Behe's design discourses are in fact rather successful: his account of the structures he describes certainly do produce the impression of design. Biological science, so far, anyway, has at best produced weak defeaters for these design beliefs.[52]

This question whether design beliefs are defeated by Darwinian suggestions is actually much more complex, involving a good deal of the epistemology of defeat and deflection. Here I will just point to

---

52. Of course this is supposing that there aren't any other defeaters here—no good argument, for example, that there couldn't be a designer, or that the only plausible candidate here—divine design—can somehow be shown to be ineligible.

some of that complexity. First, assume that in fact there is an impulse, an inclination to believe that these biological phenomena are designed, as is attested even by such opponents of divine design as Sir Francis Crick. Second, as I noted above, a belief—for definiteness, consider a basic belief—can be defeated. But such beliefs can also be deflected; we must distinguish between defeat and deflection. A *defeater* D for a belief B is another belief I acquire, such that as long as I hold that belief D, I cannot rationally (given my noetic structure) continue to believe B (and a partial defeater requires that I hold B less firmly). A belief *deflector* D* for a (potential) belief B, is, roughly speaking, a belief I already hold such that as long as I hold it (and given my noetic structure) I can't rationally come to hold B. So, with respect to the earlier example of a defeater (p. 248), I said you got a defeater for your belief that you see a sheep in the field if I, whom you know to be the owner of the field, come along and tell you that although there are no sheep in the field, there is a canine sheep look-alike that often frequents the field. But you won't get a defeater, here, if you already think that I am unreliable on this topic, or that I have a lot to gain by getting you to doubt that there is a sheep there, or if you believe that there aren't any dogs in this part of the world, or that no dogs ever look like sheep from the distance in question, and so on. In these cases the looming defeater (defeater belief) will be deflected.

The above characterization of a deflector is too broad, in that it assigns deflectorhood to almost any belief with respect to a belief that is sufficiently irrational. Thus consider the belief B that there has not been a past; this belief, I take it, is irrational, in the sense that a properly functioning human being with anything like a standard noetic structure will not form B. But then nearly any other belief I hold is (on the above account) a deflector with respect to B: any other belief is such that as long as I hold it, I can't rationally acquire B. What has to be added is a clause roughly to the effect that a deflector belief D for a belief B must be such that in the relevant circumstances, if D were not present in my noetic structure, I would have formed B. True, this account involves a counterfactual, inviting the sort of grief to which analyses involving counterfactuals often succumb; but perhaps it is close enough for present purposes. In any event, I leave as homework the project of refining the account.

The question is whether Darwinian considerations present a defeater for the design beliefs a person S forms in response to a given design discourse. To make the discussion manageable, assume that the occasion in question is the first on which S is confronted with the design discourse in question; suppose she is then confronted for the first time by relevant Darwinian considerations. Whether these Darwinian considerations defeat S's design beliefs will depend upon the rest of what S believes. If S is already a theist, S believes that these things (and indeed the whole universe) is designed. Under those conditions, Darwinian considerations will not give S a defeater for the design belief in question; her theistic belief is a defeater-deflector for the looming defeater. Here too, however, there are further complexities: what happens depends on the strength of S's theistic belief, and also on the strength of her reaction to the potential Darwinian defeating belief. If the Darwinian considerations produce a strong enough impulse to form the belief that the phenomena in question are *not* designed, if *that* impulse overwhelms her initial theistic belief, then defeat of the design belief will not be deflected, and indeed S will wind up with a defeater for her initial theistic belief.

What about the serious naturalist? She comes in varieties. One such variety is a naturalist who is wholly convinced that the biological world we find around us came to be just by the grace of unguided evolution. Such a naturalist will have a deflector for the relevant design beliefs, and will presumably not form such beliefs (she may follow Crick's advice, repeatedly telling herself that it evolved and isn't designed)—unless, of course, the impulse to form those design beliefs is overwhelming; in that case the impulse to form the design belief will outweigh the potential belief-deflector. Another kind of naturalist might believe that the biological world and its denizens have not been designed by God, but she may leave slightly ajar the door to belief that they have been designed by some other beings. If so, she might still form a design belief in the circumstances, perhaps thinking these biological phenomena have been designed by ancient astronauts, creatures from a scientifically advanced culture on another planet who intervened in the evolution of life on our planet a half billion years ago. (By now these creatures would be pretty long in the tooth.) For most of us, this scenario, though perhaps possible, is pretty unlikely; for S to come to this conclusion, both the design impulse and belief that God has not designed these phenomena would have to be strong indeed.

Finally, consider someone who had little or no opinion either way with respect to the question whether Behe's protein machines, for example, or the eye, or the universe have been designed (and whose noetic structure is otherwise like ours). For such a person, encountering a design discourse like Paley's or Behe's, or the fine-tuning considerations presented by Richard Swinburne and Robin Collins, will in all likelihood result in a design belief. But also, for such a person, encountering the relevant Darwinian considerations I think, will present her with a partially undercutting defeater for those design beliefs.

So let's suppose the Behe design discourses are at least marginally successful. What follows for the question of this chapter, the question whether theistic and or Christian belief gets support from science? Behe's design discourses certainly start from scientific conclusions; how much support, if any, do they confer upon Christian and theistic belief? Well, they offer little support for specifically Christian belief insofar as it goes beyond theistic belief; they don't support incarnation, atonement, resurrection. Do they support theistic belief? That's not entirely easy to say. For first, theism, of course, involves a great deal more than the bare claim that the living world has been designed. That claim could be true even if there were a number of designers forming a committee, with some of the drawbacks committees display, or even if (here we could follow Hume) the designer(s) are infant deities or superannuated deities, and reveal their limitations by awkward or infelicitous design. According to theism, there is but one ultimate designer, and the designer is the Designer: all-powerful, all-knowing, wholly good, loving, the Creator as well as the Designer. The design conclusion thus supports theism in that it entails one very important part of theistic belief; but it isn't clear how much it supports theism as such.

On the other hand, for many people the live options are either theism or naturalism: either there is such a person as God, or, if not, there is nothing at all like God. For people who think like this, there would be a great deal more support for theism here. Further, suppose theism is indeed true, and add that there is something like Calvin's *sensus divinitatis*; then there are many situations in which the rational response is theistic belief.[53] Here there are at least two relevant possibilities. First, perhaps some of the design situations— the situations such that the rational response to them is design belief—are also situations in which the *sensus divinitatis* works. If this were so, the rational response to those situations wouldn't be just design belief; it would be full-blown theistic belief. Design discourses—at any rate *those* design discourses—would then indeed support theism, but only by way of being special cases of the support offered by the *sensus divinitatis*. Secondly, if there is such a thing as the *sensus divinitatis*, then perhaps those Humean possibilities—a committee of designers (infant, superannuated, or in some other way incompetent)—are quite properly (that is, quite rationally)

53. See my *Warranted Christian Belief* (New York: Oxford University Press, 2000), chapter 6.

discounted. Discounting those Humean fantasies is in effect to endorse the proposition that if there is a designer, there is the Designer. And hence any support for design would indeed be support for theism. Of course these possibilities presuppose the truth of theism; presumably there isn't any *sensus divinitatis*, if theism is false.[54] It is of some interest to see that we really can't tell what sort of support, if any, design discourses offer theism without knowing whether theism is true.

On balance, then: Behe's design discourses do not constitute irrefragable arguments for theism, or even for the proposition that the structures he considers have in fact been designed. Taken not as arguments but as design discourses they fare better. They present us with epistemic situations in which the rational response is design belief— design belief for which there aren't strong defeaters. The proper conclusion to be drawn, I think, is that Behe's design discourses do support theism, although it isn't easy to say how much support they offer. I realize that this is a wet noodle conclusion: can't I say something more definite and exciting? Well, I'd love to; but my job here is to tell the sober truth, whether or not it is exciting. That obligation can sometimes interfere with telling a good story; but what can I say? That's just life in philosophy. As the saying goes, it is what it is. In the next chapter, however, we'll look into much deeper and more definitive concord between Christian belief and science.

54. See my *Warranted Christian Belief,* pp. 186ff.

Chapter 9

Deep Concord: Christian Theism and the Deep Roots of Science

Recall my overall thesis: there is superficial conflict but deep concord between theistic religion and science, but superficial concord and deep conflict between naturalism and science. In the first few chapters, we saw many allegations of conflict between science and religion. Much of this alleged conflict is merely illusory—between evolution and theistic belief, between science and special divine action (for example, miracles), and between religious faith and the scientific way of forming belief. We also saw that some conflicts— that between theistic religion and various claims and theories of evolutionary psychology—are genuine; though genuine, however, they are merely superficial, in that these conflicts, rightly understood, do not tend to offer defeaters to those who accept theistic religion. We then turned from the question whether science conflicts with theistic belief to the question whether it *supports* theistic belief, gives us some reason to *accept* theistic belief. Here we addressed considerations from contemporary science, in particular fine-tuning arguments and biological arguments of the sort offered by Michael Behe. These, we saw, can be taken either as arguments or as design discourse; either way they perhaps offer a certain limited but still non-negligible support for theism. While these arguments and discourses are interesting and relevant, there is a much deeper concord between theistic religion and science. It is time to turn to this concord.

1 SCIENCE AND THE DIVINE IMAGE

Modern Western empirical science originated and flourished in the bosom of Christian theism and originated nowhere else. Some have found this anomalous. Bertrand Russell, for example, thought of the Christian church as repressing and inhibiting the growth of science. He was therefore disappointed to note that science did not emerge in China, even though, as he said, the spread of scientific knowledge there encountered no such obstacles as he thought the Church put in its way in Europe.[1] But the fact is, it was Christian Europe that fostered, promoted, and nourished modern science. It arose nowhere else. All of the great names of early Western science, furthermore—Nicholas Copernicus, Galileo Galilei, Isaac Newton, Robert Boyle, John Wilkins, Roger Cotes, and many others—all were serious believers in God. Indeed, the important twentieth-century physicist C. F. von Weizsäcker goes so far as to say, "In this sense, I call modern science a legacy of Christianity."[2]

This is no accident: there is deep concord between science and theistic belief.[3] So I say: but why should we think so? We may begin by asking the following question: what sorts of conditions would be required for the success of science? What would contribute to its growth? What would things have to be like for science to flourish? What are the necessary (and sufficient) conditions for such flourishing?

But first, how shall we think of science? There are many opinions here. Realists think science is an effort to learn something of the sober truth about our world; instrumentalists think its value lies in its ability

1. Russell, *The Problem of China* (Charleston, S.C.: BiblioBazaar, 2006), p. 164.
2. Von Weizsäcker, *The Relevance of Science* (New York: Harper: 1964), p 163.
3. Peter van Inwagen, one of the finest philosophers of our age, cites it as one of his main reasons for believing in God; see his "Quam Dilecta" in *God and the Philosophers*, ed. Thomas Morris (New York: Oxford University Press, 1994), pp. 52ff.

to help us get on in the world; constructive empiricists claim that its point is to produce empirically adequate theories, the question of the truth of these theories being secondary. Initially (and perhaps naïvely) the realists are right: science is a search for truth about ourselves and our world. From science we learn a little about the great regularities displayed by the planets and their motions, and about how these same regularities are to be found at a more terrestrial level. We learn about the nature of electricity, about the structure of matter and the variety of the elements. We learn about the early history of our planet and about the history of our species. We learn about the incredible and enormously detailed structure of the human body, and have learned how to cope with many diseases and pathologies. By virtue of science, we have learned how to build airplanes that obliterate distance; in the nineteenth century the trip from Chicago to Beijing was an arduous months-long affair; now it takes twelve hours.

The basic idea, therefore, is simple enough: science is at bottom an attempt to learn important truths about ourselves and our world. According to Albert Einstein, a proper scientist is a "real seeker after truth."[4] Of course we don't expect science to give us the answer to just any question. Science can't tell us whether slavery is wrong, for example, though it might be able to tell us about some of the social or economic consequences of slavery. We don't expect science to tell us whether, say, Christian Trintarianism is true: that's not its business. (Nor does it make much sense to suggest that since we now have science, we no longer need any other sources of knowledge—religion, for example. That is like claiming that now that we have refrigerators and chain saws and roller skates, we no longer have need for Mozart.) Furthermore, while science is an attempt to find important truths about our world and ourselves, it isn't just any such attempt—there are other ways in which people have tried to discover truths about

4. Einstein in a letter to Robert Thornton, December 7, 1944. Einstein Archives 61–574.

ourselves and our world. Still, the fundamental class to which science belongs is that of efforts to discover truths—at any rate it is science so thought of that I mean to deal with here. More specifically, science is a disciplined and systematic effort to discover such truths, an effort with a substantial empirical involvement. While it is difficult to give a precise account of this empirical component, it is absolutely crucial to science, and is what distinguishes science from philosophy.

Now how is Christian belief relevant here? What is this deep concord I claim? The first thing to see here is simplicity itself. It is an important part of Christian, Jewish and some Islamic thought to see human beings *as created in God's image.* This doctrine of the *imago dei,* the thought that we human beings have been created in the image of God has several sides and facets; but there is one aspect of it that is crucially relevant in the present context. This is the thought that God is a knower, and indeed the supreme knower. God is omniscient, that is, such that he knows everything, knows for any proposition p, whether p is true. We human beings, therefore, in being created in his image, can also know much about our world, ourselves, and God himself. No doubt what we know pales into insignificance beside what God knows; still we know much that is worthwhile and important. Crucial to the thought that we have been created in his image, then, is the idea that he has created both us and our world in such a way that (like him) we are able to know important things about our world and ourselves.

Thomas Aquinas put it as follows:

> Since human beings are said to be in the image of God in virtue of their having a nature that includes an intellect, such a nature is most in the image of God in virtue of being most able to imitate God;

and

Only in rational creatures is there found a likeness of God which counts as an image.... As far as a likeness of the divine nature is concerned, rational creatures seem somehow to attain a representation of [that] type in virtue of imitating God not only in this, that he is and lives, but especially in this, that he understands.[5]

Here Aquinas says that a nature including an intellect is *most* in the image of God, in virtue of being most able to imitate God. Perhaps he exaggerates a bit in thinking that understanding, the ability to know, is the *chief* part of the image of God. What about being able to act, what about having a grasp of right and wrong, what about being able to love one another, what about being able, in some way, to experience God? In any event, however, this ability to know something about our world, ourselves and God is a crucially important part of the divine image.

But how, more exactly, is this supposed to go? God created both us and our world in such a way that there is a certain fit or match between the world and our cognitive faculties. The medievals had a phrase for it: *adequatio intellectus ad rem* (the adequation of the intellect to reality). The basic idea, here, is simply that there is a match between our cognitive or intellectual faculties and reality, thought of as including whatever exists, a match that enables us to know something, indeed a great deal, about the world—and also about ourselves and God himself. According to Noam Chomsky, "This partial congruence between the truth about the world and what the human science-forming capacity produces at a given moment yields science. Notice that it is just blind luck if the human science-forming capacity, a particular component of the human biological endowment, happens to yield a result that conforms more or less to the truth about the

5. *Summa Theologiae* Ia q. 93 a. 4; ST Ia q.93 a.6.

world."[6] From the point of view of theistic religion, this is not blind luck. It is only to be expected.

Science, clearly, is an extension of our ordinary ways of learning about the world. As such, it obviously involves the faculties and processes by which we ordinarily do achieve knowledge. Thus perception (whereby we know something of our environment), memory (whereby we know something of our past), a priori insight (by which we grasp logic and mathematics), broadly inductive procedures (whereby we can learn from experience), perhaps Thomas Reid's "sympathy" (by which we know about the thoughts and feelings of other people), and perhaps still others—all of these take their place in the prosecution of science. What is involved in science is these basic ways of knowing; of course it is also true that by use of these basic ways we can construct devices and instruments (telescopes, electron microscopes, and accelerators, not to mention opera glasses) that vastly extend the reach of our ordinary cognitive faculties.

For science to be successful, therefore, there must be a match between our cognitive faculties and the world. How shall we understand this fit? First, it is important to see that it is by no means just automatic or inevitable that there is such a match (as I'll argue in more detail in the next chapter). Our faculties are designed to enable us to know something about *this* world; if the world were very different, our faculties might not serve us this way at all. Visual perception of our kind, obviously enough, requires light, electromagnetic radiation of the right wavelength; in a world where everything is always obscured by thick darkness, our eyes would be of no use. Something similar, of course, goes for hearing and our other perceptual faculties. We might think that our evolutionary origin guarantees or strongly supports the thought that our basic cognitive faculties are reliable: if they

6. Chomsky, *Language and the Problems of Knowledge* (Cambridge: The MIT Press, 2001), pp. 157–58.

weren't, how could we have survived and reproduced? But this is clearly an error, as I'll argue in the next chapter. Natural selection is interested in adaptive behavior, behavior that conduces to survival and reproduction; it has no interest in our having true beliefs.

So what more can we say about this required fit or match between our cognitive faculties and the world we seek to learn about? I've just mentioned perception; clearly this is a most important source of belief about the world; and one condition of the success of science is that perception for the most part, and under ordinary and favorable conditions, produces in us beliefs that are in fact true. This isn't inevitable. It is possible that perception should produce in us beliefs that are adaptive, or meet some other useful condition, whether or not they are true.

II RELIABILITY AND REGULARITY

For science to be successful, the world must display a high degree of regularity and predictability. As we saw in chapter 4, intentional action requires the same thing: we couldn't build a house if hammers unpredictably turned into eels, or nails into caterpillars; we couldn't drive downtown if automobiles unexpectedly turned into tea pots or rosebushes. Intentional action requires a high degree of stability, predictability, and regularity. And of course the predictability in question has to be predictability *by us*. For intentional action to be possible, it must be the case that we, given our cognitive faculties, can often or usually predict what will happen next. No doubt there could be creatures with wholly different cognitive powers, creatures who could predict the course of events in ways we can't; that might be nice for them, but science as practiced by us humans requires predictability given *our* cognitive faculties. Furthermore, science requires more than regularity: it also requires our implicitly *believing* or *assuming* that the world is regular in this way. As the philosopher Alfred North Whitehead put it, "There can be no living science unless there is a widespread instinctive conviction in the existence of an *Order of Things*. And, in particular, of an *Order of Nature*."[7]

It's an essential part of theistic religion—at any rate Christian theistic religion—to think of God as providentially governing the world in such a way as to provide that kind of stability and regularity. Let me quote again the Heidelberg Catechism:

> Providence is the almighty and ever present power of God by which he upholds, as with his hand, heaven and earth and all creatures, and so rules them that leaf and blade, rain and drought, fruitful and lean years, food and drink, health and sickness, prosperity and poverty—all things, in fact, come to us not by chance but from his fatherly hand.[8]

Christian theism involves the idea that *God* governs the world; that what happens does not come about by chance, but by virtue of God's providential governance. The idea is that the basic structure of the world is due to a creative intelligence: a person, who aimed and intended that the world manifest a certain character. The world was created in such a way that it displays order and regularity; it isn't unpredictable, chancy or random. And of course this conviction is what enables and undergirds science. Whitehead, as we saw, points out that science requires an instinctive conviction that nature is ordered; he goes on to attribute this widespread instinctive conviction to "the medieval insistence on the rationality of God."[9]

What does this "rationality" of God consist in? What might the medievals have meant in saying that God is rational? When they

7. Whitehead, *Science and the Modern World* (New York: McMillan, 1925), pp. 3–4.
8. Lord's Day Ten, Question and Answer 27.
9. Whitehead, *Science and the Modern World*, p. 13.

discussed this topic, the medievals put it in terms of the question whether, in God, it is *intellect* or *will* that is primary. They thought that if *intellect* is primary in God, then God's actions will be predictable, orderly, conforming to a plan—a plan we can partially fathom. On the other hand, if it is *will* that is primary in God, then his actions would involve much more by way of caprice and arbitrary choice and much less predictability. If it is intellect that is prior in God, then his actions will be rational—rational in something like the way that we are rational; if it is will that is prior, then one can't expect as much by way of rationality. Aquinas championed the primacy of intellect in God, while William of Ockham endorsed the priority of will. This, of course, is vastly oversimplified (as is nearly anything one can say about medieval philosophy) but it conveys an essential point. Ockham seemed to think that God's will was essentially unconstrained by God's intellect (or anything else); God is free to do whatever he wants, even something that is irrational in the sense of contrary to what his intellect perceives as good or right. Ockham insisted that while in fact God chose to redeem humanity by becoming a human being, he could just as properly have chosen to do so by becoming a stone, a tree, or an ass.[10] He also claimed that God could have commanded hatred instead of love, adultery instead of faithfulness, cruelty instead of kindness; and if he had, then those things would have been morally obligatory. Aquinas, on the other hand, taught that God's commands stem from his very nature, so that it isn't so much as possible that God should have commanded hate rather than love.

The rationality of God, as Aquinas thought, extends far beyond the realm of morality. God sets forth moral laws, to be sure, but he also sets forth or promulgates laws of nature, and he creates the world in such a way that it conforms to these laws. The tendency of Ockham's

---

10. Josef Pieper, *Scholasticism: Personalities and Problems of Medieval Philosophy* (Notre Dame, Ind.: St. Augustine's Press, 2001), p. 148.

thought, on the other hand, is to emphasize the freedom (willfulness?) of God to such a degree that he becomes completely unpredictable; and to the extent that God is completely unpredictable, the same goes for his world. There is no guarantee that the world at some deep level is law governed, or lawful; there is no guarantee that God's world is such that by rational, intellectual activity, we will be able to learn something about its deep structure. In fact there is no reason to think, on Ockham's view, that it *has* a deep structure. What Whitehead points out here is that modern science required a sort of instinctive conviction that God is more like the way Aquinas thinks of him than the way Ockham does.[11] And indeed, many of the early pioneers and heroes of modern western science, the scientists propelling the scientific revolution, clearly sided with Aquinas. Thus Samuel Clarke: "What men commonly call 'the course of nature'... is nothing else but the will of God producing certain effects in a continued, regular, constant, and uniform manner."[12]

III LAW

A. Law and Constancy

This constancy and predictability, this regularity, was often thought of in terms of *law*: God sets, prescribes laws for his creation, or creates

11. There is also an important contrast here between the usual Christian and the usual Islamic way of thinking about God. This is not the place to go into detail into Islamic conceptions of God (even if I knew enough to do so), and of course there are several different Islamic conceptions of God, or Allah, just as there is more than one Christian conception of God. But on the whole it seems that the dominant Muslim conception of God is of a more intrusive, unpredictable, incomprehensible divinity. Rodney Stark points out that a common "orthodox" claim was that all attempts to formulate natural laws are blasphemous, because they would limit Allāh's freedom. See his *Discovering God* (New York: Harper, 2007), p. 367.
12. Clarke, *A Demonstration of the Being and Attributes of God*, ed. Ezio Vailati (Cambridge: Cambridge University Press, 1998), p. 149.

in such a way that what he creates is subject to, conforms to, laws he institutes. Thus William Ames in *The Marrow of Theology*: "...the establishment of law and order, which is to be observed perpetually in the thing to which ordaining power applies. The constancy of God shines forth in that he would have all creatures observe their order, not for days or years but to the end of the world."[13] Robert Boyle, the founder of modern chemistry, adds that "God [is] the author of the universe, and the free establisher of the laws of motion."[14] According to Roger Cotes, who wrote the Preface to the second edition of Isaac Newton's great work *Principia Mathematica*,

> Without all doubt this world, so diversified with that variety of forms and motions we find in it, could arise from nothing but the perfectly free will of God directing and presiding over all.
>
> From this fountain it is that those laws, which we call the laws of Nature, have flowed.[15]

Later (mid-nineteenth-century) William Whewell, an extremely influential philosopher, scientist and polymath, put it like this: "But with regard to the material world, we can at least go so far as this—we can perceive that events are brought about not by insulated interpositions of Divine power, exerted in each particular case, but by the establishment of general laws."[16] Finally, Albert Einstein again: "Every one who is seriously engaged in the pursuit of science becomes

---

13. Ames, *The Marrow of Theology* 1623. tr. John Dykstra Eusden (Grand Rapids, Mich.: Baker Book House, 1997), p. 104.
14. Boyle, *The Reconciliableness of Reason and Religion* in *The Works of Robert Boyle* ed. M. Hunter and E. B. Davis, 14 volumes (London: Pickering and Chatto, 1999–2000), vol. 3, p. 516.
15. Cotes, *Newton's Philosophy of Nature: Selections from his writings* (New York: Hafner Library of Classics, 1953).
16. Whewell, *Astronomy and General Physics Considered With Reference to Natural Theology* (Bridgewater Treatise), Cambridge, 1833.

convinced that the laws of nature manifest the existence of a spirit vastly superior to that of men."[17]

It is worth noting the connection here between moral law and natural law, or laws of nature. Boyle again: "The nature of this or that body is but *the law of God prescribed to it* [and] to speak properly, a law [is] but *a notional rule of acting according to the declared will of a superior.*"[18] Moral laws are promulgated by God for free creatures, who have it within their power to obey or disobey. Moral laws, then, are not inevitably obeyed; free creatures are able to opt for disobedience as well as obedience. The laws of nature, on the other hand, are promulgated for the inanimate world of matter; physical objects don't get to decide whether to obey, say, Newton's law of gravity.[19] In each case, however, we have the setting forth or promulgation of divine rule for a certain domain of application. It is important to see that our notion of the laws of nature, crucial for contemporary science, has this origin in Christian theism.

One thought, therefore, is that science requires regularity and lawful behavior on the part of the world: without this science would be impossible. But science involves law in another way: according to a very common view, these laws are *available* to us; we can discover them; and part of the job of science is to describe them. Recall Whewell: "But with regard to the material world, we can at least go so far as this: we can perceive that events are brought about not by isolated interpositions of Divine power, exerted in each

---

17. In Max Jammer, *Einstein and Religion* (Princeton: Princeton University Press, 1999), p. 93.
18. Boyle, *Notion of Nature*, in *Works of Robert Boyle*, 5, p. 170.
19. It's interesting to note that some contemporaries have been encouraged by quantum mechanical speculations to think of inanimate nature as in some way free, and perhaps even in some way making choices; when the wave function collapses, it isn't determined by previous history to collapse to any particular set of eigenvalues. (Of course it's a bit of a stretch to conclude that an elementary particle gets to decide how its wave function will collapse.)

particular case, but by the establishment of general laws."[20] E. O. Wilson relates that upon reading Ernst Mayr's 1942 *Systematics and the Origin of Species*, he was overwhelmed by "a belief in the unity of the sciences—a conviction, far deeper than a mere working proposition, that the world is orderly and can be explained by a small number of natural laws."[21] Finally, Stephen Hawking: "the more we discover about the universe, the more we find that it is governed by rational laws."[22] On this conception, part of the job of science is to discover the laws of nature; but then of course science will be successful only if it is possible for us human beings to do that.[23] Science will be successful only if these laws are not too complex, or deep, or otherwise beyond us. Again, this thought fits well with theistic religion and its doctrine of the image of God; God not only sets laws for the universe, but sets laws we can (at least approximately) grasp. This thought also traces back to the beginnings of modern science. According to Kepler,

> Those laws are within the grasp of the human mind. God wanted us to recognize them by creating us after his own image so that we could share in his own thoughts... and if piety allow us to say so, our understanding is in this respect of the same kind as the divine, at least as far as we are able to grasp something of it in our mortal life.[24]

---

20. Whewell, *Astronomy and General Physics Considered With Reference to Natural Theology*.
21. Wilson, *Consilience* (New York: Vintage, 1999), p. 4.
22. In Gregory Benford, "Leaping the Abyss: Stephen Hawking on black holes, unified field theory, and Marilyn Monroe," *Reason* 4.02 (April 2002): 29.
23. This is widely, but not universally accepted. For example, Bas van Fraassen, as canny a philosopher of science as there is, argues that there aren't any laws of nature.
24. Letter to Johannes George Herwart von Hohenburg, April 9–10, 1599, *Gesammelte Werke*, 13: 309, letter no. 117, lines 174–79; English tr. in *Johannes Kepler Baumgardt: Life and Letters*, p. 50.

B. Law and Necessity

There is still another important way in which theism is hospitable to science: theism makes it much easier to understand what these laws are like. The main point here has to do with the alleged *necessity* of natural law. Note first that not just any true universal statement is a law.

(1) Everyone in my house is over 50 years old

is a true universal proposition; still, it's not a law. Nor is the problem that this proposition contains a reference to a specific person (me) or specific physical object (my house).

(2) Every sphere made of gold is less than 1/2 mile in diameter

is a (presumably) true universal proposition, but is not a law, and the same goes, no doubt, for

(3) No provost of a large university climbs at the 5.12 level.

While these propositions are true and universal in form, they aren't laws. Why not? One answer: because they are merely *accidentally* true. They are accidentally true universal generalizations; laws, however, are not accidentally true.

How shall we understand this non-accidentality? Those who endorse natural laws typically think of them as in some way *necessary*; there is a certain necessity about natural laws.[25] However, it seems

25. Again, typically but not universally. David Lewis, for example, thought of laws as axioms of a deductive system describing the world containing a best balance of strength and simplicity; so thought of they need not display any kind of necessity.

that laws are not *logically* necessary; it seems logically possible that, for example, there be a pair of particles that do not attract each other with a force inversely proportional to the square of the distance between them, even if Newton's inverse square law is indeed a natural law.[26] It seems possible that God accelerate an object from a speed slower than c, the speed of light, to a speed greater than c. Still, that this doesn't happen seems necessary in some way—*causally* necessary, as people say, or *nomologically* necessary. But what kind of necessity is that? Logical necessity we know and love: but what is this causal or nomological necessity?

All we're ordinarily told is that this necessity is weaker than logical necessity (the laws of nature are not logically necessary), but still stronger than mere universal truth (not all true universal generalizations are necessary in this sense). But what *is* this necessity? What is its nature? This is the real rub. It seems impossible to say what it is. The philosopher David Armstrong at one time spoke of laws as involving a necessitating relationship among universals: a law is just the expression of a certain necessary relationship between universals.[27] But, as David Lewis pointed out, naming this relation "necessity" doesn't tell us much. It also doesn't mean that it really *is* necessity—anymore, said Lewis, than being named "Armstrong" confers mighty biceps.[28]

Armstrong added that the class of propositions necessary in this sense is larger than the class of logically necessary propositions, but smaller than that of true propositions. But this too is no real help: any class of true propositions that includes all the logically necessary propositions, but doesn't include all true propositions, meets this

26. A few philosophers demur: Sydney Shoemaker, for example, holds that natural laws are indeed necessary in the broadly logical sense. See his "Causal and Metaphysical Necessity," *Pacific Philosophical Quarterly*, vol. 79, issue 1 (March, 1998), p. 59.
27. Armstrong, *What is a Law of Nature?* (Cambridge: Cambridge University Press, 1985).
28. "New Work for a Theory of Universals," *Australasian Journal of Philosophy* 61 (1983).

condition. (For example, the class of true propositions minus the proposition *China is a large country* meets this condition: but obviously this tells us nothing about the intended sense of "necessary.") Armstrong later decided that the laws of nature are logically necessary after all, prompted no doubt by the difficulty of saying what this other brand of necessity might be. It is also this difficulty, one suspects, that prompts others who hold that the laws of nature, despite appearances to the contrary, are logically necessary.

Theism offers important resources here: we can think of the necessity of natural law both as a consequence and also as a sort of measure of divine power. Natural laws, obviously enough, impose limits on our technology. We can do many wonderful things: for example, we can fly from Paris to New York in less than four hours. No doubt our abilities along these lines will continue to expand; perhaps one day we will be able to travel from Paris to New York in under four minutes. Even so, we will never be able to travel to the nearest star, Proxima Centauri, in less than four years. That is because Proxima Centauri is about 4.3 light years from us, and c, the velocity of light, is an upper limit on the relative velocity of one body with respect to another.[29] That it *is* such an upper limit, we think, is a natural law. But the distance to *Proxima Centauri* is such that if I were to travel there (in a spaceship, say) in less than four years, my velocity with respect to the earth would have to exceed that limit. And if, indeed, this restriction on the relative velocities of moving objects *is* a law of nature, we won't be able to manage that feat, no matter how hard we try, and no matter how good our technology.

From a theistic perspective, the reason is that God has established and upholds this law for our cosmos, and no creature (actual or

---

29. Strictly speaking, what is precluded is not relative velocities greater than c (for perhaps tachyons aren't precluded) but acceleration of one body relative to another from a velocity less than c to one greater than c.

possible) has the power to act contrary to what God establishes and upholds. God is omnipotent; there are no non-logical limits on his power; we might say that his power is infinite. The sense in which the laws of nature are necessary, therefore, is that they are propositions God has established or decreed, and no creature—no finite power, we might say—has the power to act against these propositions, that is, to bring it about that they are false. It is as if God says: "Let c, the speed of light, be such that no material object accelerates from a velocity less than c to a velocity greater than c"; no creaturely power is then able to cause a material object to accelerate from a velocity less than c to one greater than c. The laws of nature, therefore, resemble necessary truths in that there is nothing we or other creatures can do to render them false. We could say that they are *finitely inviolable*.

Though these laws are finitely inviolable, they are nevertheless contingent, in that it is not necessary, not part of the divine nature, to institute or promulgate just *these* laws. God could have created our world in such a way that the speed of light should have been something quite different from c; he could have created things in such a way that Newton's laws don't hold for middle-sized objects. As we saw in chapter 7 on fine-tuning, there are many physical constants that are finitely inviolable (*we* can't change them) but could have been different and are therefore contingent. The natural laws are finitely inviolably, but not necessarily true.

Still further, these laws are not like the laws of the Medes and Persians (see chapter 3); it is not true that once God has established or instituted them, they limit or constrain his power to act. As we saw in chapter 3, this is a bit tricky. Say that God acts specially in the world when he acts in a way that goes beyond creation and conservation. We can then think of the natural laws as of the following form:

When God is not acting specially, p.

For example,

> When God is not acting specially, no material object accelerates
> from a speed less than c to a speed greater than c.

But of course that doesn't mean that *God* cannot bring it about
that some material object accelerate from a speed less than c to one
greater than c. Neither we nor any other creature can do this; it
doesn't follow that God cannot. If the laws take the above form
they are really conditionals: the antecedent of a law specifies that
God is not acting specially, and the consequent is a proposition
describing how things ordinarily work, how they work when God
is not acting specially. For example, when God isn't acting specially, no material object accelerates through the speed of light, any
two objects attract each other with a force directly proportional to
the product of their masses and inversely proportional to the
square of the distance between them, and so on. The thing to see is
that while no creatures, no finite beings, can bring about a state of
affairs incompatible with the consequent of a law, God has the
power to do so.

  With respect to the laws of nature, therefore, there are at least
three ways in which theism is hospitable to science and its success,
three ways in which there is deep concord between theistic religion
and science. First, science requires regularity, predictability, and constancy; it requires that our world conform to laws of nature. In the
west (which includes the United States, Canada, Europe, and, for
these purposes, Australia and New Zealand) the main rival to theism
is naturalism, the thought that there is no such person as God or
anything like God. Naturalism is trumpeted by, for example, three of
the four horsemen of atheism: Richard Dawkins, Daniel Dennett,

and Christopher Hitchens.[30] (The fourth horseman, Sam Harris, is an atheist, all right, but doesn't seem to rise to the lofty heights—or descend to the murky depths—of naturalism: he displays a decided list towards Buddhism.[31]) From the point of view of naturalism, the fact that our world displays the sort of regularity and lawlike behavior necessary for science is a piece of enormous cosmic luck, a not-to-be-expected bit of serendipity. But regularity and lawlikeness obviously fit well with the thought that God is a rational person who has created our world, and instituted the laws of nature.

Second, not only must our world in fact manifest regularity and law-like behavior: for science to flourish, scientists and others must believe that it does. As Whitehead put it (earlier in this chapter): "There can be no living science unless there is a wide-spread instinctive conviction in the existence of an *Order of Things;*" such a conviction fits well with the theistic doctrine of the image of God.

Third, theism enables us to understand the necessity or inevitableness or inviolability of natural law: this necessity is to be explained and understood in terms of the difference between divine power and the power of finite creatures. Again, from the point of view of naturalism, the character of these laws is something of an enigma. What is this alleged necessity they display, weaker than logical necessity, but necessity nonetheless? What if anything explains the fact that these laws govern what happens? What reason if any is there for expecting them to continue to govern these phenomena? Theism provides a natural answer to these questions; naturalism stands mute before them.

30. See Dawkins, *The God Delusion* (New York: Bantam, 2006); Dennett, *Breaking the Spell: Religion as a Natural Phenomenon* (New York: Penguin, 2006); and Hitchens, *God Is Not Great: How Religion Poisons Everything* (New York: Hachette Book Group, 2007).
31. Harris, *The End of Faith: Religion, Terror, and the Future of Reason* (New York: Norton, 2004) and *Letter to a Christian Nation* (New York: Knopf, 2006).

IV MATHEMATICS

A. *Efficacy*

The distinguished scientist Eugene Wigner spoke of the "unreasonable efficacy of mathematics in the natural sciences."[32] What might he have meant? Mathematics and natural science in the West have developed hand in hand, from the Leibniz/Newton discovery of the differential calculus in the seventeenth century to the non-Abelian gauge theory of contemporary quantum chromodynamics. Much of this mathematics is abstruse, going immensely beyond the elementary arithmetic we learn in grade school. Why should the world be significantly describable by *these* mathematical structures? Why should these complex and deep structures be applicable in interesting and useful ways?

Perhaps you will claim that no matter how the world had been, it would have been describable by mathematics of some kind or other. Perhaps so; but what is unreasonable, in Wigner's terms, is that the sort of mathematics effective in science is extremely challenging mathematics, though still such that we human beings can grasp and use it (if only after considerable effort). No matter how things had been, perhaps there would have been mathematical formulas describing the world's behavior. For example, here is one way things could have been: nothing but atomless gunk with nothing happening. I guess there could be mathematical descriptions of such a reality, but they would be supremely uninteresting. Here is another way things could have been: lots of events happening in kaleidoscopic variety and succession, but with no rhyme or reason, no patterns, or at any rate no patterns discernible to creatures

---

32. Wigner, "The Unreasonable Effectiveness of Mathematics in the Natural Sciences," in *Communications in Pure and Applied Mathematics*, vol. 13, no. I (February 1960).

like us. Here too mathematical description might be possible: event A happened and lasted ten seconds; then event B happened and lasted twice as long as A; then C happened and had more components than A, and so on. But again, under that scenario the world would not be mathematically describable in ways of interest to creatures with our kinds of cognitive faculties. Still a third way things could have been: there could have been surface variety and chaos and unpredictability with deep regularity and law—so deep, in fact, as to be humanly inaccessible.

All of these are ways in which mathematical description would be possible; these ways would also be of no interest to us. What Wigner notes, on the other hand, is that our world is mathematically describable in terms of fascinating underlying mathematical structures of astounding complexity but also deep simplicity. To discover it has required strenuous and cooperative effort on the part of many scientists and mathematicians. That mathematics of this sort should be applicable to the world is indeed astounding. It is also properly thought of as unreasonable, in the sense that from a naturalistic perspective it would be wholly unreasonable to expect this sort of mathematics to be useful in describing our world. It makes eminently good sense from the perspective of theism, however. Science is a splendid achievement, and much of its splendor depends upon mathematics being applicable to the world in such a way that it is both accessible to us but also offers a challenge of a high order. According to theism, God creates human beings in his image, a crucial component of which is the ability to know worthwhile and important things about our world. Science with its mathematical emphasis is a prime example of this image in us: science requires our very best efforts—both as communities and individuals—and it delivers magnificent results. All of this seems wholly appropriate from a theistic point of view; as Paul Dirac, who came up with an influential formulation of quantum theory, put it, "God is a mathematician of a very high order and He used advanced mathematics in constructing the universe."[33] So here we have another manifestation of deep concord between science and theistic religion: the way in which mathematics is applicable to the universe.

B. Accessibility

Just as it is unreasonable, from a naturalistic perspective, to expect mathematics of this sort to be efficacious, so it is unreasonable, from that perspective, to expect human beings to be able to grasp and practice the kind of mathematics employed in contemporary science. From that point of view, the best guess about our origins is that we human beings and our cognitive faculties have come to be by way of natural selection winnowing some form of genetic variation. The purpose of our cognitive faculties, from that perspective, is to contribute to our reproductive fitness, to contribute to survival and reproduction. Current physics with its ubiquitous partial differential equations (not to mention relativity theory with its tensors, quantum mechanics with its non-Abelian group theory, and current set theory with its daunting complexities) involves mathematics of great depth, requiring cognitive powers going enormously beyond what is required for survival and reproduction. Indeed, it is only the occasional assistant professor of mathematics or logic who needs to be able to prove Gödel's first incompleteness theorem in order to survive and reproduce.

These abilities far surpass what is required for reproductive fitness now, and even further beyond what would have been required for reproductive fitness back there on the plains of Serengeti. That sort of ability and interest would have been of scant adaptive use in

33. Dirac, "The Evolution of the Physicists's Picture of Nature," *Scientific American* 2008, no. 5 (May 1963), p. 53.

the Pleistocene. As a matter of fact, it would have been a positive hindrance, due to the nerdiness factor. What prehistoric female would be interested in a male who wanted to think about whether a set could be equal in cardinality to its power set, instead of where to look for game?[34]

Of course it is always possible to maintain that these mathematical powers are a sort of spandrel, of no adaptive use in themselves, but an inevitable accompaniment of other powers that do promote reproductive fitness. The ability to see that 7 gazelles will provide much more meat than 2 gazelles is of indisputable adaptive utility; one could argue that these more advanced cognitive powers are inevitably connected with that elementary ability, in such a way that you can't have the one without having the other.

Well, perhaps; but it sounds pretty flimsy, and the easy and universal availability of such explanations makes them wholly implausible. It's like giving an evolutionary explanation of the music of Mozart and Bach in terms of the adaptiveness, the usefulness, in the Pleistocene, of rhythmical movement in walking or running long distances.[35]

C. The Nature of Mathematics

There is a third way in which the "unreasonable efficacy" of mathematics in science points to and exemplifies deep concord between theistic religion and science. Mathematics, naturally enough, is centrally about numbers and sets. But numbers and sets themselves make a great deal more sense from the point of

---

34. Well, you never really know. Eleonore Stump, the *mater familias* of Christian philosophy, reminds me that female pheasants seem to be deeply impressed by apparently gratuitous decorative plumage; and some claim that perverse preference on the part of female Irish elk for males with gigantic horns led to the extinction of the species. Who knows what idiosyncratic romantic preferences prehistoric women might have had? Still, set theory...?

35. See chapter 5.

view of theism than from that of naturalism. Now there are two quite different but widely shared intuitions about the nature of numbers and sets. First, we think of numbers and sets as abstract objects, the same sort of thing as propositions, properties, states of affairs and the like. It natural to think of these things as existing necessarily, such that they would have been there no matter how things had turned out. (After all, we think of some propositions—true mathematical propositions, for example—as necessarily true; but a proposition can't be necessarily true without existing necessarily.) On the other hand, there is another equally widely shared intuition about these things: most people who have thought about the question, think it incredible that these abstract objects should just exist, just *be* there, whether or not they are ever thought of by anyone. Platonism with respect to these objects is the position that they do exist in that way, that is, in such a way as to be independent of mind; even if there were no minds at all, they would still exist. But there have been very few real Platonists, perhaps none besides Plato and Frege, if indeed Plato and Frege were real Platonists (and even Frege, that alleged arch-Platonist, referred to propositions as *gedanken*, thoughts). It is therefore extremely tempting to think of abstract objects as ontologically dependent upon mental or intellectual activity in such a way that either they just are thoughts, or else at any rate couldn't exist if not thought of. (According to the idealistic tradition beginning with Kant, propositions are essentially *judgments*.)

But if it is *human* thinkers that are at issue, then there are far too many abstract objects. There are far too many real numbers for each to have been thought of by some human being. The same goes for propositions; there are at least as many propositions as there are real numbers. (For every real number r, for example, there is the proposition that r is distinct from the Taj Mahal.) On the other hand, if abstract objects were divine thoughts, there would be no problem here. So perhaps the most natural way to think about abstract objects, including numbers, is as divine thoughts.[36]

---

36. Consider Thomas Aquinas, *De Veritate*: "Even if there were no human intellects, there could be truths because of their relation to the divine intellect. But if, *per impossibile*, there were no intellects at all, but things continued to exist, then there would be no such reality as truth." And see my "How to be an Anti-Realist," *Proceedings and Addresses of the American Philosophical Association*, 1982.

Second, consider sets. Perhaps the most common way to think of sets is as displaying at least the following characteristics: (1) no set is a member of itself; (2) sets (unlike properties) have their extensions essentially; hence sets with contingently existing members are themselves contingent beings, and no set could have existed if one of its members had not; (3) sets form an iterated structure: at the first level, there are sets whose members are nonsets, at the second, sets whose members are nonsets or first level sets, and so on.[37] (Note that on this iterative conception, the elements of a set are in an important sense prior to the set. That is why on this conception no set is a member of itself, thus disarming the Russell paradoxes in their set theoretical form.[38])

It is also natural to think of sets as *collections*—that is, things whose existence depends upon a certain sort of intellectual activity—a collecting or "thinking together." Thus Georg Cantor: "By a 'set' we understand any collection M into a whole of definite, well-distinguished objects of our intuition or our thought (which will be called the 'elements' of M)."[39] According to Hao Wang, "the set is a single object formed by collecting the members together."[40]

And

> It is a basic feature of reality that there are many things. When a multitude of given objects can be collected together, we arrive at a set. For example, there are two tables in this room. We are ready to view them as given both separately and as a unity, and justify this by pointing to them or looking at them or thinking about them either one after the other or simultaneously. Somehow the viewing of certain given

37. See Charles Parsons, "What is the Iterative Conception of Set?" in *Mathematic in Philosophy* (Ithaca: Cornell University Press, 1983), pp. 268ff.
38. J. R. Shoenfield, *Mathematical Logic* (Boston: Addison-Wesley, 1965) writes:
    A closer examination of the (Russell) paradox shows that it does not really contradict the intuitive notion of a set. According to this notion, a set A is formed by gathering together certain objects to form a single object, which is the set A. Thus before the set A is formed, we must have available all of the objects which are to be members of A (p. 238).
39. Cantor, *Gesammelte Abhandlungen mathematischen und philosophischen Inhalts*, ed. Ernest Zermelo (Berlin: Springer, 1932), p. 282.
40. Wang, *Mathematics to Philosophy* (New York: Humanities Press, 1974), p. 238.

> objects together suggests a loose link which ties the objects together in our intuition.[41]

If sets *were* collections, that would explain their having the first three features. (First, if sets were collections, the result of a collecting activity, the elements collected would have to be present before the collecting; hence no set is a member of itself. Second, a collection could not have existed but been a collection of items different from the ones actually collected, and a collection can't exist unless the elements collected exist; hence collections have their members essentially, and can't exist unless those members do. And third, clearly there are noncollections, then first level collections whose only members are noncollections, then second level collections whose members are noncollections or first level collections, et cetera.) But of course there are far too many sets for them to be a product of *human* thinking together. Furthermore, many sets are such that no human being could possibly think all their members together—for example, the set of real numbers. Therefore there are many sets such that no human being has ever thought their members together, many such that their members have not been thought together by any human being. That requires an infinite mind—one like God's.

The basic objects of mathematics, that is, numbers and sets, fit very neatly into a theistic way of looking at the world—vastly better than into a naturalistic perspective. Perhaps this explains the strenuous efforts, on the part of Hartry Field and others, to "reinterpret" mathematics in such a way as to make it possible for naturalism to accommodate it.[42] Again, we see deep concord between theistic religion and science.

D. *Mathematical Objects as Abstract*

There is still another way in which theism is friendly to mathematics, more friendly than naturalism is. The objects of mathematics—numbers, functions, sets—are *abstract* objects. Abstract objects, so

41. Wang, *Mathematics to Philosophy*, p. 182.
42. Field, *Realism, Mathematics and Modality* (Oxford: Blackwell, 1989).

we think, differ from concrete objects in that they do not occupy space and do not enter into causal relations. The number 3 can't cause anything to happen; it is causally inert. This is not a peculiarity of that number; the same goes for all the other numbers—real, complex, whatever—and for sets, including functions. But this creates a puzzle.[43] It seems sensible to think that the objects we can know about can causally affect us in some way, or at least stand in causal relationship with us. We know about trees. We can perceive them; this involves light waves being reflected from trees into our eyes, forming an image on the retina; this induces electrical activity in the optic nerve, finally issuing in neural activity in the brain. We know something about distant galaxies, again, only because electromagnetic radiation from them reaches us. As I say, it seems sensible to think that a necessary condition of our knowing about an object or kind of object is our standing in some kind of causal relation to that object or kind of object. If this is so, however, and if, furthermore, numbers and their kin are abstract objects, then it looks as though we couldn't know anything about them.

Once again, theism is relevant. According to classical versions of theism, sets, numbers and the like, as I argued above, are best conceived as divine thoughts. But then they stand to God in the relation in which a thought stands to a thinker. This is presumably a *productive* relation: the thinker produces his thoughts. It is therefore also a causal relation. If so, then numbers and other abstract objects also stand in a causal relation to us. For we too stand in a causal relation to God; but then anything else that stands in a causal relation to God stands in a causal relation to us. Therefore numbers and sets stand in a causal relation to us, and the problem about our knowing these things disappears.

43. See Paul Benacerraf, "What Numbers Could Not Be," *The Philosophical Review*, 74: 47–73 (1965).

V INDUCTION AND LEARNING FROM EXPERIENCE

Another and perhaps less obvious condition for the success of science has to do with our ways of learning from experience. We human beings take it utterly for granted that the future will resemble the past. As David Hume pointed out with his usual keen insight, in the past we have found bread but not stones to be nourishing (this may have been known even before Hume); we expect the former to continue to have this salubrious property and the latter to lack it. Past ax heads dropped into water have sunk; we expect the next one to do the same. Night has always followed day: we assume in consequence that today will be followed by tonight. It is only by virtue of this assumption, furthermore, that we are able to learn from experience. Of course we don't expect the future to resemble the past in *every* respect; I have no doubt, for example, that my grandchildren will be larger ten years from now. Saying precisely how we expect the future to resemble the past is no mean task; we expect the future to resemble the past in relevant respects; but specifying the relevant respects is far from easy. Nevertheless, we do expect the future to resemble the past, and this expectation is crucial to our being able to learn from experience.

We generalize what we learn to the future; but this is not the extent of our generalization of experience. Aristotle held that heavy objects fall faster than light objects; according to scientific folklore, Galileo dropped a couple of balls of unequal weights from the leaning Tower of Pisa, noted that they fell at the same rate, and concluded that Aristotle was wrong. We run a few experiments, and conclude that Newton's law of gravity is at least approximately true. In cases like these we don't conclude merely that Aristotle's theory is false for that pair of balls Galileo allegedly dropped, or for the area around the leaning tower, or on Thursdays. We don't conclude that maybe Aristotle was right in his day—two thousand years ago, maybe heavy things did fall faster than light. No; we conclude that Aristotle's theory is false generally, and that Galileo's results hold for any pair of balls that might be dropped. In experiments verifying Newton's laws, we don't infer merely that Newton's laws held in the time and place where those experiments were conducted; we think they hold much more generally. We don't necessarily conclude that they hold for all of time and space (we are open to the idea that things may have been different shortly after the big bang, or in one of those other universes of which cosmologists speak); but we do conclude that they hold far beyond the temporal and spatial limits of the situation of the experiments. The great eighteenth-century philosopher Thomas Reid claimed that among the "principles of contingent truth" is that *"in the phaenomena of nature, what is to be, will probably be like to what has been in similar circumstances"* (Reid's emphasis). What he meant is that we simply find ourselves, by virtue of our nature, making that assumption. This principle, furthermore, "is necessary for us before we are able to discover it by reasoning, and therefore is made a part of our constitution, and produces its effects before the use of reason."[44] Reid goes on to claim that having this conviction—that "in the phaenomena of nature, what is to be, will probably be like to what has been in similar circumstances"—is essential to learning from experience. This isn't exactly right, at any rate if what Reid means is that one must explicitly have this belief in order to learn from experience. A child learns from experience; "the burnt child dreads the fire." The burnt child may never have raised the question whether the future

---

44. Reid, *Essays on the Intellectual Powers of Man*, Essay VI, V, 12. A similar principle is stated by David Hume:

If reason determined us, it wou'd proceed upon that principle, that past instances, of which we have had no experience, must resemble those, of which we have had experience, and that the course of nature continues always uniformly the same. *A Treatise of Human Nature*, ed. L.A. Selby-Bigge (Oxford: Clarendon Press, first edition 1888), Book I, Part III, 6, p. 89 (Hume's emphasis).

resembles the past, and she may have no explicit views at all on that topic. What learning from experience requires is more like a certain habit, a certain practice—the habit of making inductive inferences. But that too isn't exactly right: in any event there need be nothing like explicitly thinking of premise and conclusion. It is more as if we have the experience and in direct response to it form a belief that goes far beyond the confines of the experience.

We are able to learn that unsupported rocks near the surface of the earth will fall down rather than up, that water is good to drink, that rockfall is dangerous—we learn these things only by virtue of exercising this habit. Indeed, it is only by virtue of this habit that a child is able to learn a language. (My parents teach me "red"; I get the idea and see what property they express by that word; unless I proceed in accord with this habit, I shall have to start over the next time they use "red.") Our ordinary cognitive life deeply depends on our making this assumption, or following this practice.

Of course this holds for the practice of science as well as for everyday cognitive life. According to the story noted above, Galileo dropped two balls, one heavy and one light, off the leaning Tower of Pisa, to see if Aristotle was right in thinking heavy objects fall faster than light. Aristotle was wrong; they fell at the same rate. Presumably no one suggested that Galileo should perhaps perform this experiment every day, on the grounds that all he had shown was that on that particular day heavy and light objects fall at the same rate. No one suggested that the experiment should be repeated in Asia, or that we should look for other evidence on the question whether in Aristotle's time he may have been right. A crucial experiment may be repeated, but not because we wonder whether the same circumstances will yield the same result.

David Hume, that great patron of skeptics, thought he detected a philosophical problem here:

As to past *Experience*, it can be allowed to give *direct* and *certain* information of those precise objects only, and that precise period of time, which fell under its cognizance: but why this experience should be extended to future times, and to other objects, which for aught we know, may be only in appearance similar; this is the main question on which I would insist. The bread, which I formerly ate, nourished me; that is, a body of such sensible qualities was, at that time, endued with such secret powers: but does it follow, that other bread must also nourish me at another time, and that like sensible qualities must always be attended with like secret powers?[45]

Right; it doesn't follow. There are plenty of possible worlds that match the actual world up to the present time, but then diverge wildly, so that inductive inferences would mostly fail in those other worlds. There are as many of those counter-inductive worlds as there are worlds in which induction will continue to be reliable. It is by no means inevitable that inductive reasoning should be successful; its success is one more example of the fit between our cognitive faculties and the world.

Hume goes on to claim that there is no rational foundation for this sort of reasoning, and that inductive reasoning is not in fact rational. Is this correct? Say that a kind of reasoning is rational, for us, just if a human being with properly functioning cognitive faculties (properly functioning *ratio* or reason) would engage this kind of reasoning; if so Hume is wrong. We human beings, including those among us with properly functioning cognitive faculties, are inveterately addicted to inductive reasoning. And this is another example of fit between our cognitive faculties and the world in which we find ourselves. Like the others, this fit is to be expected given theism. God has created us in his image; this involves our being able to have significant knowledge

---

45. Hume, *An Enquiry Concerning Human Understanding* (LaSalle: The Open Court Publishing Co., 1956), Sect. IV, 2, p. 34.

about our world. That requires the *adequatio intellectus ad rem* (the fit of intellect with reality) of which the medievals spoke, and the success of inductive reasoning is one more example of this *adequatio*. According to theism, God has created us in such a way that we reason in inductive fashion; he has created our world in such a way that inductive reasoning is successful. This is one more manifestation of the deep concord between theism and science.

VI SIMPLICITY AND OTHER THEORETICAL VIRTUES

Scientific theories, so we are told, are underdetermined by the evidence. This just means that these theories *go beyond* the evidence; they are not merely compendious ways of stating the evidence. Very few experiments of the sort Galileo conducted with those balls of different weights have been conducted; we still think his results hold for all or nearly all objects. The evidence for Newton's laws (as applied to middle-sized objects moving at moderate velocities with respect to each other) is extensive, but the laws go far beyond the evidence, applying to future cases of motion as well as past but unobserved cases. The same goes for any scientific theory. For example, the actual experimental evidence for general relativity is fairly slim, and is compatible with many theories inconsistent with general relativity. The evidence for Newton's law of gravitation is compatible with a "law" such as

> Any two physical objects attract each other with a force conforming to $G\, m_1 m_2$ over r^2 except on Thursdays, when G is replaced by G^*, (where G^* a value indistinguishable from G by current methods).

One way to think of this is in terms of the curve fitting problem. As Leibniz already pointed out in the seventeenth century, for any finite set of observations of the path of a comet, infinitely many different curves can be found to fit; he also points out that given any finite set of statistics, there will be infinitely many statistical hypotheses fitting the facts.[46]

So why do we choose certain hypotheses to endorse, when there are infinitely many compatible with our evidence? Because these hypotheses, as opposed to others, display the so-called *theoretical virtues*. Among these virtues the following have been proposed: simplicity, parsimony (which may be a form of simplicity), elegance or beauty, consilience (fit with other favored or established hypotheses), and fruitfulness. Nobel laureate Steven Weinberg suggests that the beauty of general relativity is what led him and others to embrace it, well before there was serious evidence for it:

> I remember that, when I learned general relativity in the 1950s, before modern radar and radio astronomy began to give impressive new evidence for the theory, I took it for granted that general relativity was more or less correct. Perhaps all of us were just gullible and lucky, but I do not think that is the real explanation. I believe that the general acceptance of general relativity was due in large part to the attractions of the theory itself—in short, to its beauty.[47]

Simplicity (which is involved in beauty) is often thought of as particularly important.[48] Thus Einstein:

---

46. See Ian Hacking's *The Emergence of Probability* (Cambridge: Cambridge University Press, 1975), p. 164.

47. Weinberg, *Dreams of a Final Theory* (New York: Pantheon, 1992), p. 98.

48. Here see Richard Swinburne, *Simplicity as Evidence of Truth* (Milwaukee: Marquette University Press, 1997).

With every new important advance the researcher here sees his expectations surpassed, in that those basic laws are more and more simplified under the pressure of experience. With astonishment he sees apparent chaos resolved into a sublime order that is to be attributed not to the rule of the individual mind, but to the constitution of the world of experience; this is what Leibniz so happily characterized as "pre-established harmony."[49]

Complicated, gerrymandered theories are rejected. Complex Rube Goldberg contraptions are ridiculed. When confronted with a set of data plotted on a graph, we draw the simplest curve that will accommodate all the data. There are any number of other curves that will accommodate the data; but these will be rejected in favor of the simplest alternative. Physics gives us a law of conservation of energy: energy is conserved in all closed physical systems. This is compatible with our evidence; but of course so are indefinitely many other "laws"—for example, energy is conserved in all closed physical systems except in months whose names start with "J," in each of which there are exactly twelve undetectable exceptions.

Simplicity, therefore, is a crucially important part of our intellectual or cognitive architecture—or rather, *preference* for simplicity is. That the world be relevantly simple is also required, of course, for the success of science. It isn't a necessary truth, however, that simple theories are more likely to be true than complex theories. Naturalism gives us no reason at all to expect the world to conform to our preference for simplicity. From that perspective, surely, the world could just as well have been such that unlovely, miserably complex theories are more likely to be true.

Theism with its doctrine of the *imago dei*, on the other hand, is relevant in two quite distinct respects. First, insofar as we have been cre-

---

49. Einstein, *Ideas and Opinions* (New York: Bonanza Books, 1954), p. 224-27.

ated in God's image, it is reasonable to think our intellectual preferences resemble his. We value simplicity, elegance, beauty; it is therefore reasonable to think that the same goes for God. But if he too values these qualities, it is reasonable to think this divine preference will be reflected in the world he has created. Second, what we have here is another example of God's having created us and our world in such a way that there is that *adequatio intellectus ad rem*. We are so constituted that our intellectual success requires that the world be relevantly simple; the world is in fact relevantly simple. This fit is only to be expected on theism, but is a piece of enormous cosmic serendipity on naturalism. It is therefore one more way in which there is deep concord between theistic religion and science. Surely the world could have been such that unlovely, miserably complex theories are more likely to be true. It could have been such that there is insufficient simplicity for science, at least our human brand of science, to be successful.

VII CONTINGENCY AND SCIENCE AS EMPIRICAL

A final but crucial point. Science, obviously, has a substantial empirical element; in this way it contrasts with, for example, philosophy and literary criticism. (Indeed, many take this as a reason for invidious comparisons between philosophy and science.) In science we don't sit in our armchair and just try to figure out the laws of motion; nor do we consult the ancients. Instead we take a look. There is a famous (but surely apocryphal) story about some medieval followers of Aristotle who wanted to know how many teeth a horse has. It didn't occur to them to open a horse's mouth and count its teeth; they tried to deduce the answer from first principles (and Aristotle's works). This is the opposite of the scientific impulse. Rather, we take a look, or in more abstruse cases, think up theories that can be tested in experience. It isn't true, of course, that every scientific assertion, just by itself, is testable or empirically verifiable or falsifiable. The proposition *there are electrons* is a scientific assertion; by itself, however, it has no empirical consequences and isn't testable. What yields empirical predictions, and thus is subject to empirical test, are whole theories; such a theory will include the assertion that there are electrons, and will also imply consequences that can be confronted with experience.

This means that we can't take assertions one by one and declare them scientific or unscientific, depending on whether they are empirically testable. The devotees of intelligent design claim, naturally enough, that an intelligent designer is involved in the creation of our world; others insist that this proposition is untestable and hence not properly part of science. Well, perhaps that proposition, like the proposition that there are electrons, isn't empirically verifiable or falsifiable *just by itself*; but many propositions entailing or including that one are testable. For example, the proposition *an intelligent designer has designed and created 800-pound rabbits that live in Cleveland* is falsifiable, and indeed false. On the other hand, the proposition *an intelligent designer has designed and created horses* entails that there are horses, and thus, like electron theory, has empirical consequences that are in fact true. It is difficult *in excelsis* to say precisely what testability is, or how we should think about it; nevertheless there is no doubt that this link to the empirical is an essential part of modern science.

Here there is another crucial connection between theistic belief and modern science. According to theism, God has created the world; but divine creation is *contingent*. Many of God's properties—his omniscience and omnipotence, his goodness and love—are, as theists think of it, *essential* to him: he has them in every possible world in which he exists. (And since, according to most theistic thought, God is a necessary being, one that exists in every possible world, he has those properties in every possible world.) Not so, however, with God's properties of being a creator and having created our world.

God is not obliged, by his nature or anything else, to create the world; there are plenty of possible worlds in which he doesn't create a world outside himself. Instead, creation is a free action on his part. Furthermore, given that he *does* create, he isn't obliged to do so in any particular way. He wasn't obliged to create people or electrons; he wasn't obliged to create matter in such a way that Newton's laws of motion hold for middle-sized objects moving at moderate velocities with respect to each other; he wasn't obliged to create a world in which quantum mechanics or relativity theory would be true. That he has created a world outside of himself at all, and that the world he has created displays the particular character and laws it does display— these are contingent matters.

It is this doctrine of the contingency of divine creation that both underlies and underwrites the empirical character of modern Western science.[50] The realm of the necessary is the realm of a priori knowledge, knowledge that is prior to experience. Here we have mathematics and logic and much philosophy. We know that $3+1 = 4$, but not by way of empirical investigation; we don't assemble a lot of pairs of groups of three things with groups of one thing, and then count up the members of those pairs to see if they make four. We can simply see that $3+1 = 4$. In the same way, we know that if all terriers are dogs and all dogs are animals, then all terriers are animals. Again, we know this a priori; we don't have to assemble packs of terriers, note that they are all dogs, and then check to see whether they are animals. Our knowledge of what is logically necessary is a priori.[51] What is contin-

50. See Del Ratzsch, "Humanness in their Hearts: Where Science and Religion Fuse" in *The Believing Primate*, ed. Jeffrey Schloss and Michael Murray (New York: Oxford University Press, 2009).

51. There are exceptions. You use a computer to calculate the product of a couple of 6 digit numbers; the computer comes up with a certain number n. Your knowledge that this product is indeed n—which is, of course, necessary—is *a posteriori*; it depends on your *a posteriori* knowledge that computers ordinarily calculate the right answers to arithmetical questions. I name the actual world "alpha"; then it is a necessary truth that (say) there was a U.S. Civil War in alpha, but your only way of knowing this necessary truth is *a posteriori*.

gent, on the other hand, is the domain or realm of a posteriori knowledge, knowledge that requires experience, the sort of knowledge produced by perception, memory, the sort of knowledge produced by the empirical methods of science.[52] We can't just sit down and figure out whether Newton's laws of motion apply; we have to resort to observation and experience. We can't tell a priori how many teeth horses have or whether heavy objects fall faster than light objects; we must take a look.[53]

This relationship between the contingency of creation and the importance of the empirical, in science, was recognized very early; indeed, the former is the source of the latter. Thus Roger Cotes, from the preface he wrote for the second edition of Newton's *Principia Mathematica*:

> Without all doubt this world, so diversified with that variety of forms and motions we find in it, could arise from nothing but the perfectly free will of God directing and presiding over all.
>
> From this fountain it is that those laws, which we call the laws of Nature, have flowed, in which there appear many traces indeed of the most wise contrivance, but not the least shadow of necessity. These *therefore* we must not seek from uncertain conjectures, *but learn them from observations and experiments.*[54]

---

52. Some have claimed that there are contingent truths of which we have a priori knowledge. Others claim this is a mistake; see my *The Nature of Necessity* (Oxford: Clarendon Press, 1974) p. 8, footnote 1.

53. Here I must correct or perhaps supplement what I said earlier about Ockam and Aquinas. The Thomists, following Aristotle, leaned towards necessity in nature; Ockham emphasized its contingency. Perhaps it was the creative tension between these that was the fertile soil for modern science. Perhaps what was required is something like a synthesis of Ockham and Aquinas: as Ockham says, God freely chooses to create this world; as Aquinas says, however, he creates a world that manifests regularity and reliability.

54. Cotes, *Newton's Philosophy of Nature: Selections from his writings*, pp. 132-33; emphasis added.

Here we have still another way in which there is deep concord between science and theistic religion.

In this chapter, we've seen that theistic religion gives us reason to expect our cognitive capacities to match the world in such a way as to make modern science possible. Naturalism gives us no reason at all to expect this sort of match; from the point of view of naturalism, it would be an overwhelming piece of cosmic serendipity if there were such a match. As a matter of fact, however, things are much worse than that for naturalism; in the next chapter I'll explain why.

PART IV

DEEP CONFLICT

Chapter 10

The Evolutionary Argument
Against Naturalism

My overall thesis: there is superficial conflict but deep concord between science and religion, and superficial concord but deep conflict between science and naturalism. So far I have developed the first half of this theme; it is now time to turn to the second.

I SUPERFICIAL CONCORD

I suppose it isn't really necessary to argue that there is (at least) superficial concord between naturalism and science; the high priests of naturalism trumpet this loudly enough. Naturalists pledge allegiance to science; they nail their banner to the mast of science; they wrap themselves in the mantle of science like a politician in the flag. They confidently claim that naturalism is part of the "scientific worldview," and that the advent of modern science has exposed supernaturalism as a tissue of superstition—perhaps acceptable and perhaps even sensible in a prescientific age, but now superseded. A particularly charming phrase, here, is the obligatory "as we now know"; we were previously wallowing in ignorance and superstition, but now, thanks to science, we finally know the truth.[1]

---

1. For example: "Natural selection, the blind, unconscious automatic process which Darwin discovered, and which we now know is the explanation for the existence and apparently

All of this, however, is error, and whopping error at that. Naturalists don't ordinarily explain just why they think science guarantees or supports naturalism; they are usually content just to announce the fact. And ordinarily what they announce is not that, say, quantum mechanics, or general relativity, or the periodic table of the elements has dethroned theism and supernaturalism, but that Darwin has. According to Stephen J. Gould (see above chapter 1), "Before Darwin, we thought that a benevolent God had created us"; but now, after Darwin, we realize that "No intervening spirit watches lovingly over the affairs of nature." George Gaylord Simpson seconds the motion: Man is the result of a purposeless and natural process that did not have him in mind.[2]

As we saw in chapters 1 and 2, however, this is the result of confusion—a confusion between guided and unguided evolution, between sober science and philosophical or theological add-on. Let me briefly recapitulate. The scientific theory of evolution just as such is entirely compatible with the thought that God has guided and orchestrated the course of evolution, planned and directed it, in such a way as to achieve the ends he intends. Perhaps he causes the right mutations to arise at the right time; perhaps he preserves certain populations from extinction; perhaps he is active in many other ways.[3] On the one hand, therefore, we have the scientific theory, and on the other, there is the claim that the course of evolution is not directed or guided or orchestrated

---

purposeful form of all life, has no purpose in mind." Richard Dawkins, *The Blind Watchmaker* (London and New York: Norton, 1986), p. 5.

2. Simpson, *The Meaning of Evolution* (New Haven: Yale University Press, rev. ed., 1967), pp. 344–45.

3. For example, he might do so in the way suggested in chapter 4: he might be active at the quantum level in such a way that (in accord with the GRW version of quantum mechanics) he selects the eigenvalues to which the wave functions associated with quantum mechanical systems collapse.

by anyone; it displays no teleology; it is blind and unforeseeing; as Dawkins says, it has no aim or goal in its mind's eye, mainly because it has no mind's eye.

This claim, however, despite its strident proclamation, is no part of the scientific theory as such; it is instead a metaphysical or theological add-on. On the one hand there is the scientific theory; on the other, the metaphysical add-on, according to which the process is unguided. The first is part of current science, and deserves the respect properly accorded to a pillar of science; but the first is entirely compatible with theism. The second supports naturalism, all right, but is not part of science, and does not deserve the respect properly accorded science. And the confusion of the two—confusing the scientific theory with the result of annexing that add-on to it, confusing evolution as such with unguided evolution—deserves not respect, but disdain.

The fact is, as we saw in chapter 9, science fits much better with theism than with naturalism. On balance, theism is vastly more hospitable to science than naturalism, a much better home for it. Indeed, it is theism, not naturalism, that deserves to be called "the scientific worldview."

II DEEP CONFLICT

In this chapter I'll take this line of thought further. I'll argue that despite the superficial concord between naturalism and science— despite all the claims to the effect that science implies, or requires, or supports, or confirms, or comports well with naturalism—the fact is science and naturalism don't fit together at all well. The fact is there is deep unease, deep discord, deep conflict between naturalism and science. I'll argue that there is a deep and irremediable conflict between naturalism and *evolution*—and hence between naturalism and science.[4] My quarrel is certainly not with the scientific theory of evolution. Nor is it an argument for the conclusion that unguided evolution could not produce creatures with reliable belief-producing faculties; I very much doubt that it could, but that it *couldn't* is neither a premise nor the conclusion of my argument.[5] Still further, my argument will not be for the conclusion that naturalism is false, although of course I believe that it is.

What I *will* argue is that naturalism is in conflict with evolution, a main pillar of contemporary science. And the conflict in question is not that they can't both be true (the conflict is not that there is a contradiction between them); it is rather that one can't sensibly accept them both. By way of analogy: I can't sensibly believe that there aren't any beliefs, or that no one has true beliefs, or that my beliefs are all false. These things are all possible, but I can't sensibly believe them. In the same way, I mean to argue that one can't sensibly believe both naturalism and the scientific theory of evolution. If my argument is cogent, it follows that there is deep and serious conflict between naturalism and evolution, and hence deep conflict between naturalism and science.

4. Among the ancestors of my argument are C. S. Lewis's argument in *Miracles* (1947) and Richard Taylor in *Metaphysics* (1963). I first proposed the argument in "An Evolutionary Argument Against Naturalism," *Logos* 12 (1991); it has also appeared in many other places, including *Warrant and Proper Function* (New York: Oxford University Press, 1993), chapter 12; *Warranted Christian Belief* (New York: Oxford University Press, 2000), pp. 227ff.; *Naturalism Defeated? Essays on Plantinga's Evolutionary Argument Against Naturalism*, ed. James Beilby (Ithaca: Cornell University Press, 2002), Introduction, pp. 1ff. and "Reply to Beilby's Cohorts," p. 204ff.; *God or Blind Nature*, internet book with Paul Draper, 2007 (available at http://www.infidels.org/library/modern/debates/great-debate.html); Plantinga and Tooley, *Knowledge of God* (New York: Blackwell Publishing, 2008), pp. 30ff.; with Daniel Dennett, *Science and Religion; Are They Compatible?*, pp. 16ff., 66ff.; and "Content and Natural Selection," *Philosophy and Phenomenological Research*, forthcoming. In the years since I first proposed it, I have learned much about the argument (from critics and supporters alike), and have repeatedly revised it. The version presented here is the official and final version (I hope).

5. Contra Daniel Dennett; see Daniel Dennett and Alvin Plantinga, *Science and Religion; Are They Compatible?*, pp. 73ff. "No Miracles Needed," where Dennett thus misconstrues the argument.

Now it is not clear that naturalism, as it stands, is a religion; there is enough vagueness around the edges of the concept of religion for it to be unclear whether naturalism does or doesn't belong there. But naturalism does serve one of the main functions of a religion: it offers a master narrative, it answers deep and important human questions. Immanuel Kant identified three great human questions: Is there such a person as God? Do we human beings have significant freedom? And can we human beings expect life after death? Naturalism gives answers to these questions: there is no God, there is no immortality, and the case for genuine freedom is at best dicey. Naturalism tells us what reality is ultimately like, where we fit into the universe, how we are related to other creatures, and how it happens that we came to be. Naturalism is therefore in competition with the great theistic religions: even if it is not itself a religion, it plays one of the main roles of a religion. Suppose we call it a "quasi-religion." I've already argued that there is no conflict between theistic religion and science; if my argument in this chapter is right, however, there *is* profound conflict between science and a quasi-religion, namely naturalism. So the real conflict lies not between science and Christian belief (or more generally theistic religion), but between science and naturalism. If we want to focus on the fact that naturalism is a quasi-religion, the truth is that there is a science-religion conflict, all right, but it is between science and naturalism, not science and theistic religion.

III THE ARGUMENT

My argument will center on our *cognitive faculties*: those faculties, or powers, or processes that produce beliefs or knowledge in us. Among these faculties is *memory*, whereby we know something of our past. There is also *perception*, whereby we know something about our physical environment—for the most part our immediate environment, but also something about distant objects such as the sun, the moon, and stars. Another is what is often called "a priori *intuition*," by virtue of which we know truths of elementary arithmetic and logic. By way of a priori intuition we also perceive deductive connections among propositions; we can see which propositions logically follow from which other propositions. In this way, starting from a few elementary axioms, we can explore the great edifices of contemporary logic and mathematics.

There are still other cognitive faculties: Thomas Reid spoke of *sympathy*, which enables us to know the thoughts and feelings of other people, *introspection* (reflection), whereby we know about our own mental life, *testimony* whereby we can learn from others, and *induction*, whereby we can learn from experience. Many would add that there is a *moral sense*, whereby we know right from wrong; and believers in God may add that there is also John Calvin's *sensus divinitatis* or Thomas Aquinas's "natural but confused knowledge of God" whereby we know something of God.[6] These faculties or powers work together in complex and variegated ways to produce a vast battery of beliefs and knowledge, ranging from the simplest everyday beliefs— it's hot in here, I have a pain in my right knee—to less quotidian beliefs such as those to be found in philosophy, theology, history, and the far reaches of science. In science, clearly enough, many of these faculties work together—perception, memory, testimony, sympathy, induction, a priori intuition are all typically involved. There is also the whole process of theory building, which may or may not be reducible to the previous abilities.

My argument will concern the *reliability* of these cognitive faculties. My memory, for example, is reliable only if it produces mostly true beliefs—if, that is, most of my memorial beliefs are true. What proportion of my memorial beliefs must be true for my memory to

6. See my *Warranted Christian Belief*, chapter 6.

be reliable? Of course there is no precise answer; but presumably it would be greater than, say, two-thirds. We can speak of the reliability of a particular faculty—memory, for example—but also of the reliability of the whole battery of our cognitive faculties. And indeed we ordinarily think our faculties *are* reliable, at any rate when they are functioning properly, when there is no cognitive malfunction or disorder or dysfunction. (If I get drunk and suffer from delirium tremens, my perception will be impaired and all bets are off with respect to its reliability.) We also think they are more reliable under some circumstances than others. Visual perception of middle-sized objects (medium-sized dry goods, as J. L. Austin called them) close at hand is more reliable than perception of very small objects, or middle-sized objects at some distance (a mountain goat from six hundred yards, for example). Beliefs about where I was yesterday are ordinarily more likely to be true than the latest high-powered scientific theories.

Now the natural thing to think, from the perspective of theism, is that our faculties are indeed for the most part reliable, at least over a large part of their range of operations. According to theistic religion (see chapter 9), God has created us in his image; an important part of this image consists in our resembling God in that like him, we can have knowledge. In chapter 9 we saw that Thomas Aquinas put it as follows: "Since human beings are said to be in the image of God in virtue of their having a nature that includes an intellect, such a nature is most in the image of God in virtue of being most able to imitate God."[7] When Thomas speaks of our nature as including an intellect, he clearly means to endorse the thought that our cognitive faculties are for the most part reliable. But suppose you are a naturalist: you think that there is no such person as God, and that we and our cognitive faculties have been cobbled together by natural selection. Can you then sensibly think that our cognitive faculties are for the most part reliable?

7. *Summa Theologiae* Ia q. 93, a. 4.

I say you can't. The basic idea of my argument could be put (a bit crudely) as follows. First, the probability of our cognitive faculties being reliable, given naturalism and evolution, is low. (To put it a bit inaccurately but suggestively, if naturalism and evolution were both true, our cognitive faculties would very likely not be reliable.) But then according to the second premise of my argument, if I believe both naturalism and evolution, I have a *defeater* for my intuitive assumption that my cognitive faculties are reliable. If I have a defeater for *that* belief, however, then I have a defeater for *any* belief I take to be produced by my cognitive faculties. That means that I have a defeater for my belief that naturalism and evolution are true. So my belief that naturalism and evolution are true gives me a defeater for that very belief; that belief shoots itself in the foot and is self-referentially incoherent; therefore I cannot rationally accept it. And if one can't accept both naturalism and evolution, that pillar of current science, then there is serious conflict between naturalism and science.

So much for an initial and rough statement of the argument; now we must proceed to develop it more carefully. The first premise, as I say, is something like the worry or doubt that our cognitive faculties would not be reliable if both naturalism and evolution (or perhaps just naturalism) were true. This worry has some eminent advocates. For example, there is Friederich Nietzsche. Ordinarily what Nietzsche says inspires little confidence, but in the following he may be on to something:

> It is unfair to Descartes to call his appeal to God's credibility frivolous. Indeed, only if we assume a God who is morally our like can "truth" and the search for truth be at all something meaningful and promising of success. This God left aside, the question is permitted whether being deceived is not one of the conditions of life.[8]

8. Nietzsche , *Nietzsche: Writings from the Late Notebooks* (Cambridge Texts in the History of Philosophy), ed. Rüdiger Bittner, tr. Kate Sturge (Cambridge: Cambridge University Press, 2003), Notebook 36, June–July 1885, p. 26.

To leap to the present, there is the philosopher Thomas Nagel, himself no friend of theism: "If we came to believe that our capacity for objective theory [true beliefs, e.g.] were the product of natural selection, that would warrant serious skepticism about its results."[9] According to another philosopher, Barry Stroud (again, no friend of theism), "There is an embarrassing absurdity in [naturalism] that is revealed as soon as the naturalist reflects and acknowledges that he believes his naturalistic theory of the world. ... I mean he cannot say it and consistently regard it as true."[10] As Patricia Churchland, an eminent naturalistic philosopher, puts it in a justly famous passage:

> Boiled down to essentials, a nervous system enables the organism to succeed in the four F's: feeding, fleeing, fighting and reproducing. The principle chore of nervous systems is to get the body parts where they should be in order that the organism may survive. .... Improvements in sensorimotor control confer an evolutionary advantage: a fancier style of representing is advantageous *so long as it is geared to the organism's way of life and enhances the organism's chances of survival.* Truth, whatever that is, definitely takes the hindmost.[11]

Churchland's point, clearly, is that (from a naturalistic perspective) what evolution guarantees is (at most) that we *behave* in certain ways—in such ways as to promote survival, or more exactly reproductive success. The principal function or purpose, then, (the "chore" says Churchland) of our cognitive faculties is not that of producing true or verisimilitudinous (nearly true) beliefs, but instead that of contributing

---

9. Nagel, *The View From Nowhere* (Oxford University Press, 1989), p. 79.
10. Stroud, "The Charm of Naturalism" in *Naturalism in Question*, ed. Mario De Caro and David Macarthur (Cambridge: Harvard University Press, 2004), p. 28.
11. Churchland, *Journal of Philosophy* LXXXIV (October 1987), p. 548; emphasis in original.

to survival by getting the body parts in the right place. What evolution underwrites is only (at most) that our *behavior* is reasonably adaptive to the circumstances in which our ancestors found themselves; hence it does not guarantee mostly true or verisimilitudinous beliefs. Our beliefs *might* be mostly true or verisimilitudinous (hereafter I'll omit the "verisimilitudinous"); but there is no particular reason to think they *would* be: natural selection is interested, not in truth, but in appropriate behavior. What Churchland therefore suggests is that naturalistic evolution—that is, the conjunction of metaphysical naturalism with the view that we and our cognitive faculties have arisen by way of the mechanisms and processes proposed by contemporary evolutionary theory—gives us reason to doubt two things: (a) that a *purpose* of our cognitive systems is that of serving us with true beliefs, and (b) that they *do*, in fact, furnish us with mostly true beliefs.

Indeed, Darwin himself expresses serious doubts along these lines: "With me the horrid doubt always arises whether the convictions of man's mind, which has been developed from the mind of the lower animals, are of any value or at all trustworthy. Would any one trust in the convictions of a monkey's mind, if there are any convictions in such a mind?"[12]

IV THE FIRST PREMISE: DARWIN'S DOUBT

Nietzsche, Nagel, Stroud, Churchland, and Darwin, nontheists all, seem to concur: (naturalistic) evolution gives one a reason to doubt that human cognitive faculties produce for the most part true beliefs. Since Darwin is the standout among this group, call this thought

---

12. Letter to William Graham, Down, July 3rd, 1881. In *The Life and Letters of Charles Darwin Including an Autobiographical Chapter*, ed. Francis Darwin (London: John Murray, Albermarle Street, 1887), vol. 1, pp. 315–16. It may be that by "convictions," Darwin means something narrower than belief.

"Darwin's doubt." How shall we construe Darwin's doubt? Can we state it a bit more exactly?

Here the idea of *conditional probability* will be useful. This is a familiar idea, one we constantly employ. The conditional probability of one proposition p on another proposition q is the probability that p is true *given that*, on the condition that, q is true.

Consider the probability that Mr. A will live to be eighty years old, given that he is now thirty-five, smokes heavily, is grossly over-weight, eats only junk food, never exercises, and had grandparents all of whom died by the age of fifty: this probability is pretty low. Contrast this probability with the probability that Mr. B will live to be eighty, given that Mr. B is now seventy, has never smoked, watches his diet like a hawk, runs ten miles a day, and has grandparents all of whom lived to be over one hundred; that probability is much higher. With this notion of conditional probability in hand, we can put Darwin's doubt as follows: the conditional probability that our cognitive faculties are reliable, given naturalism together with the proposition that we have come to be by way of evolution, is low. This is quite a mouthful: we can abbreviate it as

(1) $P(R/N\&E)$ is low.

"R" is the proposition that our cognitive faculties are reliable, "N" is naturalism, and "E" is the proposition that we and our cognitive faculties have come to be in the way proposed by the contemporary scientific theory of evolution. "$P(\ldots/\_\_\_)$" is shorthand for "the probability of…given ___". (1), that is, Darwin's doubt, is the first premise of my argument.

All of the above luminaries apparently endorse something like Darwin's doubt; nevertheless (oddly enough) there are those who seem to disagree. In what follows, therefore, I'll explain why Darwin's doubt seems eminently sensible and indeed correct.

A. *Naturalism and Materialism*

First, we must note that nearly all naturalists are also *materialists* with respect to human beings; they hold that human beings are material objects. From this perspective a human person is not (contrary to Descartes and Augustine) an immaterial substance or self that is connected with or joined to (has?) a material body. Nor is it the case that a human being is a composite that has an immaterial component; human beings do not have an immaterial soul or mind or ego. Instead, so the materialist thinks, a person *just is* her body, or perhaps some part of her body (so that talk about "my body" is misleading). I *am* my body (or maybe my brain, or its left hemisphere, or some other part of it, or some other part of my body). Nearly all naturalists would agree. They give at least three sorts of reasons for materialism. First, naturalists often argue that dualism (the thought that a human being is an immaterial self or substance intimately related to a human body) is incoherent or subject to crushing philosophical difficulties; hence, so they say, we are rationally compelled to be materialists. You can find a typical set of such objections to dualism in Daniel Dennett's book *Consciousness Explained*.[13] Most of these objections (including Dennett's) are astonishingly weak; no one not already convinced of materialism would (or at any rate should) find them at all persuasive.[14] Still, they are often trotted out as showing that we are all obliged, these enlightened days, to be materialists.

13. Dennett, *Consciousness Explained* (Boston: Little, Brown and Co., 1991). Some who don't admire the book have complained that a better title would be "Consciousness Explained Away." Dennett's book illustrates, I think, the problem for one who accepts materialism but also (like the rest of us) can't help thinking that there is such a thing as consciousness.

14. See, e.g., William Lycan (who is himself a materialist), "Giving Dualism its Due," *Australasian Journal of Philosophy*, vol. 87, Issue 4 December 2009, and Charles Taliaferro, "Incorporeality," in *A Companion to Philosophy of Religion*, ed. Philip L. Quinn and Charles Taliaferro (Oxford: Blackwell, 1999), pp. 271ff., who does a nice job of exposing some of these weaknesses. See also my "Against Materialism," in *Faith and Philosophy*, 23:1 (January 2006), and "Materialism and Christian Belief," in *Persons: Human and Divine*, eds. Dean Zimmerman and Peter van Inwagen (Oxford: Oxford University Press, 2007).

A second and somewhat better reason is this: many naturalists think it is just part of naturalism as such to have no truck with immaterial souls or selves or minds. It may not be completely easy to see or say precisely what naturalism is, but, so goes the thought, at any rate it excludes things like immaterial selves or souls. Naturalism is the idea that there is no such person as God or anything like him; immaterial selves would be too much like God, who, after all, is himself an immaterial self. This reason is really quite persuasive (for naturalists), but not wholly conclusive. That is because of the vagueness of the concept of naturalism. According to naturalism, there isn't anything *like* God; but just how much similarity to God is tolerable, from a naturalistic perspective? After all, everything resembles God in *some* respect; how much similarity to God can a decently sensitive naturalist manage to accept? Plato's idea of the good and Aristotle's unmoved mover (who is also immaterial) clearly won't pass muster, but what about immaterial soul substances? Can a proper naturalist allow such a thing? That's not entirely easy to say. Far be it from me as an outsider, however, to intrude upon a delicate family dispute among naturalists; I hereby leave naturalists to settle this issue for themselves.

A third reason is as follows. Naturalists will ordinarily endorse Darwinian evolution; but how, they ask, could an immaterial soul or self have come to exist by way of the processes that evolutionary science posits? Thus Richard Dawkins: "Catholic Morality demands the presence of a great gulf between *Homo Sapiens* and the rest of the animal kingdom. Such a gulf is fundamentally anti-evolutionary. The sudden injection of an immortal soul in the timeline is an anti-evolutionary intrusion into the domain of science."[15] According to contemporary evolutionary theory, new forms of life arise (for the most part) by way of natural selection working on some form of genetic variation—the

15. Dawkins, "The Improbability of God," *Free Inquiry Magazine*, vol. 18, no. 2 (1998).

usual candidate is random genetic mutation. Though most mutations of this sort are neutral, a few are advantageous in the struggle for survival. Those lucky organisms that sport them have a reproductive advantage over those that do not, and eventually the new feature comes to dominate the population; then the process can start over. But how, they ask, could an *immaterial self or soul* evolve this way? What sort of genetic mutation would result in an immaterial soul? Could there be a section of DNA that codes, not for the production of proteins, but for an immaterial self?[16] That seems doubtful.

These reasons clearly aren't conclusive, but most naturalists find them (or perhaps other arguments for materialism) at least reasonably compelling. For these reasons and perhaps others, most naturalists are materialists about human beings. For present purposes, therefore, I propose to assimilate materialism to naturalism; henceforth I'll think of naturalism as including materialism, and what I'll be arguing against is the conjunction of current evolutionary theory and naturalism, the latter including materialism.

B. Beliefs as Neural Structures

Now what sort of thing will a belief *be*, from this materialist perspective? Suppose you are a materialist, and also think, as we ordinarily do, that there are such things as beliefs. For example, you hold the belief that Proust is more subtle than Louis L'Amour. What kind of a thing is this belief? Well, from a materialist perspective, it looks as if it would have to be something like a long-standing event or structure

---

16. Again, this reason is far from conclusive. As we'll see below, materialists usually think that mental properties supervene on physical properties. If so, it is conceivable that the property of having an immaterial soul supervenes on physical properties of an organism; perhaps there are physical properties such that necessarily, any organism with those physical properties will also be linked with an immaterial soul. See William Hasker, *The Emergent Self* (Ithaca: Cornell University Press, 1999).

in your brain or nervous system. Presumably this event will involve many neurons connected to each other in various ways. There are plenty of neurons to go around: a normal human brain contains some 100–200 billion neurons. These neurons, furthermore, are connected with other neurons via synapses; a single neuron, on the average, is connected with seven thousand other neurons. The total number of possible brain states, then, is absolutely enormous, much greater than the number of electrons in the universe. Under certain conditions, a neuron fires—that is, produces an electrical impulse; by virtue of its connection with other neurons, this impulse can be transmitted (with appropriate modification from other neurons) down the cables of neurons that constitute effector nerves to muscles or glands, causing, for example, muscular contraction and thus behavior.

So (from the materialist's point of view) a belief will be a neuronal event or structure of this sort, with input from other parts of the nervous system and output to still other parts as well as to muscles and glands. But if this is the sort of thing beliefs are, if they are neuronal events or structures, they will have two quite different sorts of properties. On the one hand they will have *electro-chemical* or *neurophysiological* properties (NP properties, for short). Among these would be such properties as that of involving n neurons and n^* connections between neurons, properties that specify which neurons are connected with which others, what the rates of fire in the various parts of the event are, how these rates of fire change in response to changes in input, and so on.

But if the event in question is really a *belief*, then in addition to those NP properties it will have another property as well: it will have a *content*.[17] It will be the belief that p, for some proposition p. If it's the

17. It is of course extremely difficult to see how a material structure or event could have content in the way a belief does; on the face of it, this appears to be impossible. That is one of the main problems for materialism. For development of this thought, see my "Against Materialism," footnote 14.

belief that Proust is a more subtle writer than Louis L'Amour, then its content is the proposition *Proust is more subtle than Louis L'Amour.* My belief that naturalism is vastly overrated has as content the proposition *naturalism is vastly overrated.* (That same proposition is the content of the Chinese speaker's belief that naturalism is vastly over-rated, even though she expresses this belief by uttering a very different sentence; beliefs, unlike sentences, do not come in different languages.) It is in virtue of having content that a belief is true or false: it is true if the proposition which is its content is true, and false otherwise. My belief that all men are mortal is true because the proposition which constitutes its content is true; Hitler's belief that the Third Reich would last a thousand years was false, because the proposition that constituted its content is (was) false.

Given materialism, therefore, beliefs are (ordinarily) long-standing neural events. As such, they have NP properties, but also content properties: each belief will have the property of having such and such a proposition as its content. NP properties are *physical* properties; on the other hand content properties—for example the property of having as content the proposition *all men are mortal*—are *mental* properties. Now how, according to materialism, are mental and physical properties related? In particular, how are content properties related to NP properties—how is the content property of a particular belief related to the NP properties of that belief?

C. Reductive and Nonreductive Materialism

Materialists offer fundamentally two theories about the relation between physical and mental properties (and hence two theories about the relation between NP properties and content properties): reductive materialism and nonreductive materialism. According to Sir Francis Crick: "your joys and your sorrows, your memories and your ambitions, your sense of personal identity and free will, are in fact no more than the behaviour of a vast assembly of nerve cells and their associated molecules."[18] This is a pretty good statement of *reductive* materialism, according to which (naturally enough) mental content properties are *reducible to* NP properties; according to *nonreductive* materialism, content properties are not reducible to NP properties, but are *determined by* (supervene on) NP properties.[19] We could put it like this: according to reductive materialism, there is only one kind of property in the neighborhood: NP properties, some of which are also mental properties. According to nonreductive materialism, on the other hand, there are *two* kinds of properties, NP properties and also mental properties, which are not NP properties, but are determined by NP properties.

Suppose we think first about reductive materialism. Consider the property of having as content the proposition *naturalism is vastly overrated*, and call this property "C." On reductive materialism, C *just is* a certain combination of NP properties. It might be a disjunction of such properties: where P_1 to P_n are NP properties, C, the property of having the content in question, might be something like (where "v" represents "or")

$$P_1 \vee P_2 \vee P_3 \vee P_8 \vee \ldots P_n$$

More likely, it would be something more complicated: perhaps a disjunction of conjunctions, something like (where "&" represents "and")

$$(P_1 \& P_7 \& P_{28} \& \ldots) \vee (P_3 \& P_{34} \& P_{17} \& \ldots) \vee (P_8 \& P_{83} \& P_{107} \& \ldots) \vee \ldots [20]$$

18. Crick, *The Astonishing Hypothesis: the Scientific Search for the Soul* (New York: Scribner, 1995), p.3.
19. For simplicity, I ignore so-called "wide content"; nothing in my argument hinges on this omission.
20. We could put this by saying that any content property is a Boolean combination of NP properties.

If complex combinations of NP properties are themselves NP properties, content properties, on reductive materialism, are really just a special kind of NP property. According to reductive materialism, therefore, content properties—for example, the property of having *naturalism is vastly overrated* as content—are or are reducible to NP properties.

That's one of the two proposals made by materialists. The other is that a content property isn't an NP property, and can't be reduced to NP properties, but is nevertheless *determined by* NP properties. Here the basic idea is this: for any particular mental property M you pick, there is a physical property P such that necessarily, if a thing has M, then it has P, and if a thing has P, then it has M.[21] So take any mental property—for example, the property of being in pain: there will be some physical property P (presumably an NP property), such that it's true in every possible world that whatever has P is in pain, and, conversely, whatever is in pain has P.[22] Specified to content and NP properties, the idea is that for any content property C that a neural structure can have, there is an NP property P such that if a neural structure has that content property C, it has P, and conversely, any neural structure that has P also has that content property C.

According to both reductive and nonreductive materialism, mental properties are determined by physical properties (and indeed according to reductive materialism mental properties just *are* physical properties). As we go up the evolutionary scale, we find neural structures with greater and greater complexity. Near one end of the scale, for example, we find bacteria; presumably they have no beliefs at all. At the other end of the scale there are human beings, who have a rich and varied store of beliefs

21. The necessity involved could be broadly logical necessity: the sort of necessity enjoyed by, for example, true mathematical and logical propositions. Or it could be nomological necessity, the sort of necessity enjoyed by natural laws.
22. This is what philosophers call "strong supervenience." For a good account of the various kinds of supervenience, see the Stanford online encyclopedia entry on supervenience.

and whose brains contain many billions of neurons connected in complex and multifarious ways, so that the number of different possible brain states is more than astronomical. And the idea is that as you rise in the evolutionary scale, as you go through more and more complex neural structures, at a certain point there arises something we can properly call a belief, something that is true or false. At a certain level of complexity, these neural structures start to display belief content. Perhaps this starts gradually and early on—perhaps it is with *C. elegans*, a small but charismatic beast that enjoys the distinction of having its nervous system completely mapped. Possibly *C. elegans* displays just the merest glimmer of consciousness and just the merest glimmer of actual belief content, or perhaps belief content shows up further up the scale; that doesn't matter. What does matter is that at a certain level of complexity, neural structures begin to display content and the creatures that harbor those structures have beliefs. This is true whether content properties are reducible to NP properties or supervene on them.

So (given materialism) some neural structures, at a certain level of complexity of NP properties, acquire content; at that level of complexity, NP properties determine belief content, and the structures in question are beliefs. And the question I want to ask is this: what is the likelihood, *given evolution and naturalism* (construed as including materialism about human beings), that the content thus arising is in fact *true*? In particular, what is the likelihood, given N&E, that the content associated with *our* neural structures is true? What is the likelihood, given N&E, that our cognitive faculties are reliable, thereby producing mostly true beliefs?

V THE ARGUMENT FOR PREMISE (1)

We are now ready to state the reasons for the first premise of the main argument, which, as you recall is

(1) P(R/N&E) is low.

Of course we all commonsensically assume that our cognitive faculties are for the most part reliable, at least over a large area of their functioning. I remember where I was last night, that I've just had oatmeal for breakfast, that my elder son's name is not Archibald, that a year ago I didn't live in the house I live in now, and much else besides. I can see that the light is on in my study, that the flower garden is overgrown with weeds, and that my neighbor put on weight over the winter. I know a few truths of mathematics and logic, mostly pretty simple, no doubt, but still . . . The natural thing to assume, and what we all do assume (at least before we are corrupted by philosophy or neuroscience) is that when our cognitive faculties aren't subject to malfunction, then, for the most part, and over a wide area of everyday life, the beliefs they produce in us are true. We assume that our cognitive faculties are reliable. But what I want to argue is that the naturalist has a powerful reason *against* this initial assumption, and should give it up. I don't mean to argue that this natural assumption is false; like everyone else, I believe that our cognitive faculties *are*, in fact, mostly reliable. What I do mean to argue is that the *naturalist*—at any rate a naturalist who accepts evolution—is rationally obliged to give up this assumption.

A. *The Argument and Nonreductive Materialism*

As you recall, we are thinking of naturalism as including materialism, which, as we've seen, comes in two varieties: reductive and nonreductive. Let's think first about the question from the point of view of nonreductive materialism. Return to the evolutionary scale and *C. elegans*, that celebrated little worm, and suppose that it is in *C. elegans* that we first get belief. No doubt such belief will be primative *in excelsis* (and if you don't think *C. elegans* has beliefs, you can simply go up the scale until you encounter creatures you think do have beliefs), but let's suppose members of this species have beliefs. Now given that *C. elegans* has survived for millions of years, we may assume that its behavior is adaptive. This behavior is produced or caused by the neurological structures in the *C. elegans* nervous system; we may further assume, therefore, that this neurology is adaptive. This underlying neurology causes adaptive behavior; as Churchland says, it gets the body parts where they must be in order to survive. But (in line with nonreductive materialism) it also determines belief content. As a result, these creatures have beliefs, which of course have a certain content.

And here's the question: what reason is there for supposing that this belief content is *true*? There isn't any. The neurology causes adaptive behavior and also causes or determines belief content: but there is no reason to suppose that the belief content thus determined is true. All that's required for survival and fitness is that the neurology cause adaptive behavior; this neurology also determines belief content, but whether or not that content is *true* makes no difference to fitness. Certain NP properties are selected for, because they contribute to fitness. These NP properties also cause or determine belief content; they associate a content or proposition with each belief. The NP properties are selected, however, not because they cause the content they do, but because they cause adaptive behavior. If the content, the proposition determined by the neurology (the NP properties of the belief) is true, fine. But if it is false, that's no problem as far as fitness goes.

Objection: consider a frog on a lily pad. A fly buzzes by; the frog's tongue flicks out and captures the fly. If this frog is to behave successfully, adaptively, there must be mechanisms in it that register the distance to the fly at each moment, its size, speed, direction, and so on. Aren't these mechanisms part of the frog's cognitive faculties? And don't they have to be accurate in order for the frog to behave adaptively? And isn't it therefore the case that the frog's cognitive mechanisms must be accurate, reliable, if the frog is to survive and reproduce? Or consider an animal, maybe a zebra, grazing on the veldt; a lion approaches. The zebra notices the predator; this noticing consists in part of some neural structure arising in its brain, perhaps a certain pattern of firing of neurons in the optical portion of its brain, and perhaps this pattern ordinarily arises in response to the appearance of a predator in the middle distance. If this structure isn't properly correlated with the presence of predators, the zebra won't be long for this world. And wouldn't this structure, furthermore, be part of the creature's cognitive mechanisms? And don't those mechanisms have to be accurate, reliable, if the zebra is to survive?

Reply: that frog clearly does have "indicators," neural structures that receive input from the frog's sense organs, and are correlated with the path of the insect as it flies past, and are connected with the frog's muscles in such a way that it flicks out its tongue and captures that unfortunate fly. The same goes for the zebra: if it is to behave adaptively (evade predators, for example) it too will have to have indicators, neural structures that monitor the environment, that are correlated (for example) with the presence of predators, and are connected with its muscles in such a way as to cause it to flee when a predator threatens.

Now if we like, we can include these indicators under the rubric "cognitive faculties." The important point to see here, however, is that indication of this sort does not require *belief*. In particular, it does not require belief having to do with the state of affairs indicated; indeed it is entirely compatible with belief *inconsistent* with that state of affairs. For example, anaerobic marine bacteria (so the story goes) contain magnetosomes, tiny internal magnets that indicate magnetic north; in the oceans of the northern hemisphere, this direction is down, towards the oxygen-free depths.[23] These indicators are connected with the propulsion devices of the bacteria in such a way as to cause these creatures, which can't flourish in the oxygen-rich surface water, to move towards the deeper water. But this in no way requires that the bacteria form *beliefs*. Fleeing predators, finding food and mates—these things require cognitive devices that in some way track crucial features of the environment, and are appropriately connected with muscles; but they do not require true belief, or even belief at all. The long-term survival of organisms of a certain species certainly makes it likely that its members enjoy cognitive devices that are successful in tracking those features of the environment—indicators, as I've been calling them. Indicators, however, need not be or involve beliefs. In the human body there are indicators for blood pressure, temperature, saline content, insulin level, and much else; in these cases neither the blood, nor its owner, nor anything else in the neighborhood ordinarily holds beliefs on the topic. The objector is therefore right in pointing out that fitness requires accurate indication; but nothing follows about reliability of belief.

Returning to the main line of our argument, we are considering nonreductive materialism and asking about P(R/N&E), given nonreductive materialism. (Another way to put this: we are considering P(R/N&E& nonreductive materialism).) In order to avoid automatically introducing into the argument our ordinary assumptions about our own mental life, suppose we conduct a thought experiment. Consider a hypothetical species that is cognitively a lot like us: members of this species hold beliefs, make inferences, change beliefs, and the like. And let us suppose naturalism holds for them; they exist in a world in which there is no such person as God or anything like God.

---

23. All is not well with this popular little story: see W. J. Zhang, "Configuration of redox gradient determines magnetotactic polarity of the marine bacteria MO-1," in *Environmental Microbiology Reports* vol. 2, issue 5, October 2010.

Our question, then, is this: what is the probability that their cognitive faculties are reliable? Consider any particular belief on the part of one of these hypothetical creatures. That belief is a neural structure of a given sort, and one sufficiently complex to generate content. We may add, if we like, that this structure occurs or takes place in response to something in the environment; perhaps it is a certain pattern of firing of neurons in the optical portion of the brain, and perhaps this pattern arises in response to the appearance of a predator. Suppose further that a certain content, a certain proposition, is determined by the NP properties of this structure. This structure, therefore, will be a belief, and will have a certain proposition p as its content.

But now for the crucial question: what is the probability (given N&E) that this proposition is true? Well, what we know about the belief in question is that it is a neurological structure that has certain NP properties, properties the possession of which is sufficient for the possession of that particular content. We are assuming also that this structure arises in response to the presence of that predator. We can assume further, if we like, that this structure is a reliable indicator of that kind of predator: it arises when and only when there is such a predator in the middle distance. But why think it is a *true* proposition that is determined by those NP properties? These NP properties determine a proposition: but why think that proposition is true? Natural selection selects for adaptive NP properties; those NP properties determine content; but natural selection just has to take pot-luck with respect to the propositions or content determined by those adaptive NP properties. It does not get to influence or modify the function from NP properties to content properties: that's just a matter of logic or causal law, and natural selection can't modify either. Indeed, the content generated by the NP properties of this structure, on this occasion, need have nothing to do with that predator, or with anything else in the environment. True: the structure is correlated with the presence of a predator and indicates that presence; but indication is not belief. Indication is one thing; belief content is something else altogether, and we know of no reason (given materialism) why the one should follow the other. We know of no reason why the content of a belief should match what that belief (together, perhaps, with other structures) indicates. Content simply arises upon the appearance of neural structures of sufficient complexity; there is no reason why that content need be related to what the structures indicate, if anything. Indeed, the proposition constituting that content need not be so much as *about* that predator; it certainly need not be true.

What, then, is the likelihood that this proposition, this content, is true? Given just this much, shouldn't we suppose that the proposition in question is as likely to be false as true? Here's the picture: the NP properties of a belief are adaptive in that they cause adaptive behavior. Those NP properties also determine a content property. But as long as the NP properties are adaptive, it doesn't matter, for survival and reproduction, what content is determined by those NP properties. It could be true content; it could be false content; it doesn't matter. The fact that these creatures have survived and evolved, that their cognitive equipment was good enough to enable their ancestors to survive and reproduce—that fact would tell us nothing at all about the *truth* of their beliefs or the reliability of their cognitive faculties. It would tell something about the *neurophysiological* properties of a given belief; it would tell us that by virtue of these properties, that belief has played a role in the production of adaptive behavior. But it would tell us nothing about the truth of the *content* of that belief: its content might be true, but might with equal probability be false. So shouldn't we suppose that the proposition in question has a probability of roughly .5? Shouldn't we estimate its probability, on the condition in question, as in the neighborhood of .5? That would be the sensible course. Neither seems more probable than the other; hence we should estimate the probability of its being true as .5.

The probability we are thinking of here is objective, not the personalist's subjective probability, and also not epistemic probability.[24] (Of course there will be a connection between objective and epistemic probability, perhaps a connection in the neighborhood of Miller's principle; presumably epistemic probability will in some way follow known objective probability.) But then, in suggesting the first attitude above, am I not relying upon the notorious Principle of Indifference? And hasn't that principle been discredited?[25] Not really. The Bertrand paradoxes show that certain incautious statements of the principle of indifference come to grief—just as Goodman's grue/bleen paradoxes show that incautious statements of a principle governing the projection of predicates or properties come to grief. Still, the fact is we project properties all the time, and do so perfectly sensibly. And the fact is we also regularly employ a principle of indifference in ordinary reasoning, and do so quite properly. We also use it in science—for example in statistical mechanics.[26]

Given that the probability, for any belief on the part of these creatures, is about.5, what is the probability that their cognitive faculties are *reliable*? Well, what proportion of my beliefs must be true, if my faculties are reliable? The answer will have to be vague; perhaps a modest requirement would be that a reliable cognitive faculty must deliver at least 3 times as many true beliefs as false: the proportion of true beliefs in its output is at least three-quarters. If so, then the probability that their faculties produce the preponderance of true beliefs

24. See my *Warrant and Proper Function*, chapter 9. It's worth noting that the argument can also be conducted in terms of epistemic probability, although I don't have space here to show how.
25. See, e.g., Bas van Fraassen's *Laws and Symmetry* (Oxford: Clarendon Press, 1989), pp. 293ff.
26. "An astonishing number of extremely complex problems in probability theory have been solved, and usefully so, by calculation based entirely on the assumption of equiprobable alternatives." Roy Weatherford, *Philosophical Foundations of Probability Theory* (London: Routledge and Kegan Paul, 1983), p. 35. See also Robin Collins's "A Defense of the Probabilistic Principle of Indifference" (lecture to History and Philosophy of Science Colloquium, University of Notre Dame, October 8, 1998; presently unpublished), and see Roger White, "Evidential Symmetry and Mushy Credence," *Oxford Studies in Epistemology*, vol. 3.

in its output is at least three-quarters. If so, then the probability that their faculties produce the preponderance of true beliefs over false required by reliability is very small indeed. If I have one thousand independent beliefs, for example, the probability (under these conditions) that three quarters or more of these beliefs are true will be less than 10^{-58}.[27] And even if I am running a modest epistemic establishment of only one hundred beliefs, the probability that three-quarters of them are true, given that the probability of any one's being true is one half, is very low, something like .000001. So the chances that this creature's true beliefs substantially outnumber its false beliefs are small. The conclusion to be drawn is that it is very unlikely that the cognitive faculties of those creatures are reliable. But of course the same will go for us: $P(R/N\&E)$ specified not to them but to us, will also be very low.

B. The Argument and Reductive Materialism

That's how things stand for nonreductive materialism: $P(R/N\&E\&nonreductive materialism)$ is low. We can deal more briefly with $P(R/N\&E\&reductive materialism)$, the probability of R given naturalism and evolution and reductive materialism. On reductive materialism, mental properties are complex combinations of physical properties; more briefly, taking complex combinations of physical properties to be themselves physical properties, mental properties just are physical properties. What is the probability of R on N&E and reductive materialism?

Here we get the very same results as with nonreductive materialism. To see why, consider, again, any given belief on the part of a

---

27. "Independent": it could be that a pair of neural structures with content were such that if either occurred, so would the other; then the beliefs in question would not be independent. Similarly when the content of one neural structure entails the content of another: there too the beliefs in question won't be independent. My thanks to Paul Zwier, who performed the calculation.

member of that hypothetical group of creatures—say the belief *naturalism is vastly overrated*. That belief is a neuronal event, a congeries of neurons connected in complex ways and firing away in the fashion neurons are wont to do. This neuronal event displays a lot of NP properties. Again, we may suppose that it is adaptively useful for a creature of the kind in question to harbor neuronal structures of the sort in question in the circumstances in question. The event's having the NP properties it does have is fitness-enhancing in that by virtue of having these properties, the organism is caused to perform adaptively useful action—fleeing, for example. Since the event is a belief, some subset of these NP properties together constitute its having the content it does in fact display. That is, there will be some proposition that is the content of the belief; the belief will therefore have the property of having that proposition as its content; and that property, the property of having such and such a proposition as its content, will be a (no doubt complex) NP property of the belief.

Now what is the probability that this content is *true*? What is the probability that this proposition, whatever it is, is true? The answer is the same as in the case we've already considered. The content doesn't have to be true, of course, for the neuronal structure to cause the appropriate kind of behavior. It just happens that this particular adaptive arrangement of NP properties also constitutes having that particular content. But again: it would be a piece of serendipity if this content, this proposition, were *true*; it could just as well be false. These NP properties, including those that constitute its having that content, are adaptive just as long as they cause adaptive behavior. They also constitute the property of having that particular content; but it doesn't matter at all, so far as adaptivity goes, whether that content is true. So take any particular belief on the part of one of those creatures. We may suppose (given that these creatures have come to be by way of evolution) that having this belief is adaptive; its NP properties cause adaptive behavior. These NP properties also constitute the property of having such and such content; but, clearly enough, it doesn't matter (with respect to the adaptivity of these properties) whether the content they constitute is true. It could be true: fair enough; but it could equally well be false. If these properties had constituted different content, they still would have had the same causal effect with respect to behavior. Hence the probability that the content of this belief is true would have to be rated at about one-half, just as in the case of nonreductive materialism. If this is true for each of the independent beliefs of the organism in question, however, the probability that the cognitive faculties of these creatures are reliable (on N&E& reductive materialism), would have to be rated as low. The conclusion to be drawn so far, then, is that given N&E (N including materialism), it is unlikely that these creatures have reliable cognitive faculties.

C. Objection

Isn't it just obvious that true beliefs will facilitate adaptive action? A gazelle who mistakenly believes that lions are friendly, overgrown house cats won't be long for this world. The same goes for a rock climber who believes that jumping from a two-hundred-foot cliff will result in a pleasant and leisurely trip down with a soft landing. Isn't it obvious both that true beliefs are much more likely to be adaptive than false beliefs? Isn't it obvious, more generally, that true beliefs are more likely to be successful than false beliefs? I want to go from New York to Boston: won't I be more likely to get there if I believe that Boston is north of New York than if I believe it's to the south?

Yes, certainly. This is indeed true. But it is also irrelevant. We are not asking about how things *are*, but about *what things would be like if both evolution and naturalism (construed as including materialism) were true.* We are asking about $P(R/N\&E)$, not about $P(R/$the way things actually are$)$. Like everyone else, I believe that our cognitive faculties are for the most part reliable, and that true beliefs are more likely to issue in successful action than false. But that's not the question. The question is what things would be like if N&E were true; and in this context we can't just assume, of course, that if N&E, N including materialism, were true, then things would still be the way they are. That is, we can't assume that if materialism were true, it would still be the case that true beliefs are more likely to cause successful action than false beliefs. And in fact, if materialism were true, it would be unlikely that true beliefs mostly cause successful action and false belief unsuccessful action.

Here you may ask, "Why think a thing like that? What has materialism to do with this question?" Here's what. We ordinarily think true belief leads to successful action because we also think that beliefs cause (part-cause) actions, and do so *by virtue of their content*. I want a beer; I believe there is one in the fridge, and this belief is a (part) cause of my going over to the fridge. We think it is by virtue of the *content* of that belief that it causes me to go over to the fridge; it is because this belief has as content that there is a beer in the fridge that it causes me to go to the fridge rather than, say, the washing machine. More generally, we think it is by virtue of the content of a belief B that B part-causes the behavior that it does cause.

But now suppose materialism were true: then, as we've seen, my belief will be a neural structure that has both NP properties and also a propositional content. It is by virtue of the NP properties, however, not the content, that the belief causes what it does cause. It is by virtue of *those* properties that the belief causes neural impulses to travel down the relevant efferent nerves to the relevant muscles, causing them to contract, and thus causing behavior. It isn't by virtue of the content of this belief; the content of the belief is irrelevant to the causal power of the belief with respect to behavior.

Consider an analogy. I am playing catch with my granddaughter, and in a vaingolorious attempt to show off, I throw the ball too hard; it whistles over her head and shatters a neighbor's window. It is clear that the ball breaks the window *by virtue of* its mass, velocity, hardness, size, and the like. If it had been much less massive, been traveling at a lower rate of speed, had been as soft as a bunch of feathers, it would not have broken the window. If you ask "Why did the window shatter upon being hit by the ball?" the correct answer will involve the ball's having those properties (and of course also involve the window's having a certain degree of brittleness, tensile strength, and the like). As it happens, the ball was a birthday present; but it does not break the window by virtue of being a birthday present, or being purchased at Sears and Roebuck, or costing $5.00. Examples of this sort, clearly enough, can be multiplied endlessly; but examples of other kinds also abound. Sam has the right to fire the city manager by virtue of his being mayor, not by virtue of his being nice to his wife. Aquinas was a great philosopher by virtue of his acumen and insight and prodigious industry, not by virtue of his being called "the Dumb Ox."[28]

Going back to materialism and the content of belief, then, it is by virtue of the NP properties of a belief B, not by virtue of its content, that the belief causes the behavior it does cause. Among B's NP properties are such properties as that of involving many neurons working in concert: as we learn from current science, these neurons send a signal through effector nerves to the relevant muscles, causing those muscles to contract and thereby causing behavior. It is by virtue of these NP properties that it causes those muscles to contract. If the belief had had the same NP properties but different content, it would have had the same effect on behavior.

Objection: you claim that

(1) If the belief B had had the same NP properties but different content, it still would have had the same causal effects with respect to behavior;

---

28. And he was called "the Dumb Ox" by virtue of the fact that he was both taciturn and a bit corpulent, not by virtue of the fact that he wrote the *Summa Theologiae*.

but it *couldn't* have had the same NP properties but different content. (1) is not merely counterfactual; it's counterpossible. If the property of having C as content supervenes on neurophysiological properties, then (given strong supervenience) there will be a neurophysiological property equivalent to C in the broadly logical sense; hence it won't be so much as possible that the antecedent of (1) hold. Given the usual semantics for counterfactuals, the conclusion to be drawn is that (1) is true, all right, but so is any counterfactual with the same antecedent, including, for example

(2) if B had had the same neurophysiological properties but different content, B would *not* have had the same causal effects with respect to behavior.

Right. But *is* the usual semantics for counterfactuals correct? This is hardly the place to address that particular (and large) can of worms, but in fact (so I think) it isn't. It is true that if 2 had been greater than 3, then 3 would have been less than 2; it is not true that if 2 had been greater than 3, then 3 would have been greater than 2. It is not true that if 2 had been greater than 3, then the moon would have been made of green cheese. Even given that God is necessarily omniscient, it isn't true that if God had not been omniscient, he would have known that he doesn't exist. If I proved Gödel wrong, logicians everywhere would be astonished; it is false that if I proved Gödel wrong, logicians would yawn in boredom.

Furthermore, philosophers regularly and quite properly use counterpossibles in arguing for their views. Consider the philosophical view that what I really am is a member of a series of momentary person stages. One argues against this view by pointing to the truth of

(3) if this were true, I wouldn't be responsible for anything that happened more than a moment ago (a new legal defense strategy?)

Even though the view in question is noncontingent—necessarily true or necessarily false—you take that counterpossible to be true and its mate

(4) if this were true, I *would* be responsible for much that happened more than a moment ago

false. A dualist might claim that if materialism were true, the content of one's beliefs wouldn't enter the causal chain leading to behavior; a materialist might claim that if (interactive) dualism were true, an immaterial substance would (implausibly) cause effects in the hard, heavy, massy material world. One of these counterfactuals has an impossible antecedent; both, however, are properly used in the dispute between materialists and dualists.

The truth of (1) gives us some reason to think that B doesn't cause that action A by virtue of its content. As I say, however, this isn't the place to look into the difficult matter of figuring out how to reason with counterpossibles; that would take us far afield. But we can also address our question directly: is it by virtue of its content that B causes A? I should think the answer, clearly, is that it is not. It is by virtue of its neurophysiological properties that B causes A; it is by virtue of *those* properties that B sends a signal along the relevant nerves to the relevant muscles, causing them to contract, and thus causing A. It isn't by virtue of its having that particular content C that it causes what it does cause.

So once again: suppose N&E were true. Then materialism would be true in either its reductive or its nonreductive form. In either case, the underlying neurology is adaptive, and determines belief content. But in either case it doesn't matter to the adaptiveness of the behavior (or of the neurology that causes that behavior) whether the content determined by that neurology is true.[29]

VI THE REMAINING PREMISES

Now we're ready for the next step: the naturalist who sees that $P(R/N\&E)$ is low has a *defeater* for R, and for the proposition that his own cognitive faculties are reliable. A defeater for a belief B I hold—at any rate this kind of defeater—is another belief B* I come to hold which is such that, given that I hold B*, I can no longer

---

29. You might complain that it is only materialism that is important here, with naturalism playing no role. Not so. Suppose theism is true, and also (as some theists think) that materialism is true. If so, and if, as most theists think, God has created us in his image, including the ability to have knowledge, then God would presumably establish psychophysical laws of such a sort that successful action is correlated with true belief.

rationally hold B.[30] For example, I look into a field and see what I take to be a sheep. You come along, identify yourself as the owner of the field, and tell me that there aren't any sheep in that field, and that what I see is really a dog that's indistinguishable from a sheep at this distance. Then I give up the belief that what I see is a sheep. Another example: on the basis of what the guidebook says I form the belief that the University of Aberdeen was established in 1695. You, the university's public relations director, tell me the embarrassing truth: this guide book is notorious for giving the wrong date for the foundation of the University. (Actually it was established in 1495.) My new belief that the University was established in 1495 is a defeater for my old belief. In the same way, if I accept naturalism and see that $P(R/N\&E)$ is low, then I have a defeater for R; I can no longer rationally believe that my cognitive faculties are reliable.

So the second premise of the argument:

(2) Anyone who accepts (believes) N&E and sees that $P(R/N\&E)$ is low has a defeater for R.

It isn't that someone who believed N&E wouldn't have enough *evidence* for R to believe it rationally. The fact is I don't *need* evidence for R. That's a good thing, because it isn't possible to acquire evidence for R, at least if I have any doubts about it. For suppose I think up

---

30. There are several kinds of defeaters; here it isn't necessary to canvass these kinds. The kind of defeater presently relevant would be a *rationality* defeater, and an *undercutting* rationality defeater. In addition to rationality defeaters, there are also *warrant* defeaters; these too come in several kinds. For more on defeaters, see Michael Bergmann, "Deontology and Defeat," *Philosophy and Phenomenological Research* 60 (2000), pp. 87–102, "Internalism, Externalism and the No-Defeater Condition," *Synthese* 110 (1997), pp. 399–417, and chapter 6 of his book *Justification Without Awareness* (New York: Oxford University Press, 2006); and see my "Reply to Beilby's Cohorts" in *Naturalism Defeated*, pp. 205–11. See also above, chapter 6.

some argument for R, and on the basis of this argument come to believe that R is indeed true. Clearly this is not a sensible procedure; to become convinced of R on the basis of that argument, I must of course believe the premises of the argument, and also believe that if those premises are true, then so is the conclusion. If I do that, however, I am already assuming R to be true, at least for the faculties or processes that produce in me belief in the premises of the argument, and the belief that if the premises are true, so is the conclusion. My accepting any argument for R, or any evidence for it, would clearly presuppose my believing R; any such procedure would therefore be viciously circular.

So the belief that my cognitive faculties are reliable is one for which I don't need evidence or argument—that is, I don't need evidence or argument in order to be rational in believing it. I can be fully and entirely rational in believing this even though I have no evidence or argument for it at all. This is a belief such that it is rational to hold it in the *basic* way, that is, not on the basis of argument or evidence from other things I believe. But that doesn't mean it isn't possible to acquire a defeater for it. Even if a belief is properly basic, it can still be defeated. In the above example about the sheep in the field, my original belief, we may suppose, was basic, and properly so; I still acquired a defeater for it.

Here we can reuse an example from chapter 6 to show the same thing. You and I are driving through southern Wisconsin; I see what looks like a fine barn and form the belief *now that's a fine barn!* Furthermore, I hold that belief in the basic way; I don't accept it on the basis of evidence from other propositions I believe. You then tell me that the whole area is full of barn facades (indistinguishable, from the highway, from real barns) erected by the local inhabitants in a dubious effort to make themselves look more prosperous. If I believe you, I then have a defeater for my belief that what I saw was a fine barn, even though I was rational in holding the defeated belief in the basic way. It is therefore perfectly possible to acquire a defeater for a belief B even when it is rational to hold B in the basic way.

And this is what happens when I believe N&E, and come to see that P(R/N&E) is low: I acquire a defeater for R. I can then no longer rationally accept R; I must be agnostic about it, or believe its denial. Consider an analogy. Suppose there is a drug—call it XX—that destroys cognitive reliability. I know that 95 percent of those who ingest XX become cognitively unreliable within two hours of ingesting it; they then believe more false propositions than true. Suppose further that I come to believe both that I've ingested XX a couple of hours ago and that P(R/I've ingested XX a couple of hours ago) is low; taken together, these two beliefs give me a defeater for my initial belief that my cognitive faculties are reliable.[31] Furthermore, I can't appeal to any of my other beliefs to show or argue that my cognitive faculties are still reliable. For example, I can't appeal to my belief that my cognitive faculties have always been reliable in the past or seem to me to be reliable now; any such other belief is now just as suspect or compromised as R is. Any such other belief B is a product of my cognitive faculties: but then in recognizing this and having a defeater for R, I also have a defeater for B.

Objection: why should we think that premise (2) is true? Some propositions of that form are true, but some aren't. I believe that I've ingested XX, and that the probability that I am reliable, given that I've ingested XX is low; this gives me a defeater for the proposition that I am reliable. But I also believe that the probability that I live in

---

31. Other analogies: the belief that I have mad cow disease and that the probability that my cognitive faculties are reliable, on that proposition, is low. Similarly for the belief that I am a victim of a Cartesian evil demon who brings it about that most of my beliefs are false (see Descartes *Meditations*, Meditation I) and the current version of Descartes's fantasy, the belief that I am a brain in a vat, my beliefs being manipulated by unscrupulous alien scientists (see also the film *The Matrix*, Warner Bros., 1999).

Michigan, given that the earth revolves around the sun, is low, and I believe that the earth revolves around the sun; this does not give me a defeater for my belief that I live in Michigan. Why think the case of N&E and R is more like the first than like the second?[32]

Reply: Right: not every proposition of that form is true. This one is, however. What's at issue, I think, is the question what else I believe (more exactly what else is such that I believe it and can legitimately conditionalize on it in this context). If the only thing I knew, relevant to

(a) my living in Michigan,

is that this is unlikely given that

(b) the earth revolves around the sun,

then my belief that (b) and that (a) is unlikely on (b) *would* give me a defeater for (a). But of course I know a lot more: for example, that I live in Grand Rapids, which is in Michigan. I quite properly conditionalize not just on (b), but on much else, on some of which (a) has a probability of 1. But now think about N&E and R. We agree that P(R/N&E) is low. Do I know something else X, in addition to N&E, such that (a) I can properly conditionalize on X, and (b) P(R/N&E&X) is high? This is the conditionalization problem, which I address briefly on pages 346.

This brings us to the third premise:

(3) Anyone who has a defeater for R has a defeater for any other belief she thinks she has, including N&E itself.

---

32. This objection was raised by Trenton Merricks. Compare his "Conditional Probability and Defeat" in James Beilby, ed., *Naturalism Defeated?* and my reply "To Merricks" in the same volume.

(3) is pretty obvious. If you have a defeater for R, you will also have a defeater for any belief you take to be produced by your cognitive faculties, any belief that is a deliverance of your cognitive faculties. But *all* of your beliefs, as I'm sure you have discovered, are produced by your cognitive faculties. Therefore you have a defeater for any belief you have.

Still, even if you realize you have a defeater for every belief you hold, you are unlikely to give up all or perhaps even any of your beliefs. It may be that you can't really reject R in the heat and press of day-to-day activities, for example, when you are playing poker with your friends, or building a house, or climbing a cliff. You can't think dismissive Humean thoughts about, say, induction when clinging unroped (you're free-soloing) to a rock face five hundred feet up the East Buttress of El Capitan. (You won't find yourself saying, "Well, naturally I can't help believing that if my foot slips I'll hurtle down to the ground and smash into those rocks, but [fleeting, sardonic, self-deprecatory smile] I also know that I have a defeater for this belief and hence shouldn't take it seriously.") But in the calm and reflective atmosphere of your study, you see that this is in fact the case. Of course you also see that the very reflections that lead you to this position are also no more acceptable than their denials; you have a universal defeater for whatever it is you find yourself believing. This is a really crushing skepticism, and it is this skepticism to which the naturalist is committed.

The final premise of the argument is

(4) If one who accepts N&E thereby acquires a defeater for N&E, N&E is self-defeating and can't rationally be accepted.

The entire argument, therefore, goes as follows:

(1) P(R/N&E) is low.

(2) Anyone who accepts (believes) N&E and sees that P(R/N&E) is low has a defeater for R.

(3) Anyone who has a defeater for R has a defeater for any other belief she thinks she has, including N&E itself.

(4) If one who accepts N&E thereby acquires a defeater for N&E, N&E is self-defeating and can't rationally be accepted.

Conclusion: N&E can't rationally be accepted.

This argument shows that if someone accepts N&E and sees that P(R/N&E) is low, then she has a defeater for N&E, a reason to reject it, a reason to doubt or be agnostic with respect to it.

Of course defeaters can themselves be defeated; so couldn't you get a defeater for this defeater—a defeater-defeater? Maybe by doing some science—for example, determining by scientific means that her faculties really are reliable? Couldn't she go to the MIT cognitive-reliability laboratory for a check-up?[33] Clearly that won't help. Obviously that course would *presuppose* that her faculties are reliable; she'd be relying on the accuracy of her faculties in believing that there is such a thing as MIT, that she has in fact consulted its scientists, that they have given her a clean bill of cognitive health, and so on. The great Scottish philosopher Thomas Reid put it like this:

If a man's honesty were called into question, it would be ridiculous to refer to the man's own word, whether he be honest or not. The same absurdity there is in attempting to prove, by any kind of reasoning, probable or demonstrative, that our reason is not

---

33. Compare Paul Churchland, "Is Evolutionary Naturalism Epistemologically Self-defeating?, *Philo: A Journal of Philosophy* (vol. 12, no. 2); Aaron Segal and I have written a reply (forthcoming in the same journal).

fallacious, since the very point in question is, whether reasoning may be trusted.[34]

Is there any sensible way at all in which she can argue for R? It is hard to see how. Any argument she might produce will have premises; these premises, she claims, give her good reason to believe R. But of course she has the very same defeater for each of those premises that she has for R, and she has the same defeater for the belief that if the premises of that argument are true, then so is the conclusion. So it looks as if this defeater can't be defeated. Naturalistic evolution gives its adherents a reason for doubting that our beliefs are mostly true; chances are they are mostly mistaken. If so, it won't help to *argue* that they can't be mostly mistaken; for the very reason for mistrusting our cognitive faculties *generally*, will be a reason for mistrusting the faculties that produce belief in the goodness of that argument.

This defeater, therefore, can't be defeated. Hence the devotee of N&E has an undefeated defeater for N&E. N&E, therefore, cannot rationally be accepted—at any rate by someone who is apprised of this argument and sees the connections between N&E and R.

VII TWO CONCLUDING COMMENTS

First, a comment on premise (2), according to which anyone who accepts (or believes) N&E and sees that P(R/N&E) is low, has a defeater for R. Now obviously the person who believes N&E also believes a lot of other propositions. Perhaps some of those other propositions are such that by virtue of her believing *them* she doesn't get a defeater for R when she believes N&E. Perhaps she has a *defeater-deflector* for the looming defeat of R threatened by *P(R/N&E) is low* and N&E. This could happen if, for example, there were some proposition X she also

---

34. Reid, *Essays on the Intellectual Powers of Man* in *Thomas Reid's Inquiry and Essays*, ed. Ronald Beanblossom and Keith Lehrer (Indianapolis: Hackett, 1983), p. 276.

believes, such that P(R/N&E&X) is not low. Here's an example of a defeater-deflector. Go back to the sheep in the field example of a few paragraphs back. I see what I take to be a sheep in the field: the farmer who owns the field comes along and tells me that there are no sheep in that field, but adds that he has a sheep dog who looks like a sheep from this distance. That gives me a defeater. But suppose the farmer's wife had told me earlier on that her husband has developed a thing about sheep and sheep dogs, and tells everyone that there are no sheep in the field, even though there often are. Her telling me this is a *defeater-deflector*: because I believe what she says, the farmer's comments about sheep and sheep dogs don't give me a defeater for my belief that I see a sheep—a defeater the owner's remarks would otherwise have given me.

Returning to N&E and R, is there a defeater deflector for the defeat of R threatened by N&E and P(R/N&E) is low? Is there a belief X the naturalist might have such that P(R/N&E&X) is not low? Well, it certainly looks as if there are: what about R itself? That's presumably something the naturalist believes. P(R/N&E&R) is certainly not low; it's 1. But of course R itself isn't a proper candidate for being a defeater-deflector here. If a belief A could *itself* be a defeater-deflector for a putative defeater of A, no belief could ever be defeated.[35] Which beliefs are such that they can properly function as defeater-deflectors? Which beliefs are admissible in this context—that is, which beliefs X are such that if P(R/N&E&X) is not low, then X is a defeater-deflector for R and N&E and P(R/N&E) is low? This is the *conditionalization problem*.[36] It isn't easy to give a complete answer, but we can say at least the following.[37] First, neither R itself nor any proposition equivalent to it—for example, *(R v (2+1=4)) & ~(2+1=4)*—is admissible as a defeater-deflector here. Second, conjunctions of R with other propositions P the naturalist believes—for example, *(2+1=3) & R*—will not be defeater-deflectors, unless P itself is; more generally, propositions P that entail R will not be defeater-deflectors, unless a result of deleting R from P is a defeater-deflector.[38] Finally, no proposition P that is evidentially

35. See Plantinga, "Reply to Beilby's Cohorts" in *Naturalism Defeated?*, p. 224.
36. See Richard Otte's "Conditional Probabilities in Plantinga's Argument," in *Naturalism Defeated?*, pp. 143ff.; see also pp. 220–25.
37. And here I follow "Reply to Beilby's Cohorts" in *Naturalism Defeated?*, pp. 224–25.
38. Where P entails R, a result of deleting R from P will be any proposition Q such that Q is logically independent of R and such that P is logically equivalent to the conjunction of R with Q.

dependent upon R for *S*—that is, such that *S* believes *P* only on the evidential basis of R—is a defeater-deflector for R. Thus *either R or naturalism is true*, is evidentially dependent, for me, upon R (since I believe naturalism is false), as is *either R or Friesland is larger than the United States*, and *there is some true proposition P such that P(R/N&P) is high*. There is much more to be said, but instead of saying it here, I will refer the interested reader to my paper "Content and Natural Selection."[39]

Second final comment: there is a slightly different version of this argument that has somewhat weaker premises; some might find that version appealing on that account.[40] The argument as I presented it above has as a premise that P(R/N&E) is low: it is unlikely that our cognitive faculties are reliable, given naturalism and the proposition that we and those faculties have come to be by way of evolution. Here we are speaking of *all* of our cognitive faculties. But perhaps there are interesting distinctions to be made among them. Perhaps some are less likely than others to be reliable, given N&E. Perhaps those faculties that produce beliefs that appear to be relevant to survival and reproduction are more likely to be reliable than those faculties that produce beliefs of other kinds. For example, one might think that perceptual beliefs are often more likely to be relevant to adaptive behavior than beliefs about, say, art criticism, or postmodernism, or string theory. So consider *metaphysical* beliefs—for example, beliefs about the ultimate nature of our world, about whether there are both concrete and abstract objects, about the nature of abstract objects (if any), and about whether

39. Forthcoming in *Philosophy and Phenomenological Research*. In this paper I investigate whether various theories from contemporary philosophy of mind can serve as defeater-deflectors for the looming defeater for R. I examine functionalism and several theories of content, arguing that none of them can serve this purpose.
40. See Richard Otte, "Conditional Probabilities in Plantinga's Argument," and Tom Crisp "An Evolutionary Objection to the Argument from Evil," in *Evidence and Religious Belief*, eds. Kelly Clark and Rayond Van Arragon (New York: Oxford University Press, 2011) and see Michael Rea, *World Without Design* (Oxford: Clarendon Press, 2002) pp. 192ff.

there is such a person as God. Metaphysical beliefs don't seem to be relevant to survival and reproduction. And of course naturalism is just such a metaphysical belief. This belief doesn't seem relevant to survival and reproduction: it is only the occasional member of the Young Atheist's Club whose reproductive prospects are enhanced by holding the belief that naturalism is true.

So consider the faculty (or subfaculty), whatever it is, that produces metaphysical beliefs, and call it "M." And now we can ask the following question: given N&E, what is the probability that M is reliable? What is P(MR/N&E), where MR is the proposition that metaphysical beliefs are reliably produced and are mostly true? Some people may think this probability is clearly low, even if they aren't so sure about P(R/N&E). If that's how you think about the matter, I propose that you replace the first premise of the argument by

(1*) P(MR/N&E) is low;

everything else can go on as before.

It is time to bring this chapter and indeed this book to a close. I argued in the earlier portions of the book that there are areas of conflict between theism and science (evolutionary psychology for example), but that the conflict is merely superficial. I went on to argue in chapter 9 that there is deep concord between science and theistic belief; science fits much better with theism than with naturalism. Turning to naturalism, clearly there is superficial concord between science and naturalism—if only because so many naturalists trumpet the claim that science is a pillar in the temple of naturalism. As I argue in this chapter, they are mistaken: one can't rationally accept both naturalism and current evolutionary theory; that combination of beliefs is self-defeating. But then there is a deep conflict between naturalism and one of the most important claims of current science. My conclusion, therefore, is that there is superficial conflict but deep concord between science and theistic belief, but superficial concord and deep conflict between science and naturalism. Given that naturalism is at least a quasi-religion, there is indeed a science/religion conflict, all right, but it is not between science and theistic religion: it is between science and naturalism. That's where the conflict really lies.

INDEX

A priori insight, 6, 45, 149, 156, 178, 179, 233, 270, 301–302, 312

A posteriori knowledge, 301–302

Abraham, William, 45n

Abstract objects, 212, 288–291
  as divine thoughts, 288–291, 348

Adams, Robert, 42, 43

Adaptive behavior, 151, 271, 327, 331, 334, 348

Adequatio intellectus ad rem, 269, 296, 299

Agency detection, 141, 246n. *See also* HADD

Alberts, Bruce, 232, 234

Allegro, John, 157

Alston, William, 43, 45n, 46n, 48, 78n, 249n

Altruism, 134–136, 163, 164, 173

Ames, William, 275

Anthropic principle, 199–203

Ancient earth thesis, 8, 10, 11, 55–56, 144n

Aquinas, Thomas, 4, 5, 43, 60, 67, 68, 108, 135, 136, 152, 154, 178, 181, 237, 268, 269, 273, 274, 288 302n, 312, 313, 337

Aristotle, 292, 293, 294, 299, 302n, 319

Armstrong, David, 279, 280

Atkins, Peter, 75, 229n

Atran, Scott, 138, 139, 140, 143, 145, 182–183

Atheism, ix–xi, 30, 53, 142, 199, 214, 220, 223, 282

Atonement, 46, 59, 155, 164, 173, 262

Augustine, 10, 55, 89, 149, 154, 273, 318

Austin, J.L., 313

Ayala, Francisco, 254n

Barbour, John, 97

Barrow, John, 196

Barrett, Justin, 60n, 138, 140n, 141n

Basic belief, 42–49, 188, 241–247, 249–251, 270, 341–342

Bayes' theorem, 197n, 219–223, 240

Behe, Michael, 225–236, 237, 257–258, 262–264

Belief, xiv, 42–49, 60–62, 122–124, 137–143, 145–152, 163–168, 171–178, 178–183, 183–190, 240–244, 249–252, 260–262, 292–295, 309–350
  basic. *See* basic belief
  content, 321–325, 327–331, 333–339, 348n

Belief forming process/mechanism, xiv, 42–49, 137–143, 145–152, 178–183, 240–244, 249–252, 292–295, 309–350

Benacerraf, Paul, 291n

Bergmann, Michael, 167n, 340n

Bering, Jesse, 140n
Berry, Michael, 85n
Bertrand paradoxes, 332
Big Bang, 35, 121, 195–196, 212–213, 293
Big Crunch, 212–213
Bodin, Jean, 61
Bohr, Niels, 123
Boyer, Pascal, 138–140, 145
Boyle, Robert, 266, 275–276
Brading, Katherine, 95
Broadly inductive procedures, 270. See also
    induction
Brooke, John, 6n
Brown, Raymond, 155–156
Bultmann, Rudolph, 70–74, 76, 90, 96, 102n,
    105, 158–159

Calvin, John, 60, 68, 108, 145–146, 152, 154,
    178–179, 181, 263, 312
Calvinism, 145–152, 171
Campbell, George Douglas, 246n
Cantor, Georg, 289
Carr, Brandon, 194–195
Carroll, Sean, 234n
Carter, Brandon, 195n
Chance hypothesis, 198–199, 204, 232
Causal closure, xii, 70–73, 78–90, 92, 94, 96,
    99, 105, 108, 118, 119n, 130, 158, 298
Chance, 11, 16n, 29, 65, 67, 98n, 198–199, 204,
    205–206, 232, 272
Christian creeds, 8
Christianity, 4–5, 8, 11–12, 32, 41–49, 57,
    58–60, 65–68, 119–121, 140, 144n,
    149–152, 154–156, 164, 168, 173–174,
    177–178, 268–269, 272–274
Chomsky, Noam, 269–270
Churchland, Patricia, 315–316, 327
Churchland, Paul, 345n
Clark, Kelly, xv–xvi, 140n
Clarke, Samuel, 274
Classical physics, 77–78, 89, 92
Clayton, Philip, 74–75, 97–98, 105, 111, 114
Coarse-tuning arguments, 211
Cognitive faculties, xiv, 140,156, 244,
    269–271, 285, 286, 295, 311–317, 326, 328,
    325–350

reliability of, xiv, 269–271, 285, 286, 295,
    311–317, 326, 325–350. See also reformed
    epistemology
Collapse interpretations (of quantum
    mechanics), 115–116, 119n, 276n
Collins, John, 158n, 159n
Collins, Robin, xv, 78n, 197–198, 208, 211n,
    218, 262, 332
Common ancestry thesis, 9, 41n, 55
Complete Darwinian history, 15
Completeness of physics, 77, 86
Complexity of God, 26–30
Conditionalization problem, 343, 347
Consequence argument, 88–89
Conservation laws, xiii, 76, 78, 119n
Consilience, 297
Contingency of creation, 281, 299–302
Copenhagen interpretation (of Quantum
    Mechanics), 96, 114–115
    location problem for, 115
    measurement problem for, 114–115
Copernicus, Nicolaus, 185–186, 266
Copernican Revolution, 6n
Cosmological argument, 41, 42
Cosmological constant, 198
    physical constants, 194–199, 212
    fine tuning of, 194–199
Cosmology, 121, 194
Cotes, Roger, 266, 275, 302
Countable additivity, 206–211
Counterfactuals, 16n, 261, 338–339
Counterpossibles, 338–339
Coyne, Jerry, 234
Craig, William Lane, 42–43, 95, 179n, 197
Creationism, 10, 144n. See also young earth
    creationism
Crick, Sir Frances, 257, 260–262, 322–323
Crisp, Tom, xv, 152n, 348n
Curve fitting problem, 297–298

Danielson, Dennis R., 6n
Darwin, Charles, 7–9, 12, 14, 23, 56–57, 61,
    228, 245–246, 252–254, 308, 316
Darwin's doubt, 316–317
Darwinian explanation(s). See explanation,
    Darwinian

Darwinism, 9–11, 26–28, 38, 55–56, 130, 226, 240, 254, 259

Data model, 171–172

Davies, Paul, 196

Davis, Stephen, 179n

Dawkins, Richard, x, 7, 8, 13–30, 33, 37, 39, 40–41, 45n, 49, 52, 54, 55, 75, 137, 200n, 234, 252–253, 282, 283n, 307n, 308–309, 319
  blind watchmaker argument, 13–30
  Ultimate Boeing 747 argument, 28–30

Defeat
  of rationality. *See* rationality defeaters
  reduction test for, the. *See* reduction test, the

Defeater, xiii, xiv, 60, 120, 125, 130, 161, 164–167, 174–178, 183–190, 249–262, 314, 339–350
  for basic beliefs, 249–250, 260, 341–342
  partial, 252, 254n, 256, 258–260, 262
  rebutting, 165, 251, 252–254, 258
  undercutting, 165, 252, 254–258

Defeater-defeater, 345

Defeater-deflector, 346–348

Dennett, Daniel, x, 7–8, 30, 31–41, 212n, 253, 282, 283n, 310n, 318
  Darwin's Dangerous Idea, 7, 13, 31–49, 52, 54, 55, 138

Denton, Michael, 198n

Descartes, René, 43, 66–67, 89, 249n, 314, 318, 342n

Descent with modification, 9, 11, 33–34, 41n, 55, 56

Design argument, 42, 197, 219–224

Design beliefs, 244–248, 248–264

Design discourse, 247–248, 251–264

Design space, 227, 255

De Sousa, Ronald, 43–44

Determinism, 16n, 74, 80–83, 85, 88–89, 89–90, 94, 105, 110, 114–115, 119

Dirac, Paul, 285–286

Divine Action Project (DAP), 97–108, 110–114

Divine collapse causation (DCC), 116–121

Divine concurrence, 67, 72

Divine conservation, 66, 67n, 68, 79, 97, 108, 109n, 110, 111, 112, 113, 116, 281

Divine discourse, 153, 155, 156, 173

Dover trial, 170

Drake, Stillman, 7n

Draper, Paul, 31, 49–52, 219–232, 239–240, 244–245, 258, 310n
  evolutionary argument against theism, 49–52
  on Paley's design argument, 239–240, 244–245
  response to Behe, 219–232, 258

Dualism, 67n, 78, 89n, 119n, 120n, 318, 339

Duhem, Pierre, 159

Duke of Argyle, Eighth. *See* Campbell, George Douglas

Earman, John, 85n, 95

Eddington, Arthur, 202, 204

Eddy, Mary Baker, 190

Edwards, Jonathan, 43–44, 66–67, 68, 152

Einstein, Albert, 267, 275, 297

Elkana, Y., 76n

Ellis, George, 99–102, 114n

Enlightenment, the, 47, 69, 70n, 73, 155

Enlightenment case against supernaturalism, 60–62

Epistemology, 44–47, 164–168, 259–261

Essential properties, 66, 215–216, 217–218, 289–290

Euclid, 250

Evidence, xiii, 24, 29, 33, 41n, 42–43, 49–52, 118, 121, 122–124, 150, 159–160, 167–168, 172–177, 180–183, 183–186, 186–190, 200, 205, 219–220, 296–298, 340–341

Evidence base, xiii, 167–168, 172–177, 180–183, 183–186, 186–190

Evolution, xii, 7–30, 33–41, 49–52, 53–54, 55–58, 116, 129, 190, 226–234, 252–264, 270–271, 286–287, 308–309, 309–310
  guided vs. unguided, 12, 14, 16–17, 34–35, 38–41, 116, 129, 308–309
  how to think of, 8–10, 55–58
  problem of emergent order, the, 23–24
  relation to Christian belief, xii, 7–8, 10–13, 24, 49–52, 53–54, 190, 252–264

INDEX

Evolutionary argument against
  naturalism, xiv, 309–350
  given nonreductive materialism,
    326–333
  given reductive materialism, 333–335
Evolutionary psychology, xiii, 130–152, 163,
    265, 349
Explanation, 26–27, 129–133, 196–197,
    199–200, 219, 223–224, 226–228,
    239–240, 245–246, 258–259
  Darwinian, 129–133, 226–228, 239–240,
    245–246, 258–259, 287
  inference to the best, 219, 223–224
  requirements of, 196–197
  ultimate vs. particular, 26–27

Faith, 44–47, 68n, 108, 144, 156, 178–183
  as a gift from God, 68n, 108, 178
  as a source of knowledge, 44–47, 179
  Calvin's definition of, 179
  in relation to reason, 44–47, 144, 156,
    178–183
Fake barn country, 166–167, 341–342
Fantz, R.L., 243n
Feyerabend, Paul, 124
Fine-tuning argument, 194–224, 237
  anthropic objection to, 199–204
  as inference to the best explanation, 219,
    223–224
  Bayesian version of, 219–220
  coarse-tuning argument, 211
  incoherence objection to, 205–210
  likelihood version of, 220–223
  many worlds objection to, 212–218
  one-sided, 198
  "this universe" objection, 214–218
Flatness problem, the, 195
Flew, Anthony, 124, 223n
Foster, John, 67n, 89n
Four horsemen of atheism, x, 282–283.
  See also New Atheists
Free will, 87–90, 99, 102–104, 107, 117,
    119–120, 276, 311, 322
Frege, Gottlob, 288
Freud, Sigmund, 148–152
Functional interpretation of religion, 145–146

Gale, Richard, 45
Galileo, Galilei, 6–7, 266, 292–294, 296
Gardner, Martin, 200n
Galileo affair, 6–7
Gellman, Yehuda, 26
Gilkey, Langdon, 69–70, 72–74, 76, 86, 90,
    96, 159
Ghirardi, G.C., 96, 115, 119n
Ghirardi-Rimini-Weber approach (to
    Quantum Mechanics), 95–97, 115–116,
    119n, 308n
Gödel, Kurt, 338
Goodwin, Brian, 23–24
Gould, Stephen Jay, 7–9, 12, 15, 131n, 308
Gravy, half-congealed, xvi
Guthrie, Stewart, 141

Habermas, Gary, 19n
Hacking, Ian, 297
HADD (hypersensitive agency detection
    device), 141, 246n
Hands-off theologians, 74–90, 105
Harris, Sam, x, 30n, 283
Harvey, A.E., 168
Harvey, Van, 158
Hasker, William, 320
Hawking, Stephen, 195, 277
Hefner, Philip, 100, 104
Heidelberg Catechism, 4, 8, 65–67, 272
Heisenberg, Werner, 123
Hilbert's hotel, 210
Hinde, Robert A., 145
Hitchens, Christopher, x, 30n, 283
Historical Biblical Criticism (HBC), xiii,
    61, 130, 152–161, 163, 169, 173, 174, 190.
    See also scientific scripture scholarship
  Duhemian, 159–160
  Troeltschian, 174, 190
Hodge, Charles, 11
Holy Spirit, 68, 108, 152, 164
  internal witness of, 68, 108, 152
Humeanism about natural laws, 83n,
    88–89
Hume, David, 43, 74, 239, 244–245, 249n,
    263–264, 292–295
Huxley, Thomas H., 7, 16

Idealism, 201

Imago dei, xiii–xiv, 4–5, 11, 14, 120, 129, 161, 164, 181, 187, 268–269, 277, 283, 285, 295–296, 298–299, 313, 339n

Impossibility, 18, 217, 288n

Incarnation, 46, 59, 164, 173, 262

Indeterminism, 92–94, 110, 114

Indicators, 328–331

Induction, 8, 44, 45, 149, 178, 241, 292–296, 312, 344

Inference to the best explanation, 219, 223–224

Irreducible complexity, 171, 225–232

Intelligent design, 52–53, 55, 67, 170–171, 193–194, 225, 227–236, 257–264

Intentionality/aboutness, 35

Internal Witness of the Holy Spirit. *See* Holy Spirit

Intervention. 69, 71–72, 74–75, 79–83, 96–121. *See also* special divine action
alleged problems with, 71–73, 74–75, 97–108
defining, 79–83, 96–97, 108–112, 118–119

Introspection, 312

Jammer, Max, 276n

Jesus seminar, 61

Johnson, Luke Timothy, 157

Johnson, Phillip, 7

Jones, John, 171

Kaufman, Gordon, 70n

Kim, Jaegwon, 67n

Kitcher, Philip, 31, 50n, 55–63

Kant, Immanuel, 88n, 154, 288, 311

Kepler, Johannes, 277

Knowledge, xiv, 4, 5, 30, 44, 46, 48–49, 141n, 166–167, 177–181, 240–244, 267, 270, 295–296, 301–302, 311, 312, 313, 339n

Kronecker, Leopold, 210

Langford, Jerome, 6n

Laplace, Pierre, 84–90, 91, 93, 105, 109

Laplacean demon, 84–87, 93

Laplacean picture, 84–90, 91, 93, 105. *See also* causal closure; determinism

Larson, E.J., 74n

Laws of nature, xiii, 38–39, 70–71, 74–75, 76–83, 85–90, 93, 94–96, 98–114, 118–119, 130n, 217, 273–274, 274–283, 292–293, 297–298, 299, 301–302, 324, 339
conservation. *See* conservation laws
contingency of, 217, 278–281, 299, 301–302
finite inviolability of, 280–281
Humean conception of, 83n, 88
Lewisian conception of, 88–89
necessity of, 274–282, 324
relation to causal closure, xii, 78–82, 85, 89–90, 94, 108–109
suspension of, 70–71, 74–75, 79–80, 82–83, 94–96, 98–108, 108–114, 118–119, 281–282

Leibniz, Gottfried, 77n, 107, 284, 297, 298

Lent, Craig, 95

Leslie, John, 196n, 219n

Levenson, Jon, 155

Lewis, C.S., 8, 59, 310

Lewis, David, 83n, 88, 213, 278n, 279

Lewis, Peter, 115n

Lewontin, Richard, 131n

Library of Life, 16, 39

Liddel, Eric, 135

Locke, John, 17, 32, 37–38, 47–48

Luskin, Casey, 54n

Luther, Martin, 8, 86, 154

Mackie, John (J.L.), xi, 79, 80n, 82, 102, 118

Macquarrie, John, 71, 90, 96, 158n

Malebranche, Nicolas, 107

Manson, Neil, 215, 216

Materialism, xiv, 29–30, 67n, 119n, 120n, 318, 320, 321n, 322, 322–325, 326–327, 329–331, 333–335, 335–337, 339
nonreductive, 322–325, 326–327, 329–333, 335
reductive, 322–325, 326, 333–335

Mathematics, 48, 133, 172, 178, 211, 270,
    284–291, 301, 312, 326
  accessibility of, 286–287
  nature of, 287–290
  knowledge of, 48, 178, 270, 301, 326
  unreasonable efficacy of, 284–286,
    287–290
Mavrodes, George, 42
Maudlin, Timothy, 92
Mayr, Ernst, 11, 277
McGrew, Lydia, 179n, 205–208, 210–211
McGrew, Timothy, 179n, 205–208, 210–211
McMullin, Ernan, 105–106, 113, 170
Meier, John, 159, 160
Methodological naturalism (MN). See
    naturalism, methodological
Mind, 14, 27–28, 31–32, 35, 37–40, 43, 60,
    67n, 84, 132, 137, 139, 141, 151, 241–243,
    245, 246, 248, 277, 288, 290, 298, 316,
    318–319, 348n. See also dualism;
    materialism
  explanations of, 28
  Locke's argument regarding the, 17, 32,
    37–38. See also Darwin's doubt
  other minds, 43, 60, 141, 240–243,
    245, 248
Miller, Kenneth, 52–53
Miller's Principle, 332
Memory, 44–46, 48–49, 144, 149, 176–180,
    189, 270, 302, 311–313
Mental content, 323, 348n. See also belief
    content; properties, mental
Merricks, Trenton, 343n
Miracles, xii–xiii, 3, 68, 71–72, 75, 78–79, 82,
    83, 90, 94–96, 100, 104–106, 113, 118, 122,
    137, 158, 160, 163, 169, 173, 174–175, 265
  alleged conflict with science, xii–xiii, 3,
    75, 90, 91, 94–96, 104–105, 112–113, 118,
    121–125, 173, 174–178, 265
  relation to causal closure, xiii, 71–72,
    78–79, 79–82, 82–83
  relation to quantum mechanics, 94–96,
    112–113, 118
Mirandola, Pico della, 6n
Mither, Steven, 132
Mivart, St. George, 40n, 227
Monokroussos, Dennis, 26

Monton, Bradley, 95–96, 115n, 119n, 219n,
    223n
Moral argument, 42
Moral law(s), 83n, 273, 276
Moral sense, 11, 32, 51, 178, 312
Mother Teresa, 41, 135–136,
    186–188
Mouse, Mickey, 139
Multiverse, 212, 215–217
Music, 35, 132–133, 287
Mullen, John, 237n
Murphy, Nancey, 97, 114n
Murray, Michael, xv, 6, 56, 107

Nagel, Thomas, xi, 17n, 315, 316
Naturalism (N), ix–xiv, 24, 36, 50, 53–54, 56,
    122, 168–174, 174–178, 181, 189, 263, 265,
    282–283, 285, 288, 290, 298–299, 303,
    307–311, 314–320, 322–326, 329, 333–335,
    339n, 340, 346–350
  as a quasi-religion, ix–x, xiv, 311, 350
  methodological (MN), xiii, 168–174, 175,
    177–178, 181, 189–190
  metaphysical (ontological), 169, 316
  relation to science, ix–xiv, 50–52, 122,
    170–174, 174–178, 181, 189, 265, 299, 303,
    349–350 See also evolutionary
    argument against naturalism;
    Simonian science
Naturalistic origins thesis, 9
Natural selection, 9, 11–12, 13–19, 21, 23–24,
    31–32, 34–40, 55, 63, 129, 131, 135,
    139–140, 144, 147–148, 181, 227, 232, 234,
    253–254, 258, 271, 286, 307n, 313,
    315–316, 319, 330, 348
  guided, 17, 27, 34, 39, 253, 308
  unguided, 14, 17–19, 31–32, 38, 39, 40–41,
    63, 232, 234, 307n, 308
Necessity, 100, 278–280, 283, 302, 324n
  logical (broadly), 279, 324n
  nomological/causal, 100, 278–280, 283,
    302n, 324n
Necessary being, 30, 66,
    222–223, 300
New Atheism, x–xi, 45n. See also four
    horsemen of atheism

Newton, Isaac, xi, 76, 78, 164, 193, 194, 266, 275, 284

Newtonian picture, 76–77, 79, 82, 84–85, 89–90, 91, 98n

Neural structure, 320, 324–325, 328, 330–331, 333n, 336

Neurophysiological properties (NP), 321–325, 327, 330–331, 334, 336–339

Nietzsche, Friederich, 314, 316

Noetic structure, 144, 184n, 260–262

Noncontingent, 50–51, 82, 338. *See also* necessity

Normalizability, 207–209, 256

Numbers, 29, 250, 288, 290–291, 301n

Observational selection effect, 200

Ockham, William of, 273–274, 302n

Organized complexity, 26–27

Orr, H.Allen, 17n, 75

Otte, Richard, 347n, 348n

Pairing problem, 67n, 119

Paley, William, 237–240, 244–248, 251–254, 256–257, 262

Papineau, David, 85n

Parsons, Charles, 289n

Peacocke, Arthur, 85n, 97, 98n, 104

Perception, 44, 45–49, 140–141, 144, 149, 156, 178, 179, 237, 243, 245–246, 249n, 258, 270–271, 302, 311–313

Perceptual beliefs, 140–141, 242–243

Persinger, Michael, 140n

Philosophical/ontological naturalism. *See* naturalism, metaphysical

Pieper, Josef, 273n

Pinker, Steven, 132, 137

Plato, 89, 236, 288, 319

Platonism, 288

Polkinghorne, John, 97, 114–115, 196n, 197

Pollard, William, 114

Positive epistemic status, 120, 244, 249–250

Possible world(s), 20, 29–30, 35, 39, 58–59, 66, 82, 210, 212–213, 216, 217, 222, 295, 300–301, 324

Possibility, 20, 25, 38–39, 40, 83n, 102, 214, 218, 231, 254

biological, 20, 25, 38–39

(broadly) logical, 20, 40, 254

epistemic, 25, 218

Predictability, 67, 85, 102–103, 117, 120, 271–273, 274, 282

Preservation, 11, 21, 39n, 56, 72, 110, 116, 308

Principle of indifference, 332

Probability, 20, 28–30, 50, 93, 103, 151, 168, 173, 197n, 198, 202, 206–211, 213–218, 219–224, 231–232, 235–236, 314, 317, 330–333, 333–335, 342–343, 349

antecedent/prior, 219, 220, 222, 223, 224, 240

conditional, 210, 317

epistemic, 29, 223, 332

initial, 168, 173. *See also* evidence base

logical, 29, 210

objective, 29, 30, 332

of cognitive reliability, given naturalism and evolution. *See* evolutionary argument against naturalism

probability measure, 207–208

statistical, 29

subjective, 332

Problem of evil, 50n, 56–58, 61, 10. *See also* suffering

Problem of old evidence, the, 219n

Progress thesis, 9, 11, 55

Proper function, 135, 148, 150–151, 166, 178, 257, 260, 295, 313, 347

Properly basic belief(s), 341

Properties, 56–57, 58–59, 66, 141n, 145, 201, 209, 215–216, 217–218, 241, 244, 249n, 288, 289, 292, 294, 300, 320n, 321–325, 327, 330–331, 332, 333, 334, 336–339

essential. *See* essential properties of God, 66, 300

mental, 241, 320n, 321–325, 327, 333, 339

neurophysical (NP). *See* Neurophysical properties

physical 320n, 322, 324, 333

reduction of mental, 321–325, 333

Providence, 65, 106, 114n, 272
Providentialist religion, 55–56
Pruss, Alex, 15n
Ptolemy, 185
Ptolemaic theory, 7

Quantum mechanics (QM), xii, 16n, 53, 90,
    91, 92–97, 110–111, 113–121, 122, 130,
    143–144, 286, 301, 308

Randomness of genetic mutation, 11–12
Ratzsch, Del, 237n, 245n, 246n, 301n
Reason, xi, 6, 42–48, 54, 144, 155–156,
    178–180, 229n, 293, 295–196
    deliverances of, 47n, 48, 144, 156,
    179–180
    in relation to faith. See faith, in relation to
    reason
    sources of knowledge in addition
    to, 46–47, 49, 178, 267
Rationality defeater(s), 166–167, 340n
Rea, Michael, 348n
Reduction test, the, 186–188
Reconciliation, story of, 58–59
Rees, Martin, 194–195, 196n, 198
Regularity, 67, 102–104, 112, 117, 120, 271–272,
    274, 276, 282–283,
    285, 302n
Reid, Thomas, 156, 178, 237, 241, 242n, 270,
    293, 312, 345–346
Relativity theory, xii, 53, 78n, 91, 120, 122,
    143–144, 145, 176, 286, 296–297,
    301, 308
Religious belief, x, xii, 3, 5, 36, 42–45, 48, 54,
    62, 65, 123n, 124, 137, 140–141, 143, 144,
    145, 148, 150–151, 152n, 164, 168n, 169,
    181, 182, 186
    rationality of. See reformed epistemology
Religious pluralism, 61
Rimini, A., 115n
Ruse, Michael, 133–134, 142–143
Russell, Bertrand, xi, 10n, 25, 26n, 36–37,
    249, 266
Russell, Robert, 97, 111n, 114n
Russell paradoxes, 289

Resurrection, 61, 118, 153, 157–158,
    161, 262
Royden, H.L., 209

Sanders, E.P., 159
Saunders, Nicholas, 100, 104–105, 118n
Schrödinger equation, 92–93, 114–115
Schrödinger, Erin, 123
Science and naturalism. See naturalism,
    relation to science
Scientific anti-realism, 92n
Scientific realism, 92n
Scientific Scripture scholarship. See
    Historical Biblical Criticism
sensus divinitatus, 60, 148n, 181,
    263–264, 312
Scott, Eugenie, 169–170
Segal, Aaron, 345n
Set(s), 133, 171–172, 209–210, 250–251,
    286–287, 288–290, 290–291
Shapiro, James, 258
Sheehan, Thomas, 157
Shepard, Alan, 132
Simplicity, 27, 83n, 88, 257, 268, 278n, 285,
    297–299
Simon, Herbert, 134–136, 164,173
Simonian science, 164, 168, 173–174, 174–175,
    177–178, 181, 182, 184, 186, 186–189
Simpson, George Gaylord, 12–13, 308
Skepticism, 158, 315, 344
    naturalist commitment to, 315, 344
Skeptical theism, 101–102
Slone, D. Jason, 138n
Smith, Quentin, 49
Sober, Elliot, 11, 12n, 19n, 134n, 200, 202,
    220–221, 239n, 240n
Sociobiology. See evolutionary
    psychology
Spandrel, 131, 132, 137, 138, 142, 227,
    255, 287
Special divine action, xii–xiii, 20, 63, 68, 72,
    74–75, 78n, 82–83, 86, 90, 91–92, 94, 96,
    97–98, 100–101, 110–112, 113, 120–121, 122,
    125, 130, 158, 265
    divine consistency objection to, 104, 106.
    See also miracles

problem of interference/intervention, 70,
72–73, 74, 97–102, 158
problem of regularity, 102–104
Spinoza, Baruch, 155
Stark, Rodney, 137, 138, 142, 274n
Strauss, David, 156
Street, Sharon, 28n
Stroud, Barry, 315, 316
Stump, Eleonore, 44, 45n, 287n
Suffering, x, 56–59. *See also*
problem of evil
Supervenience, 88, 96, 116, 320n, 323–325,
338
Swinburne, Richard, 42, 44, 45n, 89n, 156n,
179n, 197, 208, 262, 297n
Sympathy, 156, 178, 270, 312

Taylor, Richard, 310n
Testability, 300
Theodicy, 59
Traditional biblical commentary, 152, 154,
156
Three-body problem, 84
Theoretical virtues, 297
Tillich, Paul, 104
Tipler, Frank, 194
Tracy, Thomas, 97, 111n, 114n, 118n
Tremlin, Todd, 138n
Troeltsch, Ernst, 158, 174

Unger, Peter, 3, 122
Ullman, Shimon, 243n

Van Fraassen, Bas, 92n, 95, 171, 209n, 277n,
332n
Van Horn, Luke, 110n
Van Inwagen, Peter, 44, 45n, 58n, 59n, 67n,
88n, 119n, 266n, 318n

Varghese, Roy, 124n
Vestrup, Eric, 205
Von Weizsäker, C.F., 266

Wang, Hao, 289–290
Warrant, 42, 44, 47, 48, 120, 141n, 150, 153,
166, 177, 182, 185, 188–189, 242, 244,
249–250
intrinsic, 188–189
Warrant defeaters, 166–167, 340n
Weatherford, Roy, 332n
Weber, T., 115n
Weinberg, Stephen, 297
Wells, G.A., 157
Westminster Confession, 4
Whewell, William, 245, 275, 276, 277n
White, Andrew Dixon, 6
White, Roger, 197, 214n, 332n
Whitehead, Alfred North, 272, 274, 283
Wigner, Eugene, 284–285
Wildman, Wesley, 97n, 99, 104, 111n, 112
Wiles, Maurice, 101n
Wilkins, John, 266
Wilson, David Sloan, 134n, 138, 142–143,
145–148, 150–152, 164, 171, 181
Wilson, E.O., 131, 134, 138, 277
Wish-fulfillment, 148–150
Witham, L., 74
Worldview, ix, x, 3, 122, 307, 309
scientific, x, 3, 122, 307, 309
Worrall, John, 122–124
Wolterstorff, Nicholas, 44, 45n, 46n, 153n
Wright, N.T., 179

Young earth creationism, 10, 144n

Zhang, W.J., 329n
Zweir, Paul, 333n